THE ARCHITECT'S GUIDE TO FA-CILITY PROGRAMMING is a landmark book! Conceived by the AIA's Facility Programming Task Force, this book draws on the experience and knowledge of practicing architects and programmers. It gives architects the skills they need to analyze complex design problems and expand design services in a competitive marketplace.

At the heart of this comprehensive guide are 14 case studies that illustrate actual programming processes. From initial planning and information gathering to the completed program report and its use as a tool for design, these case studies detail the state-of-the-art of programming today.

The program is an essential tool for communication with a building's users, owner and—most especially—designer. *The Architect's Guide to Facility Programming,* with over 150 charts and illustrations, puts programming techniques at the disposal of every architect.

THE ARCHITECT'S GUIDE TO FACILITY PROGRAMMING

THE AMERICAN INSTITUTE
OF ARCHITECTS

MICKEY A. PALMER

Published jointly by
The American Institute
of Architects
Washington, D.C., and
Architectural Record Books
New York
1981

Administrative editors: Robert Allan Class and Patricia Markert
Copyeditor: Carol Frances
Designer: Larry Paine, LP&A Design Studio
Production supervisors: Elizabeth Dineen and Carol Frances
Composition: Helvetica, by Unicorn Graphics
Printing and binding: Malloy Lithographing, Inc.

Library of Congress Cataloging in Publication Data

American Institute of Architects.
    The architect's guide to facility programming.

    (A McGraw-Hill publication)
    Bibliography: p.
    Includes index.
    1. Architectural design. I. Palmer, Mickey A. II. Title.
NA2728.A43 1981   720′.28′54   80-23667
ISBN 0-07-001490-6

AIA Catalog Number: 2M726

Published jointly by
The American Institute of Architects
1735 New York Avenue, N.W.
Washington, D.C. 20006 and
Architectural Record, A McGraw-Hill Publication
1221 Avenue of the Americas
New York, New York 10020

Contents

Foreword   v
Preface   vi
Acknowledgments   vii

PART ONE.   FUNDAMENTALS OF PROGRAMMING   1
1. The Role of Programming   3
The Value of Programming   3
The Meaning of Programming   4
The Nature of Programming   7
The Evolution of Programming   11
Resources on Programming   14
The Architect's Role in Programming   14

2. The Process of Programming   16
Programming Information   17
Programming Procedures   24
Program Development Process   29
Preparation, Participation and Products   32

PART TWO.   TECHNIQUES AND TOOLS OF PROGRAMMING   49
3. Techniques for Data Collection   53
Background and User Report Methods   53
Observation Techniques   70
Attitude Measurement   79
Value of Data Collection   87

4. Techniques for Data Analysis and Organization   88
Statistical Analysis   88
Analyzing Program Elements   94
Data Organization   120

5. Techniques for Communication and Evaluation   136
Participant Interaction   136
Documentation/Presentation   140
Evaluation Techniques   149
Developing Programming Competence   156

6. Computer Aids to Facility Programming   157
Computer Capabilities   158
Computerized Analysis Techniques   159
Computer Programs for Facility Programming   165
Resources on Computer Applications   166

PART THREE. APPLICATIONS OF PROGRAMMING   169

7. Program for a Neighborhood Services Center   171
Architecture One, Ltd.

8. Program for a Middle School   176
Caudill Rowlett Scott (CRS) Architects, Planners, Engineers

9. Program for Expansion of an Educational Research Facility   184
Cost, Planning & Management International Inc. (CPMI)

10. Feasibility Study and Program for a Health Clinic   191
Design and Planning Assistance Center (DPAC)

11. Feasibility Program for a Cultural Arts Center   198
The Eggers Group P.C., Architects and Planners

12. Feasibility Study and Program for Hospital Facilities   209
Kaplan/McLaughlin, Architects/Planners

13. Feasibility Study for Redesign of an Elementary School   216
Marquis Associates, Architecture/Planning/Interior Design

14. Design Criteria for a Single Family Residence   223
MLTW/Turnbull Associates, Architects and Planners

15. Master Plan Program for a Riverfront Development   228
Murphy Levy Wurman/Architecture and Urban Planning

16. User Needs Program for a Research Facility   234
School of Design, North Carolina State University

17. Program for a County Government Office Building   241
RTKL Associates Inc., Architecture/Planning-Urban Design/Engineering

18. Design Criteria for Medical Research Laboratories   247
Space for Social Systems (SPACE4)

19. Light and Color Study for Psychiatric Residence Units   256
Spivack Associates Inc., Environmental Designers and Programmers

20. Design Criteria for a Zoo Exhibit Complex   262
Zooplan Associates Inc.

21. Programming in Practice   267
Changes in the Nature and Scope of Programming   267
Contracts and Compensation   267
The Programming Practice   271
Trends in Programming   276

Bibliography   279

Index   287

Foreword

Architects have always done programming as part of their work. In earlier years, this most frequently involved only setting down the number and kinds of spaces needed in a building. Programming in those years was not distinguished as a service apart from providing solutions to architectural problems.

As client requirements grew more complex and the needs of users of facilities designed by architects required clearer articulation, the act of programming emerged as a distinct entity. The AIA's 1969 publication on the subject recognized this trend.

Today, facility programming is firmly established as an important and necessary ingredient of the design process. While philosophies of concept and application vary among its practitioners, the tools and techniques of this art are increasingly useful, sophisticated and adaptable to most architectural practices.

Programming has become a major determinant of design solutions and thus has a major impact on our buildings and other facilities. Recognizing the need to provide a comprehensive report to the profession of the latest information on this important service, the AIA commissioned the writing of this book. It is the most detailed examination of current techniques in facility programming prepared to date. I commend it to everyone who works in this area.

CHARLES E. SCHWING, FAIA
President, The American Institute of Architects

Washington, D.C.
December, 1980

Preface

This book is a guide to the meaning and methods of facility programming, to the techniques, tools, applications and opportunities, and to resources for additional information on programming procedures. It is intended to provide design practitioners and students with a firm basis for exploring, acquiring and applying the skills of investigation and analysis that will enable them to improve design and expand design services in a competitive marketplace.

In 1969, The American Institute of Architects published a booklet entitled *Emerging Techniques 2: Architectural Programming* by Benjamin H. Evans, AIA, and C. Herbert Wheeler Jr., FAIA. At that time, programming was emerging as a flourishing specialized service offered to facility owners by management and planning consultants and a few architecture firms. The report provided architects an introduction to the issues and implications of programming for design practice, as well as to many of the techniques employed.

The Architect's Guide to Facility Programming, which succeeds AIA's 1969 document, reflects the expansion of knowledge and opportunities in programming that has occurred during the past decade. It also reflects the increasing needs of owners, designers, planners, builders and facility managers for systemized procedures and analytical techniques to accommodate the diversity and complexity of design information.

Programming has emerged as a systemized process for investigating and analyzing the design requirements of a facility. As predesign decisions have increased in importance, programming has become prevalent as a means for determining project scope and function as well as assisting in determining feasibility. Its application now includes data research and analysis for other stages of the design process and its methods extend to the evaluation of facility design after construction and occupancy.

At the same time, the scope of information that must be processed has expanded. Nowhere is it more evident than in the attendance to user needs. Requirements for facility design extend beyond a listing of the owner's physical and economic criteria. They include the functional, social, psychological and aesthetic needs of those who live in, work in, operate and otherwise use a facility. Understanding and accommodating user needs has necessitated the adoption and development of research techniques that enable the programmer to analyze human factors effectively and efficiently and to incorporate them into design requirements.

Many of these techniques originate in the fields of social and behavioral research, marketing, communications and other disciplines where user or consumer needs are the primary interest. In *The Architect's Guide to Facility Programming,* I have attempted to identify and explain a variety of user research techniques that have been applied by architects and other facility programmers in practice.

However, the book does not seek to turn programmers into social scientists or vice versa. Its aim is to help achieve a comprehensive approach to facility programming that addresses all the physical, human and external influences on design projects. To that end, it will contribute to improved practice and design that produce more effective, efficient, economical and client-responsive facilities and yield greater opportunities for design professionals.

With this objective in mind, the contents of the book are presented in three parts:

—Part I, "Fundamentals of Programming," examines the definition of programming, its relationship to design, a variety of practitioner perspectives and literature on the subject, and the process and procedures of programming.

—Part II, "Techniques and Tools of Programming," describes and illustrates a variety of information-processing methods and instruments for collecting, analyzing, organizing, communicating and evaluating programming data.

—Part III, "Applications of Programming," presents 14 case studies of projects where programming has been applied and concludes with a chapter on "Programming in Practice."

Many people contributed to the development of this manuscript, as indicated in the "Acknowledgements." To these, I should add an expression of personal appreciation to several people who provided advice, encouragement, consultation, moral support, understanding and/or kind words to me during the long and arduous task of researching and writing this book. My sincere thanks to: Lyn Arillo, Michael Barker, J. Marie Beam, David Bullen, Muriel Campaglia, Robert Allan Class, Kathleen Davis, Joseph Demkin, Richard Freeman, Bryant P. Gould, Lisa Moore Hoke, Lynda Maudlin, Arnold Prima, Alan Sandler, James Scheeler, Barbara Shepherd, Frank Tavares, the late Dr. George Tolbert, Edward T. White III. Most of all, I am grateful for the support and patience of my family: Darlene, Terri, Jonathan and Tobi.

Mickey A. Palmer
Washington, D.C.

Acknowledgments

In identifying systematic practice procedures in the first half of the 1970s, the AIA's national Automated Practice Technology Committee listed facility programming among a half dozen important architectural procedures subject to systematization and ripe for development as an AIA practice program. In 1976 a small Facility Programming Task Force was created to start work on a publication on this subject and was attached to the AIA's national Project Management Committee to draw on additional resources. In a little over a year the task force produced a detailed outline and, together with a research consultant, did much of the original research that forms the backbone of this book. Task force members included: Herbert McLaughlin, AIA, chairman, of San Francisco; S. James Goldstein, AIA, Millburn, New Jersey; Bryant P. Gould, AIA, New York; Sidney E. Snyder Jr., AIA, Honolulu; and Edward T. White III, Tallahassee. The research consultant was George Miers of Oakland, California.

Following completion of the initial research, the project lay fallow for over a year. When authorized to restart, its completion was assigned as an AIA headquarters project. Additional research and preparation of a manuscript for publication became the responsibility of a manuscript development team comprising: Mickey A. Palmer, author; Paul C. Zugates, AIA, technical consultant; Douglas E. Gordon, research associate; and Robert Allan Class, AIA, staff administrator of the project.

Mickey A. Palmer, a professional writer and author of this book, earned his undergraduate degree at Wheaton College in sociology and writing and his master's degree in political science at the State University of New York at Albany. As a journalist and writer, he has served as editorial assistant, freelance writer, reporter and bureau editor for newspapers in Washington, D.C., Chicago and Albany and as writer, editor, narrator and producer of documentaries and newsletters. As a congressional assistant, he has served a U.S. Congressman in legislative research and public relations and as a special projects coordinator. During the preparation of the manuscript for this book, he served the AIA in various writing and editing consulting capacities, most notably as editor of the *Energy Newsletter* and the *Energy Notebook*.

Paul C. Zugates, AIA, architect and technical consultant for this book, is an architecture graduate of Carnegie-Mellon University and an associate in the architecture/planning-urban design/engineering firm of RTKL Associates Inc. of Baltimore, Maryland. In addition to project management expertise, his background includes development of many architectural programs for hospitals, universities, office buildings, research facilities and government buildings. His greatest concentration as a programming specialist has been in the medical field, with its attendant complexities and requirements for long-range planning.

Douglas E. Gordon, research associate for this book, earned his undergraduate degree in English at the Virginia Polytechnic Institute and State University and his master's degree in journalism at the University of Georgia. While advancing his education, he served as writer and features editor of several college newspapers and newsletters. He has been published in *Journalism Quarterly* and served as a consultant in revisions to *Introduction to Mass Communication*. During the preparation of the manuscript and additional research for this book, he served on the staff of the AIA's practice division, where he assisted in producing practice-aids publications and was co-editor of the *Time Data Bank Status Report*. During the publication period of this book, he served as a manager in the AIA's professional interest division.

Robert Allan Class, AIA, staff administrator of the manuscript development team for this book and director of the Institute's practice division, is an architecture graduate of the University of Pennsylvania, a former practitioner from Philadelphia and past president of the AIA Philadelphia Chapter. Author/editor of the AIA's 1975 *Compensation Management Guidelines for Architectural Services* and co-editor of the 1976 *Current Techniques in Architectural Practice*, he has guided many Institute practice-oriented publications, including those on development building, financing real estate development, life cycle cost analysis, personnel practices, project checklist, financial management and project management. He served on the team that developed the construction industry's *Uniform Construction Index*, published in 1972, and has written many practice-related articles. He is active in professional seminars on various management aspects of architectural practice.

Others to whom the AIA is indebted for their contributions during the development of this manuscript include those contributing substantive material for the programming applications case studies, whose names are listed in Chapters 7 thru 20, and the following architects who, in addition to the above, generously agreed to review and comment on the final manuscript:

—Bryant P. Gould, AIA, New York
—Herbert McLaughlin, AIA, San Francisco
—William M. Peña, FAIA, Houston
—Henry Sanoff, AIA, Raleigh
—Edward T. White III, Tallahassee

During the publishing phase, many valuable services were rendered and helpful ideas advanced by Patricia Markert, editor of Architectural Record Books, by Carol Frances, assistant editor, and by graphic designer Larry Paine.

PART ONE
FUNDAMENTALS
OF PROGRAMMING

**CHAPTER 1
THE ROLE OF
PROGRAMMING**

**CHAPTER 2
THE PROCESS OF
PROGRAMMING**

Programming is the analytical aspect of design. It involves types of data, procedures and techniques which may be unfamiliar or even contrary to an architect's frame of reference, but which can help improve design and practice.

Programming is an approach to the design process that extends the designer's involvement in project decision making in two directions: planning the needs of a facility and evaluating the design response to facility needs. It lays a foundation of information based on empirical evidence rather than assumption that helps the designer respond effectively and creatively to client requirements and facility parameters and constraints.

Programming is an information-processing process. It involves a disciplined methodology of data collection, analysis, organization, communication and evaluation through which all the human, physical and external influences on a facility's design may be explored.

Programming is an architectural service and an opportunity for improving and expanding practice. It aids both the client and the designer in decision making based on appropriate information and effective communication.

The two chapters which follow, "The Role of Programming" and "The Process of Programming," attempt to define the parameters and value of programming, as well as its methodology, for practical applications. The viewpoints and procedures of many programming practitioners and theorists are incorporated to aid architects and other design professionals in developing their own approaches and systems for creative, effective programming.

Chapter 1
The Role
of Programming

What is so important about facility programming that anyone would devote an entire book to the subject?

The answer is information. That is the object of programming and the subject of this book. The facility designer and his or her client, confronted with the goal of producing a functional, durable, appealing and economical facility, must recognize the vast quantity and complexity of data required to achieve it. The modern designer needs practical, systematic means of not only accumulating these data, but of analyzing, organizing and translating them into appropriate information for design decisions. Programming, as an information-processing system, accommodates the information needs of the facility designer and owner or developer.

Furthermore, decisions that affect the design of a facility—types of use, space needs, performance criteria, budget, environmental impact and energy use, for example—are often made early, much before a designer may put pencil to sketchpad. It is in the interests of the designer to participate effectively in these "predesign" decisions not only for the sake of design effectiveness and quality, but for the sake of the designer's practice as well. As a decision-making tool and as a professional service, programming has an important role in today's architectural practice.

But that is not the entire answer. Because the nature and scope of design decisions and design information have changed, the role of programming has changed as well. The traditional notion of a facility program is a list of client requirements for design. In the modern use of programming, this notion has not been displaced, but it has been extended in several directions.

First, the scope of requirements for a project's design has expanded. Awareness and accommodation of user needs have become increasingly important to both designer and owner. Energy conservation is another, and perhaps the most dramatic, example of a design-influencing factor whose impact has magnified and must be accounted for early in decision making.

Second, the depth and specialization of design information have increased as the complexity of facility use and construction has proliferated.

Third, the uses of programming have been extended from primarily acquiring and organizing information to investigating and developing information, analyzing owner and user needs, and evaluating design after construction and occupancy.

The program, and its development, have become a much more vital instrument for the architect and other design practitioners than ever before in the history of design. In order to understand the importance of programming, however, it is necessary to understand what it is, to give it a reasonably precise definition. What do the terms programming and program mean? What is the scope of programming, how does it work and what are its products? Finally and perhaps most importantly, what is the value of programming in design practice? The answers to these questions essentially outline the rest of this chapter and the contents of this book.

THE VALUE OF PROGRAMMING

Facility programs and the process of facility programming are valuable resources for both clients and designers. Programmers, both within and outside the architectural profession, cite a variety of reasons for the application of programming in architecture. Chief among them is that the complexity, quantity and variety of information necessary for design require a systemized process for developing and managing the data. There are many other benefits and, without extensive exposition, some of them are listed here.

—As a systemized process, programming helps assure the programmer of covering all the relevant issues of client need. It also provides an organizing mechanism for handling multiple, diverse factors that affect client and design requirements. It creates a structured framework for accumulating and classifying data.

—As an analytical process, it enables programmer, designer and client to base project decisions on factual evidence obtained through objective, systematic procedures rather than on assumptions, prejudices or stock experience.

—As a decision-making tool, it affords the opportunity for designers to participate effectively in predesign decisions that affect design, and for clients (owners and, particularly, users) to participate in the design process at a point where their input is most valuable.

—By comprehensively examining the facts and implications of factors that influence a design problem, a program encourages both precision and creativity in producing a design solution.

—The availability of programming services can improve the overall capability and appeal of a design firm, enhancing its marketability. Programming capability also presents opportunities for expanded practice. A programming study may lead to a contract for design phase services in the same project or to contracts for additional projects with other clients.

—Programming can reduce financial risk. A contract for programming services may act as a loss leader if a project is subsequently dropped or the scope changes. In addition, it helps clarify the scope of design phase services and establish adequate compensation levels for those services. It diminishes the risk of an owner-generated legal suit over unsatisfactory design solutions, particularly if the owner has participated in program development. Some architects who limit their practices to programming and nondesign services also report that professional li-

EXHIBIT 1-1. PROGRAMMING DEFINED BY ARCHITECTS AND OTHER PROGRAMMERS

(Unless otherwise noted, these definitions are drawn from statements provided by the individuals for this book.)

EDWARD J. AGOSTINI
Becker and Becker Associates, Inc.
New York, New York

The end product of the program is information—not design. It is a coherent, meaningful compilation of the facts needed to create facilities which will most effectively support the client's operations and organizational goals. A good, objective program should neither limit nor dictate design. It should permit wide design latitude and provide necessary criteria against which the architect can assess the validity and vitality of his [sic] design solution . . .

The program document itself should be a comprehensive report that presents in text and tabular form the detailed quantitative and qualitative requirements of the entire client organization. The recommendations should include functional space standards, department-by-department space analysis and suggested organizational groupings which respond to adjacency, work and traffic flow requirements. Guidelines for accommodating future growth in an orderly manner while preserving these interrelationships should also be included. In its format and terminology, the program document should permit all concerned to understand, abide by and implement its conclusions.

Source: "Programming: Demanding Specialty in a Complex World," *Architectural Record*, September 1968.

MICHAEL BRILL
Buffalo Organization for Social and Technological Innovation Inc. (BOSTI)
Buffalo, New York

Architectural programming tries to describe the desired range of specific human requirements a building must satisfy in order to support and enhance the performance of human activities. It is a predesign activity, but a critical part of the design process; it involves the investigation phase of a four-stage process that also includes design, implementation and evaluation.

The program is a document, the final output of the investigation phase of the design process. Its purpose is to predict those environmental conditions that are supportive and responsive to the user's activity patterns. To be relevant, these predictions are constrained by an economic framework that is related to the construction process, the resources of the client and the time constraints of the project.

A problem statement describes a present state, some of whose qualities are undesirable to someone; the program describes the qualities of some future, more desirable state. Within the total process of architectural design, the program provides a critical link between the present problem and the future solution by establishing the criteria for an intervention strategy.

GERALD DAVIS, AIA
TEAG—The Environmental Analysis Group Ltd.
Ottawa, Ontario, Canada

Programming for facilities is that part of the decision-making process that links the

ability insurance premiums are much lower for this kind of practice.

VALUE OF THE PROGRAM. The objective of the programming process is to produce information that is useful for design. As an instrument of design, the program helps ensure that the client's interests and requirements are addressed adequately and properly and that the designer's information needs are met satisfactorily. The program is useful at several stages of project development, including:

—To establish gross areas and furnish other input for site evaluation and selection

—By fixing total scope, to determine the relative balance between new construction and improvements on a project with existing facilities

—To provide gross areas and other data necessary for a preliminary budget

—To provide gross areas of different types of space in different phases for use in master planning

—To provide functional criteria and constraints for an initial design concept of building and site

—To establish the basis for assigning functions to floors and wings of a building

—To give guidelines and performance criteria for design development

—To provide information for detailed layouts of furniture and equipment

Finally, facility programs are becoming important tools for evaluating designs during their development and after projects are constructed and occupied to determine how well they meet programmatic criteria.

THE MEANING OF PROGRAMMING

Programming is a word of relatively recent origin. It was extrapolated from a noun of long standing—program—by way of a verb—to program—in order to identify the process by which a program is achieved.

Many "programming" phrases appear in modern language, such as mathematical programming, linear programming, educational programming, management programming, government programming and budget programming. The ascent of automated procedures and computer technology have spawned a whole new set of terms including: to program a robot or a missile, programmable calculators and even programmed instruction.

Perhaps the most commonly used connotation is the association of programming with the computer field. Here, it is the process of preparing and supplying instructions to a computer by which the machine may draw from its bank of data to calculate solutions to problems that are the objects of the program.

DESIGN PROGRAMMING. There is perhaps more diversity in the use of the term and its meaning within the design profession than there is outside it. The more common phrases used include architectural programming, functional programming, space programming, operational programming and facility (and facilities) programming. British architects refer to the "programme" and programming as concepts having to do with project scheduling, organizing and costing within the architect's office; in other words, planning the tasks of designing. What most American, and some Canadian, architects refer to as programming, the British describe as "briefing." A project brief contains the "information, both general and specific, assembled for the purpose and providing the circumstances and requirements" of a design of a building (from the *RIBA Handbook of Architectural Practice and Management* of the Royal Institute of British Architects).

American architects have also used programming to refer, at least in part, to project scheduling and task organization.

HERBERT McLAUGHLIN, AIA
Kaplan/McLaughlin/Diaz, Architects/Planners
San Francisco, California

In reality, programming is design; particularly contemporary programming which has become increasingly comprehensive and complex. Not only is programming design, but it is a peculiar form of design, allowing client and architect to break through many of the preconceptions and limitations which dominate the usual design process.

Design is involved from conception of a project to occupancy, but most particularly in the earliest stages when the participants (client and architect) decide what is appropriate and what is possible. It begins unconsciously the moment the building is described, even in the most abstract terms. In programming, the players begin to define the design problem and therefore begin to solve it.

More than any other part of the design process, programming involves the unprejudiced analysis of a specific problem and its context. Because of its structure and reliance on techniques of interview and analysis and presentation in written rather than graphic form, programming remains the best time for analysis and clarity. It is usually the only phase of design during which the architect, user and owner can be compelled to explore and record their own prejudices and analyses of the solutions of others.

WALTER MOLESKI
Environmental Research Group
Philadelphia, Pennsylvania

Programming is simply that part of the design process which enables the architect to identify and define the problems which must be solved, the potential effects that the solutions will have on the people who will use or come in contact with the building and the constraints that will control the design process. The information provided in an architectural program should state the requirements that satisfy the needs of all those involved with the project. The program should explicitly state the objectives of each group in terms of the goals they wish to achieve, the issues that they want to resolve and the problems that they feel must be corrected.

The programming process must investigate the organizational, social and individual aspects of overt behavior. Because behavior in any social organization is largely controlled by administrative policy, this also must be considered in the planning of new facilities. Also, the program must consider the physical, psychological, sociological and cultural attributes of the users.

No matter how complete and rigorously defined, programming does not relieve the architect of design responsibility. Its purposes are to allow the designer to delve deeper into design problems in order to reveal their complexities and to serve as a tool to find meaningful solutions that are relevant and satisfying to the people who use, manage and own buildings.

WILLIAM M. PEÑA, FAIA
The CRS Group
Houston, Texas

The first two steps of the total design process are distinct and separate: (1) programming

Generally, however, it is used in reference to the client's requirements for a facility and to the design needs of a project.

Aside from the differing terms that identify programming and its elements, there is considerable philosophical diversity regarding the meaning of programming. The disparities in opinions, which sometime blossom into intellectual controversy on the meaning of programming, can be succinctly demonstrated by the following ascriptions:

—"Programming is design."
—"Programming is not design."
—"Programming is getting ready for design."
—"Programming is an inappropriate tool for designing."

Underlying these expressions are many arguable questions about programming's purpose and place in the design process. Is programming a separate or an indistinguishable service of design practice? Is it the exclusive responsibility of the client, an area in which the architect should assist only, or a task in which the architect should play a leading role? Is programming a part of design or separate from it? Does it precede or permeate designing? The difference of opinion seems to revolve about efforts to defend and/or expand the scope of design. Perhaps it could be agreed that programming is clearly within the scope of design, whether it is viewed as a separate service or an indistinguishable part of the design process; whether the program is provided by the client, the designer or by a third party.

The "problem" metaphor is prevalent in the literature on design process. A client's project is discussed as a problem and the architect's solution is a design. Design is seen as a problem-solving process. Programming enters the picture with the recognition that problems are no simpler than solutions. A problem needs to be identified or defined before it can be solved. A program, then, is a problem definition or a problem statement. Programming is a way of defining comprehensively and precisely what the problem is, and designing is comprehensively and precisely solving the problem. To illustrate:

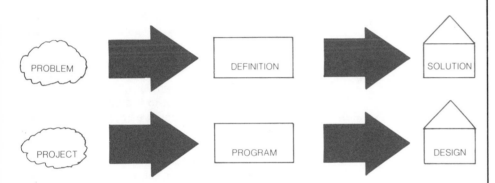

DEFINITION. What it all comes down to is information. A program is information the designer can use. It is *an organized collection of the specific information about the client's requirements which the architect needs in order to design a particular facility.* This encompasses not only the expressed requirements of the client, but all of the *human, physical and external factors which will influence the design.* A program is *communication.* It transmits and interprets the needs of the client to the designer.

Since a program is information—purposeful, specific, systemized information—then programming involves developing, managing and communicating the information. Programming is an information-processing process. For the purposes of this book, it is defined as *a process of identifying and defining the design needs of a facility and communicating the requirements of the client to the designer.*

Most architects, and others who program, agree that it is a process, but, as already mentioned, there is a range of opinions among them as to what constitutes this process and where it fits within the design process. Each practitioner has

to reach his or her own conclusions about the meaning of programming, how to use it, what techniques to employ and what information to produce. To help the individual clarify his or her own definition of programming, those of several architects and other programmers are presented in Exhibit 1-1.

THE NATURE OF PROGRAMMING

Programming has been defined as a process of identifying and defining the needs of a project and communicating the requirements of the client to the designer. It has also been described as a system of processing information. That description is meant to indicate that programming, as it has evolved in modern practice, involves more than information transfer. In response to the increasing complexity and consequence of design decisions, the need has grown for more precisely adequate and appropriate information on which to base those decisions. As a result, programming's emphasis has shifted away from delivery to development of the necessary information, and its character from that of a vehicle to that of a process.

In order to fully define the nature of programming, it will be examined in six general

categories: purpose, program audience, programmer, scope of information, process and program.

PURPOSE. An architect, engineer or facility planner must know, at least, what type of facility the client needs, what functions it will perform, the amount of space required, the restrictions on land use and facility form, and the size of the project budget. The primary purpose of programming is to supply the information needed for design.

The types and categories of information needed for any particular facility vary. Programming helps the designer organize and identify specific information needs.

The owner or developer of a project may have, more or less, all the data required to define its design objectives. In that case, programming is a relatively simple matter of preparing a program in a suitable format. The owner, the architect or a programming consultant might perform this task. Frequently, however, not all data are readily available for translation into a program, and producing the information will require a certain amount of research and interrogation. Similarly, the programmatic data a client supplies (either in the form of a program or solicited by the architect) may not be adequate or appropriate for the designer's needs. Again, a certain amount of investigation is required of the architect.

Thus, the purpose of programming a project becomes investigation and analysis of project design needs. This is even more pertinent when the client does not have a clear idea of what the project goals are or should be. For instance, the owner of a shoe factory may know how many shoes can be manufactured and sold in a year from an existing plant. But a manufacturer can't always translate that into the design needs for a new factory that can accommodate projected sales growth, new equipment, innovative procedures and planned automation. How (analysis) and (2) schematic design (synthesis). Programming is problem seeking and design is problem solving. Programming is seeking and finding the whole problem so that the design solution may be comprehensive.

Programming is an organized process based on standard procedures which can be used on large and small projects, simple and complex building types and with single or multiple clients . . .

. . . Programming is more than a process of asking questions. It is processing raw data into useful information. It is stimulating clients to make decisions.

Programming deals with the client's building program—which honors the client's goals and aspirations, ideas, needs, land and money. . . .

Source: *Problem Seeking—An Architectural Programming Primer* by William M. Peña, with William Caudill and John W. Focke. Boston: Cahners Books International Inc., 1977.

WOLFGANG F. E. PREISER
Architectural Research Consultants Inc.
Albuquerque, New Mexico

Facility programming enables communication among the eventual occupants, the providers and the managers of facilities. This communication is particularly necessary for large organizations and government agencies with highly complex and substantial construction programs, frequently consisting of repetitive building types such as offices, schools or housing.

Programming can be defined as the process that elicits and systematically translates the mission and objectives of an organization, group or individual person into activity-personnel-equipment relationships, thereby resulting in the functional program. These functional facility requirements are usually stated in performance language, and they are distinct from the architectural program, which consists of a "shopping list" of hardware assembled to match the functional program.

Source: "Introduction: Responding to the Changing Context of Environmental Design," *Facility Programming* edited by Wolfgang F. E. Preiser. Stroudsburg, Pa.: Dowden, Hutchinson & Ross Inc., 1978.

HENRY SANOFF, AIA
School of Design
North Carolina State University
Raleigh, North Carolina

A program is a communicable statement of intent. It is a prescription for a desired set of events influenced by local constraints and it states a set of desired conditions and the methods for achieving those conditions.

The program is a formal communication between designer and client in order that the client's needs and values are clearly stated and understood. It provides a method for decision making and a rationale for future decisions. It encourages greater client participation as well as user feedback. The program also serves as a log, a memory and a set of conditions that are amenable to postconstruction evaluation.

The program conveys current information on the progress of the project and its various stages of development. Frequently, it is perceived as an organizing procedure for codifying and classifying numerous bits of project information, sometimes misused,

much space will be needed over the next 20 years? Should the plant operations be reorganized and how? Are there alternative uses that could be accommodated if imported shoes flood the market and close down operations?

These types of questions can lead the architectural programmer into extensive data collection, projection analysis and even into nonarchitectural research areas such as marketing, technology applications and operations. Furthermore, the client may want to find out how automation will affect employee productivity and how different operational procedures and space utilization arrangements might improve productivity. It is easy to see that the objective of programming is much more than acquiring and organizing information; it often means developing and producing the information as well.

Another purpose of programming is communication. The program must serve the information needs of both the client and the designer. Programming enables both to understand and agree on the design goals, project needs and criteria for design. Programming helps achieve effective communication in information development and in decision making.

PROGRAM AUDIENCE. To whom is a program addressed? Who uses it? Although a program is the client's statement of design requirements, it is the designer's instrument for meeting those requirements. The program is to be used by the client in deciding the feasibility of a project, determining if facility needs have been adequately addressed (or determining what the needs are) and for making project and budget authorization decisions. The designer uses the program as a guide to the design criteria which must be fulfilled, a source of data for preparing design solutions and as a reference for making design decisions. Together, the client and designer use the program to monitor and evaluate the design as it develops and to reconcile conflicts between design needs and resources (such as space/budget conflicts).

Because it is a working resource for the designer, who must interpret the requirements and produce a design that fully responds to the client's needs, the program must be organized and presented in a manner that serves the designer's information needs. It must speak the designer's language while explaining the terms to the client. It should contain as much data as the designer requires for creative judgment, without overwhelming the lay client with technical details.

PROGRAMMER. The producer of the program for a facility might be the client, the design architect or a third-party programming consultant (who may also be an architect). In traditional client-architect arrangements, the program is the responsibility of the client, although the architect has an obligation to, at least, review the client's program of requirements and agree to an approved program. Because of the architect's specific information needs, however, the designer often ends up reorganizing or developing original data to suit his or her purposes. Some architects feel this task is a routine part of basic design services.

On the other hand, programming may be identified as a specific service in a package of services for which a design architect is retained. The design team may handle this responsibility, delegate it to the firm's programming staff, or retain the services of a programming consultant. Cost-based compensation approaches to architect's service agreements (such as those outlined in AIA Documents B161 and B162) have facilitated this kind of arrangement through designation of programming to either the client or the architect by mutual agreement.

An independent programming consultant can perform the work on behalf of either the facility owner or the architect.

Some architects specialize partially or exclusively in programming and related services. However, there are nonarchitectural programming specialists as well. Often, they concentrate on specific building types such as educational or health care institutions.

SCOPE OF INFORMATION. The scope of design information is the scope of programming information. That is, whatever data are necessary and relevant to the efficient, effective design of a facility that accommodates the needs of the client are the legitimate concerns of the programmer. This observation leaves very wide latitude for interpreting the scope of a specific program. Ideally, any program would address all factors which limit, influence and/or enable a facility's design. In ac- tuality, however, the purview of a program is determined by the programmer's inclination or routie, the client's interests and the resources of time and money available to produce it. The content of a program will differ also according to the type of program desired, the kinds of information needed and the level of detail appropriate.

Chapter 2 examines in greater depth types of design-influencing factors and the contents of programs. The types of information that programming may address can be classified in three categories: human factors, physical factors and external factors. The programmer not only investigates three areas of information, but also draws three types of information conclusions appropriate for programs: ascertainments, predictions and recommendations. Ascertainments state the objective findings of analysis; predictions project future implications and consequences; recommendations represent value judgments, the translation of findings into action concepts.

PROGRAMMING PROCESS. The nature of the programming process is investigative, analytical and systematic. This characterization runs somewhat contrary to the inclinations of designers, who tend to synthesize rather than analyze information and solve rather than define problems. The performance of programming requires a different kind of discipline than the design practitioner may be used to. It involves accumulation of all pertinent facts before making judgments or decisions; objective evaluation of data rather than application of data; making conclusions based on verified, project-specific facts rather than on intuition and previous experience. However, that doesn't mean that intuition and previous experience are excluded from programming. In fact, they are extremely important sources of preliminary data and criteria for judging conclusions.

Moreover, programming analysis does involve synthesis operations—e.g., identifying and testing relationships among data, patterns of needs and requirements, families of issues, etc. The synthesis of data in the analysis process creates the bases for the concepts addressed in schematics.

The intuitive, creative process of designing can be enhanced greatly by conclusive programmatic data that has been tested for relevance, reliability and validity through systematic, objective and analytical means. Some architects, however, feel that the difference between the natures of programming and designing is too significant for both activities to be performed by the same personnel. The two tasks are delegated to separate programming and designing specialists. On the other hand, some architects see program-

ming as a direct extension of the design process, in spite of the different perspectives of a design problem. They argue that separation of the activities inhibits the necessary continuity between handling the design problem and its solution.

Programming is still evolving as a process, and perhaps that explains the differing viewpoints on its nature and use. Some general features have emerged, however. It is recognized by its practitioners as a dynamic and interactive process; that is, the information and the program evolve through the discovery and manipulation of many factors that influence and respond to the environment and to each other, and do so differently under alternative conditions. Programming is also viewed as a decision-making process, a part of the design decision-making process. It enables and produces a progression of increasingly refined decisions involving interaction of client, programmer and designer.

Chapter 2 examines the process of programming in greater detail as well as individual procedural methodologies used by architects and others. The following overview touches on four areas: information processing, procedure, participants and techniques.

Information Processing. Programming is an information-processing system. It involves the performance of five principal functions: collection, analysis, organization, communication and evaluation of information. All the functions are continuous, occurring from the beginning to the end of a programming project, although they vary in scope and activity at various stages of information development. However, evaluation is generally more appropriate when information conclusions have been reached and are reviewed.

Procedure. There are different procedural methodologies employed by programmers, some of which are examined

in Chapter 2. Each programmer must establish a system for getting the job done efficiently and effectively. Be that as it may, a procedural model based on the commonalities of systems that appear in practice today has been developed for this book. It is merely outlined here for further discussion in the next chapter. The following are the basic steps, which may not always proceed in this order, for developing a program:

—Establish project goals
—Organize the programming effort
—Investigate issues
—Integrate data
—Interpret information
—Instruct designer and client
—Evaluate results
—Recycle information

The last step identified is a key element in the modern use of programming. Many programs today are the result of several iterations or cycles of information processing, each of which is successively more precise and specific than the preceding. Furthermore, recycling also means feeding information developed in programming into the design phases in order to monitor and evaluate the design, as well as into subsequent facility programming projects.

Participants. There are three main categories of participants in the programming process: client, programmer and designer. The roles, relationships and responsibilities of each are explained in Chapter 2 and discussed in Chapter 21, but the categories are briefly defined here.

The term *client* is used to refer to the collective body of individuals and groups that is related in various ways to the facility which is programmed. It includes not only the *owner* or developer of a facility, but the *users* and *related publics* that may affect or be affected by the facility. In a sense, the programmer "works for" all three because the program should address the needs of each one.

The *programmer* is the firm or individual who conducts the programming and produces the program. This may be the project architect, a professional (perhaps an architect) who specializes in programming, or the client's in-house facility planning and/or programming staff (again, this might include architects).

Designer identifies the architect-of-record. The firm or individual is the principal user of the program and interprets it in the development of a design.

Techniques. A wide variety of techniques and tools for collecting, analyzing, organizing, communicating and evaluating information is available to the programmer. Many have been developed by architects and other programmers in response to the specialized information needs of programming and designing. Others originate in fields such as management science, communications, computer science, statistics, market and opinion research, and planning. The awakening of interest in consumer (facility user) needs has opened access to the abundance of methods and procedures employed in the behavioral and social sciences such as sociology, psychology, anthropology and economics.

The techniques employed in programming should be appropriate to the information required, the nature and scope of the project, the client's interests and, of course, the resources of time, budget and personnel. A substantial portion of this book (Part Two) is devoted to examination of the potential and procedures of a variety of techniques for programming.

COMPREHENSIVE PROGRAMS. The content of a program, the form of the information and the format of the communication will vary from project to project, from client to client, from programmer to programmer, and from designer to designer. The goal, however, always should be to provide adequate, appropriate information that clearly communicates the specific needs of that project so that the designer may satisfy those needs through whatever creative, efficient, effective form he or she deems most suitable for the client.

There is great variety in program types. The application may be broad or narrow, simple or complex. It is possible to program both a room and an urban complex. A program may be an itemization of the physical spaces required for a building and/or an analysis of the human, physical and external factors that must be considered in its design. Depending on the focus, it may be a space program, activity program, functional program, engineering program, site program, operations program, etc.

However, for facility design—particularly architecture—the main interest is *comprehensive programs*. Comprehensive programs address the total facility in terms of the physical, human and external factors and requirements that affect its total design. Programs may be general or specific. There are essentially three levels of detail for comprehensive programs: master program, facility program and component program. They differ not only in scale of detail but also in purpose and, to a degree, in content, as will be explained in the next chapter.

THE EVOLUTION OF PROGRAMMING

The program, if not programming, is probably as old as architecture. Every design project has had a program, either implied or stated, that told what the design needed or should accomplish. There would never have been a pyramid, a Parthenon, a Westminster Abbey if someone didn't have a vision, an idea, of what could be or should be done. Once the vision was articulated and its requirements stated, it became a program.

Through most of architecture's formal history, a program has been an informal matter—a simple, verbal statement of requirements from one individual directly to another; i.e., from client or patron to architect. Such an arrangement is unlikely today, except for the most uncomplicated facility such as a simple house. Complexity in all matters of concern to the modern architect—buildings and building technology, contractual arrangements, client composition, design itself, regulation, economic and social forces, availability of resources—necessitates detailed investigation, analysis and documentation.

As facility requirements and other influencing factors have become more complex, diversified and specialized, the need for thorough and systemized methods of investigating and identifying them has intensified. The development of programming as a process and a service over the past third of a century has been a response to this need. Yet the earliest and most sustained interest in the field has been outside the province of design. Management experts were among the first to recognize the opportunities for programming, applying their expertise in operations research, systems analysis and efficiency management to organization and space planning in large office buildings. Other building types with specialized space and activity requirements, such as hospitals and educational institutions, also have seen development of professional firms devoted to programming specifications for their unique circumstances.

The intensifying of social consciousness and consumer awareness in society, extending into both the natural and built environments, has aroused the interest of social and behavioral scientists to apply their expertise to explaining the human dimension of architecture. For many years, psychologists and sociologists have researched human behavior in relation to architecture and the impact of environmental settings on activities, attitudes and

EXHIBIT 1-2. SYNOPSES OF MAJOR PROGRAMMING BOOKS

Problem Seeking: An Architectural Programming Primer. William Peña with William Caudill and John Focke. Boston: Cahners Books International, 1977, 204 pp.

A practical formula for programming, this is a description of The CRS Group's five-step method. Pena emphasizes the separation of programming (analysis) from design (synthesis), and emphasizes that programming comes before, not during, the design phase. Programming, according to Peña, reduces the guesswork of designing for users' needs, but seeks rather than solves design problems.

The programming stage consists of the five steps:
(1) Establish goals
(2) Collect facts
(3) Uncover concepts
(4) Determine needs
(5) State problem

The first four steps need not be in the particular order as listed, Peña notes, but stage five, problem statement, must be the final task as it represents the culmination of the preceding four. Problem statement is also the link between programming and design, Peña states.

Each of the five steps is defined in terms of Function/Form/Economy/Time. A matrix of the five steps as a function of Function, Form, Economy and Time is developed as a checklist of programming activities. This checklist is to be used in schematic programming and program development, according to the author.

The book also discusses information handling and organization as well as team organization and communication in the programming process. An appendix provides glossaries; problem statement examples; programming procedures; sophistication, situations and simplifications of programming, and useful techniques.

Facility Programming. Wolfgang F.E. Preiser, ed. Stroudsburg, Pa.: Dowden, Hutchinson & Ross Inc., 1978, 352 pp.

An overview of programming approaches and procedures of various individuals experienced in the discipline. An edited compilation approach is used because no one person would "have a full understanding of all the considerations and approaches that are necessary and already practiced in order to bring about a more habitable built environment," according to Preiser.

The book is divided into three main subheadings which pertain to the main thrust of the programming backgrounds of chapter authors: Facility Programming, Programming for Architecture and Design, and Research for Facility Programing.

"Facility Programming" is a collection of how-to's from five individuals specializing in programming services, and one MIT professor's theoretical explanation of applying programming data to design.

"Programming for Architecture and Design," on the other hand, is a series of five articles from architectural practitioners describing how they have applied programming techniques in the predesign phase of project development.

Both sections are similar in that they contain articles separately emphasizing adaptability of the built environment, human needs in design, and renovation of existing facilities.

"Research for Facility Programming" is devoted to six articles addressing methodologies of programming research. The described research involves general user needs, perceptions. More recently, behavioralists have begun to explore practical applications of their knowledge and techniques in areas such as programming and post-occupancy evaluation.

These nonarchitectural disciplines have created approaches—such as managing, specifying and explaining—to the handling of design complexity. On the other hand, although programming has been recognized as a distinct function, if not service, in the architectural profession, few efforts have been made to develop its potential until comparatively recently.

A notable exception is the firm of Caudill Rowlett Scott of Houston, Texas (a part of The CRS Group). The firm and one of its principals, William M. Pena, FAIA, have probably contributed more to the formalization and popularization of the programming process than any other single architect or firm.

Peña's career parallels the history of programming. It is reported that he programmed his first building in 1949, but it was ten years later that he and partner William Caudill, both founders of CRS, wrote a pioneering article in *Architectural Record* magazine that established the basic principles of a programming methodology which has become one of the firm's hallmarks.

In 1969, their first publication on architectural programming appeared under the authorship of Peña and another architect/programmer, John W. Focke, AIA. An expanded successor book was published in 1977 with the same title, *Problem Seeking: An Architectural Programming Primer.*

THE AIA AND PROGRAMMING. The first significant recognition of programming as a distinct service phase of design by The American Institute of Architects (AIA) came in 1966 in a booklet called *Emerging Techniques of Architectural Practice.* It noted the growing interest among architects in developing techniques for "the expert planning and scheduling of the programming phase of a project." There were also references to questionnaires, forms, analytical diagrams, space analysis diagrams, bar charts and "other planning techniques."

Three years later, coincident with, but not connected with, the release of Peña's initial programming guide, the AIA published another booklet, *Emerging Techniques 2: Architectural Programming.* It was the Institute's first major publication devoted to the subject and is the predecessor of this book. The 70-page booklet consisted primarily of a lengthy catalogue of summaries on techniques used in programming, many of which are still employed today.

The listing continued an emphasis on project task management, orderly data assemblage and standardized formats. However, there was a noteworthy recognition that the requirements of a project extend beyond those expressed by the client (owner). Programming, the text explained, "is the means by which data about the needs of the *ultimate building user* [emphasis added] are determined and expressed for the instruction of the architect in the development of a design solution." Such data may include, it also said, "social, spiritual, aesthetic or esoteric considerations that may or should influence the decision making."

A distinction was made also between the roles of the client and the architect in developing the program. According to *Emerging Techniques 2*, programming was clearly a responsibility of the client, although it could be delegated to the architect, and consisted of four main elements: client philosophy and objectives, functional relationships, facility space requirements and client background and research. However, the booklet then indicated there was a second program to be prepared, this one by the architect. The responsibility of the architect is best explained by an excerpt from the text: "After the collection and analysis of data

EXHIBIT 1-2. SYNOPSES OF MAJOR PROGRAMMING BOOKS (CONT'D)

postconstruction analysis, and one explanation of computer use in maximizing the use of programming data in design development.

A concluding chapter by John P. Eberhard, then president of the AIA Research Corporation, is an overview analysis of the potential of increased use of programming by the architectural profession. He has an optimistic view of the future of architectural programming, especially computer application to programming, but he warns against the sterilization of design through overemphasis of concrete purpose over aesthetics.

Methods of Architectural Programming. Henry Sanoff. Stroudsburg, Pa.: Dowden, Hutchinson & Ross Inc., 1977, 208 pp.

Sanoff defines "programming" as a communicable statement of intent that is a prescription for a desired set of events influenced by local constraints, and that states a set of desired conditions as well as the methods for achieving those conditions. In the process, the programmer normally uses decision-making tools to determine relative importance of information, to discover relationships and to resolve conflicts. The main portion of this book is devoted to the description and illustration of a variety of decision-making tools for programming.

Sanoff begins with "Preconditions to Programming" in which he illuminates some basic methods of organizing a firm's resources for problem evaluation/solving. The examples emphasize group problem-solving methods.

In "Information Retrieval Methods," Sanoff describes several specific methods of: identifying and exploring the design problem, searching for and expanding ideas, classifying and analyzing information, generating and evaluating alternatives, producing preliminary design, and conducting postcompletion evaluation. These methods are divided into categories of methodology: collective decision methods, comparison methods, rating methods, visual preference methods, descriptive and evaluative methods, and design methods.

"Methods of Transforming Design Information" explains the vital link between information collection and design synthesis. Six design models are presented as tools for standardizing the data-to-drawings procedure, each of which emphasizes maximum client input.

The book concludes with analysis of five case study programs exemplifying the concepts of: user-participation questionnaire data gathering, computer-aided programming, space planning, educational facilities programming, and simulation game data gathering.

Introduction to Architectural Programming. Edward T. White III. Tucson, Ariz.: Architectural Media, 1972, 84 pp.

A basic programming primer, this paperback manual gives the background of programming and its role in modern-day architecture, and provides how-to-program instruction. The book was written with the intent of "promoting the concept and value of programming" to architecture students, practicing architects and clients alike. The presentation introduces the reader to theoretical and practical applications of traditional programming, emphasizing three areas: the value of programming; the operations involved in producing a program; and the relationships "between issues within programming, between programming and design synthesis, and between [the] program and the final design."

EXHIBIT 1-2. SYNOPSES OF MAJOR PROGRAMMING BOOKS (CONT'D)

The book is subdivided into 10 chapters:
—Programming Paradigm
—Survey of Programming
—Research
—Philosophy and Facts
—Nontraditional Facts
—Traditional Facts
—Information Gathering
—Analysis, Evaluation and Organization of Facts
—Designing from the Program
—Program and Design Evaluation

These chapters are organized in a structured outline format. Diagrammatic illustrations are used generously to emphasize the text.

on the four elements of programming, the architect then can develop his [sic] program instrument *from which the designs are produced.*'' (Emphasis added.) The implications of this division have probably raised many questions such as why are two programs needed? Why doesn't the architect produce both? Why should the architect assume a programming responsibility without being compensated?

Since that time, other efforts and publications have promoted programming as a service. A chapter was devoted to the subject in *Current Techniques in Architectural Practice* (1976). Programming became a "designated" service under the AIA Document B162, Scope of Designated Services. Finally, since 1973, the annual guide for professional examinations published by the National Council of Architectural Registration Boards has devoted 25 percent of the test preparation and example test portions to programming.

RESOURCES ON PROGRAMMING

In the past decade, particularly near its end, the burgeoning interest in architectural programming was reflected in the publication of several books on the sub-

ject. After the above-mentioned 1969 publications, the first major document appeared in 1972, entitled *Introduction to Architectural Programming* by Edward T. White III. Then, in 1977 and 1978, three other works appeared: Peña's revised edition of *Problem Seeking; Methods of Architectural Programming* by Henry Sanoff; and *Facility Programming*, edited by Wolfgang F.E. Preiser. A synopsis of each of these four books is presented in Exhibit 1-2.

This book, *The Architect's Guide to Facility Programming*, has sought to combine elements that reflect the central themes of the other major publications. The next chapter explores the process and products of programming. Following chapters address techniques appropriate to programming, both manual and automated. Next in order is a series of case studies examining the methods, techniques and products of programming projects. The final chapter discusses some of the business aspects concerned with programming in architectural practice.

A number of other references closely related to the procedures and concerns of facility programming also have been published in recent years. A substantial portion deals with issues and techniques relevant to investigation of human needs

in the built environment. References of interest to architects are annotated in the bibliographic section of this book.

THE ARCHITECT'S ROLE IN PROGRAMMING

It is not a certainty that an architect will program every project which he or she designs. An owner may provide a perfectly adequate program or may have had one professionally prepared by a consultant or another architect before the design architect comes on the scene. However, in all probability, an architect will be involved in programming, to one degree or another, in just about every project he or she undertakes. It may involve only reorganizing the information into a more useful order or format, filling in missing data or adding elements. The design architect may play a contributory role in programming conducted by another architect or professional. On the other hand, an architect may provide a complete program for a project either to supplement or detail the client's program, as part of a design services package or as a separate service.

Programming is not exclusive to the architect's domain. It may be, and is, performed by planners, engineers, space management consultants, interior designers and other professionals. The fact is, many architects have tended to relegate comprehensive programming to specialists. Nevertheless, the trend is toward greater involvement of architects in programming, both in practice and in specific projects.

Architects bring a unique perspective to facility programming because of their coordinative and responsible position in projects, their expertise in designing and their manner of conceptualizing. The professional architect, by training and experience, is not only able to assimilate and translate the wants and requirements of a client, but to combine that information with the architectural and other requirements for design, of which the client is often unaware. The architect's predilection to synthesize information and coordinate information sources, although not always conducive to the analytical procedures of programming, is vital to the decision-making process of programming.

Where the architect may sometimes fall short is in thoroughly examining the human needs aspects relative to the physical aspects of a facility so that the form and function of design respond effectively to realistic criteria of use. However, awareness of the importance of this aspect is growing, and methods for identifying user needs are becoming integrated into the design process.

The next chapter explores how architects and other design professionals can comprehend and employ the process of programming and skillfully develop useful programming products.

Chapter 2
The Process
of Programming

"Programming is architectural analysis and designing is architectural synthesis," distinguishes William M. Peña, FAIA, in his book, *Problem Seeking: An Architectural Programming Primer*. Many architects won't accept such a differentiation, and some explicitly reject it. It is safe to say, however, that programming and designing are two parts of the same process: development of architecture primarily to accommodate the needs of the client.

In spite of this common objective, programming and designing do operate differently in their development of architectural information. They are distinct activities that require different approaches, resources and procedures, even though they might be considered "mirror images" of each other, as one programmer has put it, or one a part of the other. The distinction may become clear if examined through another optical metaphor illustrated in Exhibit 2-1.

Both a program and a design are *projected images* of reality, emanating from a client and circumstances, and progressively focused by the processes of programming and designing. Both serve to define a project, bringing the client's goal closer to the reality of a constructed, occupied, operating facility.

Through programming, information (relevant knowledge of reality) is translated from one form—client's goals, circumstances, influencing factors—into another—design requirements, performance criteria, parameters and constraints—that can be understood and used by the designer. Programming is a lens that focuses and filters information into a clear, words-and-numbers picture of what is needed for design.

The designer's lens manipulates this "image" of information and projects it in a new form: schematic and detailed drawings. The same information processed by programming is further refined and focused by designing until it becomes

EXHIBIT 2-1. PROGRAMMING AND DESIGNING PROJECT DIFFERENT IMAGES OF REALITY

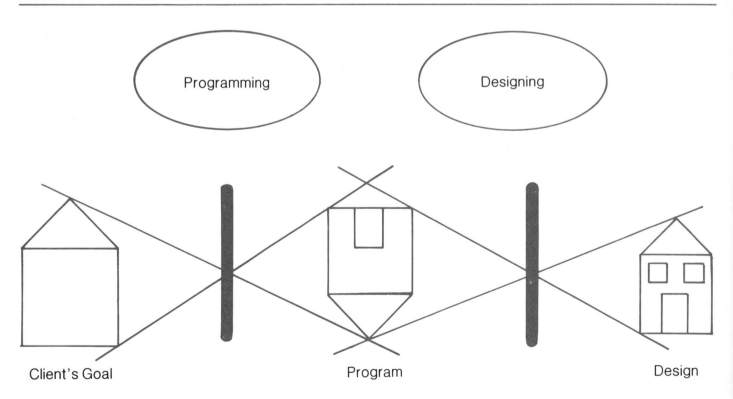

a unique and three-dimensional statement of what it was originally when the client said "I want a school," "I want a hospital," or "I want a factory."

The process of projecting an image of reality operates differently in programming and in designing. Designing is primarily intuitive, creative, synthesizing, interpretive. Programming is rational, investigative, analytical, objective. The issues and the subject matter may be the same—design information—but the perspectives and the approaches are different.

For one thing the scope of programming information is broader, not only in the kinds of issues investigated but in its perspective of routine design issues. For example, programming seeks to establish an empirical basis for support of routine architectural considerations such as types of spaces, quantities and dimensions. A sophisticated programming investigation of these issues might include an evaluation of the client's organization, analysis of personnel activities and interactions, and observation of actual space usage. The resulting program should provide a realistic appraisal of space needs based on factual evidence.

Moreover, nonroutine or nonconventional architectural issues such as behavior settings, environmental quality, organizational communication, energy consumption and market impact, may need to be addressed in programming a facility because they affect its ability to function successfully. Too often, however, the client may not have the inclination or money, nor the architect the time and resources, to pursue such matters. The systemized process of programming and use of appropriate programming techniques enable the architect to bring such matters into the realm of facility design.

PROGRAMMING INFORMATION

The primary purpose of programming is to provide the architect with the information necessary to make design decisions. The most important and difficult part of programming is deciding what information is necessary and relevant to the design of a particular facility. It may even involve determining what information is relevant to architecture, in terms of the facility or in general.

SCOPE OF INFORMATION. Many often confusing, sometimes conflicting factors affect the development of a facility. The programmer's task is to discover *which factors affect* the facility and *what are the significances* of each influence. Once important factors have been identified, the programmer then must determine *how they interact* with each other and with the potential facility to limit, enable and/or otherwise influence its design.

Before examining the types of factors and information that programming addresses, two general factors which affect programming in modern practice should be discussed.

Client/Designer Interests. Although intended primarily for the facility's designer, a program also must satisfy the client's (in particular, the owner's) information needs. In a sense, the programmer must prepare two separate programs that overlay each other, usually in a single document. One addresses the interests of the client and the other the interests of the designer.

Owners are interested in data that enable them to judge the worth of a project: costs of designing, constructing and operating; future use; functional efficiency; the amount of time it will take to build and occupy the facility. The designer is also concerned with these matters, not only because of the client's interest but because they impact the design response to the client's needs. However, other considerations usually are of more direct interest to the designer in terms of his or her ability to deliver the project. These might include: restrictions on the site and facility; functions to be accommodated; types and amounts of space required; functional relationships, space proximities and circulation; economy of form and space.

This is not to say that the interests diverge or are inconsistent. On the contrary, all the factors that affect a facility are of mutual concern; it is the emphasis that may differ, as Exhibit 2-2 illustrates. The programmer should be aware of the different emphases and accommodate them in developing and presenting the program.

Expanding Scope of Programming. As suggested earlier, the scope of programming information has changed and expanded since programming was for-

EXHIBIT 2-2. CLIENT/DESIGNER INTERESTS DIFFER IN EMPHASIS

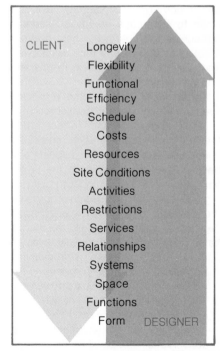

CLIENT

- Longevity
- Flexibility
- Functional Efficiency
- Schedule
- Costs
- Resources
- Site Conditions
- Activities
- Restrictions
- Services
- Relationships
- Systems
- Space
- Functions
- Form

DESIGNER

(Examples not necessarily in order of priority)

mally recognized as a distinct aspect of facility development. The traditional program might include design objectives, space requirements, space relationships, flexibility, expansibility, special equipment and systems, and site requirements.

Programmers in modern practice recognize a wider range of issues that have an impact on design as well as the value of accumulating adequate information at the earliest possible stage of project decision making. Community and public interest issues, for instance, are addressed in a growing number of programs: e.g., environmental and economic impact, preservation, neighborhood use and aesthetic compatibility, land use, and, perhaps the most recent, solar access.

Two factors, however, have had the greatest impact on changing the scope of program information: energy conservation and user needs. The rising costs of conventional fuels for heating, cooling, lighting and operating facilities, and the public recognition of energy scarcity have combined to encourage *energy conservation* through design. Energy use control affects facilities at all stages of their development and use, from site selection to operation and maintenance.

Facility worth has become very sensitive to energy costs and conservation. As a result, decisions which affect project feasibility, size, configuration, orientation, space use and many other aspects have been pushed back earlier in the project timetable. Methods of incorporating energy concerns into the design process and the tools and techniques for analyzing energy use at various stages in the process have been developing rapidly over the past five years. The role of programming in addressing energy use includes:

    —Comparison of fuel costs by types
    —Cost-benefit analysis of alternative energies such as solar
    —Identification of alternative energy conservation strategies for the facility
    —Preliminary HVAC load analysis

—Preparing and recommending energy use goals and/or budgets
—Identifying space utilization arrangements to reduce energy consumption
—Projecting life cycle costs of energy use in budget planning
—Site orientation to take advantage of and ameliorate climatic conditions
—Site selection using energy conservation as one criterion
—Analyzing availability of energy resources

The other major influence on the changing nature of programming and its scope is *user needs*. The worth of a facility can be measured by its ability to accommodate its intended use. Unfortunately, the people who have the most direct and extensive relationship with use—the occupants, operators, consumers and those who otherwise use the facility—have often been overlooked in designing efficient, effective, economical form and function.

The reason for the neglect of users is twofold. First, the owner's concern for operational efficiency and economy often focuses on technology, resources, systems and costs rather than on the people who make operations efficient and cost-effective or inefficient and ineffective. The consideration of the human dimension of facility operations is secondary, if it is a concern at all.

Second, designers base their design judgments of appropriate facility use on their own experiences, values, attitudes and behavior. These may be quite different from those of general population and, in particular, the users of a specific facility.

User needs are not intended to refer primarily to such esoteric things as how many people in an office drink their coffee black or how home life affects work performance. In facility programming, user needs pertain to those aspects of attitude and behavior that are, more or less, directly related to efficiency and effective-

ness of facility use. The objective of investigating user needs is to obtain, firsthand, a realistic accounting of such things as how operations are performed; how people interact with each other and their surroundings; what effects lighting conditions, noise and comfort have on productivity; what equipment and furnishings are necessary; how organizational and communications structures affect space allocation and arrangement; how environment influences perception and how perception influences environment; what user preferences can be accommodated to achieve efficiency and effectiveness, and so forth.

Programmers more frequently go directly to the source—the users themselves—for this information rather than relying on their own assumptions or taking the word of owners. The questionnaire, interview, perception and preference test, observational study and other techniques of direct data collection have become standard practices in many programming efforts. The result is that programs more precisely and reliably reflect the real needs of facility use to which the design can respond appropriately.

THREE CATEGORIES OF INFORMATION. The factors, and information about them, which are relevant to design are many and varied and don't lend themselves to easy categorization. Peña has created a simplified classification that includes Form, Function, Time, Economy and Energy; each is further divided into three subcategories. *Introduction to Architectural Programming*, by Edward T. White III, contains seven pages of "typical" factors that he considers "traditional" architectural considerations or "facts." He breaks them into nine categories:

    —Similar projects and critical issues
    —Client
    —Financial
    —Building codes
    —Planning by related organizations

—Function
—Site
—Climate
—Growth and change

Another way to categorize the factors which should be taken into consideration in developing program information is a three-way classification: human factors, physical factors and external factors.

Human factors include all aspects that pertain to the owner, users and public relevant to the facility. They might encompass, for example, the client's organizational structure, client objectives, number of people and demographic characteristics, activities, perceptions, comfort, productivity, etc.

Physical factors are more easily identifiable within their category. They include such things as space types and dimensions, functions, adjacency, operations, circulation, equipment/furnishings, aesthetic qualities, internal and external environments, and durable life of the facility.

External factors are those which influence the facility and its design but may be outside the control, more or less, of the client or designer. These include codes, standards and regulations; development or construction time; costs; climate; topography; future conditions; and energy resources.

A more extensive, but not exclusive, list of design-influencing factors, divided according to the three categories, is presented in Exhibit 2-3. These represent a sampling of the kinds of issues and data that might be investigated in programming a facility. The categorization also represents a possible way of organizing a programming study and/or of organizing a program.

SCOPE OF INVESTIGATION. It should be clear that it would require an inordinate amount of time and resources to analyze thoroughly the impacts and implications of all human, physical and external factors

EXHIBIT 2-3. FACTORS THAT INFLUENCE FACILITY DESIGN

HUMAN FACTORS	PHYSICAL FACTORS	EXTERNAL FACTORS
Activities	Location	Legal Restrictions
Behavior	—Region	(Codes/Standards/
Objectives/Goals	—Locality	Regulations)
Objectives/Goals	—Community	—Building
Organization	—Vicinity	—Land use
—Hierarchy		—Systems
—Groups	Site Conditions	—Energy
—Positions		—Environment
—Classifications	Building/Facility	—Materials
—Leadership		—Safety
	Envelope	—Solar access
Characteristics	Structure	
(Demographics)		Topography
	Systems	
Social Forces	—Engineering	Climate
	—Communications	Ecology
Political Forces	—Lighting	
	—Security	Resource Availability
Interactions		
—Communication	Space	Energy Supplies/Prices
—Relationships	—Types	—Conventional
—Transfer of materials,	—Dimensions	—Solar
etc.	—Relationships	—Alternatives
Policies/Codes	Equipment/Furnishings	Economy
Attitudes/Values	Materials/Finishes	Financing
Customs/Beliefs	Support Services	Time
	—Storage	—Schedule
Perceptions	—Parking	—Deadlines
	—Access	—Operations
Preferences	—Waste removal	
	—Utilities (water,	Costs/Budget
Qualities	sewage, telephone)	—Construction
—Comfort		—Materials
—Productivity	Uses	—Services
—Efficiency		—Operations
—Security	Functions	
—Safety	Behavior/Activity Settings	Costs/Benefits
—Access		
—Privacy	Operations	
—Territory	Circulation	
—Control		
—Convenience	Environment	
	—Comfort	
	—Visual	
	—Acoustical	
	Energy Use/Conservation	
	Durability/Flexibility	

for a particular facility—even of the limited listing exhibited here. Depending on the nature and scope of a project, programming may address primarily one of the categories or focus on a single issue such as economic feasibility, activity analysis or space use.

However, in most cases (even those listed in the last paragraph), programming must be comprehensive; it must, at least, address as many factors as possible from all three categories. The influences which limit and enable the design of a facility are interdependent and interactive. To exclude any for the sake of time and economy, for instance, may distort the meaning or significance of others and result in inaccurate or inappropriate recommendations for design.

Energy conservation is a good example. If only the engineering systems, the envelope and the climatic conditions of a building are considered in assessing thermal energy requirements, this may achieve the objective of reducing energy consumption. However, it can limit the designer's options for not only conserving energy but also satisfying other criteria of design. The energy analysis should take into consideration the effects of heat gain from people and equipment, the comfort requirements imposed by various human activities, the arrangement of spaces, desired aesthetic qualities and availability of energy supplies and of alternative energy technologies. The objective is to optimize the energy performance, rather than to merely cut back energy use, while, at the same time, optimizing the other functional criteria of the facility.

For each project, the programmer must select what is relevant and important for the particular facility. The following are a few guidelines on defining the scope of investigation.

—Certain factors are fundamental. Most programs, unless specially oriented, address these basic types of information extracted from Exhibit 2-3:

HUMAN FACTORS
Activities
Objectives
Organization
Interactions
Policies
Preferences

PHYSICAL FACTORS
Site conditions
Building/facility
Systems
Space
Functions
Circulation
Internal environment
Useful life
Energy use

EXTERNAL FACTORS
Legal restrictions
Climate
Time
Costs

—Specific factors will have prominent influence on the facility. They may be determined by circumstances (e.g., energy shortage, operational problem, facility purpose, site restrictions), client's goals or public interests. Identifying which factors have the most significant impact on the facility will give the programmer direction for conducting the investigation. The prominent factors may not be obvious at the outset of programming, but that is one of its objectives: to identify them so that none are excluded from the designer's consideration.

—Time and money constrain the scope of investigation. Without neglecting any important considerations, the programmer must estimate the amount of time and resources needed to develop the program information. If it requires more than the client is willing to support or than the programmer is willing to commit, then the scope will have to be scaled down. In some cases, this may be to the detriment of the project.

—The designer's information needs and how he or she will use the program information determine the scope of the program and, to a certain extent, the scope of the investigation of program information. The programmer should be aware of designers' needs in general and of the needs of the particular facility designer in developing the program.

SOURCES OF INFORMATION. When the planned facility is a replacement or a renovation, the existing facility is one of the principal resources of programming investigation. Direct observation of its elements and functions, and of how users interact with it and in it, provide a substantial portion of the base data for programming the proposed facility. Construction drawings, floor plans and previous programs are also valuable sources of data.

The other primary source of information for the programmer is the client. The owner may provide data in anticipation of programming, but the programmer— theoretically the expert on what to look for on behalf of the designer—must also elicit data from the owner. The users— occupants, operators and consumers— are even more important sources, having direct knowledge of a facility's contents, functions, problems, advantages, dysfunctions, etc. Unless the owner has investigated user-related issues prior to programming, data from this source will not be as accessible or available and the programmer must employ sometimes sophisticated techniques of gathering relevant information from users.

The designer's and the programmer's own experiences with the facility type will also provide useful data, but caution should be exercised against the assumption that it is routinely applicable for the facility under study. Experiential data is useful in establishing investigation goals and in testing and verifying programming conclusions.

Other sources of programming information might include:
—Observation of similar facilities
—Drawings and programs of similar facilities as well as other literature on the facility type
—Research findings, literature and reports on behavior, attitudes, user needs, environmental design, etc.
—Computerized inventories of existing space and equipment
—Owner's mandatory standards
—Owner's records, reports, promotional literature
—Local authorities such as planning, zoning and building code officials, utility companies, government agencies

The programmer also may retain consultants and other experts to address specific aspects of programming or to participate on the programming team. The use of consultant specialists for programming studies is discussed in Chapter 21.

PROGRAM CONTENTS. A program is a culmination of the information development process. Some programmers call it the final stage of programming and the first stage in designing. It contains facts and conclusions that have been distilled from raw data and preliminary parameters. The program enables the designer to focus on relevant information, improv-

ing the capacity for both precision and creativity in design.

The content of a program will depend on the nature and complexity of the project and on the information the programmer has agreed to provide as a service to the client (see discussion of contracts in Chapter 21). The issues may be reported in any organized manner that clearly communicates the facility needs and/or requirements. Examples of organizing frameworks of various programs are shown in the case studies presented in Part Three. Another method of organizing the program is according to the three categories of design-influencing factors discussed previously and the three types of programming conclusions discussed next.

Program Conclusions. A program is a document that states the requirements of the client and the needs of the project for design. It may be expressed in terms of directions for the designer, component prescriptions, design goals, alternative solutions or performance criteria. Since the designer is the primary user of the program, the latter must clearly present conclusions in conformance with the methodology and terminology of designers in general and, where possible, of the specific designer in particular.

The program is deficient if it is merely a compilation of the data collected and analyzed in the course of programming. The programmer must distill what is important and relevant from a veritable mountain of materials in order to present the designer with the essential facts and conclusions. Otherwise, it will be of little use to the designer, who may have neither the time nor inclination to sort through a program document to extract what might be worthwhile information.

Program conclusions define the issues and present the concepts or precepts that must be addressed in design. They give the designer not only evidence of design-influencing factors but ideas and strategies for accommodating specific needs.

There are three types of conclusions useful for the designer's purposes: ascertainments, predictions and recommendations.

Ascertainments are statements of conditions, processes and events that influence, restrict and/or enhance the facility's design and that should be accommodated or created. Included in this category are statements about existing conditions that are relevant to design decisions.

Predictions are forecasts about the influences of certain factors, projections of future conditions and expectations of the consequences of design decisions.

EXHIBIT 2-4. MATRIX OF PROGRAM CONCLUSIONS AND INFORMATION FACTORS

	HUMAN FACTORS	PHYSICAL FACTORS	EXTERNAL FACTORS
ASCERTAINMENTS			
PREDICTIONS			
RECOMMENDATIONS			

Recommendations are specific directions or proposed actions as to what should be done to accommodate or create desired conditions, processes and events for effective design.

In combination with the three-factor classification explained earlier, the three conclusion types can create an organizing framework for a programming project and for the resulting program, as depicted in Exhibit 2-4. Not every program will contain every type of conclusion.

In fact, specific programs or special program reports may be expressed in only one form, such as an ascertainment of user needs or a long-range plan. In general, however, most programs present a combination of at least two types of conclusions.

Each type of conclusion is not necessarily appropriate for all the information factors a program includes. The programmer should not try to fit an ascertainment, a prediction and a recommendation to each issue addressed unless it helps the client and/or the designer understand the issue and make reliable decisions. Nevertheless, that is one way to present the program report, as shown in Exhibit 2-5.

Another way is based on the fact that recommendations are the real heart of the program. These represent the clearest refinements of program information and the most relevant to the designer. As Exhibit 2-6 shows, a program can be divided into three sections: one summarizing the ascertainments, another summarizing predictions, and the bulk of the program presenting the specific recommendations for design action. If the ascertainment and prediction summaries are brief, they may be combined into one section, with more detailed background material on these included in an appendix to the report.

Comprehensive Programs. Programs vary in levels of comprehensiveness and detail. As mentioned in Chapter 1, a program may focus on a specific aspect or group of issues; for example, space program, functional program, energy conservation program, site program, operations program, equipment/furnishings program, etc. However, the type of program most suitable for facility design is a *comprehensive program*.

Just as the design of a facility integrates all of its parts, a program should be an integration of the key elements and factors that pertain to its design. A comprehensive program addresses both the client's wants, needs and interests for the facility and the architectural and other parameters, constraints and requirements of direct concern to the designer. In short, it recommends action for the total design of a facility.

That doesn't mean it includes a specification for every detail of design. On the contrary, the intent of a comprehensive program is to provide an overview of design needs, integrating the range of human, physical and external controlling elements relevant to the facility. Although the program should address all significant factors, technical analyses and specifications will respond only to unique conditions and the specific interests of the client and designer. To be sure, certain aspects of a facility design may require additional or separate investigation, which should be identified by the program.

The depth of detail of a comprehensive program varies according to its purpose. Gerald Davis, AIA, has devised three levels of detail for programs: general fit, specific fit and occupancy fit. Peña recommends two types of programs: one that provides appropriate information for schematic design and another for design de-

EXHIBIT 2-5. PRESENTING ALL THREE CONCLUSION TYPES FOR EACH ISSUE ADDRESSED IS ONE WAY TO ORGANIZE A PROGRAM

	ASCERTAINMENTS	PREDICTIONS	RECOMMENDATIONS
HUMAN FACTORS			
1. Personnel 2. 3. 4.	A1. Current number and classifications A2.	P1. Anticipated growth and reorganization P2.	R1. Accommodation for current personnel and expansion plan R2.
PHYSICAL FACTORS			

EXHIBIT 2-6. A PROGRAM MAY BE ORGANIZED BY SECTIONS FOR EACH CONCLUSION TYPE

SECTION 1:   ASCERTAINMENTS

1. The site is 24 acres located at the southeast corner of the intersection of two major thoroughfares.
2. The R-3 zone limits development density to 25 units per acre. (See Appendix C.)
3. A neighboring development consists of four low-rise buildings containing approximately 20 units each.
4. The developer will install an inground swimming pool and a recreation center.
5. The principal market for the units includes young couples and 3-person families; middle-income.

SECTION 2:   PREDICTIONS

1. Planned growth for the community anticipates a population of 40,000 by the year 1990.
2. Only two other similar developments are planned for the vicinity.
3. Construction costs are expected to increase by 15 percent by the time the development gets under contract.
4. The local community board is considering adoption of an ordinance requiring all new dwelling units to include smoke detectors.

SECTION 3:   RECOMMENDATIONS

A. *Human Factors*
B. *Physical Factors*
C. *External Factors*

velopment. Other programmers develop programs in a sequence of progressively refined detail for various stages.

There appear to be three levels of comprehensive programs, each appropriate to the type of information and depth of detail needed at different points in design decision making. They are designated here as master program, facility program and component program.

As comprehensive problem statements, the master, facility and component programs should be seen as different versions of the same program. They all address the same issues or aspects of a particular facility. The amount and detail of information about issues or aspects each provides varies, however. Consequently, each will be particularly useful for different design decisions. The matrix in Exhibit 2-7 shows a sampling of kinds of design decisions and the relative usefulness of information contained in each program level to particular decisions. As indicated, certain information may be more or less appropriate for one type of decision. The absence of a matrix match in the exhibit indicates that although a program level may address a particular design issue, the data are generally too detailed or inadequate to support a particular decision about the issue.

A *master program* presents the most general type of information, providing an overview of all the significant design issues and summarizing the principal programmatic conclusions. It identifies and outlines the principal issues, defines the overall design goals and establishes the limits of the program. A master program plays a unique role in the development process. At the outset, it acts as a preliminary program, establishing a framework for program investigation. At the conclusion of programming, a revised master program summarizes the results and presents the essential facts and concepts for design. It should be the most useful of the three for client decision making, particularly in determining project feasibility and preliminary budget and in assessing a schematic design response.

The designer, on the other hand, has greater interest in the facility and component level programs. A *facility program* defines identified issues; identifies specific goals and provides evidence to support, revise or displace goals; and documents conclusions on the human, physical and external factors that affect the design. The facility program supplies a base for designing all the primary components and the integrated total of the facility and for evaluation of design progress (e.g., verifying area and volume calculations).

The *component program* is the most specific of the three levels and relates directly to the most specific design detailing. It provides precise requirements for design of individual components of the facility, such as the various engineering systems and the individual space units. The component program also most specifically reflects the needs of the individual facility users.

Putting the Program to Work. On occasion, a program may act as a stand-alone document. It can be used for non-design purposes. For example, a program may help a client decide not to build or

DESIGN DECISION	MASTER	FACILITY	COMPONENT
Site selection	●	○	
Economic feasibility	●	○	
Functional feasibility	●	○	
Design feasibility	●	○	
Project budget	●	●	●
Project schedule	●	●	●
Geometric proportions	●	●	○
Configuration	○	●	○
Orientation	●	○	
Site plan	●	●	
Sitework plan	○	●	○
Massing plan	○	●	○
Envelope design		●	○
Gross volume calculation	○	●	○
Gross area calculation	○	●	○
Net area calculation	○	●	○
Circulation area calculation		●	○
Space unit area calculation		●	●
Space unit design		○	●
Floor plan layout		●	●
Space layout		●	○
Circulation design		●	○
Operations design		●	●
Design energy budget	○	●	○
Engineering systems selection	○	●	
Engineering systems design			●
Nonengineering systems selection	○	●	
Nonengineering systems design			●
Lighting systems selection	○	●	
Lighting systems design			●
Structural design		●	○

to determine the economic feasibility of a project. Such a document, generally, is a special purpose program and is clearly identified in that way. In most cases, a program is intended to be used for making design decisions.

More broadly, a program may be said to be an initiating step in the development and delivery of a facility. It is an integral part of the design/construction/operation process. Exhibit 2-8 illustrates a conceptualization of the relationship between facility programs and facility development and the particular usability of three levels of comprehensive programs in various design phases.

The following sections of this chapter examine how the process of programming interacts with and relates to the designing process.

PROGRAMMING PROCEDURES

The many individual programming methodologies employed by architects and others have several characteristics in common, to one degree or another. They are systemized, iterative and progressive. Programmers establish systemized procedures for accomplishing work. *Systemization* enables a programmer to process information rapidly, accurately, reliably and economically. A system of procedures that also matches compatible techniques with each other and with the types of information investigated is developed by the individual through experience and trial-and-error.

Although systemization is necessary for efficiency and effectiveness, the programming process must be flexible and cumulative. The large amounts of complex data that accompany sophisticated programming efforts are generally accumulated and managed in "iterations" or cycles. The *iterative process* enables the programmer to expand and refine the data base in a logical, useful manner. Once enough factual information has been ac-

EXHIBIT 2-7. DIFFERENT PROGRAM INFORMATION LEVELS VARY IN USEFULNESS FOR DIFFERENT DESIGN DECISIONS(CONT'D)

DESIGN DECISION	MASTER	FACILITY	COMPONENT
Support service design		○	●
Fenestration		○	●
Designed energy performance		●	○
Landscape design		●	●
Code compliance	○	●	●
Project cost estimate		●	○
Construction cost estimate		●	○
Operating cost estimate		○	●
Life cycle cost estimate		●	●
Construction schedule	○	●	○
Economic analysis	○	●	○
Solar system sizing		○	●
Construction materials selection		●	●
Exterior finishes		○	●
Interior finishes		○	●
Equipment furnishing selection		○	●

● primary usefulness of information to design decision

○ = secondary usefulness of information to design decision

NOTE: Assignment of degree of usefulness and exclusion or inclusion of design decisions will vary with each program. Illustrated is a sample.

quired to make a judgment on its relativity, relevance, adequacy, etc., a written or verbal statement of the data is reviewed, evaluated and responded to.. This is followed by a statement of what the information means in terms of what should be done with it in the next iteration. The cycle is illustrated in Exhibit 2-9.

For example, at the beginning of a project, the programmer may explore possible project objectives with the client. After preparing a statement of proposed objectives, the programmer and the client review them for such things as appropriateness, resulting issues to be studied, tasks required to explore the issues, and resources available. The feedback is then incorporated into a restatement of the objectives in terms of what must be done to achieve the objectives.

In the evaluation process, some objectives may be discarded, others added and some revised. The result is that the programmer receives a clear direction of how to proceed to the next stage of the work. Ensuing iterations may include progress reviews, evaluation of proposed initial and succeeding program versions, and evaluation of subsequent design in relation to program criteria.

The iterative process of review-and-evaluation may not be so conspicuous in the methodology of some programmers, but most appear to apply it to one degree or another. However, it is obvious that programming, in general, is *progressive*. Tasks are organized and information is acquired in a manner that enables the programmer to build the program successively toward a statement of what the design ought to do or what the designer needs to know. It proceeds from the general to the specific, as illustrated by the example of objectives development above.

PROGRAMMING/DESIGNING INTERFACE. The interdependent relationship between programming and designing is unquestioned by facility programmers. However, among them there are different views of the manner in which this relationship operates in the development of facility design information. There are three basic approaches to the programming/designing interface in professional practice, as depicted in Exhibit 2-10: integrated, segregated and interactive.

The *integrated* approach takes the view that programming should not be separated from designing. One of the chief proponents of this approach is Herbert McLaughlin, AIA, of the San Francisco, California firm of Kaplan/McLaughlin/Diaz, Architects/Planners. He states succinctly: "Programming is design." To McLaughlin and others, programming is not a "predesign" service, but rather an integral first part of the design process.

Because it is a "peculiar form of design," the implication is that an architect must program and that a programmer should be an architect.

Those who opt for the *segregated* approach see programming as an initial step in the design process. They say, however, that it should be a separate, distinct activity performed prior to initiation of designing. Furthermore, it is seen as preferable that separate individuals or teams perform the two activities. According to Peña, "Programmers and designers are separate specialists because the problems of each are very complex and require two different mental capabilities: one for analysis, one for synthesis."

Others take the segregated approach one step further by dividing programming into two distinct activities: functional programming and architectural programming. Gerald Davis, AIA, of the Ottawa, Ontario, Canada firm, The Environmental Analysis Group Inc. (TEAG), has articulated this viewpoint, explaining that functional programming is the client's responsibility (performed by staff or a professional programmer) and the architectural program is developed by the design architect from the functional program.

Finally, in the *interactive* approach, a design project may begin with programming or a part of it. As the project proceeds, however, segments or versions of the program and of the design are developed in alternating sequence and in re-

EXHIBIT 2-8. PROGRAM RELATIONSHIP TO FACILITY DESIGN, CONSTRUCTION AND USE

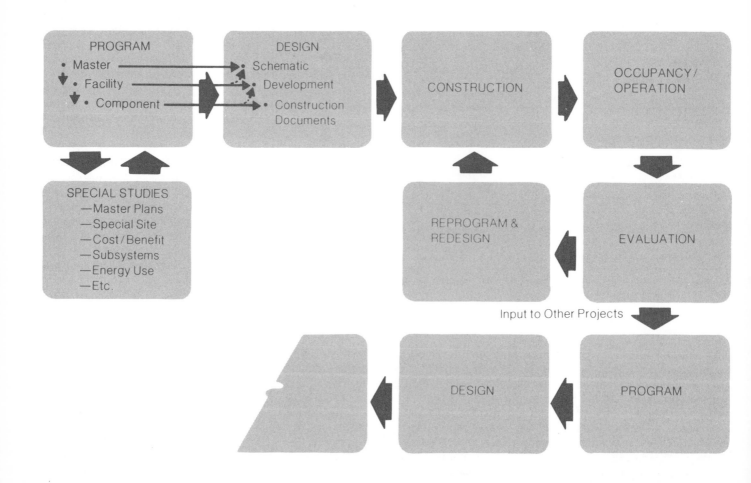

sponse to each other. The individual iterations of programming information feed the design; the design response iterations feed the programming, and so on, until final, closely aligned program and design are achieved. The link between iterations is review and evaluation by the participants in the programming/designing process. Those who employ this approach, such as John M. Kurtz of Booz, Allen and Hamilton, Bethesda, Maryland, believe it is a more efficient decision-making process and is more responsive to owner/user needs than traditional design approaches.

SAMPLE PROGRAMMING PROCEDURES. There is no single standard operating procedure for programming. The best method is that which works for the individual programming firm. The methodologies that have been articulated by practicing programmers vary in complexity and detail, in comprehensiveness and specificity. They have been developed and refined through the experience of the individuals to match their work habits, judgments of program content, and philosophies.

To provide an indication of the variety, as well as the commonality, of the programming methods in use, several models devised by practitioners are presented in Exhibit 2-11. Other systems are described in the case studies in Part Three, ''Applications of Programming.''

EXHIBIT 2-9. ITERATIVE PROGRAMMING CYCLE

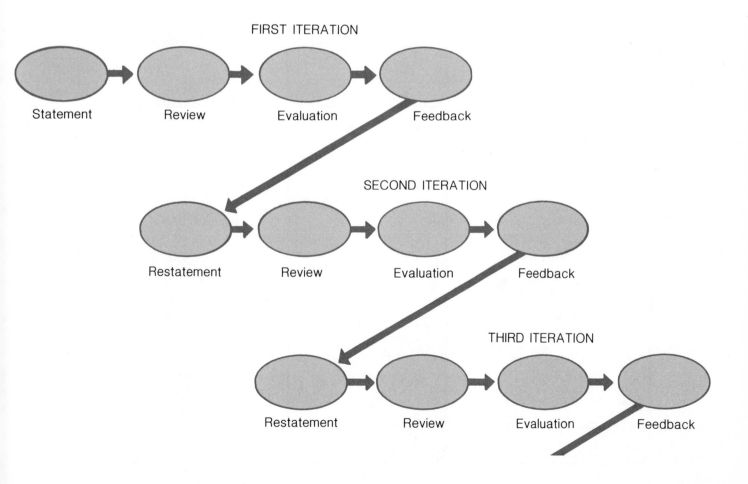

FIRST ITERATION

Statement   Review   Evaluation   Feedback

SECOND ITERATION

Restatement   Review   Evaluation   Feedback

THIRD ITERATION

Restatement   Review   Evaluation   Feedback

EXHIBIT 2-10. THREE APPROACHES TO THE PROGRAMMING/DESIGNING PROCESS

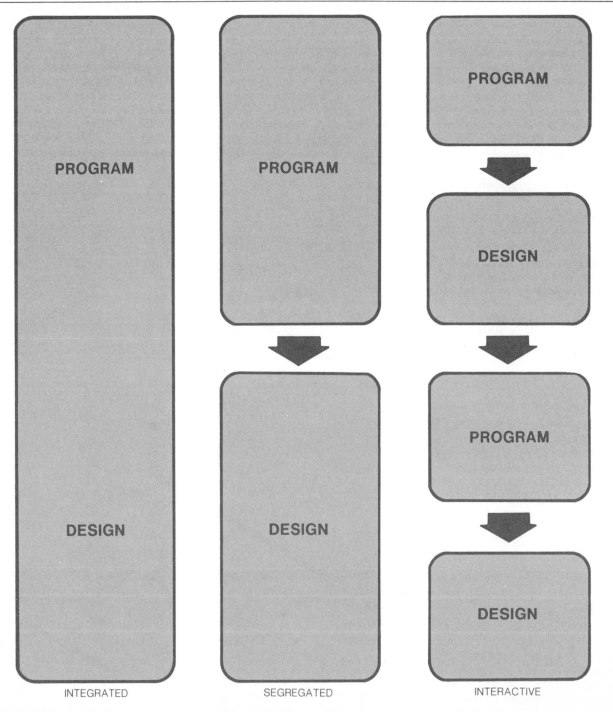

INTEGRATED   SEGREGATED   INTERACTIVE

PROGRAM DEVELOPMENT PROCESS

Programming is a decision-making process for determining the design and/or other requirements of a facility. The numerous decisions in programming, especially the final conclusions relevant to designing a specific facility, are based on objective, analytic, systematic, iterative information processing. The programming process is intended to assure the designer and client of the availability of adequate, accurate, reliable and relevant information for design decisions.

INFORMATION PROCESSING. Effective program development involves the performance of five information-processing functions: collection, analysis, organization, communication and evaluation of data.

Data collection is the process of gathering information needed to produce the program. It involves not only acquiring data, but generating and eliciting it from the client and other pertinent sources by direct and indirect means. Recording data is an important aspect of this function. Although the programmer begins work with specific data objectives, early programming tasks involve a certain amount of exploration and generality to establish the data base. As the program is refined, later data collection efforts will be more focused and may involve confirming previous conclusions and filling in missing information.

The raw or base data collected are sorted, verified, compared, tested and interpreted in order to determine validity, reliability, relevance and importance in the *analysis of data*. In programming, a great mass of data is likely to be obtained. Through analytical procedures, it is reduced to manageable proportions and useful quality. Analysis involves developing preliminary conclusions about data, testing and verifying them. The programmer continuously analyzes data as it is col-

EXHIBIT 2-11A. EXAMPLE PROGRAMMING MODEL—DAVIS

GERALD DAVIS, AIA
TEAG—The Environmental Analysis Group Ltd.
Ottawa, Ontario, Canada

(From the *Manager's Guide to Programming of Facilities*, second edition, 1979, prepared by TEAG for the federal government of Canada. Reprinted with the permission of Gerald Davis and Francoise Szigeti.)

Davis has been involved in programming and architectural research for many years. Although an architect, his consulting firm specializes in prearchitectural programming. This activity involves development of two of the three distinct types of program that Davis has identified: functional program, technical program and design program. The first two are the responsibility of the client and may be developed by consultants such as Davis. The other is prepared by the design architect of a project in response to its functional and technical programs. Davis believes the two activities should be performed separately and by separate teams. The "Range of Possible Programming Tasks" excerpted here describes a checklist of activities that a predesign programming consultant might perform for a client in developing his or her functional and technical programs. Davis and Szigeti have explained the process of functional and technical programming in "Functional and Technical Programming: When the Owner/Sponsor is a Large or Complex Organization," a paper printed in the *Proceedings of the Fourth International Architectural Psychology Conference*, Louvain-la-Neuve, July 10-14, 1979.

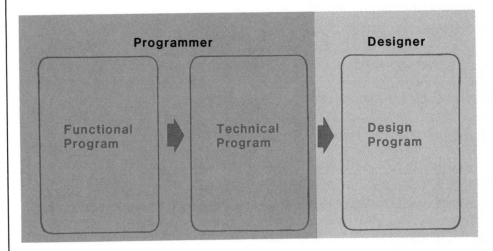

INITIAL DATA GATHERING

—Assess the context and develop an overview of the objectives and needs for facilities

EXHIBIT 2-11A. EXAMPLE PROGRAMMING MODEL—DAVIS (CONT'D)

ORGANIZATIONAL REQUIREMENTS

—Review client's corporate, business and operational plans
—Identify explicit and implicit aspects that may be affected by the quantity or character of physical facilities
—Study possible options and provide recommendations as appropriate

USER NEEDS: ANALYZE/SYNTHESIZE

—Analyze the user organization(s), its functions, activities, human milieu and external environment
—Synthesize its needs for facilities to house its approved functions and programs

FACILITIES COMPONENT OF THE CLIENT PLANNING CYCLE

—Provide the facilities component of client's business, operational and functional plans
—Specify functional requirements for facilities at various time horizons, i.e., long-range (10-20 years) and mid-range (5-10 years)
—Evaluate suitability of existing and planned facilities to satisfy these requirements
—Provide recommendations to management regarding use and/or change of existing facilities and needs for other facilities

SELECTIVE DATA-GATHERING

—Conduct selective investigations of prototypical details of user needs

DATA BASES FOR FACILITIES REQUIREMENTS

—Design and establish the data bases required for corporate planning for facilities and for programming of specific projects

OPERATIONAL USER SYSTEMS

—Provide special analyses as appropriate
—Develop options and recommendations to management to take better advantage of proposed or new facilities by modifying user/occupant operating systems

PHYSIOLOGICAL REQUIREMENTS

—Identify, analyze and provide recommendations and criteria for those ambient conditions that affect health and safety of staff, and physical performance of tasks and other activities

BEHAVIORAL REQUIREMENTS

—Analyze and develop strategies and criteria for those "humane" aspects of facilities that affect motivation, learning, perception, attitudes toward the organization, intergroup communications, group functioning, image and status, control or sharing of territory, psychological well-being and so on

INTERNAL IMPACTS

—Assess and provide recommendations regarding impacts of the proposed move or changes on:
  • The functioning of the organization
  • Its operating systems and procedures

lected or developed throughout the process.

Organization occurs at various stages of program development. At the outset, data objectives are identified and ordered for logical fulfillment, procedures are outlined and tasks assigned. When base data have been collected and analyzed, they are sorted and categorized for further investigation. Finally, information conclusions are put into meaningful order and arranged to show relationships, patterns, groupings and priorities. In preparing the final report, information is organized in appropriate format for presentation, according to which data should appear in the report and which should be compiled for background.

Communication ties the programming process together.. It is not just a matter of making sure the program states clearly and concisely the project needs. It involves making sure the client understands what data the programmer needs, fostering information exchange among the participants and enhancing effective decision making. Communication also interprets program evidence through documentation, effective presentation and, most of all, translation into the designer's terms. An architect can't design a facility that will satisfy the client's needs unless the architect understands what they are and what they mean.

The conclusions about facility needs should be *evaluated* by the client, the programmer and the designer. Ideas, concepts and data should be weighed against personal judgment, established criteria and the initial goals of the project. Evaluation is not a final step, however. Once judgments are passed, the information is recycled into the information development process in order to respond to those judgments. Depending on the procedure of the programmer, the whole cycle of data collection, analysis, organization, communication and evaluation will be repeated any number of times, yielding a succession of progressively refined program conclusions.

It should be clear from these descriptions that programming is not just fact gathering. On the other hand, it is not interpretation either. It is a little of both, but most importantly, it is translation of gathered facts into interpretable information. Some other descriptors of information-processing functions are shown in Exhibit 2-12.

The performance of the individual data-processing functions is not necessarily sequential, but is interdependent. Analysis of data depends on their prior or simultaneous collection. Evaluation depends on the availability of analyzed data and, to a degree, on their prior organization, although information is repeatedly evaluated as it is developed. Communication also operates in relation to the performance of the other functions, linking them together.

A PROCEDURAL MODEL. As seen in the examples of programming procedures that have been devised in practice (Exhibit 2-11), programmers divide the process into steps, stages or phases of work or categories of information development. The divisions reflect completion of a series of related operations or of sets of information. From these and other methodologies (for example, see the case studies in Part Three), an appropriate composite model of the programming procedure can be created. The pattern of operations proceeds as follows:

—Establish project goals
—Organize programming effort
—Investigate issues
—Integrate data
—Interpret information
—Instruct designer and client
—Evaluate results
—Recycle information

This pattern includes the activities performed, the general types of information

EXHIBIT 2-11A. EXAMPLE PROGRAMMING MODEL—DAVIS (CONT'D)

• Its staff
—Assist and provide recommendations
—Assist management in its corporate planning studies, special analyses as appropriate, internal information programs and so on

EXTERNAL IMPACTS

—Assess and provide recommendations regarding impacts of the proposed move or changes on the external environment of the organization, including its visitors and the publics it serves, the community in which it is located and/or the natural ecology

COSTS, ELAPSED TIME AND SCHEDULES

—Establish objectives, constraints and basis for making tradeoffs regarding cost, elapsed time and schedules
—At each stage of development, obtain the latest cost estimates and schedules
—In the early stages of planning, provide the cost estimator with hypotheses on which to base the early cost estimates
—Analyze, identify options and prepare recommendations for management action

FUNCTIONAL REQUIREMENTS AT EACH STAGE

—Recommend to management which user needs should be satisfied, i.e., define what the users should be able to accomplish in or at the facility
—Express these needs as performance requirements, in non-technical language so that the managements of both user/occupants and user/owner can directly evaluate what is being proposed
—At each stage of the project, specify requirements to a level of detail suitable to the needs of management and designers
—Identify options, analyze the costs and benefits of satisfying user needs, and evaluate tradeoffs
—Prepare the program document specifying functional requirements for facilities

ESSENTIAL CRITERIA FOR DESIGN AT EACH STAGE

—Create the link into conceptual design by synthesizing the essence of the design problem
—Establish those essential criteria that the design of a facility must satisfy

TECHNICAL REQUIREMENTS AT EACH STAGE

—Translate the functional requirements for each building functional system into technical criteria by which architectural and engineering designs can be directly evaluated
—At each stage of the project, specify requirements to a level of detail suitable for the needs of management and designers, expressed as performance criteria in order to avoid unnecessary constraints on the design

STANDARD REQUIREMENTS, GUIDELINES AND PLANNING MANUALS

—Select from available material of the user/owner and user/occupant those standard requirements and guidelines applicable to the design

EXHIBIT 2-11A. EXAMPLE PROGRAMMING MODEL—DAVIS (CONT'D)

—Identify and synthesize any additional functional or technical requirements that can be treated as standard for that facility
—Prepare standard requirements and guidelines in those situations where they have not been developed

EVALUATION OF DESIGN PROPOSALS

—At each stage as the design for a facility is developed, evaluate the emerging design for compliance with the performance criteria and advise management
—Identify options and provide recommendations when problems arise
—Provide feedback to the design team, and interim "crits" as required

SPACE PLANNING

—Develop functional and technical requirements at the level of detail necessary for fit-up and for placement at move-in of furnishings and equipment
—Provide criteria and guidance to management for final interior design, furnishings and finishes
—Develop functional strategies for space planning, to take into account organizational, physiological and behavioral needs
—Prepare functional and technical layouts for use by the design team in final placement of partitions, equipment, telephone outlets and access points to utilities

COMMISSIONING

—Assist management and users to move smoothly into the facility and to limit disruption
—Fine-tune at move-in and follow up with user/occupants as required

SPACE UTILIZATION

—Assist and instruct facility operations groups and user/occupants to utilize the facility effectively
—Provide guidance, instruction and user/occupant manuals
—Assist management in resolving problems in effective space utilization

DOCUMENTATION

—Prepare formal presentations and documentary reports for management, users, design team and others involved with the project

EVALUATION OF FACILITY DURING ITS USE

—Evaluate the original context, purposes and requirements for the facility, and the context and purposes now applicable to its use
—Establish or confirm with management the criteria by which the facility should be evaluated
—Identify issues and options, and provide recommendations for management action
—When appropriate, assess and evaluate the requirements and criteria that were used in planning the facility

processed and the sequence. The sequence of operations is not strict, nor are their boundaries rigidly defined. Activities overlap and the order of operations may change depending on the needs of the project, the time and budget constraints, and the interests of the client and designer. The concept is basically a pattern that helps organize and visualize the logical progression of program development.

The progression is cyclical and cumulative, as illustrated in Exhibit 2-13. Program information is first built up and then refined through a series of conclusion/review/evaluation feedback cycles. The number of information or program iterations is only as many as needed to produce conclusive evidence and agreement on the needs for design.

The recycling process does not conclude with presentation of the final program report. It continues into the design, construction and operation phases of facility development (as represented in Exhibit 2-8 earlier), where the program is used to guide and evaluate design progress and to test performance of the constructed, operating facility. The program, although directed to a specific facility, contains information that also is useful for similar projects, and may be recycled in the originator's and/or others' practices.

In each step or operation of programming, one or more information-processing functions are performed. Because these functions are interdependent and because various data develop at varying rates, any one stage is likely to include concurrent operation of various functions at one time. Nevertheless, certain activities are predominant during each stage of program development. Exhibit 2-14 indicates which information processes are most relevant to each programming operation.

PREPARATION, PARTICIPATION AND PRODUCTS

The achievement of useful programming

products and the processing of masses of multivariate data require skillful management and coordination. A programmer should be not only knowledgeable in programming techniques and procedures and design-oriented, but an able administrator as well, capable of managing information, resources and people. A successful programmer will be adequately prepared to undertake a complex task, understand the roles of participants in the process and be able to deliver the appropriate products for different programming purposes. Chapter 21 explores some of these matters in greater detail.

PREPARATION FOR PROGRAMMING. There is a vital procedural step that is discussed frequently in the literature on programming, but which sometimes fails to find a place in the various procedural models. That step is preparation: organizing the programming effort. This second step in the programming procedural model usually can be accomplished simultaneously with the process of establishing project goals. It involves several administrative tasks, including identifying programming goals, organizing the programming team, assigning responsibilities and establishing timetables, fees and other contractual matters.

Programming Goals. These are not the same as the project goals, but they will be largely determined by them. Identified programming goals establish the scope of the project. Although a client's objectives may not be clearly defined or specifically identified at the outset of a project, the programmer still must decide what types of information are to be obtained and what are the possibilities and means for obtaining them.

Before starting the programming effort, the programmer has to have a clear idea of what direction to take. This will depend on how fully the scope and goals of the project (as opposed to the programming

EXHIBIT 2-11B. EXAMPLE PROGRAMMING MODEL—FARBSTEIN

JAY FARBSTEIN
Sullivan Farbstein Associates
San Luis Obispo, California

(From a program for a juvenile corrections facility also featured in *Facility Programming*, Wolfgang F.E. Preiser, ed., Stroudsburg, Pa.: Dowden, Hutchinson & Ross Inc., 1978)

Farbstein has used a five-phase methodology that involves both the owner and the users in the development of information (primarily for evaluation of conclusions and for decision making). Each phase contains specific tasks and data considerations. User needs are a major consideration.

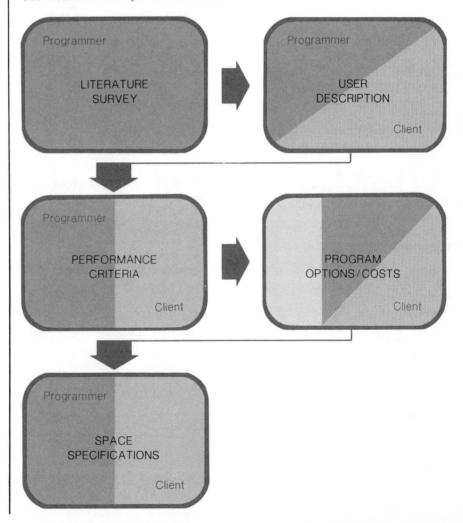

EXHIBIT 2-11B. EXAMPLE PROGRAMMING MODEL—FARBSTEIN (CONT'D)

1) LITERATURE SURVEY

Programmer

—Identify/review pertinent research findings on specific behavior environment
—Examine standard professional practices related to facility type

2) USER DESCRIPTION

Client/Programmer

—Identify potential users and key roles in relation to facility:
  • activities, attitudes, other behavior
  • characteristics, groupings
—Refine information as phase progresses
—Identify user objectives for facility
—Identify policies governing facility use
—Document activity patterns
—Identify socio-cultural factors influencing user behavior in setting
—Identify future trends

3) PERFORMANCE CRITERIA

Programmer

—Establish criteria for:
  • area needs
  • circulation
  • ambient environment
  • safety and security
  • surfaces
  • furnishings
  • flexibility
  • site design

Client

—Review criteria

4) PROGRAM OPTIONS AND COSTS

Programmer

—Identify design issues
—Develop program options for each issue
—Measure costs/benefits/tradeoffs of options

Client/Programmer

—Assess user satisfaction with options
—Review cost effectiveness of options
—Select options

5) SPACE SPECIFICATIONS

Programmer

—Develop specifications for facility spaces (three parts):
  • program summary sheet for each activity area
  • listing of total number of each type of activity area recommended for inclusion in facility
  • set of adjacency diagrams showing relationships among activity areas

Client

—Approve program
—Approve budget

goals) have been defined. Goals should be clearly stated so that the work stays on track and so there is definite contractual understanding between client and programmer on the scope of the work.

Team Organization. The composition of programming teams varies depending on two factors: 1) the operating preferences of the programmer, designer and client, and 2) the resource needs of the project. The first relates to the manner in which the programmer, client and designer expect to participate in the programming process. On one hand—especially when a designer has not been selected for a project or it is not clear that a design will result from it, as with a feasibility study—the programmer may be expected to perform most of the work and make most of the decisions independently, perhaps drawing on the expertise of a designer and the data available from a client. By and large, the designer and client are resources for the programmer rather than partners in the effort. The team, in this case, will consist of programmer and necessary consultants.

In another situation, the programmer and client (usually, owner) may work in a close partnership, making joint decisions about the program. (The client is always involved in decision making whether independently or jointly with the programmer.) This is the type of working relationship preferred by CRS, where programming teams and designing teams are segregated from each other. In the CRS operation, there are two teams in the programming stage of a project: the programming team consisting of the programmer and appropriate consultants and the client team consisting of authorized representatives and consultants. The teams come together at key points to exchange information and make decisions.

The committee is another approach to composition of a programming team. It is both a decision-making and an informa-

EXHIBIT 2-11C. EXAMPLE PROGRAMMING MODEL—KURTZ

JOHN M. KURTZ
Booz, Allen & Hamilton
Bethesda, Maryland

(Interpreted from "Habitable Schools: Programming for a Changing Environment" by John M. Kurtz in *Facility Programming*, Wolfgang F.E. Preiser, ed. Stroudsburg, Pa.: Dowden, Hutchinson & Ross Inc., 1978)

According to Kurtz, "programming is never complete because users and needs will change continuously, therefore requiring continuous reprogramming. The process is hierarchical and proceeds sequentially from the most general requirements to the most detailed. Only generalized long-range programmatic decisions are made prior to beginning building design. Programming is thus carried on in an increasing degree of detail *simultaneously and interactively* [emphasis added] with the phases of design, construction and occupancy."

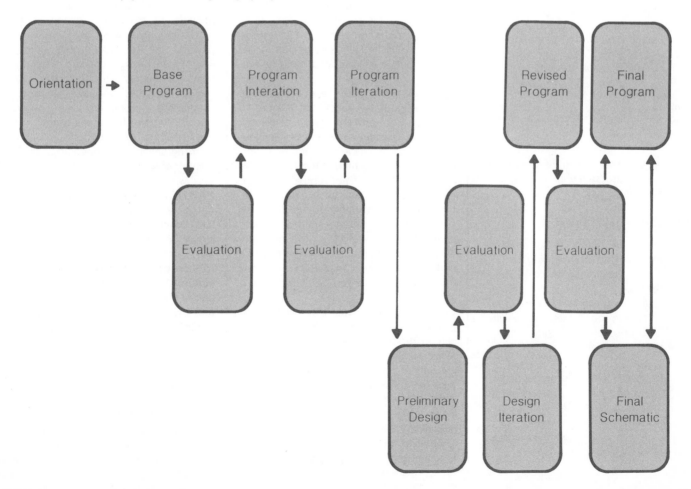

EXHIBIT 2-11C. EXAMPLE PROGRAMMING MODEL— KURTZ (CONT'D)

1) ORIENTATION

—Review client's current operations
—Identify client philosophy
—Determine project objectives

2) BASE PROGRAM

—Review client operating requirements
—Review literature on similar buildings
—Draft preliminary program including:
  • building organization
  • activity and other areas
  • space sizes and relationships

3) ITERATIVE PROGRAMMING

—Present base program to owner/users
—Obtain feedback on program from owner/users
—Draft new program
—Repeat presentation, feedback, revision of program until general agreement is reached

4) DESIGN-AS-FEEDBACK

—Develop schematic design (during later iteration of programming)
—Present preliminary design to owner/users
—Obtain feedback from owner/users
—Develop revised schematic design
—Repeat process until agreement reached on design ·

Successive iterations of program and design respond to each other and are revised accordingly. By the time final design is complete, it is in virtual agreement with program and in harmony with the needs expressed.

tion-producing group and consists of programmer, designer, client (owner, user, related publics) and relevant consultants, if any. Some programmers consider this the best approach to incorporating user needs into design decision making. In this case, the same group may also participate in design decisions. All parties represented on the team may participate equally in generating information, evaluating conclusions, making decisions. Technical work such as calculations, social measurements, interpretation and drawings are performed or at least supervised by the team professionals.

Regardless of the approach to team composition, it is important that the roles of the various groups represented be clearly established at the outset, as should the decision-making procedure to be employed.

The second factor in team composition is a matter of the resources needed to investigate the problem. This also relates to the roles that the client and the designer have in developing the program. However, the principal issue here is the type of expertise the programmer requires in order to produce and analyze appropriate information efficiently and effectively. When specialists are needed—such as behavioral scientists, engineers, economists— they should be brought onto the team as early as possible. Chapter 21 examines this aspect.

Task Assignments. The client, programmer and designer each have roles to play in developing the program, and the responsibilities of each must be clearly delineated at the beginning of the project. Who will provide what types of information? Who will make the decisions? What is the working relationship among the programming participants?

Specific tasks must also be assigned to members of the programming team. Project leadership, questionnaire development and administration, computer pro-

gramming, client liaison, special studies, report writing, graphics and production are among the types of assignments.

The role and task assignments must also be coordinated and timed so that the appropriate pieces of information for the program can be fitted together at appropriate times. The schedule for delivery of the program should also be integrated into the overall project schedule. It may be that the program can be divided conveniently into parts that can be delivered in stages so that other project team members are able to perform their tasks while the rest of the program continues to develop.

Another program planning consideration is the kinds of procedures, techniques and resources that will be employed in producing the program information. Also, client and programmer must agree on the products that will be delivered at the conclusion of programming: e.g., comprehensive program, space program, functional program, feasibility report, backup data, explanation of programming methodology, environmental impact statement.

PARTICIPANTS. There are three main categories of participants in the programming process: client, programmer and designer. These categories are rather arbitrary for the purpose of defining roles, relationships and responsibilities. For instance, the programmer and designer may be the same firm or even the same person, and thus there would only be two categories of participants for a specific project.

Roles. The term *client* is used to refer to the collective body of individuals and groups that is related in various ways to the facility which is programmed. Anyone that is affected by or that affects the facility, to one degree or another, is included. The programmer has a responsibility to consider the impact of the facility on them and their impact on the facility.

EXHIBIT 2-11D. EXAMPLE PROGRAMMING MODEL—MOLESKI

WALTER H. MOLESKI
Environmental Research Group
Philadelphia, Pennsylvania

(Moleski explains his approach more thoroughly in
"Environmental Programming for Human Needs," *Facility
Programming* edited by Wolfgang F.E. Preiser, Stroudsburg,
Pa.: Dowden, Hutchinson & Ross Inc., 1978)

Moleski uses a four-phase sequence of activities interspersed
with two specific, scheduled reviews by client, architect and
programmer together. Programming extends into the design
phase in the form of consultation and evaluation with architect
and client on design progress. Particular emphasis on user
needs and behavior in relation to facility.

Moleski adds an extended phase to programming after the
design has been completed and the facility constructed. The
EVALUATION phase should measure the effectiveness of both
the program and the design to insure that the facility satisfies
its intent and use. He suggests that an evaluation be conducted
both immediately after construction and after two years of
occupancy.

This sequence of activities is illustrated graphically on page 38.

1) AWARENESS—Identify problems,
issues, objectives

—Identify programming participants
and roles
—Review background reports
provided by client
—Conduct nondirected interviews
with selected representatives to
ascertain:
  • nature of organization (client) and
  image
  • organization functions and communication processes
  • satisfaction with current facility
  • problems of inefficiency and/or
  dysfunction
—Review similar projects
—Outline problem areas for further
investigation

2) DIAGNOSIS   Collect, analyze,
organize data

—Collect data through:
  • structured interviews with key personnel (organization functions)
  • systematic observation of selected areas
  • detailed questionnaire administered to users
—Analyze data to determine and
document:
  • activities, user characteristics,
  linkages, settings, image
  • problem issues and client needs
—Organize data to discover and
develop concepts for solution of
problems and satisfaction of client
needs

3) FIRST REVIEW

—Meet with client representative
(building committee) and design
architect to discuss preliminary
problem statement and solution
concepts
—Select concepts for further
development

4) STRATEGY—Establish performance
criteria

—Organize the specific set of design
needs and/or issues to be addressed
by design
—Develop recommended characteristics that would accommodate
activity patterns and settings of users
including:
  • spatial characteristics
  • physical conditions
  • symbolic attributes
  • space arrangement

5) SECOND REVIEW

—Meet with client representatives and
design architect to discuss recommended program
—Approve program
—Establish architectural intent of
facility

6) ACTION—Follow-up decisions

—Consult with architect during design
on program intent, possible revisions
—Evaluate design satisfaction of program criteria
—Discuss design decisions with client
and architect

EXHIBIT 2-11D. EXAMPLE PROGRAMMING MODEL—MOLESKI (CONT'D)

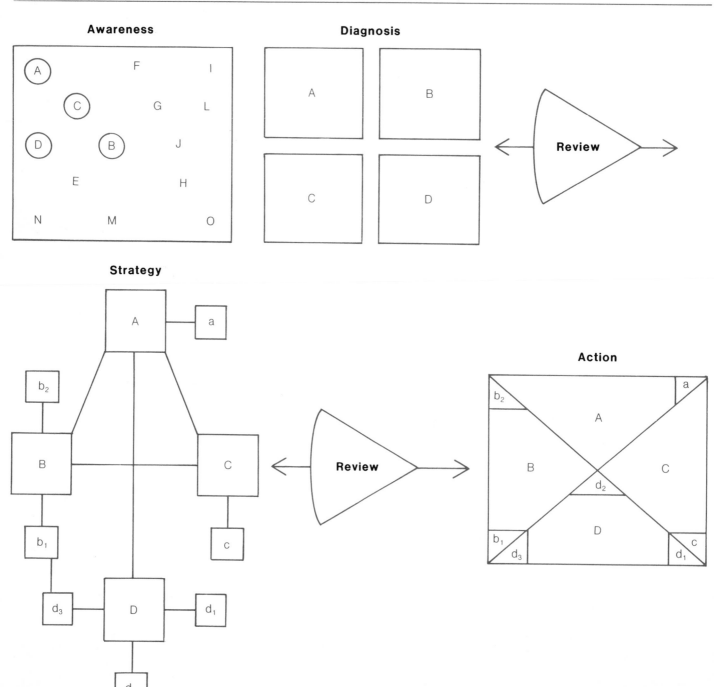

EXHIBIT 2-11E. EXAMPLE PROGRAMMING MODEL—PEÑA

WILLIAM M. PEÑA, FAIA
Caudill Rowlett Scott (CRS)
Houston, Texas

(Extracted from *Problem Seeking: An Architectural Programming Primer*, William M. Pena with William Caudill and John W. Focke, Boston: Cahners Books International, 1977; and from *Energy Estimate Analysis*, a report of the CRS Energy Task Group, 1978)

Pena and his firm have developed and refined their well-known methodology over more than 30 years of experience in programming facilities. It is characterized by clarity, efficiency and economy in both procedure and product. The CRS programming matrix represents five procedural steps: establishing goals, collecting and analyzing facts, uncovering and testing concepts, determining needs and stating the problem. These procedures operate on five basic design considerations which are the objects of program investigation: form, function, economy, time and energy (added to the matrix as a fifth element in the 1978 publication). Pena believes programming is a separate process from designing and should precede it in any project. He also advocates delivery of program information to the designer in two phases: schematic program for schematic design and development program for design development.

	Function	Form	Economy	Time	Energy
Goals					
Facts					
Concepts					
Needs					
Problem					

—Kickoff meetings with client/owner to:
• identify decision-makers
• provide and explain specifications for data from existing records or separate surveys
—Kickoff meetings with client/users (as one group) to:
• explain approach
• explain what interviewer needs to know and when

IN-OFFICE ANALYSIS
—To analyze data sent by mail
—To prepare presentation for the round of interviews

MAIN BODY OF INTERVIEWS
—With client/owner to:
• confirm previous data
• reveal new data
—With client/users (in many groups) to:
• collect specific data
• plan for next level of detail

ANALYSIS AND DOCUMENTATION
—To classify and interrelate responses
—To identify conflicts needing reconciliation
—To summarize and document information

WORK SESSIONS
—To balance space requirements, quality of construction and the total budget
—To feed back information to the client/owner and the client/users for confirmation and/or decision

FINAL DOCUMENTATION
—To obtain formal approval on the program from the client and/or funding agencies.
—To feed forward information to the designer—mostly in graphic form

EXHIBIT 2-11F. EXAMPLE PROGRAMMING MODEL—WHITE

PREPROGRAMMING

Role	1. Formulate and agree with client on process, ground rules and responsibilities	2. Confirm with client the necessary program content	3. Collect, organize, review and verify previous work produced for project	4. Define additional program information needed	5. Determine with client who will provide the information	6. Establish information dependencies and gathering sequence	7. Assemble programming team and orient the members to the process to be followed and the responsibilities	8. Schedule work sessions
1	●	●	●	●	●	●	●	●
2	○	○	○	○	●		○	○
3			○	○			○	○
4			○	○			○	

PROGRAMMING

Role	1. Gather information	2. Analyze, evaluate, correlate, organize information	3. Document results	4. Submit information to sources for review and approval	5. Review approved results with client administration	6. Test space needs against budget	7. Recycle allowable space information back to sources, if necessary	8. Extract planning and design implications	9. Review planning assumptions with client	10. Make precepts as directives for designer	11. Design alternative organizational concepts for building	12. Review total program with client
1	●	●	●	○	○	●	●	●	●	●	●	○
2	●					●	●	●		●	○	●
3	●		●			●		●		○	●	●
4	●		●									

● Primary responsibility   ○ Involvement

POSTPROGRAMMING

	Produce programming document	Distribute document as required	Give presentations on program as appropriate	Make transition to schematic design
	1	2	3	4
	●	●	●	●
		○		○
	○			

EDWARD T. WHITE III,
Architecture One Ltd.
Tucson, Arizona

(From programs produced by White)

White, author of a textbook on programming (*Introduction to Architectural Programming*), academician and practitioner, expresses a programming methodology in a series of tasks divided into three phases: preprogramming, programming and postprogramming. The actual investigation or research work is what he calls programming. The tasks required for any particular project vary and others, in addition to the ones identified below, may be necessary.

PREPROGRAMMING

1) Formulate and agree with client on process, ground rules and responsibilities
2) Confirm with client the necessary program content
3) Collect, organize, review and verify previous work produced for project
4) Define additional program information needed
5) Determine with client who will provide the information
6) Establish information dependencies and gathering sequence
7) Assemble programming team and orient the members to the process to be followed and the responsibilities
8) Schedule work sessions

PROGRAMMING

1) Gather information
2) Analyze, evaluate, correlate, organize information
3) Document results
4) Submit information to sources for review and approval
5) Review approved results with client administration
6) Test space needs against budget
7) Recycle allowable space information back to sources, if necessary
8) Extract planning and design implications
9) Review planning assumptions with client
10) Make precepts as directives for designer
11) Design alternative organizational concepts for building
12) Review total program with client

POSTPROGRAMMING

1) Produce programming document
2) Distribute document as required
3) Give presentations on program as appropriate
4) Make transition to schematic design

EXHIBIT 2-12. ACTIVITIES INVOLVED IN PROGRAM INFORMATION DEVELOPMENT

Data Collection	Data Analysis	Data Organization	Data Communication	Data Evaluation
questioning	sorting	relating	writing	reviewing
interviewing	selecting	ordering	illustrating	verifying
surveying	comparing	ranking	interacting	decision making
reading	decomposing	combining	explaining	optimizing
observing	screening	diagramming	documenting	prioritizing
searching	simulating	categorizing	discussing	weighing alternatives
studying literature	weighting	composing	debating	questioning
recording	rating	grouping	exchanging	
experimenting	testing	integrating	translating	
generating	computing	arranging	interpreting	
stimulating	segregating			

The animals to be housed by a zoo, for example, would be considered as members of the client group. The programmer could be said to "work for" all of them, even though his or her contract may be with only one of the individuals or groups that comprise the client group.

That one contracting individual or group is called the *owner*; the owner has the controlling interest in the project since the individual or group is paying for it and has responsibility for its successful completion. More often than not, the owner of a corporate or institutional project will consist of a group, and the programmer will be dealing with them individually and/or with a representative committee; in this case, a single responsible contact should be named to avoid confusion.

The term client also includes the *users*, the people (or animals and even plants) who have a more or less direct and constant relationship with the facility. These would include occupants, operators and managers. Another client category is called *related publics*, who have less direct and usually only occasional involvement with the facility. Related publics may include the owner's market or clientele, neighbors or even passersby. Regulatory agencies representing the general public

to a degree and responsible for enforcement of facility-related codes and laws, would also be considered a related public which, in most cases, must be addressed by the programmer.

The *programmer* is the firm or individual who conducts the programming investigation and produces the program. Different types of programmers include:

—Architect or firm which provides programming services separately or as part of design services.
—Professional programmer, who may or may not be an architect, and who specializes in programming.
—Programming specialist, who offers services for particular building types such as health care, educational or correctional facilities.
—Consulting programmer, who may not be called a programmer at all but who provides expert or technical advice to the principal programmer in areas of specialized concern. Behavioral or social scientists are frequently engaged by programmers to conduct studies of user needs aspects of a program. Other experts might include financial analysts, computer firms, environmentalists, statisticians, organizational communications analysts, group dynamics coun-

selors, lawyers, etc.

The *designer* is the architect-of-record and principal interpreter of the program for the design of the facility. The designer's role is to receive the program and produce the design response to it. Depending on circumstances, this role may include participation in phases of programming.

Responsibilities. The designer, in addition to interpreting the program, has a great deal of influence on its development, directly or indirectly. It is primarily the designer's information needs which must be addressed in the program. If the programmer and designer are one and the same, the program clearly will be tailored in the appropriate fashion. In addition, the designer, who may be a representative of the same firm that is programming the facility, can contribute useful information to the program and, at the same time, gain time-saving, early understanding of its intent and rationale if involved in the programming from the beginning.

The programmer's responsibility is obvious. Essentially, it involves insuring that the right information is obtained from the right sources, that it is sufficiently and properly analyzed and organized, and that it is presented in an orderly, meaningful manner—all accomplished as economically as possible. The programmer must be no less imaginative and resourceful in his or her approach to the design problem than the designer. The development of a conclusive program document entails not only coordination of information flow, but anticipation of client, designer and project needs. Perhaps most important, the programmer's job is to facilitate interaction among all the participants in the process so that information can be obtained expeditiously and so that it is understood clearly.

The owner's task is *not* to sign the programming services contract and then sit back. Today's programming encourages active participation of the owner and of the other members of the client group directly affected by the outcome of the program and eventual design. The client is a chief source of information for the program, and the many decisions required as the program develops necessitate client involvement. As a programming participant, the client can understand the reasons for decisions and can more readily identify with and accept the eventual outcome.

Owner understanding of the program

and the process which produced it is important to the programmer and the designer. Time-consuming, costly revisions to a final program can be avoided if the owner is kept informed and participates in decisions during program development. It also can help the working relationship between the architect and the owner proceed more smoothly during design.

Finally, it should be noted that the owner is the ultimate provider of the program. It is his or her (or their) statement of what the design should accomplish, whether it is prepared by an outside programmer or in-house. And, when the owner approves a program and autho-

EXHIBIT 2-13. PROGRAM DEVELOPMENT CYCLE

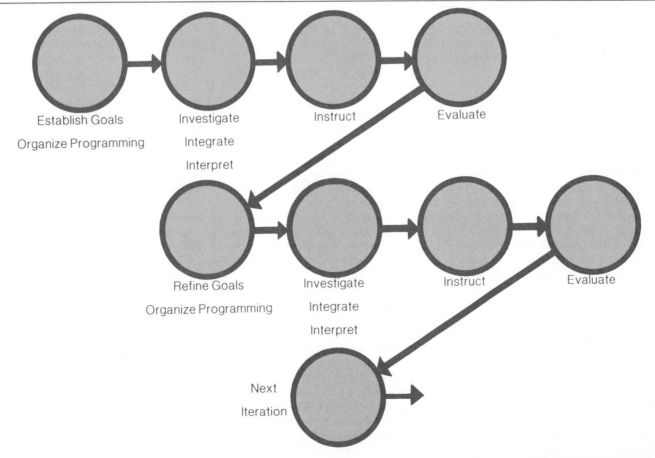

EXHIBIT 2-14. PREDOMINANT ACTIVITIES DURING PROGRAM DEVELOPMENT STAGES

	Collection	Analysis	Organization	Communication	Evaluation
Establish project goals	●	●	●	●	●
Organize programming effort			●	●	
Investigate issues	●	●		●	
Integrate data		●	●		
Interpret information		●	●		●
Instruct designer and client			●	●	
Evaluate results	●			●	●
Recycle information	●	●	●	●	●

rizes design to proceed, it is an agreement with the architect as to what will be incorporated in the facility.

PROGRAMMING PRODUCTS. Communication ties the programming process together. More importantly, it links the program with the design. A program is the essential communication between the client and the designer and between the programmer and the facility owner. It states what the client needs done so that the designer can do it. The program must not only communicate its contents effectively, but the contents must be appropriate for the purpose. The chief means of communicating program information are written, graphic program reports and/or oral and audiovisual presentations.

Program Reports. The apt observation of Marshall McLuhan, the media guru of the 1960s, that "the medium is the message" is particularly pertinent to programming. The means by which the program document communicates its information will determine how effectively (and, perhaps, if) it is used as an aid to designing an appropriate facility. And, as a consequence, it may well determine a client's interest in programming services for future projects. Following are a few guidelines for preparing effective program reports and presentations:

—Conclusions should be stated concisely and clearly, expressing authority and confidence in the data. Recommendations should be expressed in terms of results to be achieved, not necessarily actions to be performed. Many designers accept design performance goals more readily than prescriptive requirements, even from their own firms.

—Only the essential and immediately usable facts and recommendations should be presented in the body of the program report. The rationale for specific conclusions may be summarized, but the bulk of explanation, methodology and support data is, generally, best reserved for appendices or a separate report.

—The program must communicate with its specific audience. Usually, this is the designer, and so the document should speak the language of design and be organized in a format that eases retrieval of data. Language is particularly important in reports that concentrate on user needs and behavioral data. The jargon of the social scientist must be translated effectively, even if it means employing the jargon of the designer. However, clients also must be kept in mind, realizing they are at an even greater disadvantage in understanding technical issues and terminology.

—Along the same lines, the program should address the particular information needs and interests of both the designer and the client, since both will make decisions based on the contents.

—A program should be graphical in content as well as in format. It should be easy to follow and comprehend. Charts, diagrams and even cartoons are superb conveyors of information, which can be backed up with statistics and narrative appropriately placed. The format of written reports should be balanced between text and illustration, and the layout of each page should not be crowded with information, even if it increases the number of pages. A hierarchy of data importance can be achieved by spacing, indentations and heading sizes, but they must be consistent throughout the report. It should go without saying that neatness, grammar and spelling count. Typesetting and professional layout are possibilities (relatively expensive) which may depend on the permanence of the document.

—Every report should include "front matter" comprising various housekeeping items such as a table of contents (essential), identification of participants in pro-

EXHIBIT 2-15. EXAMPLES OF TYPICAL PROGRAM ORGANIZATIONS

PROGRAM A

Table of Contents

Background
  Project Purpose
  Programming Objectives
  Scope of Program
  Programming Methodology
  Project History
  Participants
  Summary Conclusions

PROJECT GOALS
  Human Concerns
  Physical Concerns
  External Concerns

ASCERTAINMENTS
  Human Factors
  Physical Factors
  External Factors

PROJECTIONS
  Human Factors
  Physical Factors
  External Factors

RECOMMENDATIONS
  Human Factors
  Physical Factors
  External Factors

Appendices
  Relevant Backup and Background Data
  Techniques
  Data Compilation

PROGRAM B (Physical emphasis)

Table of Contents

Background

(See "Program A")

HUMAN FACTORS

EXTERNAL FACTORS

PHYSICAL FACTORS
  Location

Site
Facility
Envelope
Structure
Systems
Space
Equipment / Furnishings
Materials / Finishes
Support Services
Special Needs

Appendices

PROGRAM C

Table of Contents

Background

(See "Program A")

DESCRIPTION
  Activity (services, tasks, etc.)
  Organization (structure, hierarchy)
  Sociocultural Aspects

CONSTRAINTS
  Legal (codes, ordinances, agencies)
  Physical (site, workload, policies)

FLEXIBILITY
  Long Range
  Short Range

ECONOMY
  Operational Costs
  Capital Costs
  Life Cycle Costs / Benefits
  Energy / Environment Considerations

IMPLEMENTATION
  Schedule
  Strategy

PHYSICAL / SOCIAL CRITERIA
  Quantity (space, equipment, etc.)
  Adjacencies (internal and external)
  Environment (HVAC, lighting, acoustics)
  Social (user emotions, character of facility)

SPACE PROGRAM

Table of Contents

Introduction
  Purpose
  Scope of Program
  Participants
  Summary Conclusions

FUNCTIONS
  Classification
  Types of Spaces

STANDARD UNITS
  Number Per Function
  Dimensions
  Unit Areas

RELATIONSHIPS
  Adjacencies
  Other Proximity Needs

ORGANIZATION
  Horizontal Proximities
  Vertical Proximities
  Circulation
  Support Space

DESIRED CONDITIONS
  Environment
  Social
  Equipment / Furnishing Needs

AGGREGATE NET / GROSS AREAS

COST ESTIMATE
  Unit Costs
  Optimized Costs
  Budget

Appendices

EXHIBIT 2-16. TYPES OF PROGRAMS

Ascertainment Program
Forecast Program
Recommended Program
Preliminary Program
Final Program
Master Program
Facility Program
Component Program
Performance Program
Design Requirements
Design Specifications
Design Log
Master Plan
Long-Range Plan
Social Impact Assessment
Economic Impact Assessment
Engineering Program
Feasibility Study / Program
Site Requirements
User Needs Survey / Program

Regional Plan
Site Plan
Community Plan
Neighborhood Development Program
Lighting Program
Interiors Program
Activity Program
Organizational Plan
Goals / Objectives Statement
Service Program
Systems Program
Space Program
Equipment Program
Functional Program
Energy Conservation Plan
Energy Management Plan
Energy Analysis
Operations / Maintenance Program
Cost / Benefit Analysis
Environmental Impact Assessment

gram development, identification of client and programming firm, funding sources if appropriate, title page and copyright notice if appropriate. There is nothing inappropriate about including a programmer's address and telephone number for promotional purposes.

—An introductory section could include a summary of the contents and highlights of principal conclusions, purpose of the project and justification for programming, brief history or background of project, synopsis of programming methodology, and explanation of how the program is organized.

—The program should be organized to proceed from the general to the specific and from the most important to the less important. The essence of the program and of individual sections should be presented up front so that the principal concepts are grasped before reader attention wanes.

Program Organization. This is a matter of dividing up information content so that it is easily understood and data can be efficiently extracted for use. There are as many ways to organize a program as there are programmers. Some are shown in the case studies of Part Three.

A program need not be a single document. It may be a series of reports relating definable issues or phased accomplishments; e.g., feasibility study, user needs survey, functional program, space program, design requirements. A comprehensive program may be limited to one or two levels of detail or it may consist of all three levels. It may be presented as a single document containing various levels or it may be divided into individual documents representing differing levels of detail. The organizing theme may be a focus on human factors, physical factors, external factors or some specific issue.

Exhibit 2-15 presents three different content organizations for comprehensive programs and an outline of a specific purpose program. These are only examples of the many ways in which a program may be organized.

Types of Programs. The variety of different types of programs, from comprehensive programs to special purpose programs, have been indicated throughout the chapter. Exhibit 2-16 presents a sample listing of the various kinds or names of programs and program-type studies that have been recognized.

HOW A PROGRAM HAPPENS. It doesn't happen by itself. The programmer, client and designer cooperate in the processing of information to develop the conclusions and content. The programmer has the prime responsibility not only to produce the essential information, but also to develop it. The next part of this book explores some of the many techniques available for collecting, analyzing, organizing, communicating and evaluating programmatic data.

PART TWO
TECHNIQUES
AND TOOLS
OF PROGRAMMING

CHAPTER 3
TECHNIQUES FOR
DATA COLLECTION

CHAPTER 4
TECHNIQUES FOR DATA ANALYSIS
AND ORGANIZATION

CHAPTER 5
TECHNIQUES FOR
COMMUNICATION
AND EVALUATION

CHAPTER 6
COMPUTER AIDS TO
FACILITY PROGRAMMING

Like a magician, the well-prepared programmer not only is equipped with an organized, standard routine but carries a bag of varying techniques from which to choose in addressing different opportunities and problems. There is no magic in the development of appropriate information for unique situations, clients and facilities. The trick is to match suitable techniques and tools with information needs.

The chapters of Part Two present an extensive survey of procedures, techniques and tools for the collection, analysis, organization, communication and evaluation of programming information. Some may be mastered from the information provided; others require further study, reading and practice. Most techniques are described in terms of "products," the data results that may be produced or the uses to which they may be put; "procedures," rules-of-thumb or directions for applying the technique; and "resources," guidance to sources of additional or more detailed information. Complete references for all sources cited in the text can be found in the bibliography at the back of the book.

An overview of applications of automated data processing for programming and special computer-aided techniques is presented in Chapter 6. Techniques and tools described in Chapters 3, 4 and 5 have been classified among the five information-processing functions: data collection, analysis, organization, communication and evaluation. Although each is assigned to a category, many methods are appropriate for one or more other functions. The matrix in Exhibit Two-1 is a master index that indicates the primary and secondary uses of each technique for various information-processing functions.

Chapter 3

TECHNIQUE	Collection	Analysis	Organization	Communication	Evaluation
Background Data Research	●	○	●		
Surveys	●	○			○
Interviews	●				○
Questionnaires	●				○
Data Logs	●		○	○	
Standardized Data Forms	●		●	○	
Direct Observation	●	○	○		
Tracking	●	○			
Participant Observation	●			○	
Behavior Mapping	●	○	○	●	
Behavior Specimen Record	●	○			
Instrumented Observation	●			●	
Semantic Differential	●	●			○
Adjective Checklist	●	●			○
Attribute Discrimination Scale	●	●			○
Ranking Chart	●	●		○	○
Preference Matrix	●	●		○	○

Chapter 4

TECHNIQUE	Collection	Analysis	Organization	Communication	Evaluation
Descriptive Statistics	○	●		○	
Inferential Statistics		●			●
Behavior Setting Survey	●	●	○		●
Activity Site Model	●	●	●	○	●
Time Budget Analysis	●	●	○		
Pattern Language	○	○	●	●	○
Space Unit Standards	●	●	○	○	
Space Program		○	●	●	
Energy Budgeting	○	●			○

	Collection	Analysis	Organization	Communication	Evaluation
Project Cost Estimating	○	●	●		
Construction Cost Estimating	○	●	●		
Life Cycle Cost Analysis		●			●
Value Analysis		●			●
Cost-benefit Analysis		●			●
Bar Chart/Milestone Chart		●	●	○	○
Activity Time Chart	○	●	●		
Critical Path Method (CPM)		●	●	○	●
Program Evaluation & Review Technique (PERT)		●	●	○	●
Precedence Diagramming Method (PDM)		●	●	○	●
Relationship Matrices	○	●	●	●	○
Social Map		●	●		
Sociogram		●	○		
Behavior Map	●	○	○	●	
Bubble Diagram		○	●	●	
Link-Node Diagram		○	●	○	
Block Diagram			●	●	
Interaction Net		●	●	○	
Dual Graph		●	●	○	
Adjacency Diagram	○	○	●	●	
Functional Relationship Diagram	○	○	●	●	
Layout Diagram			●	●	
Flow Diagram		●	●	○	
Organizational Chart	○	○	●	●	
Analysis Cards	●	●	●	●	○
Worksheets	●	●	●	○	○

Key

● = Primary use

○ = Secondary use

Chapter 5

TECHNIQUE	Collection	Analysis	Organization	Communication	Evaluation
Brainstorming	●	○		●	
Synectics	○	●		●	
Buzz / Rap Session	○			●	
Role Playing		●		●	○
Gaming	○	○		●	●
Group Planning	○	○	●	●	○
Narrative				●	
Graphics			○	●	
Audio / Visual Aids			○	●	
Oral Presentations				●	
Forums	●			●	
Panel Discussions	○			●	
Work / Charrette / Primer Books	●			●	
Rating and Rating Scales		○			●
Ladder Scale	○	○			●
Rating Chart	○	○			●
Evaluation Matrix	○	○			●
Weighting		●			●

Key

● = Primary use

○ = Secondary use

Chapter 3
Techniques for
Data Collection

Effective programming depends on thorough, objective and efficient data collection and on obtaining appropriate, reliable, representative and accurate information. In achieving these goals, the programmer will amass much more data than can be used to reach meaningful conclusions about a facility and its possible design. It is necessary, however, to probe extensively into the physical conditions, human behavior and attitudes, and the contextual influences to analyze and understand the whole of a particular design problem and to respond with creative, effective design solutions.

The efficacy of data collection involves knowing what types of data are needed and selecting the appropriate means of eliciting, obtaining and documenting them. It also involves using more than one data collection approach in order to cross-check results and ensure completeness of data. Conclusions that may appear obvious from the results of interviewing a client, for example, may be significantly altered after evaluating them on the basis of observations of the client's organization and activities.

The techniques described in this chapter offer a variety of approaches for obtaining factual and perceptual information from user reports, programmer's insights and independent resources. Their use may be better understood by remembering that in data collection the programmer does three basic things: asks questions, observes, and records data.

BACKGROUND AND USER REPORT METHODS

The primary source of data for programming is the client—owner, user and related publics. The following techniques include most of the traditional means of obtaining information directly from primary sources. Aside from certain aspects of background data research, the techniques depend on various forms of user report; that is, they require subjects to supply data from their personal knowledge, experience and perception related to the facility being programmed.

Different techniques are suitable for different types of data. Surveys are used primarily for collecting opinions and measuring attitudes. Data logs and standardized forms seek to document factual, descriptive information. Interviews and questionnaires, the most versatile techniques of this group, can be used to obtain both descriptive and evaluative data and can be applied at various points in the programming project.

These are basic data collection techniques, and at least one type is essential for any programming study. More often, however, two or more are combined. A survey is conducted by use of interviews and/or questionnaires. A questionnaire may be a part of an interview. Data logs and forms are often included in questionnaires.

BACKGROUND DATA RESEARCH.
Every programming project should begin with background data research. This preliminary investigation of project needs, relevant issues and existing information is necessary for establishing project goals, organizing the programming effort and documenting whatever data are available before further investigation.

A great deal of relevant information about a particular facility or project may have been produced in one form or another before programming. If it is already available, there is no need to recreate it. However, existing data may not have been compiled or organized for program purposes, and obtaining such data will require some digging.

The scope of background investigation depends on the purpose and nature of the project and on:

—The type of information needed
—How well relevant issues have been defined

—Availability of appropriate and reliable resources
—The originality of the project (if the facility to be programmed is unique to the client, the client likely will not be able to provide much background data)

The objective of background data research is to obtain and organize as much useful information as possible on a project and to analyze existing data by sorting out relevant information and determining what needs further investigation and analysis. Background research helps to:

—Define data needs and programming tasks
—Identify sources of information
—Familiarize the programmer with the client's objectives, philosophy, organization and operations
—Create a data base for verification and further investigation

Types of Information. Some of the data obtained through preliminary research will be conclusive and usable for the program. Other data will be preliminary and will merely establish the issues requiring further study. Still other data will include tentative conclusions or hypotheses that must be researched more substantially. Certain data can be obtained from the owner and users of the facility, while others will come from outside sources and from the programmer's own observations and insights. Among the types of information that a programmer might expect or hope to find from background data research are:

—Client's general objectives and specific goals for the facility
—Client's philosophy and history
—Client's organization and policies
—Design, use and technology of the facility type
—Specific design issues that may be involved with the facility
—User needs issues
—Codes, standards and regulations pertinent to the facility

—Functional and operational issues relevant to the facility
—Problems in the client's existing facilities
—Growth projections
—Demographic data
—Project constraints
—Site conditions
—Programming techniques useful for the project

Obtaining Background Data. There are three principal activities involved in preliminary investigation: exploratory observation, unstructured interviews and literature and records search. (See Exhibit 3-1.) Either before or after initial discussions with the client, the programmer can learn a great deal about the proposed facility by *observing* the existing one, other similar facilities and the intended site. Early explorations give the programmer an opportunity for unprejudiced examination of existing conditions, operations and space use.

Notes should be taken on general dimensions, activities and both positive and negative aspects of the facility or site. Exploratory observation is preliminary and the programmer only needs to identify general characteristics, obvious problems and unique or special conditions. Later, structured observation studies will provide detailed data based on preliminary observation or other sources.

Unstructured interviews with the owner, and sometimes with the users, of the facility also provide the programmer with a sense of the scope and nature of the project. They enable both the client and programmer to raise the issues that are of most concern and to identify significant problems, general constraints and program information needs. Unstructured interviews are especially useful in conjunction with a walkthrough of the client's existing facility. Interviews with other sources—e.g., local public officials, tech-

EXHIBIT 3-1. THREE PRINCIPAL ACTIVITIES IN OBTAINING BACKGROUND DATA

Observation   Interviews   Literature Search

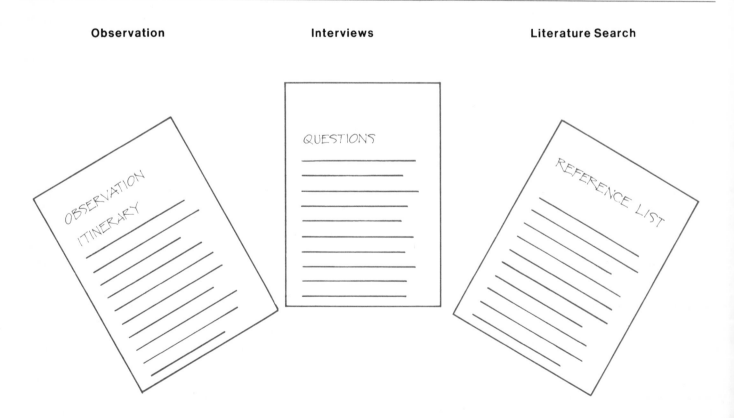

nical experts and other programmers and designers—may be more structured, seeking answers to specific questions about an issue, conditions or a problem.

The greatest effort in background data research will likely go into a *literature and records search*. Here the programmer lays a foundation for further investigation and preliminary conclusions. It involves searching through client records and documents for data directly related to the facility as well as surveying technical and other literature that might yield data on the type of facility, user needs, design issues and programming methods.

A detailed description of the technique of literature searching is found in *Design Methods: Seeds of Human Futures* by J. Christopher Jones. Jones identifies generic sources of published information and explains some of the uses and pitfalls of literature searching. The procedure he outlines is as follows:

—Identify the purposes for which published information is being sought.

—Identify the kinds of publications that are likely to contain information that can be relied on for such purposes.

—Select the most relevant of the standard methods of beginning a literature search.

—Minimize the search cost by allowing for retrieval delays and by continuously evaluating both the choice of sources and the applicability of the data collected.

—Keep accurate and complete references to documents that are found to be usable.

—Keep local collections of publications sufficiently small and temporary to permit rapid retrieval.

Sources of Information. The two primary sources of background data are the client and the technical literature. However, there are many other sources, some of which require imaginative use on the part of the programmer. The yellow pages of the local telephone book, for instance,

may provide preliminary information on the number and types of establishments that offer services or products similar to those of the client. Or, it may yield additional sources of information on specific issues or aspects of a project. Some communities have directories that list each address and identify the type of property at the location (i.e., residence, store, public building, industry, etc.). Local news publications are an excellent source of recent history on development issues, public concerns, community needs and the local political climate.

The matrix in Exhibit 3-2 lists some of the typical sources of information a programmer might employ for a project as well as the type of information each might provide.

Resources. "Unobtrusive Measures: Their Nature and Utility for Architects" by Arthur H. Patterson in *Designing for Human Behavior*, Jon Lang et al., eds. Stroudsburg, Pa.: Dowden, Hutchinson & Ross Inc., 1974.

"Literature Searching" in *Design Methods: Seeds of Human Futures*, J. Christopher Jones. New York: John Wiley & Sons Ltd., 1970.

"An Approach to the Study of Environmental Quality" by Amos Rapoport in *Proceedings of the First EDRA Conference*, Henry Sanoff and Sidney Cohn, eds. Stroudsburg, Pa.: Dowden, Hutchinson & Ross Inc., 1970.

"Toward Assessing Social Impacts: The Diachronic Analysis of Newspaper Contents" by Anabelle Bender Motz in *Methodology of Social Impact Assessment*, Kurt Finsterbusch and C.P. Wolf, eds. Stroudsburg, Pa.: Dowden, Hutchinson & Ross Inc., 1977.

SURVEYS. The Gallup or Harris opinion polls are the most easily recognized version of the broad range of scientific data collection devices known as surveys. Surveys are a well established feature of

modern society and are used, in their more popularized forms, to gauge political trends, analyze economic markets, establish television ratings and measure the sundry characteristics of the nation's population in the decennial census. They are also widely used in all the social science disciplines, particularly in fields of applied research, to study the perceptions, attitudes, opinions, motivations, preferences and characteristics of relatively large groups of people. In architectural research and in programming, the survey is becoming a standard feature of systematic efforts to identify relevant attitudes and characteristics of the users of a particular facility or type of facility.

A survey can be defined as any systematic collection of data about a population (a specified group) through direct contact with members or a representative sample of that population. To put it plainly, it is getting the information from the horse's mouth. Data are usually collected through interviews (personal or telephone) or questionnaires administered to individuals in the population. The collective responses are analyzed to reveal the patterns of attitudes, characteristics or behavior (as perceived by the survey subjects) of a specific group in a particular setting. Except in opinion polls or other simplistic surveys, the results of a study won't reveal a single "majority" view, but rather several "measurable" patterns that are useful in making judgments about the population and the client's needs. (See Exhibit 3-3.)

Because surveys and other tests of people's attitudes and perceptions measure only what they think or feel about something, there are limits to the usefulness of such information, particularly for facility designers. What people say about their behavior is not necessarily consistent with how they actually behave; or what they perceive about the functioning of a building is not necessarily a true measure of how or even how well the building serves its purpose. Furthermore, survey results enable only statistical generalizations about attitudes, perceptions and values of a large and diverse group of people. The interpretation of these generalizations requires skill and knowledge in social and behavioral sciences and may necessitate the use of a professional consultant. Nevertheless, when survey research is properly applied and used in combination with other data collection techniques, it can provide valuable insight into the needs of facility users. This information can help the designer and the owner (whose interests and perceptions in relation to the facility may be quite different from those of the users and operators) to develop a design that performs more effectively and efficiently.

Products. Survey research can provide the programmer information that describes, explains or predicts how people act in and react to their surroundings. The data may include statistical measurements of the attitudes, values, beliefs, perceptions, preferences, motivations and characteristics of the group that is using or will use the facility being programmed.

These inferences about the attributes of relatively large populations (as in an office building, neighborhood, community, etc.) are based on the collective responses of individual members of the population to specific, directed questions. The raw data are analyzed by various methods in order to reach meaningful conclusions about the results, usually verification or repudiation of the programmer's hypotheses. The use of scientifically designed surveys enables the programmer to discover and isolate patterns that are not readily apparent even to the members of the group which is surveyed.

Procedure. A survey can be designed for almost any group and for almost any kind of information relevant to a facility design. The design, administration and

EXHIBIT 3-2. TYPES AND SOURCES OF INFORMATION FOR BACKGROUND DATA

SOURCES OF INFORMATION	Client objectives	Client philosophy/history	Client organization	Facility type	Design issues	User needs issues	Codes, standards, etc.	Functions/operations	Existing problems	Growth projections	Demographic data	Project constraints	Site conditions	Programming techniques
Client (owner/users)	●	●	●			●	●	●	●	●	●	●	●	
Existing facility				●	●			●	●			●		
Existing facility plans/drawings				●	●				●			●		
Other facility plans/drawings				●	●				●			●		
Facility programs				●	●	●	●	●				●		●
Owner records/archives	●	●	●			●			●	●	●			
Owner literature (promotional documents, employee handbooks, organizational charts, etc.)	●	●	●			●				●				
Related programming/planning studies				●	●	●	●	●			●	●	●	
Research findings—user needs					●	●								●
Research findings—facility performance				●	●									
Community leaders							●		●			●		
Local authorities —Planning							●			●	●	●	●	
—Zoning							●					●	●	
—Building							●					●		
—Utilities							●					●	●	

SOURCES OF INFORMATION	Client objectives	Client philosophy/history	Client organization	Facility type	Design issues	User needs issues	Codes, standards, etc.	Functions/operations	Existing problems	Growth projections	Demographic data	Project constraints	Site conditions	Programming techniques
Data banks														
— Programmer's				●	●	●		●						●
— Project files				●	●	●	●							●
— Architecture libraries				●	●	●		●						●
— Abstracting services				●	●	●					●			
Technical libraries				●	●	●		●			●			●
Technical experts				●	●	●	●	●	●	●	●			●
Other programmers/designers				●	●	●	●	●						●
Publications (books, reports, etc.)				●	●	●	●	●					●	
Journals/periodicals				●	●	●		●						●
Local newspapers	●					●			●			●		
Design guides				●	●		●	●						
Visits to other sites				●	●	●	●	●	●			●	●	
Census records						●				●	●			
Public records									●	●	●	●	●	
Telephone book yellow pages				●							●			
Community directories/profiles											●			
Local associations						●	●				●	●		

analysis of surveys involve many procedural steps that may vary depending on the type of survey selected for the project. The following procedures generally apply to all survey research:

—One of the first steps in preparing to survey is to identify the population. In other words, decide who has the information that is needed and identify, if possible, the characteristics of that population which might be pertinent to the evaluation of the data. Of course, population characterization may be one of the objectives of the survey. In many cases, identifying the population involves selecting a small portion or sample of the group which can be assumed to represent the attributes of the total group.

—Decide what information is needed. What does the programmer want to find out about this population that is pertinent to the facility design? In most surveys, this means developing preliminary conclusions, or hypotheses, about the population that will be tested through the survey.

—The programmer may collect preliminary or background information that will enable him or her to postulate hypotheses or identify characteristics of the population that will aid in interpreting the survey results. This may include identifying such characteristics as the male-female distribution, the age groups represented, the specific activities of the individuals, etc.

—Choose the type of survey that is appropriate for the particular group to be studied and for the particular information needed.

—Design the survey instrument. This involves preparing questions (or a questionnaire), scales of measurement, forms and other devices that will be used to collect the data from the individuals in the population. The manner of presentation to the individuals and the manner in which the results are to be analyzed will be determining factors in developing the format. For example, it is important, especially when large quantities of data are involved,

EXHIBIT 3-3. TYPICAL GRAPH OF SURVEY RESULTS

●THINGS LIKED

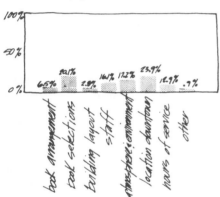

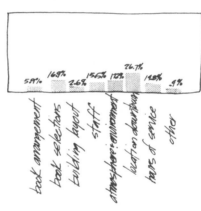

●THINGS DISLIKED

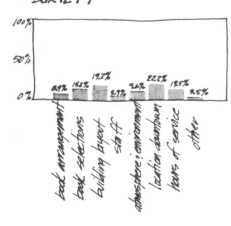

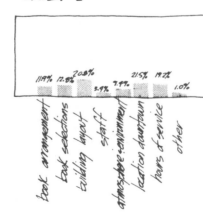

to precode answers so that they can be tabulated easily; e.g., transfer of data to keypunch cards for computer analysis.

—Administer the survey. As mentioned earlier, this may be by interview or by questionnaire; techniques are discussed later.

—Analyze the results. The collection of individual responses is nothing more than a conglomeration of raw data until it has been statistically analyzed.

Types of Surveys. There are a variety of survey techniques that can be applied in obtaining programming information. The selection of a particular survey type will often be a practical matter of cost, time or complexity. The choice may also depend on the nature of the research. Three commonly used types of surveys are the cross-section survey, the longitudinal survey, and contrasting sample survey.

The *cross-section survey* is the most widely used, mainly because it is simple and inexpensive. The objective is to determine information about a population at a fixed point in time. Characteristics, attitudes and perceived behavior are the principal outcomes of the survey and are usually presented in the form of "distributions," or breakdown of the total number of responses into categories.

Repeated cross-section surveys given at successive points in time can show the patterns of change in attitude, experience or characteristics of a group. Another approach is the *longitudinal survey* or reinterview panel, which involves tracking the same group and interviewing the individuals several times over an extended period. However, this is a more costly method and produces data more suitable for long-range planning than for immediate design projects.

The third basic survey approach is the *contrasting sample*. This is a way of cross-checking survey results. A sample of the population related to a particular project is surveyed and compared with another or several sample(s) of a similar population that is not related to the project. For example, a programmer might wish to test the attitudes of neighborhood residents toward a proposed highrise complex. The survey is administered to a representative sample of the residents and to sample groups in other similar neighborhoods which don't anticipate highrise construction. The contrast between the responses of the primary group and those of the other samples can help the programmer identify more easily the significant attitudes of the residents toward the new highrise building.

Sampling. One of the chief benefits of survey research is that it enables the programmer to make reliable generalizations about a variety of attributes of a large group without necessarily interrogating the entire group. This is possible through the use of sampling procedures. A sample is a kind of social "scale model" of the whole population. It is assumed to represent the same characteristic and attitude patterns of the full population, or "universe." There are several methods of selecting a sample, most of which are designed to insure a reliable degree of representativeness of the total population. These are called probability or random sampling techniques. Another category is called nonprobability sampling.

Probability samples are based on selection methods that permit all members of a universe (total population) an equal chance of being a part of the sample. The equality of opportunity insures that the sample, in all probability, represents the same attributes that would be found by surveying the total population. In other words, the probability that the sample deviates from the true population is minimal. Statisticians use a factor known as "sampling error" to correct the probable deviation. Generally, the larger the sample, the smaller the sampling error.

Among the probability sampling procedures, there are several commonly used varieties: simple random sampling, stratified sampling, systematic sampling and cluster sampling. All these procedures start with a list, or sample frame, of all the members of the universe. The size of the sample will depend on the complexity of the survey, the nature of the research and the cost and time available to conduct the survey. In *simple random sampling*, each member of the universe is assigned a number (ordinal scale) and the surveyor uses a standard "table of random numbers" to select the numbers from the frame, picking as many as are called for in the sample size.

Systematic sampling is a simplified version of this procedure. Instead of using a table of random numbers, the surveyor makes the random selections based on a constant interval; i.e., every item appearing at a predetermined interval on the sample frame is selected. The constant interval is determined by the ratio of the size of the population to the size of the total sample. Say, for instance, a programmer wished to interview 100 of the 900 students on a college campus. The interval would be 900 divided by 100, or nine. Every 9th name on the enrollment list would be selected for the interviews. Picking a random starting point less than nine—six, for instance—the surveyor would then pick the 6th, 15th, 24th, and so-on names on the list until a total of 100 names had been chosen for the sample.

Another procedure is *stratified sampling*, in which the total population is divided into homogeneous groups according to common characteristics. The college enrollment in the example above could be divided into strata (groups) by majors, by class years, by married and unmarried categories or by grade-point averages, for instance. Each student is allowed to appear in only one category. A sample from each of the categories would then be selected randomly. The in-

dividual samples would be surveyed and the results could be compared and combined to produce views of both the entire student population and the individual categories of students. The advantage of this method, which requires previous knowledge in order to create the strata, is that it permits the surveyor to minimize the variation of responses within each stratum and sharpen the variations among the strata.

Finally, *cluster sampling* is a method by which survey costs can be reduced through taking a sample of a sample. As in stratified sampling, it involves identifying groups or clusters—usually related by physical proximity—and then taking a sample from each cluster. If the college surveyor wished to examine the attitudes of students toward their housing conditions, the students could be clustered according to the dormitories or off-campus locations of their residences. A sample from each dormitory and from off-campus residential areas would be taken and, once the survey was administered, the results would be combined to form conclusions. The total number in the combined samples would be smaller perhaps than random sampling of all students, but would still be representative.

Sometimes it is not possible to know the limits of a population and therefore not possible to estimate a precisely representative sample. In these cases, it is necessary to use *nonprobability samples*. The members of the population are sampled on the basis of the personal judgment of the surveyor or on the basis of predetermined criteria such as a simple quota. "Person-on-the-street" interviews are examples of nonprobability sampling; a specified quota of shoppers entering a store is another. Although sometimes necessary, the reliability of findings from nonprobability surveys have to be taken with a grain, at least, of salt.

Resources. *Survey Sampling*, L. Kish.

New York: John Wiley & Sons, 1965.

"Information Retrieval Methods" in *Methods of Architectural Programming*, Henry Sanoff. Stroudsburg, Pa.: Dowden, Hutchinson & Ross Inc., 1977.

"Surveys, Questionnaires and Interviews," by Ronald J. Goodrich in *Designing for Human Behavior*, Jon Lang et al., eds. Stroudsburg, Pa.: Dowden, Hutchinson & Ross Inc., 1974.

"Survey Research" by Robert W. Marans in *Behavioral Research Methods in Environmental Design*, William Michelson, ed. Stroudsburg, Pa.: Dowden, Hutchinson & Ross Inc., 1975.

INTERVIEWS. This is perhaps the most common, and certainly the most direct, means of obtaining detailed information for programs. It is a versatile technique that produces a wide variety of information, works well in eliciting data from a variety of sources, and can be easily applied at various stages of program development. Interviewing is simply asking questions in a more or less structured manner. It works best in one-to-one situations, but can be used in group sessions. The purpose is to obtain specific data on client attitudes, needs, activities, tasks, existing conditions, perceptions, preferences, projections, etc.

The interview serves the same purpose as a questionnaire: to obtain specific and detailed data. The difference, however, is that interviews permit the programmer and the client to interact directly and immediately—the client's doubts about the meaning of interview questions can be answered and the programmer can probe for additional data or immediately clarify questionable responses. The interview session might follow a structured questionnaire, seeking quick responses to specific questions, or it might be open-ended to allow the client to freely express opinions and volunteer information that might not otherwise be revealed. The procedure

chosen will depend on the nature of the information desired.

Although the one-to-one interview is most effective, group interviews are sometimes useful. For example, when the programmer wants to find out the best sources of information or issues that need further exploration, a group interview will often reveal these. The programmer can then follow up on the initial interview by holding individual sessions with the most appropriate sources of information.

The chief drawback of the interview technique is that individual responses are subjective, or even opinionated. People sometimes give answers they believe the questioner wants to hear, or try to put a best or worst face on a situation. What people think and say about their behavior and environments may be somewhat different from the way they actually behave or respond to a setting. A corporate director's estimate of the amount of space needed for the board room in the new headquarters building may turn out to be extravagant compared to actual use of the space or to what the project budget will say is needed.

The subjectivity of human responses to interviews and questionnaires is one of the main reasons for using proper survey procedures. Interviews with all the corporate directors about the hypothetical meeting room above will likely yield a variety of suggestions on its size, but will provide a more reliable basis for judging what size will satisfy most of their requirements. These data, however, still represent subjective opinion—although it might be very knowledgeable opinion—and do not measure how well the group's preference stacks up to the actual use of board room space. Observation of a board meeting may show, for instance, that the expressed need for more space is based on the fact that the conference table is too large for the present board room, or that the way the meeting is conducted requires the presence of too many support

staff at one time. Measuring preferences alone—even with the most sophisticated interview procedures—is not the way to write an economical, efficient program. (See Exhibit 3-4.) Following up interviews with observation techniques or checking responses against questionnaire data can verify and substantiate the data obtained.

Another limitation of interviews is that they are time-consuming. For projects that require a large sampling of client representatives, it might be best to limit the use of interviews unless personnel and time resources permit. It will be more efficient to obtain data through other techniques and to interview only selected client representatives who can provide comprehensive or specialized information.

Products. Despite the limitation on the quality of data, interviewing is an essential technique for programming. The programmer must know what the client thinks and wants before client needs can be determined. Interviews provide a wide variety of necessary data, such as:

—Client goals and philosophy
—Background and historical data
—Demographic and social data
—Preferences, values, attitudes, opinions
—Identification of conflicts and problems
—New ideas, personal evaluations
—Descriptive information on operations, procedures, activities, settings, use of space, etc.
—Projections of space, equipment, operational and other needs

Procedure. The programmer begins by identifying what information is needed, deciding who to interview, and organizing a set of questions, a checklist, a data sheet or other response form. Interviews are scheduled to allow sufficient time for each individual to complete the predetermined questions and for free discussion, if desired. It is also important to arrange interviews so that they do not interfere with the individual's work or take too much time. Conducting the interview in the individual's own workplace or surroundings may help him or her relax and respond more freely to questioning. It also provides the interviewer an opportunity to observe the space used by the individual and to raise questions about it that might have been overlooked in preinterview preparation.

Accurate recording of responses is vital if the information is to be of any use. Having a prepared form with the questions and spaces for writing down answers serves the purpose well. Use of a tape recorder to ensure accuracy and detail is an option that has two drawbacks. First, people may be intimidated or nervous in the presence of a recorder, although this has become less of a problem in the age of electronic media. Second, transcription of tapes for analysis adds another time-consuming step in the data collection process. One other option is for two people to conduct the interviews: one to question and one to record. This enables both to concentrate on individual tasks, and after the interview, the two will be able to collaborate on the results. However, this option can be very costly.

Unstructured Interviews. In unstructured or open-ended interviews, the programmer may not be seeking answers to questions as much as the right questions to ask. This is mainly an exploratory mission to gain a general understanding of the client (organization and individuals), learn the client's interests and vocabulary and discover what information is needed for the program. An unstructured interview consists of general questions that probe the client's knowledge rather than pinpoint information. Answers to such questions as "What do you think are the main problems with the space in your department?" will help the programmer focus on the primary issues that need further, more methodical

EXHIBIT 3-4. SUBJECTIVITY VS. OBJECTIVITY IN USER DATA

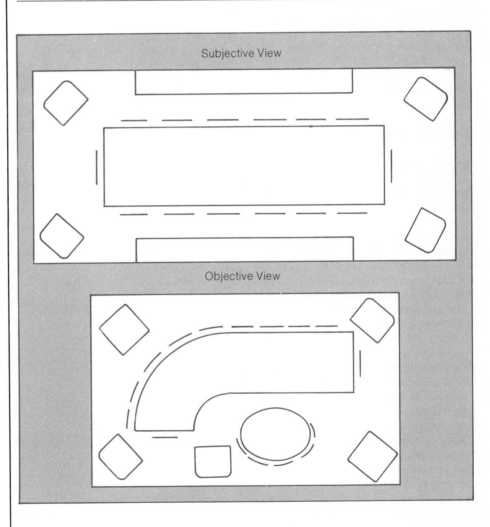

investigation. The unstructured nature of the interview enables programmer and client to discuss whatever issue might arise in the conversation. As part of a *structured interview*, the open-ended questioning provides an opportunity for the client to bring up new issues and information and to freely express views unbound by specific questions.

Structured Interviews. This type of session follows a prearranged format and attempts to obtain measurable data. The programmer has already identified the issues to be studied and is trying to "fill in the blanks" or gather from several people a set of answers that can be compared to produce conclusive evidence; e.g., 68 percent of the clerical workers interviewed say that dim office lighting is the biggest problem in performing their tasks. The structured interview includes a set of specific questions for each interviewee to complete. Some questions will call for verbal descriptions, while others will ask the client to choose among alternative answers, rank in order of preferences, or assign values to options.

Interviews often are used in tandem with questionnaires and/or data forms. Data that can be supplied in a straightforward manner can be recorded by questionnaire or form, while interviews are used to verify the results and explore issues not fitting a rigid format.

Questionnaires or forms may include quantitative data that take some time to prepare. Interviews, on the other hand, may cover subjects involving an exchange of information or requiring that the client be guided to conclusions. The client should be fully briefed in the methods of developing data and given an agenda beforehand on the topics of an interview.

In requesting information from a client about facility needs, the programmer should ask respondents to visualize their needs outside the context of the existing space. Although sometimes difficult to ac-

EXHIBIT 3-5. EXAMPLE OF A QUESTIONNAIRE

A

III *Courts/Sections*
In this section of the interview we are interested in your viewpoints concerning the particular court (homes) or section (apartments, townhouses) in which you live, in this case _____.

(22) Defining "neighborhood" with the following characteristics (people at least knowing the names of other people, people saying hello to one another, perhaps borrowing things or doing favors once in a while), do you feel that a strong sense of neighborhood exists in your section or court:

a _____ Strong sense of neighborhood   Explain:
b _____ Some sense of neighborhood
c _____ No sense of neighborhood
d _____ Conflict
e _____ No feelings on the subject

Using the following characteristics describe your particular court or section:

noisy	____	____	____	____	____	quiet
attractive	____	____	____	____	____	unattractive
unfriendly	____	____	____	____	____	friendly
poorly kept up	____	____	____	____	____	well kept up
crowded	____	____	____	____	____	uncrowded
similar people	____	____	____	____	____	different people
transient	____	____	____	____	____	permanent
liberal	____	____	____	____	____	conservative
adult oriented	____	____	____	____	____	child oriented
active	____	____	____	____	____	inactive
lack of privacy	____	____	____	____	____	private
others	____	____	____	____	____	

Explain extreme responses:

_____

With respect to the various characteristics just given, do you feel that there are significant differences between courts (or sections) within Pine Run:

_____

If yes, describe these differences (refer to map if necessary).

B

If you had the opportunity, would you move to another section/court:

_____

If yes, which one _____ and why:

_____

Have you made any complaints to the management:

_____

If yes, how many _____ and what were they about:

_____

How responsive has the management been to these complaints:

a _____ Very responsive   Explain:
b _____ Responsive
c _____ Mixed feelings
d _____ Unresponsive
e _____ Very unresponsive

(28) Read the following 2 definitions of friendships.

    Neighbors: People you know by name, have occasional short conversations with, borrow things from, share car pools, etc.

    Friends: People you see on a more regular basis and with whom you do things socially (parties, visiting, going out, etc.).

    Do you agree with these definitions: _____

    If no, give us your own definition of different friendship levels:

_____

Considering the above definitions (or your own) answer the following two questions:

How often you socialize with your "neighbors" as compared with your previous residence:

a _____ Socialize more   Explain (including differences among family members)
b _____ Same as before
c _____ Socialize less
d _____ No thoughts on the subject

---

complish, it is a good way to get the client to take a fresh look at operations and space needs.

Resources. "Surveys, Questionnaires and Interviews" by Ronald J. Goodrich in *Designing for Human Behavior*, Jon Lang et al., eds. Stroudsburg, Pa.: Dowden, Hutchinson & Ross Inc., 1974.

Planning the Research Interview, J.C. Scott and Eliska Chanlette. Chapel Hill, N.C.: Laboratories for Population Statistics, University of North Carolina, 1973.

"Using Interviews of Present Office Workers in Planning New Offices" by Gerald Davis in *EDRA 3 Proceedings*, William J. Mitchell, ed. Los Angeles: University of California, 1972.

The Dynamics of Interviewing, R.L. Kahn and C.F. Cannell. New York: John Wiley & Sons Ltd., 1957.

Interviewing in Social Research, H. Hyman. Chicago: University of Chicago Press, 1954.

QUESTIONNAIRES. The purpose of the questionnaire is basically the same as that of the interview: to elicit detailed data on client activities, attitudes, characteristics, needs, etc. It is a written set of questions that generally call for written responses. A questionnaire may be used as a guide for interviewing or may be made part of an interview. The most beneficial application is in surveying large numbers of people to collect precise responses to specific sets of questions. The ideal situation is to administer a questionnaire to a captive audience, such as a student body or a housing tenants meeting, so that the members of the group are expected to complete and turn in their answers within a time limit.

The questionnaire technique is a quick, efficient and inexpensive method of obtaining a large quantity of varied information from a broad cross section of the population affected by a project. It can

EXHIBIT 3-5. EXAMPLE OF A QUESTIONNAIRE (CONT'D)

C

How often you socialize with "friends" as compared with your previous residence:

a ＿＿＿ Socialize more   Explain (including differences among family members)
b ＿＿＿ Same as before
c ＿＿＿ Socialize less
d ＿＿＿ No thoughts on the subject

(29) How do you feel about the number of residences located within your court/section:

     a ＿＿＿ Very crowded   Explain:
     b ＿＿＿ Somewhat crowded
     c ＿＿＿ Adequate
     d ＿＿＿ Not close enough

(30) Do you believe that there are better or worse locations within your section/court: ＿＿＿＿

If yes, describe and identify these differences:

_____

(31) If you had the opportunity, would you move to another location within your section/court: ＿＿＿＿

If yes, where ＿＿＿＿＿＿ and why would you move there:

produce descriptive data or measurable data, depending on the types of questions asked. Like the interview, questionnaires can tell the programmer what a client thinks, believes and feels about behavior and environments. Again, however, this information is based on the client's own experience and subjective understanding and should be tested against data obtained by other means.

Nevertheless, questionnaire procedures enable the programmer to quantify and measure as precisely as possible attitudinal information, such as preferences, values and feelings, and to document factual data. The questionnaire requires the client to focus on questions that isolate the information desired and often forces a choice among limited options. Such constraints are necessary in order to quantify qualitative information, but they also may yield data that are not entirely representative of the client's real attitudes. An interview, on the other hand, provides an opportunity for the client to explain an answer or the reason for a particular choice.

Products. The objective of questionnaires is to obtain data that the programmer uses to define group attitudes, activities, use of space, characteristics, preferences, problems, issues. The programmer seeks to compile comparable and representative data for a group rather than to examine individual ideas and opinions. There are two kinds of data derived from questionnaires: fact or objective data and opinion or subjective data.

Fact data is that which the client knows about his or her own characteristics, surroundings, actions and interactions with others, and reasons for behavior. This includes demographic or census-type data such as age, sex, religion, income, type and value of home, education, occupation and family size. *Opinion data* includes beliefs, feelings, values, standards, viewpoints and preferences. Questions can be designed to produce either kind of data and most questionnaires contain both types of questions. For purposes of programming, fact data and identification of preferences are the main information concerns, while most subjective data has usefulness in particular projects.

Procedures. The quality of the information obtained is as important as obtaining it. The design of the questionnaire and the questions, the question types, the distribution of the questionnaire and the form in which the answers are to be given are all factors which must be considered in order to ensure reliability and usefulness of the data.

A useful way to design a questionnaire is to think of it as having four parts: introduction, preliminary questions, main questions and demographic questions. These are not meant to be categories for laying out the questionnaire, but only represent an organizing sequence. The introduction is a brief explanation of the nature and purpose of the questionnaire and includes instructions for filling it out. Preliminary questions are easily answered and help the respondent feel comfortable and get used to the questioning procedure. The main questions of the study are presented next and constitute the major portion of the questionnaire. The final group of questions refers to personal data, providing the respondent an easy conclusion to what may have been a tiring task. An example of a relatively simple questionnaire is presented in Exhibit 3-5.

Questionnaires, like interviews, pose essentially two types of questions: open-ended or unstructured and closed or fixed-response alternative. The closed question type provides the respondent with a choice between two opposites, a multiple choice, or an opportunity to rank a set of options or rate a single factor. This type of question provides short-form answers that are easier to manage in quantifying and analyzing data. The questions are usually precoded for tabulation and convenient entry into a computer analysis program. *Open-ended questions* encourage the respondent to describe or explain behavior, settings, attitudes, etc.

Other considerations in developing an effective questionnaire (most of which apply to interviews also) include:

—Keep it as brief as possible without neglecting necessary data.

—Ask questions that require definite, simple answers. This is easy in fixed-response questions which ask for yes/no, true/false or choice answers.

—Phrase questions in a way that will not bias the response. For instance, it is preferable to ask "What is your job title?" rather than "Are you a mechanic or a service operator?"

—Make sure that meanings are clear and that the vocabulary is appropriate for all respondents.

—Avoid emotionally charged words.

—Order questions so that they flow naturally from one to another without influencing each other's responses.

—Lay out the questionnaire so that it is easy to understand and use, provides adequate space for response, and is attractively presented.

—Most importantly, be sure that the questions ask for the type of information required to meet the specific program objective.

Programming projects that involve user needs research require carefully designed questionnaires or interview questions. Use of a behavioral consultant or survey researcher can save time, worry and money for the programmer in the design, administration and/or analysis of questionnaires and their results.

Resources. "Surveys, Questionnaires and Interviews" by Ronald J. Goodrich in *Designing for Human Behavior*, Jon Lang et al., eds. Stroudsburg, Pa.: Dowden, Hutchinson & Ross Inc., 1974.

Questionnaire Design and Attitude Measurement, A.N. Oppenheim. New York: Basic Books, 1966.

"Questionnaires" in *Design Methods: Seeds of Human Futures*, J. Christopher Jones. New York: John Wiley & Sons Ltd., 1977.

DATA LOGS. A log, such as a ship's log, is a means of keeping track of events over a period of time. In programming, a variety of such devices is used to obtain measurable data on human activity and/or use of space. Logging may be a self-observation technique in which individuals record their activities (Activity or User Log) or their use of space (Space-Time Log) or both over the course of a day, a week or a longer period of time. The logs are usually preorganized forms, divided into time intervals (e.g., 15 minutes, an hour, etc.), so that the programmer can receive reliable, comparable data. It is a relatively inexpensive technique since most of the time-consuming recording is done by members of the client group. Analysis of the data obtained can help determine space needs, both quantitative and qualitative, and other requirements. (See Exhibit 3-6.)

Products. Logging provides fairly complete detail for certain kinds of information, such as activities and/or time use. As a self-report technique on uniform matters, data from a broad cross section of a population can be obtained. Among the quantifiable data that can be obtained through logging are:

—Kinds of activities

—Frequency of specific activities

—Uses of spaces

—Amount of use of spaces

—Record of time spent in activity or space use

—Record of individual activities and/or use of space

—Use of equipment/furniture

—Sequential relationships among ac-

EXHIBIT 3-6. EXAMPLE OF DATA LOG

Name _____   Position Title _____

Workstation Location _____   Date _____

Time	Activity	Location	Participants	Result	Explanation/ Comment

tivities and/or space use

—Identification of participants in activities

—Record of interactions among people

Procedure. The following are some guidelines for using data logs to study user activities:

—Select the subject of study—activity, space use or both.

—Seek cooperation of the widest possible membership of the group; in a large group, select a representative sample for participation.

—Provide the loggers with advice (preferably in a group meeting to allow questions) on the purpose of the study, the reasons for organizing the log forms in the prescribed manner, and how to fill out the forms.

—Determine the time period that is to be studied—workday, 24-hour day, week—depending on the information desired.

—The loggers record their own activities or use of spaces, making brief notation of what they did and/or where they were at the time in the appropriate time slot on the form.

—Collate and tabulate the results for analysis.

The data log form must be easy to use and organized to provide the data needed. It is basically a blocked time sheet with predetermined time intervals marked on the vertical or horizontal edge. The blocks for entering data correspond to the time intervals. There may be columns or blocks for recording activity, space, purpose, equipment, and identity and number of participants.

STANDARDIZED DATA FORMS. The collection and recording of data are probably the most time-consuming and tedious aspects of programming. Anything that can be done to reduce the amount of time and paperwork for these tasks without compromising the quality of information will make the effort more economical and efficient. With experience, the programmer soon realizes that certain types of data are repetitive from one project to another and, within a specific project, from one part or element to another.

EXHIBIT 3-7. ROOM REQUIREMENTS FORM

| ROOM REQUIREMENTS
REHABILITATION INSTITUTE   C F MURPHY ASSOC
CHICAGO   ILL   CHICAGO   ILL | DEPARTMENT   PHYSICAL THERAPY SCHOOL
                              (N.O.)
SCHOOL DIRECTOR'S OFFICE | CODE
10 |

FURNITURE — EQUIPMENT	MECHANICAL	ARCHITECTURAL	RELATIONSHIP TO OTHER SPACES

FURNITURE
 	
DESK W/CHAIR
CONFERENCE TABLE (1)
SIDE CHAIRS (6)
BOOKSHELVES 15 L./FT.
 	
EQUIPMENT
 	
FILE DRAWERS 15" X 30"
	HEATING, VENT., AIR COND.
	
	           special
	
	PLUMBING
	
	           special
	
	COMMUNICATIONS
	TELEPHONE
	DICTAPHONE
	
	ELECTRICAL
	receptacles _____
	special loads _____
	other _____
		FLOORS
		CARPETING
		           special
		
		WALLS PARTITIONS
		           special
		
		CEILINGS
		           special
		
		DOORS WINDOWS
		           special
		
		ACOUSTICAL
		           special
			PRIMARY
			MEDICAL DIRECTOR'S OFFICE
			ASSISTANT DIRECTOR'S
			OFFICE
			
			SECONDARY
			
			REMARKS

| NUMBER PEOPLE
staff ___1___ male
_____ female
patients _____ | DIMENSIONS
15' x 15'
area ___225___ s.f. | NO. ROOMS REQUIRED
1
total ___225___ s.f. | EXISTING AREA

total _____ s.f. | OTHER |

Source: *Emerging Techniques 2: Architectural Programming* by Benjamin H. Evans and C. Herbert Wheeler. Washington, D.C.: The American Institute of Architects, 1969

To economize the time and effort required to collect routine or repetitive data, programmers use standardized forms. Such preorganized, preprinted data sheets identify the type of information to be collected and provide space for inserting the data. A typical data form calls for several types of data regarding a standard unit (e.g., a room, a building system, a function). Thus, a standardized room requirements form may ask for data on primary and secondary functions, net square footage required, environmental conditions necessary, equipment and furnishing needs, relationship to other spaces, etc. The same form can be used to collect and record similar data for every room in the facility. An example of a room requirements form is presented in Exhibit 3-7.

Products. Standardized data forms are most commonly used in programming to identify and tabulate routine information on space use, dimensions, criteria and/or requirements. However, there are other applications. A programmer may devise forms to record data on:

—Client objectives, philosophy and policies
—User activities
—Equipment and furnishings inventories
—Personnel growth projections
—Site conditions
—Applicable codes and standards
—Energy consumption
—Lighting requirements
—Mechanical and electrical systems requirements
—Space relationships

Another type of form, one for recording lighting conditions and energy use in an existing facility, is shown in Exhibit 3-8.

Data sheets not only provide a convenient and consistent means of compiling brief descriptive or numerical data, they offer additional advantages. A compendium of forms may organize a data collection effort as a means of insuring that certain information is acquired for any project or for each appropriate part of a facility. Standardized forms may also help organize data in a consistent format so that they are easy to identify and re-

EXHIBIT 3-8. LIGHTING SURVEY FORM FOR ENERGY USE

BUILDING DATA

E. Lighting

Room No.	Use	Lights On	Footcandles	Lights Off	Difference	Control (1)	Remarks (2)	No. Fixtures	Lamps/Fixture	Watts/Lamp	Lamps Removable or % Possible Reduction	Saved (3)
100	LOBBY	150		100	50	SWITCH IN MECH RM	↓½ GENERAL (↓100% DAYTIME - D.L. ADAQUATE	6	2	40	6	240
101	STAIRS	25		5	20	"	OK	2	1	40		
102	CORRIDOOR	40		0-10	40	"	↓½ CHECK - ON 24 HRS? (LGT-11)	20	2	40	20	800
110	CLASS RM	50-150		0-100	50	SWITCH	D.L. - SOUTH WINDOWS (100 F.C.) REWIRE - USE OF D.L. (LGT-4)	10	4	40	50%	800
120	CLASS RM	50-150		0-100	50		(110) (NOTE - WINDOW TINTING WILL REDUCE D.L.)	8	4	40	50%	640
130	CLASS RM						(110)	12	4	40	50%	960
140	REST RM	50		0	50	"	↓½	3	2	40	3	120
141	STAIRS	10-20		10-20			(101)	2	1	40		
150	CLASS RM	50-75		0-25	50	SWITCH	DL - NORTH WINDOWS, NOT SUFF. FOR REWIRE	10	4	40		
160	CLASS RM						(150)	8	4	40		
170	MECH RM	10-20		0	10-20	SWITCH	OK	3	1	40		
180	CLASS RM	(150)					(TRACK LIGHTS NOT USED BUT ON CIRCUIT)	6	4	40		
							Incad. TRACK LIGHTS - DISCONNECT	4	1	100	4	400

(1) Switch, Timeclock, Photocell, Motion Sensor, etc.

(2)
E = Windows to East
DL = Daylight Available
Zone = Zone Control Needed
Dirt = Dirty Fixtures
Incand = Incandescent Fxts.
Dark = Dark Wall Color
Waste = Rm. Unoccupied—Lights On
230 = Remarks and/or Fixture Schedule same as Rm 230
½ = Lighting Level Can Be Reduced by Half

(3) If D is %: E = A X B X C X D
If D is #: E = C X D

Source: *Energy Audits*, prepared by Energy Management Consultants Inc. of Los Angeles for the *AIA Energy Notebook*, Washington, D.C.: The American Institute of Architects, 1979.

EXHIBIT 3-9. CHECKLIST TYPE OF ROOM DATA FORM

trieve. The programmer may use a data sheet as a central repository for compiling data as they accumulate. In other cases, forms may serve as or be attached to standardized questionnaires distributed for owner/user completion. Data sheets may be used to inventory existing conditions or to identify desired ones for new facilities. Finally, a programmer may use a standardized evaluation form (such as the evaluation matrix discussed in Chapter 5) to judge recommendations or alternative proposals.

Procedure. A standardized form or data sheet consists of three essential parts:

—Identification of the unit about which data are to be collected (type of space, room, function, issue, activity, system) including identifying features such as location, title, room number or code

—Identification of the variables or information categories to be measured or defined

—A method of recording data (checkmark, fill-in space, tally)

There are innumerable ways of organizing the data sheet, depending on the type of information desired, the number and kinds of variables and the creativity of the form designer in devising an economical and convenient format. Some have been illustrated already and another format is presented in Exhibit 3-9.

Usually, a form attempts to accumulate data on several variables related to a single unit either on a single sheet or on a series of sequential sheets. However, too many variables on an individual sheet may create more confusion than convenience in tabulating and retrieving information.

Standardized forms also can be applied as a self-report mechanism for client users. Such data as room type assignments, personnel listings and growth projections, and inventories can all be assembled by the users and entered on forms designed by the programmer. It is important, in this situation, for the programmer to provide

---

CHRISTIE, NILES & ANDREWS — ARCHITECTS ; JOB NO: 10
9. SPECIFIC ROOM DATA TYPE: NAME: NO ROOM: SIM. NO: DATE: LAST REV:

Column 1	Column 2	Column 3	Column 4
A. PURPOSE OF AREA	**G. SERVICE TYPES**	**L. FLOOR FINISH**	**S. AIR**
1. MAIN	1. MAIL	1. RESILIENT	1. TEMPERATURE
	2. SUPPLIES	2. CONDUCTIVE	2. HUMIDITY
	3. RECORDS	3. STAIN RESISTENT	3. SEP. THERMOSTAT
	4. TRASH REMOVAL	4. NON-SLIP	4. EXHAUST (NORMAL)
2. SECONDARY	5. FOOD	5.	5. EXHAUST SPECIAL
	6. LAUNDRY	**M. BASE FINISH**	6. ODOR CONTROL
3. HOURS OF USE	7. FLOWERS	1. SANITARY	7. CLEANLINESS
4. PEAK USE	8. SPECIAL EQUIP.	2. STAIN RESIST.	8. ULTRA-VIOLET
5.	9. ICE	3. HEIGHT	9. RADIATION CONTROL
	10. SPECIMENS	**N. WALL FINISH**	10.
B. PEOPLE	11. FILMS	1. WASHABLE	**T. PLUMBING**
1. MAXIMUM NO.	12.	2. SOUND DROP DB.	1. WATER — COLD
2. AVERAGE NO.	**H. SERVICE METHODS**	3. STAIN RESIST	2. WATER — ICE
3. TYPES	1. PNEUMATIC TUBE	4.	3. WATER — HOT
4. MANAGEMENT	2. ELEVATOR	**O. CEILING FINISH**	4. DISTILLED WATER
5. EMPLOYEE	3. DUMBWAITER	1. ACOUSTICAL	5. SANITARY SEWER
6. MEMBERS	4. CONVEYOR	2. FLEXIBLE	6. SPECIAL LAB. DR.
7. VISITORS	5. CARTS	3. SOUND DROP DB	7. STORM DRAIN
8. SERVICE	6. STRETCHERS	4. MOISTURE RESIST.	8. FLOOR DRAIN
9. PUBLIC	7. WHEELCHAIRS	5. MIN. CEILING HT.	9.
10.	8. PEOPLE	6.	**U. PLUMBING FIXTURES**
C. ACCESS	9.	**P. LIGHT**	1. DRINKING FOUNTAIN
1. NEAR PUBLIC ENT	**I. FURNITURE**	1. DAYLIGHT	2. WATER COOLER
2. ON MAIN CIRC	1. DESK	2. SUNSHINE	3. LAVATORY
3. ON SECONDARY CIRC	2. TABLE	3. SUN CONTROL	4. TOILET
4. OUTSIDE EXIT	3. CHAIRS	4. BEST EXPOSURE	5. URINAL MEN
5. NEAR SERVICE ENT	4. SOFA	5. INCANDESCENT	6. URINAL WOMEN
6. NEAR PARKING	5. BOOK SHELVES	6. FLUORESCENT	7. SHOWER
7. EMERGENCY ENT	6. BEDS	7. DRAMATIC	8. BATHTUB
8.	7. BUREAU	8. SUBDUED	9. SINK
D. SOUND	8. COAT RACK	9. NIGHT LIGHT	10. CLINIC SINK
1. NOISE GENERATION	9. DRAPERIES	10. FOOTCANDLES GEN	11. SERVICE SINK
2. IN NOISY ZONE	10. RUGS	11. FOOTCANDLES	12. TOILET RM. ACCESS
3. IN MODERATE ZONE	11. SCULPTURE	12. REFLECTION FACTORS	13.
4. IN QUIET ZONE	12. PICTURES	13. MAX BRIGHTNESS	**V. MECHANICAL SERVICES**
5. ISOLATE	13. CLOCK. ELEC	14. COLOR CORRECT	1. STEAM
6. FOR SPEECH	14. DISPLAY AREA	15. EMERGENCY	2. COMPRESSED AIR
7. FOR MUSIC	15. BULLETIN BOARD	**Q. POWER ELECTRIC**	3. VACUUM
8.	16.	1. NUMBER OF OUTLETS	4. GAS COMMERCIAL
E. CONTROL	**J. EQUIPMENT**	2. VOLTAGE	5. VACUUM CLEAN
1. SECURITY	1. TYPEWRITER	3. CONTROL IN ROOM	6. OXYGEN
2. VISUAL	2. ADDING MACHINE	4. EXPLOSION PROOF	7.
3. ISOLATE	3. DUPLICATING EQUIP	5. WEATHER PROOF	**W. FIRE PROTECTION**
4.	4. IBM RECORDS	6. EMERGENCY	1. COMB. CONTENTS
F. EXPRESSION OF SPACE	5. FILES LETTER SIZE	7.	2. SPRINKLERS
1. FORMAL	6. FILES LEGAL SIZE	**R. COMMUNICATIONS**	3. STANDPIPE
2. DIGNIFIED	7. FILES SPECIAL	1. FIRE ALARM	4. PORTABLE EXTING.
3. QUIETNESS	8. STERILIZER	2. A.D.T.	5.
4. ORNAMENTAL	9. HOOD	3. EMERGENCY LIGHTS	**X. STRUCTURES**
5. PURPOSEFULNESS	10. REFRIGERATOR	4. TELEPHONE	1. LIVE LOAD
6. SENTIMENTAL	11. FREEZER	5. INTERCOM.	2. VIBRATION ISSOL.
7. WARM	12. INCERATOR	6. PAGING SYSTEM	3.
8. OPENNESS	13.	7. PUBLIC ADDRESS	**Y. CONTROL DIMENSIONS**
9. ACTIVENESS	**K. STORAGE**	8. TELAUTOGRAPH	1. REASON
10. EXCITEMENT	1. LOCKERS	9. MUSIC	2. LENGTH
11. TEXTURAL	2. SIZE	10. T.V. CLOSED CKT	3. WIDTH
12. EFFICIENT	3. STORAGE UNITS	11. T.V. (NORMAL)	**Z. AREA OF SPACE**
13. FUNCTIONAL	4. BASE LIN. FT.	12. T.V. AERIAL	1. ASSUMED
14. UTILITARIAN	5. WALL LIN. FT.	13. RADIO AERIAL	2. DESIGN MIN.
15.	6. SPECIAL CABINETS	14.	3. ACTUAL

Source: *Emerging Techniques 2: Architectural Programming* by Benjamin H. Evans, AIA, and C. Herbert Wheeler Jr., FAIA, Washington, D.C.: The American Institute of Architects, 1969.

precise instructions and examples for completing the forms.

OBSERVATION TECHNIQUES

Aside from asking questions, observation is the most direct and reliable means for the programmer to get information about the way people act in their environments. Through a variety of observation techniques, the programmer can learn how people use space, the effect of their surroundings on behavior, and how they act toward each other in particular settings. Observation can verify information obtained by other means and elicit new data not revealed by a previous interview or questionnaire. It is a fundamental device for the programmer's toolchest.

Observation alone, however, is not adequate for determining client user needs. It is limited to identifying only existing conditions and activities and cannot reveal, except by inference, how people feel about their environment or how they perceive it. Nor will it indicate how the environment should be changed to better accommodate behavior or client needs. Nevertheless, observational data will provide the programmer a definitive picture of what people do in a physical and/or social setting and what the physical setting is.

Resources. *Direct Observation and Measurement of Behavior*, S.J. Hutt and C. Hutt. Springfield, Ill.: Charles C. Thomas, 1970.

"User Needs Techniques" in *Neighborhood Spaces*, Randolph T. Hester. Stroudsburg, Pa.: Dowden, Hutchinson & Ross Inc., 1975.

"Unobtrusive Measures: Their Nature and Utility for Architects" by A.H. Patterson in *Designing for Human Behavior*, Jon Lang et al., eds. Stroudsburg, Pa.: Dowden, Hutchinson & Ross Inc., 1974.

"Direct and Instrumented

Observation Techniques: A Comparison" by Robert B. Bechtel in *Man-Environment Interactions—Part II* (EDRA 5). Stroudsburg, Pa.: Dowden, Hutchinson & Ross Inc., 1974.

"Systematic Observation Methods" by K. Weick in *The Handbook of Social Psychology* (Vol. 2, Research Methods), G. Lindsey and E. Aronson, eds. Reading, Mass.: Addison-Wesley Publishing Co., 1968.

DIRECT OBSERVATION. Systematic observation in its simplest form is merely watching people's behavior in specific environmental settings and recording what is observed. It is a matter of finding out who does what and where. Like a good news reporter, the programming observer must take care to watch and record objectively, noting the facts as they exist and the events as they actually happen, without interpretation or extrapolation. Systematic observing, however, is not random recording. The behavioral data obtained by observation must be meaningful to the program, and eventual design, of the facility. The three data objectives of direct observation, and all observation techniques to one degree or another, are:

—Activities (kinds, frequency, duration, sequence)

—Environmental settings (physical and other characteristics)

—Interactions (among people and between people and environmental settings)

In observing behavior, it is also important to know what kinds of people are involved in the activity observed. These data are usually obtained by other methods, but some information can be noted during observation; e.g., sex, approximate age, race, etc.

Direct observation may be used to record the behavior of an individual or a group. It may also be either exploratory or structured and is usually a little of both. An *exploratory* observation is informal and

often precedes a more structured study. The purpose is to gain a general understanding or "feel" for the subjects to be observed, what activities occur and the setting. It is often an effort to discover what data need to be collected so that the programmer can focus attention on significant behavior. In *structured* observation, the programmer is seeking to identify the patterns of behavior. The interest is focused on measuring and detailing activity, settings, interactions and relationships between people and environment.

Most of the other observation techniques presented in this section are variations of direct observation.

Products. Observation techniques are particularly useful for programming because they can provide factual data on how people actually use facilities. Although attitudes toward environments and perceptions and descriptions of needs and wishes are important, actual behavior is a concrete test of a facility's capacity to meet human needs. Observation is a way of discovering and recording environment-significant behavior. It can show the programmer:

—Patterns of behavior in a setting

—Patterns of use of spaces

—Relationships among spaces

—Influences of environment on behavior and vice versa

—Amount of space needed for particular activities

—Dysfunctions in the environment

—Characteristics of a setting

—Grouping of people

—Uses of furnishings and equipment

Procedure. As with all systematic data collection, proper preparation is essential for obtaining meaningful information from the observation of multi-varied human behavior. The programmer must have a clearcut idea of what behavior is to be observed, unless he or she is exploring a situation. The three "Rs" of data col-

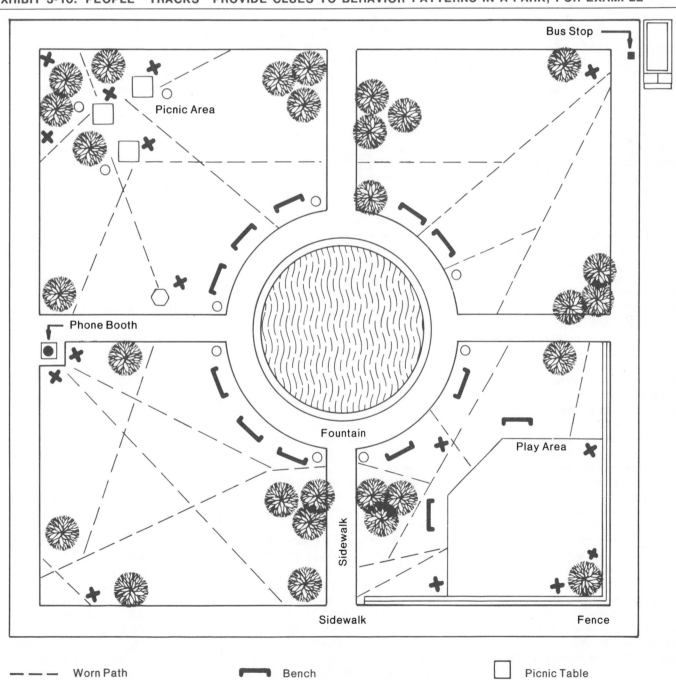

– – – Worn Path	▬ Bench	☐ Picnic Table
✖ Heavy Litter	○ Trash Receptacle	⬡ Water Fountain

lection are particularly pertinent to observational procedures: representativeness, reliability, recording. A study should be structured to insure that the behavior observed is "representative" of the kind of behavior that usually occurs in the particular setting. Data obtained must be "reliable" or based on objective, double-checked observations. This means use of trained observers in many cases, clear instruction on purpose and procedure, and repetition. Neither representativeness nor reliability can be attained without accurate, complete "recording" of data.

TRACKING. Much as the American Indians stalked game and learned the habits of their prey by following track paths and broken branches, the modern social tracker can discover human behavior patterns by examining the physical traces of human activity. Carpet wear, trash deposits, footpaths across a campus green, handprints on glass cases and wear marks on corridor walls and floors are the trails unknowingly left by people as they pursue their daily routines or respond to environmental "cues." The floor of a building lobby on a snowy day will have its route patterns revealed by the slushy boots and rubbers of people entering the building. An example of behavior pattern "tracks" is shown in Exhibit 3-10.

The tracking observer is like an archaeologist of contemporary social activity, trying to reconstruct the patterns of use of the environmental setting from the marks and "artifacts" left there. A far-fetched, but not totally unrealistic, case is that of an enterprising journalist who attempted to portray the personal habits of a high government official by analyzing his trash. A great deal of inference went into that analysis, which reveals the chief drawback of the tracking technique: the need to verify the validity of data.

Products. Tracking provides clues to behavior patterns, particularly to how people use the physical aspects of a setting. It is used most frequently to identify circulation and movement patterns. However, any evidence of prolonged or frequent use is an indication that the place where it is found is a significant activity area. Yet the significance must be tested by other methods, such as direct observation.

Procedure. To successfully use this technique requires patience, an eye for detail, strong deductive reasoning ability, and the willpower to verify conclusions. Knowledge of the kinds of activities that occur in the area of investigation will help identify the information the tracker is seeking. Narrowing the focus of the search to specific activities—such as circulation, furniture rearrangement, paper flow, use of particular equipment—will concentrate attention and save time. Of course, the search may be strictly exploratory, an effort to discover what activities do occur.

Evidence of activity is best discovered when people are absent from the scene, eliminating distractions and allowing the "tracks" to be clearly visible.

PARTICIPANT OBSERVATION. In most observation studies, the programmer is an outsider looking in. In fact, the observer usually makes a conscious effort to remain unnoticed, so that those being observed do not alter their behavior in any way. The extreme example is the use of a one-way mirror to totally screen the observer from the subjects of observation. At the other extreme is the participant observer, who actually takes part in the activity under investigation, joining the group or "living in" the situation in order to experience the activity or setting as do those who are actually involved in it.

The experience of the white journalist who wrote *Black Like Me* after chemically changing his skin color to that of a black man, was an extraordinary example of participant observation to discover discrimination patterns. Anthropologist Margaret Mead pioneered the technique in such popularized studies of cultural life as *Coming of Age in Samoa*, written after she lived with the islanders of Samoa to document adolescent life in that culture. Herbert Gans' sociological study of a Boston neighborhood, described in *The Urban Villagers*, was accomplished by Gans becoming a part of the neighborhood group.

Architects have applied the technique in less extensive studies to get, for example, a prisoner's perspective of jail or a mental patient's view of an institution by allowing themselves to be institutionalized for a short time before starting work on a new facility design. (See Exhibit 3-11).

Products. Use might include: obtaining data on activities and characteristics of an environmental setting, gathering and verifying behavioral data, understanding the purpose of an environment and its meaning to occupants and users, obtaining data on relationships among activities, and seeking knowledge of specialized procedures which can be gained only by trying them. A well-organized, long-term research project will provide the programmer a comprehensive picture of the nature of a group, its activities, the significant parts of its environment, and how and why members of the group interact with each other and their surroundings.

Procedure. Participant observation may be exploratory in nature. The observer wants to get in close to discover what is significant about a particular use of a particular place. The next objective is to discover and document patterns of behavior, particularly in relation to an individual's or group's surroundings. Before participating, the programmer will usually do some preliminary research—e.g., obtaining existing data on the subjects and the environmental setting as well as on the technique. Nonparticipant observation beforehand will help identify the areas on which to focus attention.

NOTE: Architect Joseph N. Ladd, AIA, of Richmond, Virginia, taking part in an AIA-sponsored conference on the design of correctional facilities, "went to jail" as a participant-observer.

Remaining incognito enables the observer to avoid behavior deviations that might occur if people are aware they are being "studied." However, it might cause resentment in the group if members, once they've discovered the investigation, feel their privacy has been invaded. For short-term and specific studies, asking permission or even help for the study can be beneficial. People like to feel they've made a contribution to something. As a member of the group, the researcher's image of outsider quickly dissolves and people act and react in their routine manners.

Comprehensive studies of organizations require practiced skill in the tech-nique and a thorough understanding of social dynamics. In these situations, the programmer usually engages a consultant with social science training and experience in participant observation.

Resources. *The Participant Observer*, G. Jacobs, ed. New York: George Braziller Inc., 1970.

BEHAVIOR MAPPING. Also referred to as Activity or Ecology Mapping, this technique is a method of recording and displaying behavioral data in relation to physical settings. An observer notes activities and their frequencies on a map sketch or floor plan, which when completed will show the layout of behavior for a particular place at a particular time. A partially completed behavior map is illustrated in Exhibit 3-12. Observation can be for short periods of time, repeated for the same setting to ensure completeness and validity of observations. Or, the observation may be conducted over the period of an entire event or episode. The observer identifies and records all participants in the setting and/or activity as well as the frequency of activities.

This is a relatively simple procedure to administer, but for large or complex studies it is best carried out by trained

EXHIBIT 3-12. EXAMPLE OF A BEHAVIOR MAP

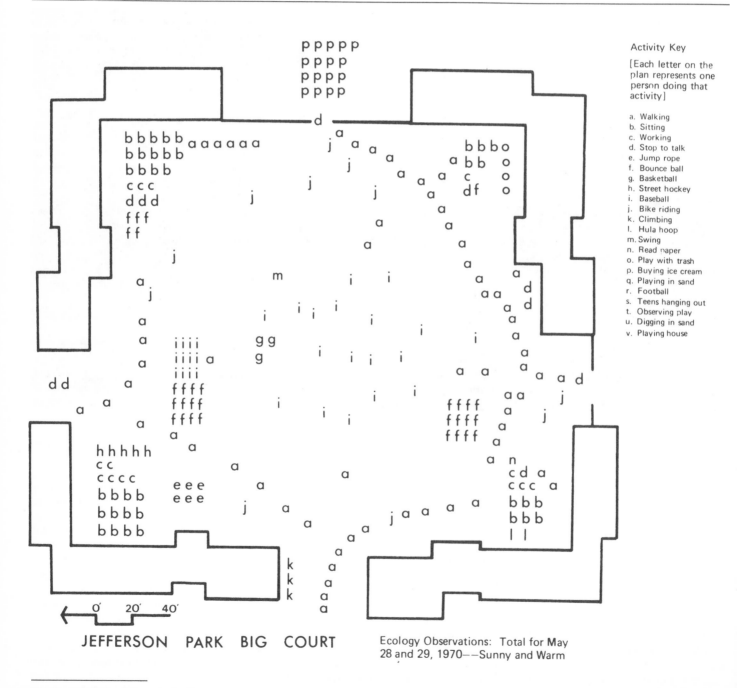

JEFFERSON PARK BIG COURT

Ecology Observations: Total for May 28 and 29, 1970——Sunny and Warm

Activity Key

[Each letter on the plan represents one person doing that activity]

a. Walking
b. Sitting
c. Working
d. Stop to talk
e. Jump rope
f. Bounce ball
g. Basketball
h. Street hockey
i. Baseball
j. Bike riding
k. Climbing
l. Hula hoop
m. Swing
n. Read paper
o. Play with trash
p. Buying ice cream
q. Playing in sand
r. Football
s. Teens hanging out
t. Observing play
u. Digging in sand
v. Playing house

Source: *Neighborhood Space* by Randolph T. Hester Jr. Stroudsburg, Pa.: Dowden, Hutchinson & Ross Inc., 1975.

observers guided by specific instructions as to what to look for. However, with clear instructions to users, behavior maps can be completed by individuals to record the location of their activities during specific time periods as well as to record interactions with other people.

Products. Behavioral maps are especially helpful in programming because this kind of visual display of behavioral data can be easily translated by the designer. The data produced by mapping includes:
—Location of activities
—Frequency of activities in locations
—Movement of people
—Relation of people to the setting
—Influence of setting on behavior
—Recurrent patterns of behavior
—Intensity of activities
—Differences in behavior among categories of people (male/female, adult/child, foreman/line worker, etc.)

Procedure. The first thing is to determine what activities are to be observed. It would be impossible for an observer to record all the varied and subtle forms of behavior that occur even in a very short time. Preliminary random observation will help identify and categorize the activities the programmer wishes to record. Behavioral researchers recommend that the activities to be recorded be overt and easily identifiable by an observer. Nothing should be left to inference. Other steps in the procedure include:
—Prepare an observation schedule that will produce a representative sampling of activities.
—Provide map sketches or floor plans of area to be observed. They should include all pertinent items in the setting such as partitions, furnishings, equipment, signs, etc.
—In a small area, station the observer so that his or her presence does not disrupt the subjects and so that an unobstructed view of the entire setting is avail-

able. In a larger setting, such as an office floor, the observer may travel around noting what individuals are doing in each location of the observed area.
—As mentioned, the time period for observing is usually short—as little as 15 minutes—but should be repeated a number of times for the same setting to ensure completeness and representativeness of observations. The time of the observation should also be recorded.
—A code identifying each activity, category of participants, and possible levels of activity intensity must be provided the observer to aid efficient recording. This can be simple alphabetical or numerical symbols or graphic symbols.
—The observer notes each new individual who enters the setting and records the activity and location.
—The results are tabulated for evaluation and a master map showing patterns of behavior and setting use may be prepared for presentation.

Resources. "Research Methods in Environmental Psychology" in *Introduction to Environmental Psychology*, William H. Ittelson et al. New York: Holt, Rinehart and Winston Inc., 1974.

"The Use of Behavior Maps in Environmental Psychology" in *Environmental Psychology: Man and his Physical Setting*, W.H. Ittelson and L.G. Rivlin, eds. New York: Holt, Rinehart and Winston Inc., 1970.

BEHAVIOR SPECIMEN RECORD. This is like taking a blood sample to analyze the properties of all the blood from which it was drawn. If samples were taken from a number of people and compared, it would be discovered that all have some identical properties, several have similar properties and a few have unique characteristics. Making a behavior specimen record is taking a sample individual from a group and documenting, in the minutest detail, this person's behavior over an ex-

tended period of time, usually a day. It is assumed that the "specimen" is representative of the group; i.e., that he or she participates in the same kind of activities as the rest of the group, responds to environments in similar ways, and expresses similar attitudes. However, group patterns are not the objective of the technique at this point, but rather an inventory of the individual's behavior, activity settings, and use of the environment. A compilation of specimen records can be compared and evaluated to reveal meaningful patterns needed for a program.

Products. An individual behavior specimen record provides a complete, detailed and sequential account of an individual's activities, time use, use of settings and interactions with other people. It may also be useful in detailing specialized procedures. The form is a narrative record of everything an individual does and says wherever he or she might be. Accumulating a number of these specimens from a group enables the programmer to analyze patterns of use of an environment, whether it is a community, a building, an open space or a room, or the furnishings and equipment in a room.

Procedure. This is a "no-stone-left-unturned" technique. It involves continuous observation of a single individual over an extended period of time. In environmental psychology research, where the method has been developed by Roger Barker and Herbert Wright, the time period is usually an entire day. The programmer, however, can adjust the study time to cover the period of use of a particular environment or setting—a factory worker's eight-hour shift at the plant, for example, or a child's afterschool use of a playground.

The observer records every detail of the subject's activity, movement, conversation and interactions, as well as the time and the behavior setting. Because this work can be exhausting over long periods, a team of observers is often assigned to spell each other. Observers are free to record their own remarks that would help clarify or interpret the behavior observed.

A transcript, including margin-indexed time and setting notations, of the observations is divided into "episodes" of behavior. This helps in quantifying behavior for analysis. Episodes of behavior of several individuals are compared to show similarities and differences according to a variety of factors; e.g., amount of time required, effect of setting on one group or individual compared to others, effects of different settings on behavior of same group.

Recording instruments are essential tools. Often, the instrument is a sheet with coded information about the individual or group to be used in analysis later. This also insures anonymity. Electronic recording is more reliable in securing as much detail as possible, but it may be more time consuming because of the need to transcribe the recording. A tape recorder is a frequently used device, sometimes including a funnel-shaped instrument called a stenomask that insulates the operator's voice.

Resources. *Recording and Analyzing Child Behavior*, Herbert Wright. New York: Harper & Row, 1967.

"Direct and Instrumented Observation Techniques: A Comparison" by Robert B. Bechtel in *Man-Environment Interactions—Part II* (EDRA 5). Stroudsburg, Pa.: Dowden, Hutchinson & Ross Inc., 1974.

INSTRUMENTED OBSERVATION. A number of the observation techniques already discussed can be performed or enhanced with the aid of certain mechanical or electronic devices for recording behavior. Among the audio and visual recording techniques are tape recording, still and time-lapse photography, motion pictures

and videotape. Among the benefits of observing with recording instruments is that they are able to capture data in greater detail, accuracy and quantity than possible by a human recorder. But perhaps the primary disadvantages are the greater time and effort required to sort and analyze this abundance of information and the inhibition of free discussion or action by the mere presence of these devices.

Some equipment, such as a cassette tape recorder or a 35mm still camera, can be employed in routine tasks and for simple uses with a modicum of training or skill. However, use of this equipment and of 8mm motion picture cameras and videotape mini-cameras for extensive or complex observational studies, brings into play a whole range of considerations that a programmer or a behavioral scientist normally would not think about, much less be prepared to handle. It is not that the apparatus is too complex for an amateur with training to operate. Rather, it is that there are additional factors to consider in planning and executing the observation.

For instance, how does an observer film shoppers in a mall without being obvious? The act of filming can turn the actions of the shoppers into acting for the camera. Or how can photographs be taken indoors without attention-attracting flash or strobe lights? What about film speed? What's the difference (in use and cost) of film editors (machines) and videotape editors? What about lighting levels? sound levels? background noise? There are answers to all these questions. The point is, these questions have to be answered if instrumented observation is to be a useful technique.

Products. The main product, and perhaps the primary benefit, of instrumented observation is a detailed, permanent record of the event observed. The observer does not have to be as concerned (although it is still important) about selecting and noting only significant data while conducting the observation. There are

many tasks in an observation: keeping track of the people who move in, out and around the setting, monitoring a multiplicity of activities, watching how people respond to environmental cues, recording interactions between people and between people and the many features of the setting, etc. Data extraction can be performed later and more conveniently when the recording is examined, with the added benefit that the observation sequence can be reexamined. This also means that the actual event, and not a reconstruction from the observer's notes and memory, is available to the programmer for repeated examination and analysis. The ability to repeatedly reproduce an event or a setting enables the programmer to verify the accuracy of observations and to identify data that might have been overlooked earlier.

Procedures. Architects have long used still photography to record existing conditions such as site topography, surrounding facilities and architectural details of significance. A modification of this technique is the *annotated photograph*. If a picture is worth a thousand words, a photograph annotated with a few words can be of great value to the programmer. The technique involves noting on a photograph of a building, a room or other space the features that are relevant to the use or function of the space. Of course, still photographs don't have to be marked up in order to accomplish this. However, annotation helps to focus on such data as evidence of activity patterns, arrangement of the space and its contents for users, and features that influence behavior. It can be used, often in conjunction with a data form, to inventory the features and contents of spaces. The annotated photograph is particularly useful in pinpointing space arrangements and features which are dysfunctional or hinder efficient use of the space. Aside from their value in collection and analysis of data, annotated

EXHIBIT 3-13. ANNOTATED PHOTOGRAPHS HELP VISUALIZE SPACE USE

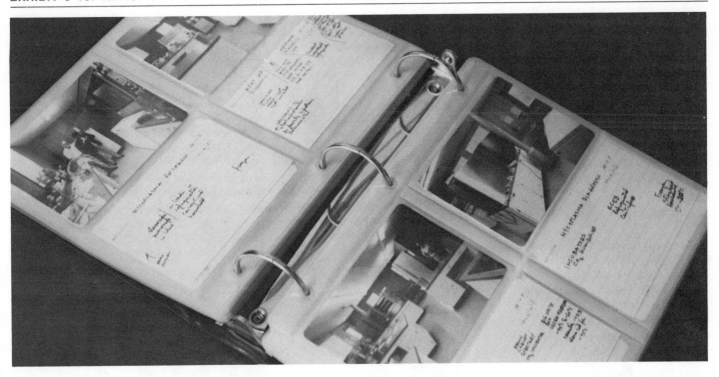

NOTE: Photographs of settings can be annotated on index cards. Here both photos and annotations are compiled in a looseleaf notebook project file.

Source: Gerald Davis, AIA, The Environmental Analysis Group Inc., Ottawa, Ontario, Canada.

photographs are effective graphic aids for illustrating these data in the programming reports or other presentations, as shown in Exhibit 3-13.

This indirect observation technique is one of the simpler uses of instrumented observation. Another indirect method, akin to tracking, is the use of a *hodometer*. This apparatus is a series of pressure-sensitive floor mats connected to a counter which records the number of times that each square foot of floor space is walked over. Such data can help define circulation patterns or density of foot traffic. A similar device is used in measuring highway traffic.

Time-lapse photography, motion pictures and videotape improve examination

of the dimension of sequence in the recording of observations. They enable the observer to see the actions which precede and follow each other, helping to interpret individual actions and to give the context of a complete activity. *Time-lapse photography* involves the use of a camera set to automatically shoot a frame or frame sequence of film at timed intervals, enabling the observer to capture samples of a complete activity or setting use. Although a similar effect can be accomplished by manually taking timed still photographs, the advantage of the automatic camera is that it can be left unattended for long periods and is less obtrusive. There are still photography cameras or attachments which provide time-lapse ca-

pability, but motion picture cameras which permit adjustment of exposure rate (frames per second) and shooting interval offer greater versatility and longer observation periods. *Motion picture filming*, shot at normal speed, also offers the opportunity to reproduce events as they actually occurred. The sequence of actions shown in the Exhibit 3-14 photographs helps the programmer understand a behavior pattern and determine how to accommodate it with the form or contents of the setting.

Film, either still or motion picture, has to be chemically processed in order to develop the images for projection. *Videotape* provides the time-saving advantage of instant image development because it is electronically produced (like an audiotape

EXHIBIT 3-14. STILL OR MOTION PHOTOGRAPHY HELPS THE PROGRAMMER DECIPHER BEHAVIOR PATTERNS

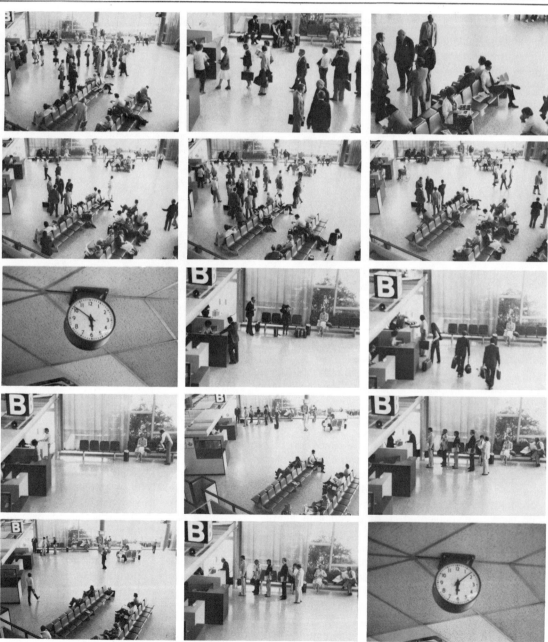

NOTE: A photographic study of queuing behavior in an airport terminal.

Source: Gerald Davis, AIA, The Environmental Analysis Group Inc., Ottawa, Ontario, Canada.

recording) with ionized particles rather than physiochemically produced. This permits an instant replay of the scene recorded. And it permits the operator to erase and reuse the videotape (although the reproduction quality gradually deteriorates with repeated reuse). Another capacity of videotape is simultaneous recording of sound on the same tape, so that the observer has auditory as well as visual access to events recorded. Videotape provides the same benefits as still and motion photography.

Technological development in audio and visual communications equipment has been rapid recently. New equipment and capabilities are coming on the market every year. Particularly important to the observing programmer are the improvements in compactness and lightness of recording hardware. Mini-cassette tape recorders, lightweight compact 35mm cameras, 8mm movie cameras and film and audio-video film cassettes are only a few examples. The most recent development, as of this writing, is the availability of portable videotape recorders. Sometimes referred to as portapaks or mini-cams, they are part of what the television industry calls "electronic news gathering" or ENG systems that enable reporters to go almost anywhere and instantly transmit recordings of events as they are occurring. The programmer doesn't have to be concerned about instant transmission, but the portability of the video mini-camera enables him or her to apply the broad capabilities of video recording to a larger range of instrumented observation situations.

Resources. Only a few of the procedural questions and possibilities of instrumented observation have been raised in this section. A great many more, with many practical tips, have been addressed in a paper by Gerald Davis, AIA, and Virginia Ayers of The Environmental Analysis Group (TEAG) of Ottawa, Canada. The paper is entitled "Photographic Recording of En-

vironmental Behavior" (*Behavioral Research Methods in Environmental Design*, William Michelson, ed., Stroudsburg, Pa.: Dowden, Hutchinson & Ross Inc., 1975). This programming team shares its experience with still and time-lapse photography. The uses they have identified for this technique are summarized below. However, the paper also reports on equipment selection and use, the role of photography in environmental research, methods of coding the vast quantities of data obtained, and the ethical questions involved in recording people's behavior. The uses of photographic observation identified by Davis and Ayers include:

—Cataloging an inventory of a physical environment (spaces, buildings, interiors, and their contents)
—Recording people or things for later counting, grouping, identification, etc.
—Studying selected details of an activity or function
—Studying a sequential experience (observer moving through the environment recording selected aspects) or of an event sequence (subjects' activities)
—Studying the visual components of the image of a place
—Analyzing functional systems, including activities and physical components (examining a behavior setting)
—Analyzing individual behavior, group dynamics and roles
—Supplementing data collection in a participant observation study

Other readings on the subject include:
"An Analysis of Unobtrusive Observation of Pedestrian Movement and Stationary Behavior in a Shopping Mall" by Wolfgang F.E. Preiser in *Architectural Psychology: Proceedings of the Lund Conference*, Rikard Kueller, ed. Stroudsburg, Pa.: Dowden, Hutchinson & Ross Inc., 1973.

"Photographic Methods of Research on Behavior in Human Milieu: New Developments and Critique" by Davis and

Ayers in *Environmental Design Research*, Wolfgang F.E. Preiser, ed. Stroudsburg, Pa.: Dowden, Hutchinson & Ross Inc., 1973. (An earlier abbreviated treatment of the subject of the paper that was cited above.)

Visual Anthropology: Photography as a Research Tool, John Collier Jr. New York: Holt, Rinehart and Winston Inc., 1967.

ATTITUDE MEASUREMENT

Among the instruments used to survey what people know, think and feel about their social and physical environments and about their behavior, there is a variety of "tests" which mainly measure attitudes. Although they may be referred to as tests, or paper-and-pencil tests, they generally do not rate what or how much people know. Attitude measurements are more concerned with identifying and quantifying patterns of group values, feelings, perceptions, priorities, preferences and goals so that they can be measured, studied and related to other factors that influence the design of a facility.

Many differing, and often conflicting, attitudes exist within any large, complex organization or diverse group. Isolating specific attitudes and determining the relative importance of each are not simple tasks. Even individual attitudes are hidden within a complex relationship of personality, social structure and culture. Nevertheless, it may be important for the programmer to understand the values, preferences, aspirations, priorities or perceptions of the group that will use a facility. And, it may be especially important for the facility designer who may discover that his or her own interests and perceptions differ significantly from those of the facility users.

Attitude tests serve the double purpose of not only articulating and quantifying individual attitudes, but of identifying and measuring the attitude patterns that exist within a group of individuals. Aside from

EXHIBIT 3-15. DIFFERENCES IN PERCEPTIONS OF THE SAME OBJECT

"HOT"

helping the programmer and designer understand differences between their own attitudes and those of users, attitude measurement studies can also help identify client goals, establish priorities among issues and needs, compare alternatives and isolate and evaluate the variations among significant attitude patterns.

Sophisticated attitude measurements may be beyond the scope of a specific programming project. Furthermore, the programmer may be able to interpret user perceptions and feelings or obtain a sense of major attitude patterns through interviews, background research, observations and questionnaires. On the other hand, there have been some costly ex-

amples of designs that did not "work" because user needs were not adequately understood or interpreted.

Proper utilization of attitude tests requires knowledge of personality and social behavior research as well as experience in applying such tests and related statistical analysis procedures. The assistance of a consultant with experience in psychological or sociological research and statistical measurement will enable the programmer to employ attitude measurements efficiently and effectively.

SEMANTIC DIFFERENTIAL. One of the most widely used "tests" of people's attitudes toward architectural concepts

and features, the semantic differential is also one of the most criticized. The main issue that nurtures the intellectual controversy about the method is the very aspect it is intended to measure: meaning. Meaning is such a subjective matter that researchers who use the semantic differential have been pressed by others to verify the validity of their measurements. (See Exhibit 3-15.) If an individual were asked to tell what a picture of a flower garden means to him or her, the description will be based on a variety of factors. That person's feelings about it will depend on his or her background and experience, mood at the time the picture is seen, the quality of the picture, and even the light and the individual's eyesight. The influence of these factors on another individual's judgment about the garden likely will be quite different. How, then, can a landscape designer say that this particular garden was judged by a group of people to be pleasant or unpleasant, too small or too large, or anything else if it cannot be verified that the basis of judgment was consistent among the individuals in the group? The meaning of the basic concept of ''garden'' may vary from one individual to the next.

The semantic differential tester might respond that, of course, you can't eliminate subjectivity from meaning, but you may be able to find a consistency of subjective meaning within a specific group toward a particular object or concept. And, you might also be able to find that the meaning pattern in one group differs significantly from the meaning pattern of another.

This last point brings out the special value that this type of test has in programming. Semantic differential findings can reveal a difference between the perceptions or preferences of the users of a facility and those of the designer. It can help keep the designer from barking up the wrong tree or help identify an attitude that had not been taken into consideration. In the garden example, the landscape architect might have put forward what was considered a good design for a flower garden, while the potential users might have judged it inadequate; the collective score of the semantic differential test might show they consider the proposal aesthetically pleasing but functionally unpleasant. Of course, the findings won't tell the designer that the reason for this response was that half the people suffer from hayfever and wouldn't go near a flower garden anyway. At least, the test would reveal that there is a problem that could be investigated further.

Products. The semantic differential does not directly identify group preferences or perceptions. These are determined by interpretations of the measurements of descriptive meanings, which are the direct products of the test. The original text on the subject by Osgood, Suci and Tannenbaum in 1957, *The Measurement of Meaning*, identified three major classifications of human meanings: evaluation (as in good-bad), potency or power (as in strong-weak), and activity (as in fast-slow). These basic measures of meaning can themselves be measured, which is the objective of the semantic differential. The rationale of the process is to limit the range of meanings that a person could ascribe to an object, and at the same time allow latitude for the variations within those meaning limits that could be expressed. By narrowing the scope of subjectivity, it is expected that individual responses can be compared, grouped and collectively measured. Scientific interpretation of the results can tell a programmer the relative value or importance of a group's preferences, perceptions or other attitudes.

Procedures. The device used for narrowing the scope of meaning is an adjective scale, sometimes referred to as a ''bipolar scale.'' It consists of one or more pairs of adjective antonyms, such as good-bad, pleasant-unpleasant, large-small, hot-cold, etc. These are the *factors* which the individual is to use in judging the *concepts* presented. The concept of storefront, for instance, might be presented to a group of individuals in the form of pictures of several storefronts. Each individual would be asked to judge the appearance of each storefront (as pictured) based on several factors, such as friendly-unfriendly, tasteful-untasteful, colorful-bland. The factors selected depend on what information is desired.

The tester has tried to improve the precision of the findings by limiting the descriptive factors to a few choices between extremes. But because these adjective words have differing connotations (emotive meanings as opposed to denotative meanings) for each individual, the tester also tries to increase precision of responses by allowing a range of choices between each extreme. An example of a semantic scale should help here.

Storefront #1

friendly _ : _ : _ : _ : _ unfriendly

Now the individual can indicate whether the appearance of Storefront #1 is more or less friendly, more or less unfriendly, or in between by marking one of the spaces along the scale. A seven-interval scale is the one most used in semantic differential tests, although fewer may be used as indicated above.

Usually several factors will be measured for each of several examples of a concept. Since programming is concerned with architectural or environmental concepts, they are usually presented in the form of diagrams, pictures, slides, scale models, or even film or videotape. An example of a multifactor semantic differential scale is shown in Exhibit 3-16. The scales can be presented in one of several ways, such as the interval spaces shown above to be checked off or as a series of numbers or letters to be circled.

Tabulating the collection of marked scales is simply a matter of totaling the marks for each interval for each factor scale for each concept example.

friendly ⫴ : ⫶ : ⫼ : ⏐ : _ unfriendly
        +2 +1   0   -1 -2

An arithmetic mean can be produced for each factor to measure its relative value in the judgment of storefront appearance. A weight is assigned to each interval as shown by the bottom row of numbers above (+2 to -2). The weight is multiplied by the number of marks for the interval;

EXHIBIT 3-16. EXAMPLE OF MULTIFACTOR SEMANTIC DIFFERENTIAL SCALE

simple	:	:	:	:	:	complex
beautiful	:	:	:	:	:	ugly
passive	:	:	:	:	:	active
strong	:	:	:	:	:	weak
rational	:	:	:	:	:	intuitive
unique	:	:	:	:	:	common
ambiguous	:	:	:	:	:	clear
exciting	:	:	:	:	:	calming
plain	:	:	:	:	:	ornate
interesting	:	:	:	:	:	boring
generalized	:	:	:	:	:	specialized
confined	:	:	:	:	:	spacious
delicate	:	:	:	:	:	rugged
good	:	:	:	:	:	bad
accidental	:	:	:	:	:	controlled
open	:	:	:	:	:	closed
gloomy	:	:	:	:	:	cheerful
superficial	:	:	:	:	:	profound
permanent	:	:	:	:	:	temporary
welcoming	:	:	:	:	:	forbidding
chaotic	:	:	:	:	:	ordered
uncomfortable	:	:	:	:	:	comfortable
bold	:	:	:	:	:	timid
continuous	:	:	:	:	:	broken
revolutionary	:	:	:	:	:	reactionary
delightful	:	:	:	:	:	dreadful
considered	:	:	:	:	:	arbitrary
tight	:	:	:	:	:	loose
annoying	:	:	:	:	:	pleasing
straightforward	:	:	:	:	:	contradictory

Source: "A Study of Meaning and Architecture" by Robert G. Hershberger in *Proceedings of the First Annual Environmental Design Research Association Conference*, Henry Sanoff and Sidney Cohn, eds. Stroudsburg, Pa.: Dowden, Hutchinson & Ross Inc., 1970.

these are added together and then divided by the total number of marks for this scale. This arithmetic mean can then be compared with the means produced for the other scales to show which factor or combination of factors is important in the judgment of the group.

Another method of comparing is to create a profile of each person's responses to each concept example. This is done by drawing a line that connects the intervals selected on each scale. The zigzag profiles for all respondents can be overlaid to reveal the pattern of responses. Or, instead of overlaying the profiles, a different type of line or color can be used for each respondent and plotted on a single blank scale sheet. The profile method also creates a very good graphic for presentation to the client. (See Exhibit 3-17.)

The method most frequently used to analyze the results of semantic differential tests is called "factor analysis," a means of reducing a large quantity of raw data to manageable proportions. It is a statistical technique for discovering and understanding correlations among factors, and will be discussed in the next chapter under statistical analysis techniques.

As can be seen in this explanation of the procedure, there are many opportunities for slips in judgment by the programmer. Giving the test to a group and tallying the results are fairly simple matters. But deciding which concepts to present, which factors will provide valid measures, the proper adjective antonyms to select and, especially, analyzing the results of the measurements require precision and understanding of human attitudes. The use of a professional consultant can save time in performing these tasks and should prevent unreliable results.

Resources. The original text explaining the rationale and procedures of the semantic differential technique was produced in 1957 under the title *The Measurement of Meaning* by Charles E.

EXHIBIT 3-17. GROUP RESULTS OF SEMANTIC DIFFERENTIAL PLOTTED BY HISTOGRAM

Group 1   Group 11

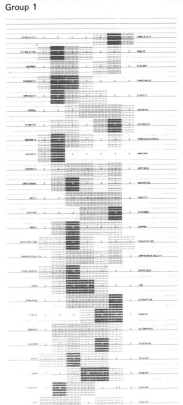 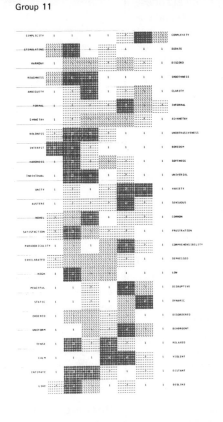

NOTE: The diagram represents two groups' responses to an environmental display of a street scene (pictured above). Respondents from each group rated the picture on a seven-point semantic scale. The histogram is a computer graphic representation of the frequency distribution of all responses; the darkest tone indicates the highest degree of rating similarity among respondents (also indicated by numerical values not clearly depicted here).

Source: "Measuring Attributes of the Visual Environment" by Henry Sanoff in *Designing for Human Behavior*, Jon Lang, et al. eds. Stroudsburg, Pa.: Dowden, Hutchinson & Ross Inc., 1974.

Osgood, George J. Suci and Percy H. Tannenbaum. Champaign, Ill.: University of Illinois Press, 1957.

"Toward a Set of Semantic Scales to Measure the Meaning of Architectural Environments" by Robert G. Hershberger in *Environmental Design: Research and Practice* (EDRA 3). Los Angeles: University of California, 1972.

ADJECTIVE CHECKLISTS. Another kind of measure of user perception of an environmental setting or architectural space is an adjective checklist. It is simply a list of adjectives which individuals can use, by checking off the appropriate ones, to describe a particular object. An adjective checklist can also be arranged so that it consists of pairs of antonyms, as in the semantic differential test, allowing individuals to choose between opposite descriptions or (also like the semantic differential) among a range of degrees between opposite descriptions. Joyce V. Kasmar has devised an adjective checklist, using paired antonyms in laymen's terms, that can be used to measure user perception of building performance; for instance, soft lighting-harsh lighting, well scaled-poorly scaled, good acoustics-poor acoustics.

Resources. "The Development of a Usable Lexicon of Environmental Descriptors," by Joyce V. Kasmar. *Environment and Behavior*, Vol. 2, No. 2, September 1970.

ATTRIBUTE DISCRIMINATION SCALE. Similar in procedure and purpose to the semantic differential and the adjective checklist, this test attempts to establish a common understanding of the terms and concepts being used to evaluate a particular environmental setting or architectural space. Instead of limiting the bipolar terms on an interval scale to adjective descriptors, however, the scale includes both adjectives and nouns with opposite meanings. Generally, the terms

EXHIBIT 3-18. BOX MATRIX RELATING SIX VARIABLES TO EACH OTHER

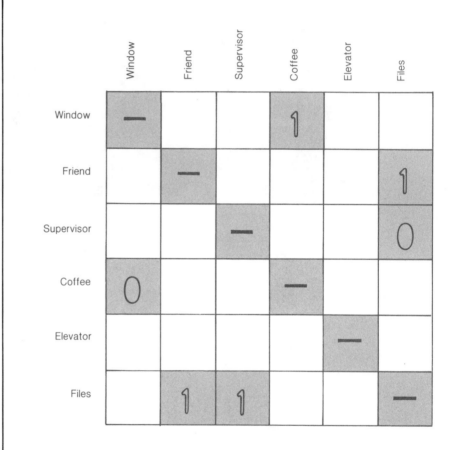

reflect concepts commonly used by designers, and are arranged on an interval scale in the same fashion as the semantic differential to allow a range of precise choices. The results can be used to show how different groups respond to the same setting or how the same group compares different settings.

Resources. *Methods of Architectural Programming*, Henry Sanoff. Stroudsburg, Pa.: Dowden, Hutchinson & Ross Inc., 1977.

RANKING CHART. Another way to find

out what people like or dislike, prefer among alternatives or want in their surroundings is to ask them to rank or rate various attributes or factors. A device that enables an individual or a group to rank the priority of a series of variables that may appear to be equally important is the *ranking chart*. In this technique, individuals are asked to make a series of choices between all possible pairs of specified variables. The variables are then ranked by the individuals according to the number of times each was chosen over the others. The one variable that was selected the most times is ranked first (Number 1) and

EXHIBIT 3-19. BOX MATRIX AND RANKING

	Window	Friend	Supervisor	Coffee	Elevator	Files	Sum	Rank
Window	—	0	1	1	1	1	4	2
Friend	1	—	1	1	1	1	5	1
Supervisor	0	0	—	1	1	0	2	4
Coffee	0	0	1	—	0	0	0	5
Elevator	0	0	1	1	—	1	2	4
Files	0	0	1	1	0	—	3	3

of several in a questionnaire distributed to the office workers concerning their location preferences and other attitude variables. In this section of the questionnaire, each worker is asked to compare each factor in the vertical column with each factor in the horizontal row. The idea is to choose one of each pair that is more important to the individual in positioning his or her work station. Preferences are marked with either a "1" or a "0." If a column factor is preferred, the box matching it with one of the row factors is marked with a "1;" if the row factor is preferred, the box is marked "0." For instance, if being near to a window is more important than being near the coffee room, the individual would mark a "1" in the box that is across from the "window" factor and below the "coffee" factor. Logically, when the worker reaches the column (vertical) factor "coffee," the same choice would be made in comparing it with the row (horizontal) "window" factor and thus would mark a "0" in that box, indicating he or she still preferred access to a window instead of to the coffee room.

Unfortunately, one of the problems with this device is that people do not always respond logically and sometimes may switch choices in the second comparison. The worker completing the sample matrix in Exhibit 3-18 did just that when choosing between access to a friend and access to the central files. Another problem, along the same lines, is that the logic of choices may not progress among the variables; e.g., "window" may be selected over "coffee" and "coffee" over "supervisor," but then "supervisor" may be selected over "window." If this occurs frequently, it can produce a statistical error that is too large to provide valid results. The investigator should randomly examine several of the completed matrices to determine if this is a problem.

After completing the matrix, the individual totals each row of boxes, marking the sum to the right of each. This identifies

the one that was selected the least number of times is ranked last (Number 6 in a list of six variables, for instance.) This shows the individual his or her highest priority or preference as well as the relative order of importance of the other variables. The group's preferences are ranked by totaling the individual rankings received by each variable, so that the variable which receives the lowest score is the top-ranked priority or preference.

Procedures. An example will help explain the procedures of the ranking chart technique. An architect designing an of-

fice floor layout wants to find out which factors are most important to the workers in determining the arrangement of their work stations. In interviews, six factors emerged as considerations in preferred location: access to a window, a friend, the supervisor, the coffee room, the elevator, and the central files. The architect decides to use a ranking chart to identify the relative importance of the six factors.

A box matrix is created and the six variables are listed vertically on the left side and horizontally along the top, both in the same order. (See Exhibit 3-18.)

More than likely, this study will be one

the rank order of the six preferences; the factor receiving the highest total is the most important, while the factor with the lowest score is the least important. The ranking can also be marked next to the sums, as shown in Exhibit 3-19.

In order to identify the order of preference among the factors for the entire group of office workers, the individual rank orders are tabulated as shown in Exhibit 3-20 (assuming seven workers took this test) and the ranks of each factor (the rows) are added together. The sum of the individual rankings of the "window" factor is 19, for example. These figures are the sums of ranks, not the sums of choices, and therefore the highest rank for the group will be the factor which received the lowest score. Likewise, the lowest factor of importance to the workers will be the one which received the highest score. Now the architect should have a clear idea of which factors are of priority concern to the office workers in determining the office layout.

PREFERENCE MATRIX. A modified version of the ranking chart, a preference matrix also can be used to establish a priority ranking of group preferences. Although it simplifies the process of choosing between pairs of variables, the operation may be confusing to some unsophisticated groups. By using a half matrix, individuals need only compare factor pairs once, instead of twice as with the box matrix of the ranking chart. With the preference matrix, the group's ranking is also determined from the rankings of the individuals.

Procedures. Using the same office worker example, the six factors to be matched are listed in a vertical column only (Exhibit 3-21). A number is assigned to each factor (1 through 6). Again, the workers are asked to choose one in each pair of factors that is more important to them. One factor is compared with each

EXHIBIT 3-20. RANK ORDERING OF FACTORS

FACTOR	WORKERS' INDIVIDUAL RANKINGS							SUM	GROUP RANK
Window	2	1	6	4	2	1	3	19	1
Friend	1	3	2	6	5	4	4	25	4
Supervisor	4	2	4	5	1	3	5	24	3
Coffee	5	6	1	3	3	6	2	26	5
Elevator	4	5	3	2	6	5	6	31	6
Files	3	4	5	1	4	2	1	20	2

EXHIBIT 3-21. HALF MATRIX

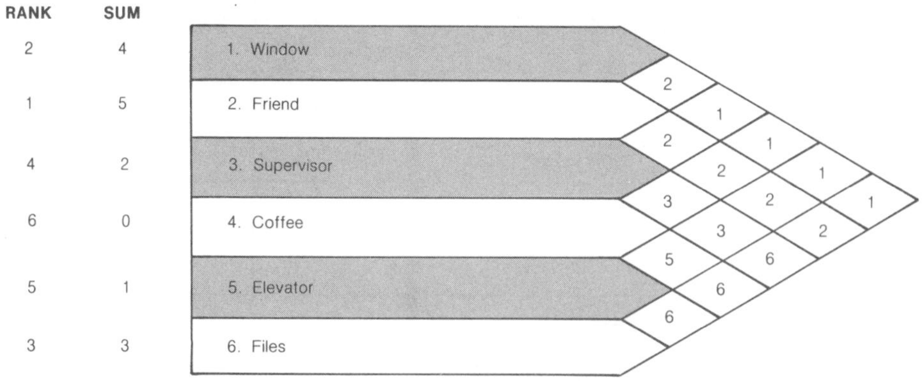

other factor only once, with the choice marked in the box that matches the two variables. The individual's choice is indicated by writing the number assigned to that variable in the box. If access to a window is chosen over access to central files, the individual finds the appropriate box by going down the diagonal row associated with window and up the diagonal row associated with files to the point where the two rows overlap. A "1" is marked in the box.

The individual's rank order of preferences is determined by first totaling the number of times that each factor's number appears in the matrix; in the case of "window," the figure "1" appears four times. The factor with the highest score is the first ranked preference (in this case, "friend"), and the factor with the lowest score is ranked last ("coffee").

The method of determining the group's priority ranking is the same as that used in the ranking chart.

VALUE OF DATA COLLECTION

Data collection has always been one of the most important functions of programming, but it is often one of the least carefully performed. Perhaps due to tradition, lack of awareness or limits of time and money, the collection of program data too frequently is limited in scope, source and technique. Proper attention to the mission and methods of data collection for programming should save time and money in the design process and provide a realistic and adequate foundation upon which to base design decisions. In applying data collection techniques, the programmer should:

—Use techniques that are appropriate to the type of information desired and to the sources of information.

—Consider the amount of time, effort and resources required for performing the operation in relation to the amount of time, money and resources available for completing the work.

—Seek the broadest possible input to the data collection effort from client owners and users and other sources.

—Make sure the data obtained are reliable, relevant and representative.

—Use a variety of techniques in order to cross-check results and address comprehensive issues.

The data collection effort of programming must provide an adequate and relevant base for the analysis and organization of program data, concepts and conclusions.

Chapter 4
Techniques for
Data Analysis
and Organization

One old saying goes, "you can't see the forest for the trees." But sometimes you can't see the forest without looking at the trees first. The abundance of data generated by programming may be meaningless in its initial compilation and it won't take on significance until the programmer starts looking at it one part at a time. The role of analysis is to sort and break down data into manageable portions, to test the relevance and validity of individual pieces and to determine the relation of individual data and groups of data to the whole design problem or issue.

Analytical procedures range from reducing and measuring data through statistical methods to isolating independent factors and systems so that their various roles and impacts can be clearly established. The programmer can gain insight into the physical requirements users have for a facility, for example, by examining their behavior system in relation to the physical system.

The organization function of information processing is almost the opposite of analysis: to gather together the individual parts of a problem or issue in order to visualize its component relationships and total relationship patterns. Methods of organization can also help in generating and analyzing information in a consistent and comprehensive manner.

STATISTICAL ANALYSIS

The word statistics brings to mind lists of numbers, tables of figures, graphs, and charts representing numerical data. Census population figures, baseball batting averages, EPA mileage ratings and political voting results are examples of what are commonly thought of as statistics. These numerical results of mathematical manipulations are, indeed, one valid use of the term statistics.

However, statistics also refers to the process by which these results are derived. Statistical research is a discipline

of applied mathematics, complete with its own terminology, methodology and body of knowledge. Statistical methods are invaluable tools in all the physical sciences, economics, engineering and the behavioral and social sciences. Statistical analysis has a place in any work or study where the variables can or should be quantified and especially in any area where decisions must be inferred on the basis of incomplete information.

Put another way: "Whenever anything is measured numerically, even though the attempt to make an assessment results in numbers no more refined than simple counting, there arises the desire for judging the significance of the data and for making the maximum use of the information gathered. These are the principal problems with which statistical methods are concerned." *(Introduction to Statistical Analysis,* second edition, by Wilfred J. Dixon and Frank J. Massey Jr.)

Statistics is the use of numerical data and mathematical procedures to measure, differentiate and correlate variables. The abstraction of information into numerical data simplifies management and manipulation and can improve the precision of interpretation. Furthermore, the use of probability-based techniques enables the statistician to predict possible results of combinations and comparisons of simpler data forms.

There is a wide range of statistical procedures, from relatively simple descriptive measures—such as averages, percentages, distributions and variances—to sophisticated methods of predicting outcomes and interpreting data based on inference from sample data—such as factor analysis, multidimensional scaling, regression analysis and analysis of variance. They are generally classified in two categories: descriptive statistics and inferential statistics. The latter group is useful in drawing conclusions or predicting results about a large population based on calculations from a representative sample

of the population.

Areas in programming where statistical analysis may be useful include cost estimates, economic analysis, market analysis, site evaluation, feasibility predictions, energy analysis, space use and requirements analysis, attitude and behavior measurement, evaluating alternatives and projecting future needs and trends. In general terms, statistics may assist the programmer in:

—Simplifying the description and calculation of factors

—Reducing mixed variables to a common quantifying basis for comparison and correlation

—Testing the validity and reliability of data and conclusions

—Predicting the varying impacts of problem components on each other and on the whole problem

—Optimizing elements and combinations of elements

—Improving precision of calculations

In all likelihood, the facility programmer will use statistics in some way for analyzing design needs, even if it is merely to summarize conclusions with numerical descriptions. And, although a programmer generally may not apply some of the more sophisticated analytical methods, he or she should have a working knowledge of basic statistics and, at least, be familiar with more complex procedures that may be applied by architectural researchers or consultants.

The discussion of descriptive and inferential statistics which follows provides an overview of some of the statistical tools of value or potential value in programming. There are numerous texts on statistics that explain its principals and applications in greater detail. One of the most readable and comprehensible is a college textbook by William Mendenhall and Madelaine Ramey called *Statistics for Psychology* (North Scituate, Mass.: Duxbury Press, 1973). Others include:

—*Basic Statistical Methods,* fourth edition, N.M. Downie and R.W. Heath. New York: Harper & Row,. 1974.

—*Statistics Made Simple,* H.T. Hayslett Jr. Garden City, N.Y.: Doubleday & Company Inc., 1968.

—*Introduction to Statistical Analysis,* second edition, Wilfred J. Dixon and Frank J. Massey Jr. New York: McGraw-Hill Book Company, 1957.

Geoffrey Broadbent, ARIBA, a British architect, relates, in a simplified fashion, statistical methods to design in his book, *Design in Architecture* and also describes their application in design-related fields such as operations research, information systems and ergonomics. Other references are cited in the following text.

DESCRIPTIVE STATISTICS. The most straightforward use of statistics in programming is to describe or characterize quantities of data. Descriptive statistics may be expressed in numerical or tabular form or in graphical form. The principal descriptive devices are tabulations, classification, frequency, measures of location or central value, and dispersion or variation. An example will help illustrate some of the rudiments of statistical measures. Suppose some kind of study were to be conducted on one type of workstation (activity area) in an existing office building. The variable considered is size in terms of area. There are 100 workstations of the particular type which vary in size from 42 square feet to 121 square feet, each having been measured previously.

Tabulation, Classification and Frequency. The first order of business in the statistical analysis is to record all the *observations* (the general term used for the relevant items in statistical analysis); in this case, it would be the individual areas of all 100 workstations. The tabulation is shown below with observations recorded in random order.

RANDOMLY ORDERED OBSERVATIONS

80	90	56	72	108
90	72	48	64	88
72	81	60	56	42
48	60	70	49	60
99	63	88	100	54
81	48	80	88	100
64	108	96	64	72
48	96	99	96	56
60	81	108	110	49
56	110	121	54	88
56	56	110	70	72
96	42	64	81	54
49	121	48	60	49
42	100	80	54	80
88	80	72	63	64
70	72	110	96	56
63	54	99	72	90
54	63	81	88	72
96	56	49	54	54
72	49	90	63	88

For some purposes, it is useful to reorganize the tabulation in rank order from the smallest to the largest, as shown below.

RANK ORDERED OBSERVATIONS

42	54	64	80	96
42	54	64	80	96
42	56	64	80	96
48	56	64	81	96
48	56	64	81	96
48	56	70	81	99
48	56	70	81	99
48	56	70	81	99
49	56	72	88	100
49	56	72	88	100
49	60	72	88	100
49	60	72	88	108
49	60	72	88	108
49	60	72	88	108
54	60	72	88	110
54	63	72	90	110
54	63	72	90	110
54	63	72	90	110
54	63	80	90	121
54	63	80	96	121

Rather than deal with 100 individual workstations, however, the data would be more manageable if reduced to a smaller number of items. The grouping indicated by enclosures above results in a set of 20 different *classes* of data. Twenty sets may be a larger classification than desired for statistical manipulation and more frequently, observations are not as repetitious as shown here. It is standard to classify data into no more than 10 to 15 sets. The standard procedure is to group data into classes of equal *class intervals.* The interval is determined by figuring the difference between the largest and smallest observation (121 – 42 = 79) and dividing the difference by the arbitrarily selected number of classes, in this case, 10 (79 ÷ 10 = 7.9, or rounded to 8). The total number of observations is then ordered into 10 classes with intervals of 8 (e.g. 42 to 49, 50 to 57, etc.).

It is much easier to work with ten classes of data than with 100 individual items. What is significant about the data, however? One significant description is the *frequency* with which the data occur within each class. The frequency is determined by simply counting the number of observations (workstation sizes) that fall within the individual *class limits,* as shown below.

CLASS	CLASS LIMITS	FREQUENCY
1	42– 49	14
2	50– 57	16
3	58– 65	15
4	66– 73	13
5	74– 81	10
6	82– 89	7
7	90– 97	10
8	98–105	3
9	106–113	7
10	114–121	2

With the class frequencies established,

and likewise the *frequency distribution* of the total observations, a significant pattern begins to emerge. For this type of workstation, the prevalent size is 50 to 57 square feet and there tend to be more workstations of smaller size than of larger.

There are two other ways to describe the frequency distribution, both graphical: *histogram* and *frequency polygon*. Exhibit 4-1 shows a frequency polygon (the line graph) superimposed on a histogram (a kind of bar graph). The horizontal axis of the graph represents the equidistant class intervals and the vertical axis, the frequencies.

Central Tendency, Value or Location. These are different ways of identifying a statistic which represents the entire set of observations. Very simplistically, each refers to the "middle" number of the set. However, there are several different kinds of middle numbers, only one of which comes close to fitting that title. Exhibit 4-2 illustrates four central location values for 11 data items (not drawn from the workstation example).

The *median* is the observation which falls in the middle of the set of data; in other words, half the data is smaller than the median and half is larger. It is found by, first, arranging the data in rank order from smallest to largest, and then counting to the halfway point in the list. If there is an odd number of observations (11, for instance), the median is the sixth one—the first five falling below and the last five falling above. In the workstation example, there are 100 observations and the median has to be calculated since it falls between the 50th and the 51st ranked observation. This is done by adding the two and dividing the result by 2. In the example, both the 50th and 51st numbers are 72 and the median, therefore, comes out to be 72 also. If the figures had been 72 and 76, the median would have been 74.

The median is one of the most frequently used measures of central tendency. Even more frequently used is the *mean,* or *arithmetic mean.* It is also the simplest to determine, especially in a large number of randomly ordered observations. The values of all observations are added and the result divided by the total number of observations. In the example, it is 7365 divided by 100. The mean is 73.65 and rounded off, it is 74.

There are two other measures of central value that are sometimes used: mode and midrange. The *mode* is the observation that occurs most frequently in the set—72 in the example, which occurs ten times. The *midrange* is the middle of the *range* (also a statistical descriptor) between the smallest observation and the largest. The range is 79 and the midpoint, 39.5, is added to the smallest observation (42) to yield the midrange of 81.5.

The procedures for determining the median and the mean of classified data are a little more complicated than for calculating those values for the total set. Nevertheless, they are useful when individual observations are not known and only classified data are available. Looking back at the frequency distribution table or the histogram, the *median of classified data* can be found by the following procedure:

EXHIBIT 4-1. A HISTOGRAM OR FREQUENCY POLYGON IS A GRAPHIC DESCRIPTION OF DATA

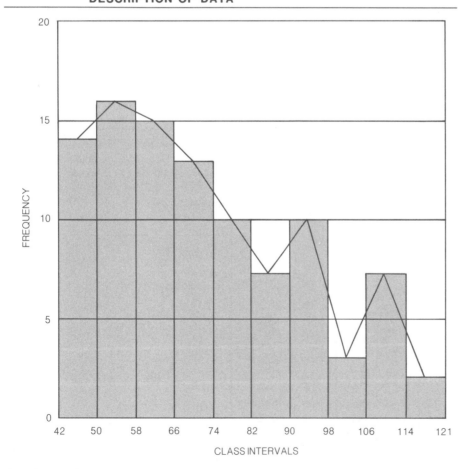

—Locate the class in which the 50th observation falls by adding the frequencies (14 + 16 + 15 = 45 + 13 = 58). It is in the fourth class, or the fifth observation after the end of the third class (45 + 5 = 50).

—Estimate the increment by which each of the 13 observations in Class 4 can be determined. Without the exact observations, it is not possible to know which one is the 50th. It can be statistically predicted, however, because the estimator knows there are 13 observations in the class and each class has an interval of 8. Each of the 13 will be equal to 1/13 of 8.

—Estimate the location of the median in the fourth class. Since the total observations is even (100), the exact median is not the 50th, but rather the 50.5th observation. The median would be the value that is 5.5 observations after the 45th which is 65; that is, 65 plus 5.5 increments (1/13 + 1/13 + 1/13 + 1/13 + 1/13 + .5/13 = 5.5/13 = .423) multiplied by 8 (which equals 3.384) to yield a sum of 68.384, the median.

Again referring to the frequency distribution, the *mean of classified data* can be figured by the following procedure:

—Assume that each unknown observation in a class has a value equal to the midpoint of the class. In the first class, it would be 45.5; in the second, 54.5; the third, 62.5, and so on. Multiply this value by the number of observations (frequency) in the class and repeat for each class (e.g., 45.5 × 14 = 637).

—Sum the resulting products for each class (7016.5).

—Divide the sum by the number of observations (7016.5 ÷ 100 = 70.165). The mean of the classified data is 70.165, or approximately 70.

Variation or Dispersion. Each of the devices explained above helps to illuminate the significance of a mass of data by organizing the individual items and by reducing the total to more manageable proportions. They show how statistics

EXHIBIT 4-2. MEASURES OF CENTRAL LOCATION ILLUSTRATED

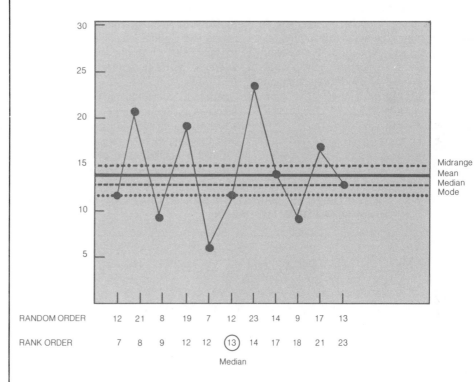

RANDOM ORDER 12 21 8 19 7 12 23 14 9 17 13

RANK ORDER 7 8 9 12 12 (13) 14 17 18 21 23

Median

provides a kind of shorthand for data. It can be very handy for purposes of describing a large quantity of data, such as the sizes of 100 workstations, to say the median size is 72 square feet or the average (mean) size is 74 square feet.

However, those single values do not even hint at the wide variation that exists among the individual workstations or that there is little or a great deal of variation. *Measures of variation or dispersion* are also single values, but they provide an indication of the degree of difference among the observations in a set. Thus, it could be said that the sizes of the workstations

vary from the smallest of 42 square feet to the largest of 121 square feet. Or, the size *range* is 79, which is the difference between the two extremes.

The range is the simplest, but least explicative measure of variation. Others include the mean absolute deviation, the variance and the standard deviation. Each of these three are indications of the ''average'' difference between an individual item and the mean of all the items. See Exhibit 4-3.

The *mean absolute deviation* relies on absolute numbers; in other words, when a negative value occurs in calculation, the minus sign is ignored and the number is treated as though it were positive. The mean absolute deviation is determined by calculating the difference between each observation and the mean, adding the results and dividing the sum by the number of observations. To illustrate, take a small sample of five out of the 100 workstation sizes (80, 56, 72, 110 and 48). The mean of these is approximately 74. The individual deviations are:

80 – 74 =   6
56 – 74 = –18
72 – 74 = – 2

110 – 74 = 36
48 – 74 = –26

Change the signed (negative) deviations to absolute numbers and add to yield 88. Divide this by the 5 sample observations to get 17.6, or approximately 18. The average, or mean absolute, deviation is 18.

Another measure that avoids signed numbers is the *variance*. It is based on squaring the values, and everyone knows that the square of a negative number is a positive number. The procedure is the same as for the mean absolute deviation,

except the values are squared:

80 – 74 =   6, squared =   36
56 – 74 = –18, squared = 324
72 – 74 = – 2, squared =   4
110 – 74 = 36, squared = 1296
48 – 74 = –26, squared = 676

The sum of the squared values is 2336, which divided by 5 observations equals 467.2, or approximately 467. The variance is also called the *mean squared deviation* in statistics.

The *standard deviation* is determined directly from this value and is more useful in many cases because it enables the statistician to compare figures on the same level. For instance, it is very difficult to relate 467 as a measure of variation to a mean size of 74 or any individual workstation size. However, if the square root of the mean squared deviation or variance is calculated, then the variation is at a comparable level with the observations. The standard deviation for the five-sample set would be the square root of 467, or approximately 22. It is the same thing as saying that, on the average, any individual observation may vary by 22 square feet from the average size of 74 square feet.

These various descriptive statistical measures are useful for their own purposes. However, they also provide a working basis, in combination with rules of statistical probability, for performing a wide range of tests and other calculations to predict similar conclusions about complex data. Such statistical manipulations are categorized as statistics of inference or inferential statistics.

INFERENTIAL STATISTICS. When the mean, median, variance, standard deviation or other measure is used to describe the entire set of members of a defined group—such as all the workstations of a particular type—it is referred to as a *parameter*. Parameters are quantities that define or characterize a *population*, the full set of members of a group.

EXHIBIT 4-3. MANY FORMS OF VARIATION ARE EXPRESSED AS DEVIATION FROM THE MEAN

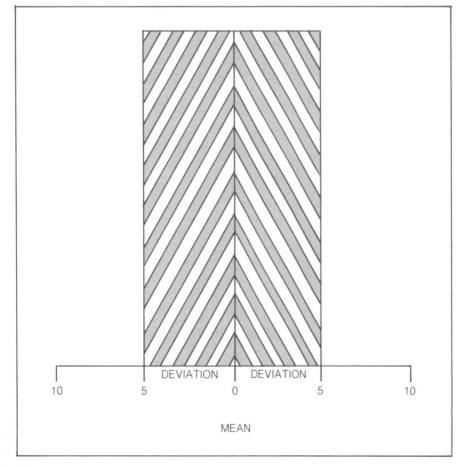

Often, however, it is not feasible or workable to deal with a population in its entirety, especially when it consists of hundreds or thousands of individual items. The computations that must be performed to determine the significant parameters of the population would be long and tedious and would work against one of the objectives of statistical analysis, which is to simplify and clarify large quantities of data. Statistics, most often, deals with representative *samples* of a population, as discussed in Chapter 3 under "Surveys."

A sample is a group of observations selected from a population that is assumed to represent the entire population. The most usual way to ensure proper representation is to select members of the sample randomly. *Random sampling* provides each member of the population an equal chance of being selected for the sample.

The various descriptive measures calculated for a population sample are called *statistics*, which refers to individual quantities instead of the body of knowledge and procedure. A statistic—sample mean, sample variance, etc.—represents a parameter; a parameter represents a population. Sample statistics are used to *infer* the parameters of a population. The inferences are based on the likelihood or *probability* that the statistics truly represent the parameters.

Inferential statistics, then, combines sampling, probability and descriptive measures to predict outcomes or conclusions about the data of a population. There are a large number of procedures—many of which relate to hypothetical conclusions or *statistical hypotheses* that the analyst wishes to prove or disprove—that are used to *test* predictions or determine the reliability, limits and freedom of the inferences. In addition to testing hypotheses, inferential statistical analysis (the word "inferential" is actually redundant here) is used to:

—Measure *correlations* among variables
—Determine values of one variable from the relationship between it and another variable, as in *regression analysis*
—Determine *confidence limits* and *degree of freedom* of statistical inferences

Nonparametric Statistics. As the name of this group of statistical tests of hypothesis implies, they refer to procedures which can be applied without regard to the parameters of a population. They are concerned not with the numerical values or quantities that characterize a population, but rather with the order of the data and the frequency distribution of the population. Obviously, tests that are concerned with parameters come under the heading of *parametric statistics*.

Nonparametric statistical tests are used, primarily, for data that are difficult to quantify and where the form of the population distribution is uncertain. They apply to data that are measured by rank ordering rather than by quantification and, therefore, are particularly useful in the behavioral sciences.

Tests of this sort are particularly appealing for the novice statistician because they are relatively quick and easy to use, require few computations and assumptions and have wide applicability. However, they may require lengthy computations of probability or extensive use of tables to display data for analysis. Some nonparametric tests are identified (from *Statistics for Psychology* and *Statistics Made Simple*) below for further reference:

—Sign test for comparing two population distributions
—Rank correlation coefficient
—Rank-sum test
—Signed-rank test

Resources for additional information on nonparametric statistics include *Nonparametric Statistics* by J. Hajek and *Nonparametric Statistics for the Behavioral Sciences* by S. Siegel.

Multivariate Statistics. In the example used in this section, various statistical procedures were applied to a single variable: the size of workstations. It was the significant variable of interest. However, in real design situations there may be more than one significant variable that the programmer wishes to analyze simultaneously or in relation to one another. In many cases, such analysis is necessary because the variability of one variable may affect the variability of others and vice versa.

For instance, a programmer might wish to relate size to such things as cost, shape, user satisfaction, comfort criteria or even to measure various dimensions of these relationships, such as area in relation to energy use, area in relation to cost of materials, area in relation to shape.

Procedures of multivariate statistics enable an analyst to simultaneously examine, measure or relate several variables or multiple dimensions of variables. Some techniques help to reduce unmanageable quantities of dimension measurements to a significant few which predict representation of the entire set. Most such procedures are highly complex and involve numerous statistical iterations, requiring the use of electronic data processing. A few that appear to hold potential for programming applications are identified here with references to relevant publications:

—*Analysis of variance* is said to be one of the most powerful tools of the statistical analyst. It involves classifying the variation within a sample population into separate components so that each can be tested. See *Statistics Made Simple, Statistics for Psychology, Introduction to Statistical Analysis.*

—*Factor analysis* is a means of statistically determining the most important factors that could be said to account for the results of a study or test out of numerous factors that may have been identified. The effect of the procedure is to group or collapse the multiple factors into fewer categories or "artificial" factors that are common to the individual members.

Factor analysis is based on interpretation of interaction or correlation matrices and measures the degree of relatedness of individual factors to the common factors. Geoffrey Broadbent describes the technique briefly in *Design in Architecture*. More detailed discussion is found in *Factor Analysis of Data Matrices* by P. Horst.

—*Multidimensional scaling* is a nonparametric procedure and deals with factor relationships on the basis of rank order of variables. There are numerous multidimensional scaling methods, many of which are still under development. In general, they attempt to represent relationship data as points in multidimensional space. The dimensions of the geometric space represent the factors by which the individual items are compared or related. Several articles exploring applications of multidimensional scaling are included in *Architectural Psychology: Proceedings of the Lund Conference* edited by Rikard Kueller. The theory and application of the technique, as well as an extensive bibliography and guide to computer applications, are examined in *Multidimensional Scaling and Related Techniques In Marketing Analysis* by Paul E. Greene and Frank J. Carmone.

Appropriate Statistics. The variety of procedures and applications of statistical analysis is immense. The programmer's use of statistical methods depends on his or her skill in the field and on appropriateness for particular tasks. The programmer should also remember that statistics is an attempt to abstract and quantify information. Its application to human factors and the dynamic variables of design are approximations, at best.

ANALYZING PROGRAM ELEMENTS

A comprehensive facility program consists of a combination of various elements that together define the whole of a facility's design needs and/or requirements. Although they may not be categorized as such in a program, the principal components of many contemporary programs include:

—Analysis of the functional and/or activity system to be accommodated
—Determination of the kinds, amounts and criteria of space corresponding to functional needs
—An estimate or analysis of the cost implications of physical requirements
—Establishment of schedules for performing the programming, designing, construction and, sometimes, occupation and operation of the facility
—Analysis of the requirements and implications of energy use

These five component categories do not cover the entire scope of any one program. Site analysis, engineering systems requirements and building code requirements, for instance, are often necessary ingredients of a comprehensive program. Nevertheless, the five listed appear to be fundamental components and may include many other elements not specifically cited above.

FUNCTION AND ACTIVITY ANALYSIS. Underlying a client's need for a particular physical entity called a facility is another entity that defines its use. This is the functional system—the operational system of activities and relationships that is organized for the accomplishment of specified objectives. A facility "facilitates" the existence and performance of this system. Understanding the functional system is essential in order to project a corresponding physical system of elements, relationships, organization and configuration. The definition of the client

organization's operational system requirements is often referred to as a "functional program."

The functional system consists of separate, but frequently overlapping, functions that can be classified in three categories:

—*Primary functions,* those related to achievement of the organization's objectives
—*Secondary functions*, those related to support, maintenance or performance of individual primary functions
—*Support functions*, those related to support and maintenance of the functional system (these include operations generally common to different types of facilities such as communications, lighting, comfort conditioning, circulation, mechanical and electrical service, waste disposal)

The performance of the functional system depends on activities and operations, which may be accomplished by human and other living beings or by mechanical and electrical devices.

The activities/operations, their interconnections and groupings, form a system that is a unique dimension of the functional system. The activity system—particularly the behavioral or human activity system—can be examined as a distinct entity or as a subsystem of the functional complex in analyzing and creating a model on which a facility's physical system may be based.

Through the analysis of functional and/or activity systems, the programmer can create a model or nonphysical infrastructure on which to base the analysis and recommendations pertaining to physical needs. Such analyses consist of:

—Identifying functional or activity components
—Assessing relevant dimensions or attributes of individual components
—Rating or ranking components according to relative significance and organizational status

—Identifying relationships among components

—Grouping components according to interdependencies

—Establishing performance goals, requirements or criteria

—Resolving conflicts among components

—Organizing or reorganizing components into an efficient, effective system

Function Analysis. The functional framework of a facility is based on the client's goals and operational objectives. When programming a facility that is unique to a client's experience, the programmer may begin by helping to develop and identify the primary objectives and the various operations and activities necessary to achieve them. If the client has previously defined and categorized functions, it might be well to reassess these in relation to objectives in order to accommodate changes that may occur in the new facility.

Categorization of primary functions enables the programmer to manage the analysis of each category. The analysis will include determining if primary functions have been adequately identified, defining necessary secondary functions, and tentatively identifying system-supporting functions. The latter should also be grouped together and categorized so that each category subsequently can be applied to the system components in a consistent manner. Exhibit 4-4 depicts the categorization of primary, secondary and support functions that could be associated with a religious congregation.

The analysis of primary functions may involve a variety of aspects, depending on the level of detail of the intended program. The programmer might break each down into lesser components such as subfunctions or activities, performance criteria, conditions necessary for functional performance, existing or desired attributes, or space and environmental requirements. Once the common system-support functions have been identified, these will be related to primary functions to determine whether and to what extent each is needed for functional performance. However, since support functions are generally easily translated to physical counterparts (e.g., engineering systems, lighting, circulation), this correlation might be postponed until primary functions have been translated to physical requirements.

The relative importance or status among the functions within the system can be a significant determinant of system organization. However, the most relevant factor in determining organization is the relationship among the individual functions. Analysis of the interaction or relationship among functional elements can be based on various criteria such as operational interdependence; frequency and duration of contact; and need for services, equipment, space or other functions. The easiest way to determine relationships is by a pairing method such as a matrix. (See "Data Organization" later in this chapter.)

A precise definition of the overall relational pattern among primary functions often is based on analysis of their subfunctions, the common secondary functions or activities/operations. Once connections among individual activities or base functional units have been identified, the programmer can develop the conceptual relationships among the primary functional groupings.

The data to be obtained from functional interaction analysis include the fact of individual relationships, the type of connection and the strength or importance of the association. This information is useful for determining such physical dimensions as adjacency and proximity, hierarchy of locations, space use scheduling and circulation.

Activity Analysis. Another approach to establishing a programmatic model for determining the physical requirements of a facility is activity analysis. The basic procedure is essentially the same as function analysis, but it focuses on a more precise dimension of facility use. An *activity* is an accepted and specific pattern of behavior, or series or group of actions, that can be expected to be repeated periodically or routinely over any given duration. It may be dependent on or independent of location and may be goal- or nongoal-directed.

A strict functional analysis of an organization, unless based on examination of its component activities, will yield a usable model for determining general physical needs. An activity analysis, because it deals with the more precisely defined unit, enables the programmer to recognize all the essential elements of the functional system and, therefore, produce a more complete indication of functional needs. It also recognizes elements that may be necessary to the operation of the system but not necessarily related directly to organization objectives or system support (e.g., informal communication, car pools, overtime).

Data from activity analysis is useful in helping to determine how much space a facility and its components require, effective organization of space, dimensions of the energy system, current and future personnel needs, and subsystem requirements. The procedure of analysis involves:

—Identification of individual activities

—Definition of activities

—Assessment of similarities and differences

—Classification by similarities or functional category

—Assessment of activity attributes such as number of people required, conditions necessary for performance, amount and periods of time, etc.

—Identification of interdependencies and other relationships

—Grouping according to similarities and interdependencies

EXHIBIT 4-4. PRIMARY, SECONDARY AND SUPPORT FUNCTIONS OF A CHURCH

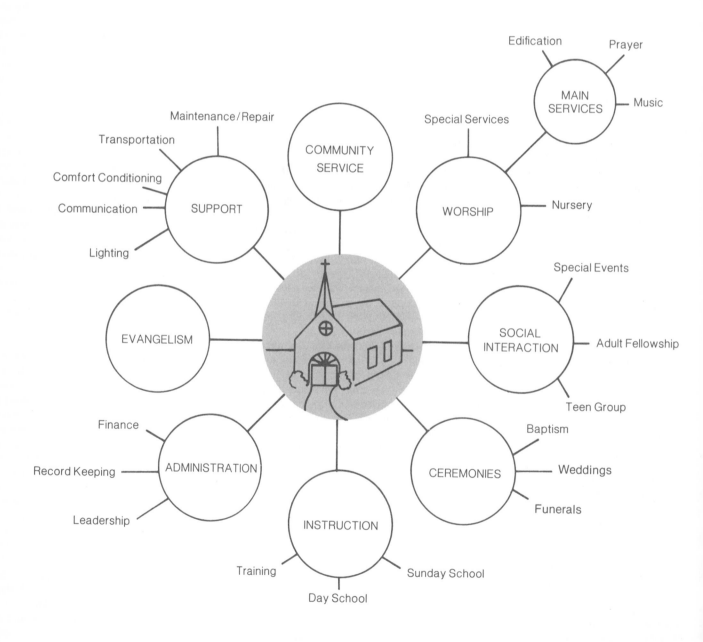

—Reconciliation of duplications and conflicts

—Organization into the system (existing or desired)

Sociophysical Analysis Models. The examination of a functional or activity system as though it exists independently of a physical context is a trick of analytical thought processes. In reality, such a situation does not exist. It is virtually impossible to engage in almost any kind of activity without doing so some place. The place has an influence on the activity, and the activity affects the place. Nevertheless, the segregation of social-behavioral and physical reality can be a handy device to use to discern clearly the relevant factors of interest to the examiner.

Social and behavior researchers, unless investigating the interface between environment and behavior, tend to purify the context of their research by focusing on their own area of interest: e.g., social organization, attitude, personality, perception, interaction, etc. Dismissal of physical context is the extreme opposite of the approach of many architects and engineers who, in designing facilities and operational systems, tend to exclude human perception, attitude and performance in their creation of mechanical and material artifacts.

There is growing recognition among both social behaviorists and designers—perhaps most clearly seen in the field of environmental design—that function and form, activity and place, are integral dimensions of design. Despite a willingness to talk a common language, environmental designers and design theorists have been struggling for a long time to develop a conceptual unit that satisfactorily represents the interactive quality of space and activity. To have such a workable tool would not only save the programmer a difficult transitional step between developing sociofunctional data and corresponding physical requirements or criteria, but

would more realistically represent the owner-user-facility needs.

Five models for analyzing sociophysical environments are presented in the following paragraphs. They have been developed by behavioral scientists or designers. The models are based on the concept of reciprocal influence between activity and space. Except for time budget analysis, each model relies on a base environmental component that serves as a consistent unit of analysis and design; i.e., behavior setting, activity cells and zones, activity site, pattern.

The concept of *behavior setting* was developed by environmental psychologist Roger Barker at the University of Kansas. It is a naturally occurring unit, a standing pattern, of behavior that is defined by both recurring activity and place. This sociophysical unit is the basis of Barker's methodology for researching and defining environmental behavior called *behavior setting survey*. A survey results in a detailed portrayal of the many integrated settings which comprise a particular environment such as a school, a community, city or a region. In order to ensure that the environment has been comprehensively defined by all the relevant settings, such a survey generally covers the period of a year.

A survey of such a duration would not be practical for most programming studies. However, the concept has powerful implications for programmers and designers:

—Use of the behavior setting as a standard unit for defining the socio-physical needs of a facility

—Use of setting types that have already been developed for specific types of facilities as a framework for analyzing a similar facility

—Use of findings from behavior setting research projects as a basis for evaluating user needs in a specific project

A great deal has been written on be-

havior setting studies since Barker's work began to be published in the 1950s. Barker has written *Ecological Psychology: Concepts and Methods for Studying the Environment of Human Behavior* (Palo Alto, Calif.: Stanford University Press, 1968). However, Robert B. Bechtel brings the concept closer to the design perspective in *Enclosing Behavior*, a very readable book published by Dowden, Hutchinson & Ross Inc. Other references include:

—"Observing Environmental Behavior: The Behavior Setting" by Dagfinn Aas in *Behavioral Research Methods in Environmental Design*, William Michelson, ed. Stroudsburg, Pa.: Dowden, Hutchinson & Ross Inc., 1975

—"Behavior Settings as Data-Generating Units for the Environmental Planner and Architect" by William F. LeCompte in *Designing for Human Behavior*, John Lang et al., eds. Stroudsburg, Pa.: Dowden, Hutchinson & Ross Inc., 1974

The *activity site model* is perhaps a more practical methodology for the programmer for analyzing project-specific behavior settings. The procedure was developed by Walter Moleski of the Environmental Research Group of Philadelphia, and he explains it in "Behavioral Analysis and Environmental Programming for Offices" (*Designing for Human Behavior*). An activity site, Moleski explains, "is a physical area within the organizational boundaries in which a prescribed activity recurrently and regularly takes place; this activity is purposive in that it is directed toward the achievement of organizational or corporate objectives and is controlled by organizational rules." He adds, "The primary attribute of the activity site is the relationship between the behavior patterns and the physical site in which they take place. Because of this interdependency, an activity site can be described in either its physical or behavioral components."

This is essentially the same concept as

a behavior setting, but it is taken a step further by being integrated with the idea of the required performance of the setting. The sociophysical performance characteristics are the basis of a transitional analytical step in the development of programs that enable the programmer to translate the behavioral system of an organization into an appropriate physical system.

Two matrix forms Moleski has developed to accomplish the transition from behavioral system to sociophysical characteristics to physical system requirements are shown in Exhibit 4-5.

Another method for modeling facility use is *activity system analysis*. Donald Watson, AIA, Yale University professor and architect, presents the model in an article, "Modeling the Activity System," which was published in the *Proceedings of the First Annual Environmental Design Research Association Conference* (Henry Sanoff, AIA, and Sidney Cohn, editors). Watson inferentially testified to the importance of activity analysis in his opening statement: "Of all the types of information on which an architectural designer depends, the category of activity is often the least developed. It is no wonder that many contemporary buildings are unresponsive to behavior requirements."

Recognizing that any defined unit of an activity system may by useful for analytical purposes but unstable in reality, Watson defines three generic elements of an activity system:

—Linkages, connecting circulation paths between activity-space units
—Activity zones (public, semipublic and private), areas that have various use potentials due to their locations or assigned activities
—Activity cells, units of activity that develop spontaneously or as programmed

An activity system is dynamic—constantly changing with new actions, new activities, remodeling, changes in technology. The

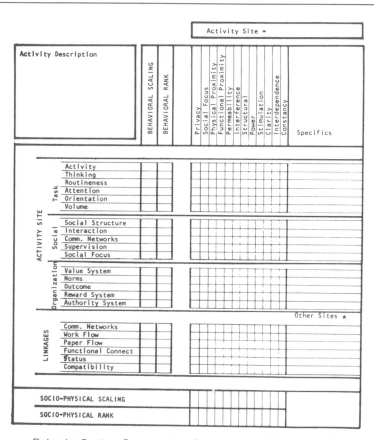

Behavior System Converted to Sociophysical Characteristics

activity program which depicts an existing activity system or predicts a new one must take into account the fact that the system may have changed by the time a program report is printed, may change again as the design develops and most certainly will be altered by users after the facility is occupied.

The elements of Watson's activity system model are shown in the diagram in Exhibit 4-6.

Time budget analysis is somewhat different from the preceding models in that it does not postulate a standard sociophysical unit. Rather it permits the analysis of activities within and among any given spaces. The integrating unit of analysis is time—duration, amounts and points of time in use of and connection between settings. William Michelson and Paul Reed describe time budget analysis in an article, "The Time Budget," which appears in *Behavioral Research Methods in Environmental Design* (William Michelson, editor). The data that can be generated via time budgets may include:

—Total amount of time allocated to specified activities, with variations by time of day, day of week, or season
—Frequency with which activities and

Perceptual Quality: Mood · Image · Symbols · Status Consideration · Graphics

Attributes: Style · Texture · Materials · Color · Lighting · Acoustics · Thermal

Environ. Components: Location · Traffic · Organization · Arrangement

Spatial Configuration: Boundary · Physical definition · Networks/Linkages · Visibility through · Positioning · Scale

SOCIO-PHYSICAL SCALING · **SOCIO-PHYSICAL RANK**

Privacy
Social Focus
Physical Proximity
Functional Proximity
Permeability
Interference
Structural
Power
Stimulation
Power
Stimulation
Clarity
Interdependence
Constancy

PHYSICAL SCALING

PHYSICAL RANK

Sociophysical Characteristics Translated to Physical System

Source: *Designing for Human Behavior: Architecture and the Behavioral Sciences.* Jon Lang, et al, eds. Stroudsburg, Pa.: Dowden, Hutchinson & Ross Inc., 1974.

types of activities are engaged in
—Patterns or clusters of typical activities

A data collection device for activity-time research is shown in Exhibit 4-7. It is similar to an activity or space use data log described in Chapter 3. Procedures for collecting, analyzing and using time budget data are explained in "The Time Budget" and in *Time-Budgets of Human Behavior* by Pitirim Sorokin and Clarence Berger. A computerized system for analyzing time budgets is presented in an article by Peter Kranz, "What Do People Do All Day?" (*Behavioral Science* journal, May 1970).

Pattern language is a system for conceptualizing and designing environments. It is also a vehicle for collaboration between environment users and professional designers, providing a common "language" for mutual discussion and resolution of design problems. The language consists of an extensive set of patterns—each representing a discrete segment of the total socio-cultural-functional-physical environment—and a set of rules for combining patterns into other patterns, each itself a discrete segment of the environment.

The concept, the generic patterns and the rules of "grammar" for constructing any unique language that accommodates any particular design situation were developed over several years by Christopher Alexander and his associates at the Center for Environmental Structure at Berkeley, California. The entire system is expounded in a series of three books: *The Timeless Way of Building, A Pattern Language* and *The Oregon Experiment* (publication data cited in "Bibliography").

The system rests on a fundamental unit called a pattern. A pattern is not a standard physical unit; its scope, size and purpose vary according to the situation examined. It is a planning principle that has proven itself successful in ordering or arranging the environment to accommodate the particular needs it addresses. *The Oregon Experiment* defines a pattern as "any general planning principle which states a clear problem that may occur in the environment, states the range of contexts in which this problem will occur and gives the general features required by all buildings or plans which solve this problem."

A pattern language appears to bridge the artificial gap between programming and designing which is usually necessary in order to ascertain user needs on one side and to create responsive form for needs on the other. Examples of patterns from a pattern language are illustrated in Exhibit 4-8.

SPACE ANALYSIS. As any architect knows, space is the single most important element of a facility. It is the clay with which the designer sculpts artistic accommodation of client needs. All the many other aspects and elements of a facility depend on and support the various kinds, amounts and conditions of space that comprise the facility. It is not surprising, then, that the programmatic analysis of human, physical and external factors which influence a design converges in an assessment of space needs.

EXHIBIT 4-6. ELEMENTS OF AN ACTIVITY SYSTEM

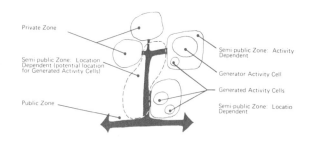

Source: "Modeling the Activity System" by Donald Watson, AIA, in *Proceedings of the First Annual Environmental Design Research Association Conference*, Henry Sanoff and Sidney Cohn, eds. Stroudsburg, Pa.: Dowden, Hutchinson & Ross Inc., 1970.

The purpose of space analysis is to determine the physical characteristics—the quantity and conditions—that can accommodate a client's objectives, philosophy, organization and activities. Although space needs are based on specific functions and activities and, to one degree or another, on user perceptions, preferences, priorities and personal needs, these criteria ultimately must be translated into a physical dimension.

Products. The physical elements that comprise a space needs assessment might include types and numbers of different spaces; area (square footage) requirements; visual, acoustical and comfort criteria; equipment, apparatus and furnishings needed to make space usable; and space relationships. A part of a space analysis might be an estimate of the costs of providing space; i.e., construction, financing, purchase, life cycle. Identification of space needs also might include or provide a basis for determining support system requirements such as lighting, electrical, mechanical and utility systems.

Although space analyses vary in the form of their conclusions, most include some or all of the following:

—Identification and categorization of appropriate units of space

—Space unit requirements; desired conditions or performance criteria

—Space inventory; a catalog of individual spaces or space types, number of each, associated requirements, area calculations

—Equipment/furnishings inventory; another catalog

—Space plan or layout based on unit sizes and adjacency needs

—Space program summary; a listing of the area requirements of major space unit groupings or categories and tally of total area or volume needs, both net and gross (see Exhibit 4-9)

—Space program; a detailed report that includes a space inventory, space relationship data, other relevant program conclusions affecting space use, and a cost estimate analysis

—Space budget or cost estimate, which may parallel a space inventory or program and indicate per-square-foot and total predicted cost of providing the space

Procedure. Depending on the scope of the program and the purpose for which it is to be used, the assessment of space needs may be general or specific. In other words, it may vary according to the scale or level of program detail desired (master, facility, component). At different scales,

the programmer works with different space units, which are classifications or category groupings defined for purposes of the project-specific analysis.

In developing data for space needs—particularly area calculations—the programmer may rely on one or a combination of sources. These include existing conditions of the replaceable or a similar facility, the programmer's own experience and judgment, estimates by owner and users, and industry or architectural research standards. It is generally best to rely on user estimates and compare them or evaluate them on the basis of other information.

Regardless of the source of data, effective space analysis requires frequent, if not continuous, interaction between client and programmer. The client knows best what his or her space needs are, even if unable to describe or analyze them technically, and, just as important, the client should know the limits of the budget and the extent of willingness to pay for one thing or another. The programmer, on the other hand, provides guidance on the meaning of terms and concepts analyzed (which ensures mutual understanding of space needs), as well as advice on the implications of client space decisions.

There are any number of procedures for analyzing space needs, including those sociophysical models examined previously. Some sociophysical analysis methods, however, can be more socio than physical. Ultimately, the social and operational criteria of a facility must be translated into physical requirements. At the same time, the analysis of physical space needs cannot neglect other dimensions, particularly user needs and budget limits. These latter two elements frequently conflict, and one of the objectives of space analysis will be to resolve conflicts and optimize the balance between user needs and resource limits.

Generally, most procedures for space analysis include three tasks:

EXHIBIT 4-7. A TIME-USE DIARY FOR DATA COLLECTION

Please complete this activity record for your activities during waking hours on

______ (day of week) ______ (month) ______ (day) ______ (year)

NOTE: Any time spent working at your job (or jobs) should simply be recorded as "At work". However, please rember to include any lunch or coffee breaks.

	ACTIVITY	Office use only	STARTING TIME	FINISHING TIME	OTHERS PARTICIPATING: 1 Alone, 2 Family, 3 Friends, 4 Work associates, 5 Other	LOCATION: 1 At home, 2 At work, 3 Travelling, 4 Other	
01							(if other, specify)
02							(if other, specify)
03							(if other, specify)
04							(if other, specify)
05							(if other, specify)
06							(if other, specify)
07							(if other, specify)
08							(if other, specify)
09							(if other, specify)
10							(if other, specify)
11							(if other, specify)
12							(if other, specify)
13							(if other, specify)
14							(if other, specify)
15							(if other, specify)
16							(if other, specify)
17							(if other, specify)

Source: "The Time Budget" by William Michelson and Paul Reed in *Behavioral Research Methods in Environmental Design*, William Michelson, ed. Stroudsburg, Pa.: Dowden, Hutchinson & Ross Inc., 1975 (from the Department of Secretary of State, Ottawa, Canada).

—Define and itemize space units
—Specify requirements of each unit
—Calculate total space needs

Define and itemize space units: The specific categorization of space for any project is dependent on the facility characteristics and the programmer's inclinations. Classification for the three levels of scale might include:

—Master or general facility-wide units (site, total conditioned and total unconditioned enclosure or activity, connective and support space totals
—Facility or functional scale units (individual primary functional areas and the secondary and supporting functions that may or may not be defined by space, but which help define primary space; includes connective space and ancillary space such as parking or storage)
—Component or activity scale units (individual activity or operational areas, support and connective space, plus ancillary and site components

Specify requirements, criteria and parameters of each identified space unit that will enable it to be used effectively, efficiently and economically: The necessary or preferred conditions that facilitate use of space include physical, functional, social, psychological and even spiritual elements. Some may be:

—Net area and/or volume
—Dimensions
—Visual, acoustical, other sensory qualities
—Equipment, apparatus and furnishings
—Lighting requirements
—Significant thermal conditioning requirements, e.g., for computers
—Adjacency and/or proximity to other spaces
—Communications requirements

Numbers	Topic	Problem	Tendencies conflicting	Pattern	Transformations
					A
1	Entrance to architect's office—transparent	Visitors feel that they are not welcome when they approach the office.	1. Visitor feels uncomfortable about entering an alien professional world. 2. "Architects" fear complete exposure to public realm.	If: Entrance to any architect's office. Then: Entrance facade has transparent surfaces on either side of door and/or door can be transparent also.	
3	Entrance—position of reception desk in relation to entrance	Office has to control entrance of visitors.	1. Visitors want a route. 2. Some visitors want to come into office unobserved. 3. Visitors want to prepare "face." 4. Receptionist wants to observe visitor as soon as he enters and be unobserved. 5. Receptionist wants another direction to face.	If: Entrance to any architect's office that maintains a reception desk. Then: Visitor faces wall as he enters, then turns right angle. Receptionist nearest to entrance has clear view of entry; can turn in 2 directions faces visitor, no way ino office except by R desk.	
5	Staff and path to drawing office	In many offices there is nowhere for the staff to get together. There is nowhere to go (except at the work table), nowhere to sit, nowhere to prepare coffee, snacks, etc.	1. Staff tend not to meet each other except when they are actually collaborating on a problem. 2. Staff tend to learn more from each other if they meet informally away from workplace. 3. Staff tend to get jaded, need breaks, light relief.	If: Any architect's office. Then: Kitchen near receptionist. breakplace in center of office where all circulation joins & BETW. All workplaces and entrance, library niche can be used as breakplace but should be opposite BP if have both, breakplace near R & K.	
6	Partners and contact with staff	Partners must keep in contact with staff yet want a place of their own in the office.	1. Partners tend to make special "places" for themselves in the office. 2. Staff tend to lose contact with partners	If: Office where partners and staff are in danger of being separated. Then: Common circulation for each and staff and partners work together in teams in drawing office.	
8	Two workplaces	People want to work in groups as well as work as separate individuals	1. People tend to want relief from a single task. 2. People tend to want to work in groups—realize that it's more efficient for certain kinds of arch problems.	If: Any architect's office. Then: Library is equipped with carrels for individual study & is large enough to store books and materials. Open on one side of main circulation route. Space large enough for 1/3 maximum office staff at any time.	
9	Conference room	Not all meetings can be held in the drawing office.	1. Need for meetings with limited outside contact 2. Need for staff and partners to keep in touch (see pattern 6).	If: Any architect's office. Then: Conference room just off main circulation route. entrance not through workplace, receptionist can give easy directions to it. distractions controllable to and from workplace.	

1.3 1.3.8 1.3.8.6 1.3.8.6.9 1.3.8.6.9 +

Source: "A Progress Report on the Pattern Language" by Francis Duffy and John Torrey in *Emerging Methods in Environmental Design and Planning*. Gary T. Moore, ed. Cambridge, Mass.: The MIT Press, 1970.

—Special accommodations
—Psychic qualities such as privacy, security, territory

Calculate total space needs: This task is not simply a matter of totaling up the needs of each individual unit, although that is a necessary step. It also involves:
—Grouping space units according to types for further analysis and according to functional relationships
—Determining gross area based on net area requirements (the conversion factor varies according to the facility type and the programmer's experience)
—Estimating anticipated construction costs based on gross area
—Comparing anticipated costs with preliminary budgets
—Organizing space units according to functional relationships, hierarchy of need and other criteria
—Adjusting space allotments and totals to resolve conflicts among individual needs and account for use scheduling overlaps and conflicts, and resolving budget-space conflicts

Space Unit Standards. A facility for a large organization such as a school, hospital or commercial office will house many individual activities that are recurrent or similar. The space requirements for repetitive activities will be similar, if not identical, in terms of size, accommodations and conditions. Teaching spaces in a school, for example, may include several lecture rooms, science laboratories, media laboratories, workshops, etc. Hospitals contain numerous inpatient rooms, treatment areas, nursing stations and operating rooms. Offices generally are composed of hundreds of similar workstations, although they may be of several different types.

In specifying requirements for activity spaces, each separate unit may be taken individually to catalog its size, furnishing and equipment needs, lighting requirements and so forth. However, the pro-

EXHIBIT 4-9. SPACE PROGRAM SUMMARY (PARTIAL)

NON-RESIDENTIAL					LINCOLN—COSTS
COMPONENT	NET SF	+ % NET	GROSS SF	COST/SF	COMPONENT COST
EXECUTIVE AND PUBLIC					
Executive Administration	2,145	.50	3,217.5	40	$ 128,700
Reception	260	.50	390.0	40	15,600
Mail Sorting	200	.20	240.0	40	9,600
Visiting	3,750	.50	5,625.0	40	225,000
CONTROL					
Custody Administration	1,290	.50	1,935.0	40	77,400
Inmate Reception	865	.50	1,297.5	40	51,900
Hearing Room	305	.20	366.0	40	14,640
PROGRAM AND ACTIVITIES					
Program Administration	1,105	.50	1,657.5	40	65,300
Psychological Services	1,065	.50	1,597.5	40	63,900
Media Center	1,600	.20	1,920.0	45	86,400
Legal Service Center	485	.20	582.0	40	23,280
Academic School	2,625	.50	3,937.5	45	177,188
Vocational Services	9,000	.20	10,800.0	45	486,000
Multiservice Center	1,080	.20	1,296.0	40	51,840
Recreation/Gym	8,995	.20	10,794.0	45	485,730
Auxiliary Services	685	.50	1,027.0	40	41,080
SUPPORT					
Support/ Maintenance	3,000	.50	4,500.0	40	180,000
Central Stores	3,000	.20	3,600.0	40	144,000
Food Service	6,030	.20	7,236.0	75	542,700
Medical	2,995	.20	3,594.0	70	251,580
Total: Non-Residential	50,480	.30	65,612	42	3,122,838

Source: Master Plan for Nebraska State Medium-Minimum Security Facilities by Kirkham, Michael and Associates, Architects, Engineers, Planners of Omaha, Nebraska; and Gruzen & Partners, Architects Planners of New York.

grammer can simplify the task by reducing the total number of spaces—often in the hundreds—to a group of 5 to 15 standard types of space, depending on the facility type and its specific functions. It is not only easier and more efficient to work with only a handful of standard space units in enumerating applicable criteria, but standardization also aids in organizing space units and in cost estimating.

The criterion most often standardized for activity spaces is size or area. However, it is possible to incorporate several criteria in standardized space units. Exhibit 4-10 shows a series of six different standard units organized in a uniform chart that includes the criteria of area, preliminary form (diagrams), number of people to be accommodated, equipment requirements, lighting needs, comfort and scheduled use. A second chart lists nine standard support function spaces with the same criteria applied. For any particular functional group or area—in this case, the civil engineering department—only the task and function spaces necessary are marked to indicate the number of standard units needed and the resulting area calculations.

The type of space unit that may be standardized is usually no larger than a room and no smaller than an individual workstation, or the stationary space required for an individual to perform a given task. However, as seen in Exhibit 4-10, it may be appropriate to standardize ancillary functions separately so they can be matched to groups of related task spaces.

A programmer may use stock space standards for a particular facility type based on previous experience. However, standard units generally are developed, or at least modified, for an individual project. The general procedure is as follows:

—Identify individual activity spaces and determine desired requirements for each; usually based on interview and/or questionnaire results.

—Group individual space units according to similarity in task, function and/or principal criteria.

—Based on user-identified requirements for each unit in a group, determine the optimum criteria for the space type and repeat for each group. William J. Mitchell discusses methods of standardization in Chapter 12 of his book, *Computer-aided Architectural Design*.

—Test the resulting space unit standards by user evaluation and modify as necessary.

—Allocate standard units to each functional area, activity group or department.

—Calculate total space needs for each group and for the total facility.

Space Program. The space program element of a facility program generally includes an itemization of requirements for each space unit (standardized or individual), categorized according to the primary functional or activity groups, and the total area requirements of each category and the total facility. The catalog of spaces may be abbreviated in a single- or multipage summary of program requirements, as illustrated in Exhibit 4-9, which may show net square footage, net-to-gross percentage conversion factors for various types of space, gross area, unit cost estimates and total cost estimates. The space unit catalog may be accompanied by or include an inventory of the equipment and furnishings required for individual units.

The functional or activity groupings of the facility may be further analyzed to determine various relationship needs. The adjacency requirements of individual activity spaces within a functional group can be itemized and summarized by diagram, as shown in Exhibit 4-11. In this case, the primary circulation directions are shown also. The interdependencies among different functional groups for the total facility may also be analyzed in a space program and illustrated by sketch diagrams, floor plans and/or stacking plans.

ENERGY ANALYSIS. The 1973 oil embargo gave energy conservation its first shot at stardom in the consciousness of Americans. But after the shock of shortages and first price hikes wore off, conservation became more or less a fad—like disco, the "in" thing to do. Gradually, with prices continuing a steady, steep rise, social obligation characterized the need to save energy (remember the oil-company slogan "saveagallonagasaday") and soon it took on the tone, if not the proportions, of a political imperative.

Even if fuel resource depletion were a contrivance of energy company executives and political campaigners, the reality is that the prices of conventional energy resources are high and, by everyone's account, won't stop going higher for some time. From a practical standpoint, energy conservation is a matter of economics. It is prudent business to save energy. This is especially so with respect to buildings, which, it has been reported widely, waste as much as 50 percent of the energy they consume, due to inefficient design and use.

While it is politically and socially important to conserve energy supplies and reduce dependence on imported fuels, the practical rationale for energy-efficient facilities is to save money and improve the value of the properties. Energy consumption takes a bigger and bigger bite out of each annual operating budget, and this has a significant impact on the life cycle value of a facility. Reduced energy consumption, and consequently reduced operating costs, increase the economic efficiency and the long term value of a facility.

An energy-efficient design may require a higher initial investment in construction, but many energy conservation strategies require minimal or even no added costs. The initial cost of any measure must be weighed against its benefits—immediate

EXHIBIT 4-10. TASK AND FUNCTION SPACE UNIT STANDARDS

TASK (OFFICE) SPACE STANDARDS

GROUP SUB-GROUP

DESIGNATION	TYPICAL SPACE LAYOUTS	DESCRIPTION	SQ. FT./ TASK	NO. SPACES	TOTAL SQ. FT.	NO. PEOPLE /SPACE (DESIGN)	EQUIP/ SPACE (TYPICAL)	LIGHTING /SPACE TASK	LIGHTING /SPACE GEN	COMFORT LEVEL S	COMFORT LEVEL W	VENT CFM	TIME OF USE	REMARKS
TASK E	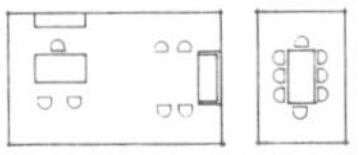	•EXECUTIVE (Conf.)	380 + CONF			1		70 ESI	35 FC	75 °F / 55% RH	72 °F / –	.25/ S.F.	8-5	
1	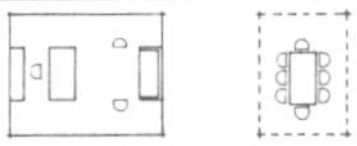	•VICE PRESIDENT (Conf.) •MANAGERS (Share a Conf.) •CHIEF ENGS. (Share a Conf.)	260 + CONF			1		70	35	75 / 55	72 / –	.25/ S.F.	8-5	
2	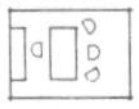	•ASSISTANT TO •ASSISTANT MANAGER •SUPERVISORS	170			1		70	35	75 / 55	72 / –	.25/ S.F.	8-5	
3	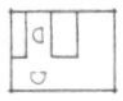	•STAFF •FINANCIAL ANALYST •ENGINEERS	120			1		70	35	75 / 55	72 / –	.25/ S.F.	8-5	
4	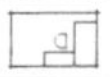	•SECRETARY •KEY PUNCH •CLERICAL	75			1		70*	35	75 / 55	72 / –	.25/ S.F.	8-5	*KEY PUNCH 150 ESI/50
5	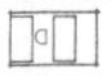	•DRAFTING •BOOKKEEPER •SUPPORT STAFF	80			1		70*	35	75 / 55	72 / –	.25/ S.F.	8-5	*DRAFTING 200 ESI/70
TOTALS														

FUNCTION / TASK ORIENTED SPACE STANDARDS

GROUP SUB-GROUP

DESIGNATION	TYPICAL SPACE LAYOUTS	SQ. FT./ FUNCTION	NO. SPACES	TOTAL SQ. FT.	NO. PEOPLE /SPACE (DESIGN)	EQUIP / SPACE (TYPICAL)	LIGHTING / SPACE FUNCT	LIGHTING / SPACE GEN	COMFORT LEVEL S	COMFORT LEVEL W	VENT CFM	TIME OF USE	REMARKS
CONFERENCE / MEETING	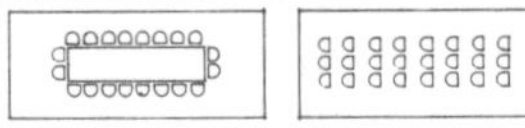	CONF. RM. 360 MEETING			20-24		70 ESI	35 FC	75 °F / 55% RH	72 °F / –	5/ PER-SON	8-5	
CONFERENCE / MEETING	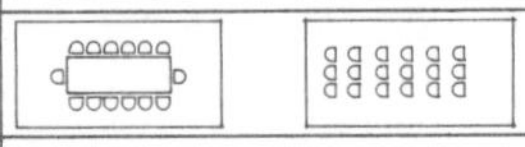	CONF. RM. 280 MEETING			12-16		70	35	75 / 55	72 / –	5/ PER-SON	8-5	
CONFERENCE (TASK)	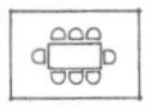	150			6-8		70	35	75 / 55	72 / –	5/ PER-SON	8-5	
SUPPLY AREA		40			–		–	35	75 / 55	72 / –	.25/ S.F.	8-5	
FILE AREA		50			–		–	35	75 / 55	72 / –	.25/ S.F.	8-5	
FILE AREA (FLAT)		50			–		–	35	75 / 55	72 / –	.25/ S.F.	8-5	
REFERENCE STORAGE or WORK AREA		100			–		80	35	75 / 55	72 / –	.25/ S.F.	8-5	
COAT AREA		20			–		–	35	75 / 55	72 / –	.25/ S.F.	8-5	
COMPUTER TERM. AREA	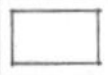	75			–		150	50	75 / 55	72 / –	.25/ S.F.	8-5	
CIRCULATION													
TOTALS													

Source: Program for Georgia Power Company headquarters in Atlanta, Georgia, developed by Heery & Heery, Architects and Engineers, Atlanta, Georgia.

EXHIBIT 4-11. DIAGRAM OF ADJACENCY REQUIREMENTS AND CIRCULATION DIRECTION

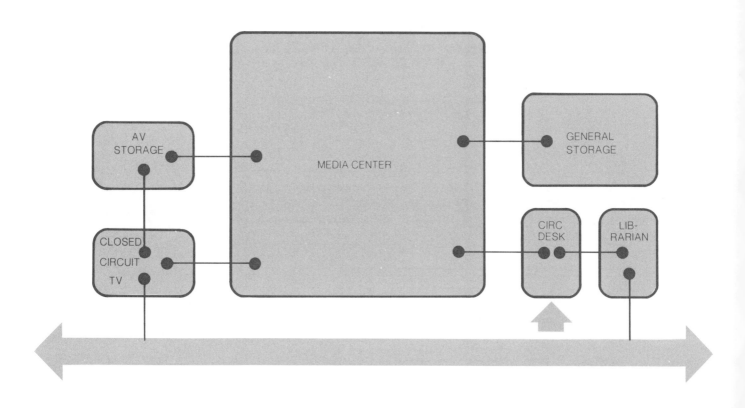

Source: Master Plan for Nebraska State Medium-Minimum Security Facilities by Kirkham, Michael and Associates Architects, Engineers, Planners of Omaha, Nebraska; and Gruzen & Partners Architects Planners of New York.

and life cycle—in order to judge its worth.

Energy conservation can be achieved through use of more efficient building components and heating-cooling-ventilation, process and lighting equipment, and through more efficient use of equipment. But it also can be achieved through proper manipulation of the design elements and strategies involved in space organization and sizing, facility orientation and configuration, siting, use scheduling, envelope design and fenestration, among others.

The facility programmer can contribute information and recommendations pertaining to various energy-conserving design and systems elements. These as-

pects, however, don't tell the whole story of the relationship between energy use and a facility. As illustrated in Exhibit 4-12, the energy considerations of a program may include several issues listed under the following four broad categories:

—*Energy supplies*. This might include energy prices and availability; efficiency and cost of producing energy and delivering it; the social costs of energy production in terms of air pollution, nuclear radiation risk, centralized control, etc.

—*Construction*. The significance of the amount of energy required to build a new facility compared to rehabilitation of an existing one is vastly underrated. Pro-

grammer, designer and client may wish to consider the energy consumption involved in getting construction materials to a site, operating construction equipment and producing building materials. A feasibility analysis, taking energy into consideration, may conclude it is more cost-effective to upgrade a facility than to replace it with a new one.

—*External operations*. Energy is consumed by activities not directly related to the physical facility but involved in performance of the client's organizational objectives. The energy needed to transport people and materials to and from the facility may have an effect on site location,

EXHIBIT 4-12. ENERGY CONSUMPTION FACTORS RELATED TO A FACILITY

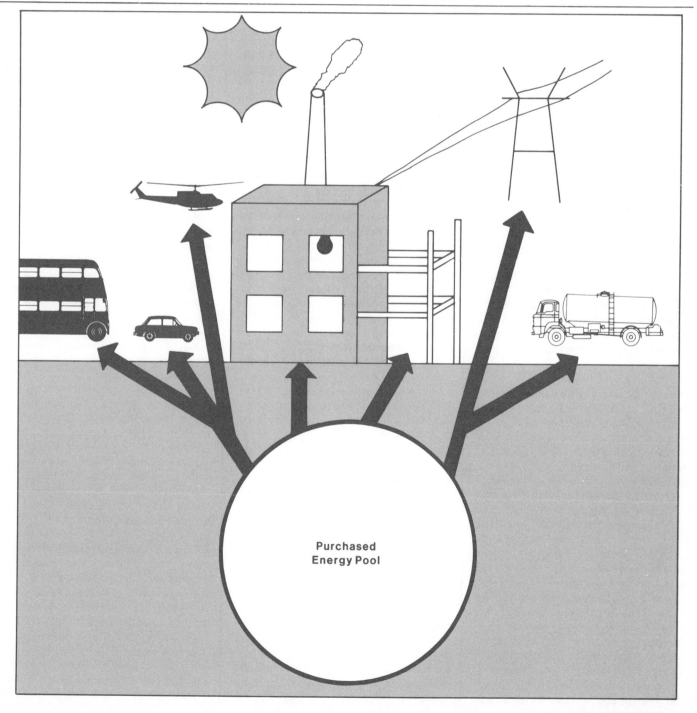

Purchased
Energy Pool

for example. Likewise, services, materials and products brought in to support facility operations consume energy in their manufacture and performance, and their costs affect the fiscal integrity of the facility and owner.

—*Internal operations.* Within a facility, energy is used for space heating and cooling, service water heating and cooling, ventilation, lighting and operating process equipment (e.g., computers, elevators, conveyors, appliances).

A facility program may consider any or all of these factors, as well as others. However, the principal focus is generally on those factors that directly influence the design; in other words, the considerations involved in organizing, using and operating the facility.

In order to determine how the programmer can contribute to the designer's task of developing an energy-efficient design, it's necessary to look at how energy use relates to facility operations and how to recognize energy conservation opportunities.

Energy Conservation and Facility Design. Not many years ago, energy consumption was an afterthought in the design equation of a facility, and energy conservation came after that. Each system and component of a facility was designed to achieve optimum performance of its function without regard to the energy implications of the design. A heating or cooling system, for example, would be sized to meet thermal comfort needs, often achieved by overcoming maximum possible heat loss or gain. On the other hand, efforts to minimize heat gain or loss through envelope design were aimed not at saving energy but at maintaining control of internal environment conditions. Likewise, lighting systems would be designed to meeting illumination needs regardless of the amount of electricity consumed or of heat generated and added to the cooling load. The effect of one system on another

in terms of energy consumption or the energy use results of any combination was generally ignored.

Now that energy conservation is becoming much more of a forethought in the minds of facility owners and designers, energy-consuming systems are being designed for efficiency of energy performance as well as of primary function performance. However, a more fundamental change has occurred in the energy perspective of some designers. They recognize energy performance of a facility in terms of a total system rather than of a group of individual systems. To them, energy performance is the result of the interaction of many variable elements and influencing factors in the total facility design. Thus, energy conservation is less a matter of overcoming individual problems (such as heat gain or loss) one by one than it is of manipulating and integrating all the energy-related elements and factors to achieve a balanced and efficient total performance system.

The potential list of factors that influence a facility's energy performance, and their interdependencies, could be endless. The reason is that energy performance is dynamic; it varies for each facility type, responding to particular climatic conditions and to specific requirements of design and use. Some of the factors that may influence energy use or that represent opportunities to apply energy-conserving strategies are listed in Exhibit 4-13. The exhibit illustrates that the designer has more direct control over physical elements than over human or external factors.

The traditional emphasis in energy-conserving design has been on the physical areas, with particular attention to improving individual systems efficiency. Human and external influences typically have been regarded as parameters to be met or constraints to be overcome by control of physical components. For example, the influence of climate typically is controlled—in large facilities, at least—by ex-

cluding it. In other words, heat loss and external heat gain are controlled by a tight thermal envelope. The designer then works to exercise maximum control over the internal climate—frequently, a matter of overcoming internal heat gain by air conditioning.

However, if a designer sees climate as a dynamic influence on a facility that can be manipulated to use its advantages as well as control its negative impacts, then climate becomes an integral element of total facility design. It represents an opportunity not only for energy conservation but for creative design response.

Designing to achieve balance and efficiency in the total energy performance system involves incorporation of human and external factors into consideration of physical factors, but it also involves recognition of the dynamic relationship among the three parts. Exhibit 4-14 illustrates that the energy performance of a facility is the result of the overall interaction of all three elements or, as shown, of the natural environment, the built environment and people.

A facility's energy performance system is only one element in design, but one which permeates design integration; it can't be slipped in and out of the design equation as though it were an independent variable. Energy conservation in design is more a matter of energy effectiveness than of energy efficiency or even of reducing energy consumption. Energy conservation is a design function.

Energy Considerations in Programming. The programmer can play a very important role in development of a design that uses energy effectively. Several ways in which the program helps develop energy-effective design strategies are:

—Development of data on factors that directly influence energy such as climatological factors, current and future prices and availabilities of energy supplies, status of new energy conservation technologies and alternative energy sources, energy budgets

—Determining the energy use implications of other design factors; e.g., functional requirements for energy use, area requirements and space organization, facility use scheduling, lighting requirements, comfort requirements, equipment needs

—Identification of potential energy conservation opportunities and strategies appropriate to the particular facility; e.g., climatic orientation, grouping of energy-intensive functions, space use scheduling, recycling waste heat, operation and maintenance scheduling, passive solar energy concepts

—Development of energy budgets, or performance goals, that are appropriate for the particular facility types, functions and climatic conditions

—Preliminary analysis of energy-using systems to compare relative significance of individual allocations

Energy Budgeting. An energy budget is a tool for a programmer or designer to use in establishing an energy performance goal for a facility's design and in evaluating the energy performance of a design after it is completed. It can be used also in the analysis of relative allocations of energy use among energy-consuming systems in a facility design to discover energy conservation opportunities.

An energy budget is an estimate of the rate of energy consumption of a design over a specified period of time. The standard expression for energy budgets is British thermal units (Btu) per gross square foot per year. The annual consumption rate pertains to the facility's total energy performance without regard to specific design systems or components. It is a desired energy use level or a limit, rather than a prediction of the result of a design.

An energy budget for a facility can be determined based on historical evidence of performance of similar facilities in the

EXHIBIT 4-13. ENERGY-RELATED DESIGN VARIABLES

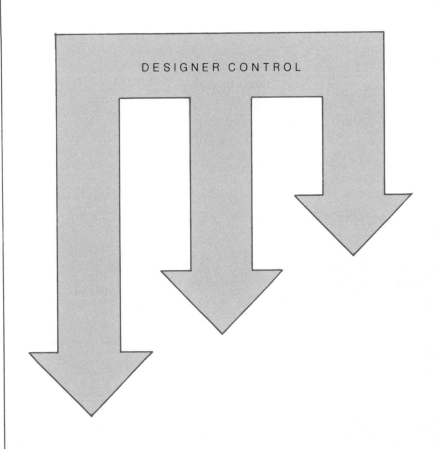

DESIGNER CONTROL

PHYSICAL FACTORS	HUMAN FACTORS	EXTERNAL FACTORS
Space Unit Size	Objectives	Energy Prices
Total Space	Activities	Energy Supplies
Space Organization	Use Scheduling	Climate
Functions	Operation and	Site Location
Configuration	Maintenance	Site Conditions
Envelope Design	Comfort Requirements	Solar Access
Structure Massing	Attitudes/Values	Codes/Standards
Environmental Control		Cost of Materials/
Lighting System		Equipment
Mechanical System		Alternative Energy
		Sources

EXHIBIT 4-14. INTERACTION OF ENERGY-RELATED FACTORS DETERMINES ENERGY PERFORMANCE

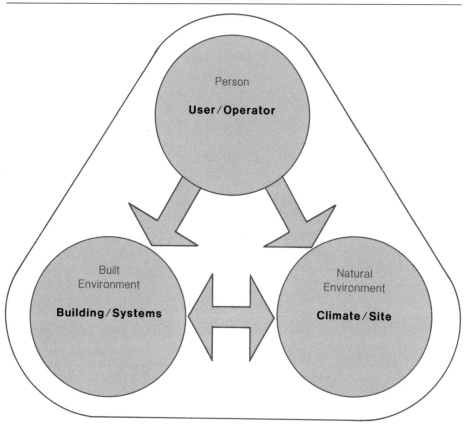

same climate, if energy use data are available. From the performance records of several such buildings, a statistical median or mean is determined that sets an arbitrary limit of how much energy the proposed facility should use. Such a procedure was used in establishing both an energy consumption budget and summer and winter peak load budgets for the Georgia Power Company headquarters building in Atlanta, Georgia, which was programmed and designed by Heery & Heery, Architects and Engineers, of Atlanta. Exhibit 4-15 shows a table of the energy use data for several Atlanta office buildings that were used to select the energy budget figures for the project.

The federal government has simplified the process of selecting an energy budget by performing the statistical analysis on a national scale and using the results to establish uniform energy budget levels. The federal building energy performance standards (BEPS) establish reasonable limits of design energy use for different building types in different climatic regions. The standards specifically state that total performance is the basis for the energy conservation requirements and that materials, methods and system components for achieving a goal are left to the discretion of the designer.

Before BEPS were developed, the principal energy conservation standards were based on a prescriptive approach rather than a performance approach. Prescriptive standards are based on values applied to individual building components, systems and equipment and determined by test experience. The theory of energy conservation design under this approach is that if the performance of individual components is energy-efficient, then a resulting combination of components would be energy-efficient as well. This all but ignores the dynamic and interactive effects of diferent elements and doesn't consider the influences of climate and user/operator on energy performance. It also limits the designer's creativity in selecting design strategies and components that take advantage of climatic resources and that meet functional criteria other than energy conservation.

The federal BEPS require a facility designer to establish an energy budget for the design, using standardized data (budget levels) based on facility type, function and size, and the climatic conditions of the area in which it is located. The designer is free to employ any energy-conserving methods and materials that will result in a design energy consumption rate which does not exceed the budget. Once the design is developed, it is analyzed by a standardized evaluation technique (BEPS includes one) to determine if the design can perform within the goal limit.

The BEPS provide a uniform procedure for incorporating energy analysis in the design process and standardize building energy conservation goals. A BEPS budget is a maximum, not a minimum, and a facility owner and designer may wish to establish a different budget level (within the standard) that is suitable to the objectives and circumstances of the project. Furthermore, although the BEPS procedure bases an energy budget on preliminary design concepts, it can be developed also in the programming stage. In fact, the programmer and designer may develop a series of energy budgets corresponding

EXHIBIT 4-15. ENERGY BUDGET BASED ON SURVEY OF SIMILAR BUILDINGS

	PEAK DEMAND (BTU/SQ. FT.)		CONSUMPTION (BTU/SQ. FT./YR.)
	S	W	
TOTALS	673.74	910.19	2,924,952.68
NO. OF BUILDINGS	31	31	31
AVERAGE	21.73	29.36	94,353.31
70% OF AVERAGE	15.21	20.55	66,041.31
65% OF AVERAGE	*14.12	19.08	61,652.05
60% OF AVERAGE	13.03	17.61	56,909.59
55% OF AVERAGE	11.95	*16.14	*51,894.32
50% OF AVERAGE	10.86	14.77	47,447.16

*SELECTED AS BUDGET FIGURES

	PEAK DEMAND		CONSUMPTION
ENERGY BUDGET	14	16	51,000.00

ATLANTA BASE ENERGY BUDGET CALCULATIONS

BUILDING NO.	TYPE ENERGY	PEAK DEMAND (BTU/SQ. FT.) S	W	CONSUMPTION (BTU/SQ. FT./YR.)	BUILDING NO.	TYPE ENERGY	PEAK DEMAND (BTU/SQ. FT.) S	W	CONSUMPTION (BTU/SQ. FT./YR.)
16	G-E	34.64	62.57	150,092.72	18-1	E	24.55	26.66	113,884.75
9	E	34.01	39.71	168,014.39	18-2	E	18.27	20.69	86,015.33
20	E	23.82	31.44	82,014.39	39	G-E	18.92	37.88	84,778.01
10	G-E	16.91	*16.30	72,715.42	77	E	18.20	23.56	79,089.95
19	E	20.40	26.91	79,067.08	27	E	18.58	28.33	69,675.38
15	E	18.37	29.70	70,940.00	33	G-E	24.88	35.14	92,215.53
21	G-E	22.06	34.69	117,203.43	79	E	24.62	34.27	134,080.43
25	G-E	16.83	25.93	81,769.47	24	E	18.17	21.34	84,916.99
17	G-E	20.90	20.33	88,989.85	76	E	*14.08	18.78	66,963.81
26	E	26.40	29.61	154,392.60	60	E	21.55	27.55	66,920.59
38	G-E	29.43	31.81	91,737.09	59	G-E	15.88	27.14	*53,606.08
46	G-E	25.57	40.53	119,889.34	58	G-E	23.93	38.33	104,446.96
48	E	15.07	17.73	60,206.50	1-1	E	15.75	20.53	61,677.06
54	G-E	28.12	39.28	108,284.95	1-2	E	17.39	21.24	80,724.31
72	E	19.64	26.39	95,217.23	57	E	20.90	28.20	106,999.76
7	E	25.40	27.62	98,432.28	TOTALS		673.74	910.19	2,924,952.68

Source: Program for Georgia Power Company headquarters, Atlanta, Georgia, by Heery & Heery, Architects and Engineers, of Atlanta, 1977.

to refinements in data and design. For instance, energy budgets may be established:

—At the outset of programming based on preliminary determination of facility function, size and climatic data to serve as a guide in development of other programmatic criteria and concepts

—As one conclusion of the program based on final program requirements and more precise data to guide development of design concepts

—After preliminary design to firmly establish the limit of design energy consumption, the performance goal

—During design development to evaluate progress toward meeting the goal or to revise the goal based on better data

A facility's energy budget can be used also in programming as the basis for analysis of the major energy-consuming components of the facility design. The budget figure can be divided proportionally among the different elements to show the relative amount of energy consumption of each component. Data on actual consumption by similar facilities in the same climate, broken down into component allocations, are necessary to perform this analysis. A percentage distribution can be obtained also from statistical data contained in BEPS technical backup reports or similar study reports. As shown in Exhibit 4-16, the percentage breakdown is applied to the total budget figure to provide the energy consumption estimates in Btu/gross square foot/year. The component energy allocation serves as a guide to which areas might offer the greatest opportunities for energy use reductions.

Resources. Very little material has been published on energy analysis in programming. At the time of this writing, the *AIA Energy Notebook* of The American Institute of Architects was developing a practice guide on the subject, however. In 1978, Caudill Rowlett Scott's Energy Task Group produced a booklet called *Energy Estimate Analysis*, which explained a procedure for energy use estimating in programming. Other sources of information on related topics include:

—*Energy Audits*, a supplement of the *AIA Energy Notebook*. Washington, D.C.: The American Institute of Architects, August 1979.

—*Energy Planning for Buildings*, by Michael M. Sizemore et al. Washington, D.C.: The American Institute of Architects, 1979.

—*Energy Conservation in Buildings: Techniques for Economical Design* by C.W. Griffin. Washington, D.C.: Construction Specifications Institute, 1974.

—*Energy Conservation Through Building Design*, Donald Watson, ed. New York: Architectural Record Books, 1979.

COST ANALYSIS. All too often, project costs are not considered adequately until the architect is well into the design. Finding out at that time that costs exceed budget or that operating expenses will be prohibitive usually means the architect must alter the program or change the design. This can be time-consuming and costly for the architect and/or the client, although some changes are inevitable and necessary. It is better to begin analyzing costs at the earliest possible stage of a project and to plan revisions at several points in the design process than to be forced to revise the design because some factor was neglected earlier.

A variety of cost analyses and cost elements are involved in cost planning and control. The programmer's principal concern is the project cost estimate, which is usually based mainly on an estimate of building construction costs. Other types of analysis may come within the purview of the programmer, however, either as part of programming or as separate services. These include life cycle cost analysis, cost-benefit analysis and value analysis. Each of the three is concerned with the worth of a project beyond the initial outlay of funds to get a facility designed, built and operating.

Project Cost Estimate. Cost estimates are, or should be, evolutionary, reflecting a series of refinements that lead toward the estimator's best prediction of how much money will have to be expended to complete the project. As program requirements are more precisely defined for a project and design solutions are proposed and selected, the estimate of their costs becomes increasingly definite and precise. Cost estimate revisions should be scheduled for each phase of work completion; e.g., program, schematic design, design development, construction documents.

At the predesign stage, major decisions are made about project feasibility, scope and function. These have direct bearing on the costs of a project, the client's budget and, consequently, on the limitations of the design. A determination of the cost implications of these factors, to the extent possible, not only will provide a more precise framework for design, but also can contribute to predesign decision making itself. If tradeoffs between design requirements and affordable design are to be made—and they are inevitable—it is sensible to begin making them, or at least identifying potential conflicts and opportunities, when design requirements are being determined in the program.

A program or other predesign cost estimate is a preliminary prediction of the probable cost of a project. Actually, all cost estimates are predictions, but the program estimate is the initial and roughest approximation. It is based on program requirements, the client's budget limits and current, local market conditions in terms of materials, labor and other economic factors. The main elements of a total project cost estimate include:

EXHIBIT 4-16. HYPOTHETICAL ENERGY BUDGET COMPONENT ANALYSIS

		Btu/sq. ft./yr.
A. Building Envelope	**10.5%**	**6,825**
1. Walls and windows	9.0%	5,850
2. Roof, floor and skylights	1.5%	975
B. Building Contents	**39.5%**	**25,675**
3. Occupants	2.5%	1,625
4. Ventilation	12.0%	7,800
5. Appliances	5.0%	3,250
6. Elevators, motors, fans and misc.	15.0%	9,750
7. Water heating	5.0%	3,250
C. Lighting Systems	**50.0%**	**32,500**
8. Task and general illumination	48.0%	31,200
9. Outdoor and special	2.0%	1,300
D. Total Energy Budget	**100.0%**	**65,000**

Source: *Energy Estimate Analysis*, CRS Energy Task Group. Houston, Texas: Caudill Rowlett Scott, Architects Engineers Planners, 1978.

—Building construction and site development costs

—Professional fees

—Management or administrative expenses of the client

—Allowances for contingencies and for movable equipment and furnishings

The project cost estimate also might include cost of land acquisition and/or demolition and analysis of interim and permanent financing costs. In addition, it might be possible to anticipate general operating costs, which is important in determining project feasibility and life cycle value.

One of the most important functions of predesign cost estimating is to ensure that all the major cost elements are included in the analysis, even if only rough approximations of value can be determined for some of them at the time. Once the cost element breakdown has been determined, it tends to become fixed for the duration of the project. Overlooking of one factor can, when it turns up later, change the effect and proportions of all the others and usually change design work completed.

In addition to identifying all significant cost elements, at the predesign stage, it is important to:

—Identify special conditions that might affect costs so that they can be investigated and analyzed

—Provide a reasonably accurate and complete prediction of costs, given available information and the preliminary nature of design requirements

—Anticipate escalation of costs during the term of the project

—Establish a procedure and schedule for reviewing and revising the cost estimate

The project cost estimate included in or accompanying the program is very preliminary and may be calculated by approximate methods such as the quick and easy technique illustrated in Exhibit 4-17. It indicates that estimates of most cost elements can be based on various per-centages of the building construction cost estimate. The percentage levels are usually developed from analysis of past experience and will vary depending on the type of facility, size and the quality and extent of work involved. Of course, if more exact figures are available for any item, they should be used instead.

Construction Cost Estimate. Construction is usually the largest single element of project costs, larger by many times than any other factor. It is important to predict construction cost as accurately as possible, even in the programming stage. A difference in calculation of only a fraction will affect other elements based on the construction estimate and alter the total project cost significantly. Such a difference can invalidate feasibility decisions, reduce or increase project scope and change the facility design.

There is a wide range of variables that affect and determine construction costs, such as building type, size and quality of construction. Construction estimates take into consideration the local costs of materials and labor, contractor's overhead and profit, unusual project requirements, contingencies and escalation of costs during the life of a project. These factors must be analyzed in increasing detail as the design becomes more completely delineated.

There also are various methods for analyzing cost factors and elements, each applicable to different stages of the design's development. For preliminary estimates, the primary method is the application of a unit cost standard to the sum total of units. Although unit standards take into account most of the cost-influencing factors, it is still important to examine specific factors in order to adjust for specific conditions of locale and current time.

The unit factor sometimes can be a *use unit* (e.g., cost per bed for hospitals, cost per student for schools) or a *building component unit* (such as floors and walls, fe-

EXHIBIT 4-17. HYPOTHETICAL PROJECT COST ESTIMATE

A. Building Costs	199,543 sq. ft. at $32.00/sq. ft.		$ 6,385,360
B. Fixed Equipment	(8% of A)		510,830
C. Site Development	(15% of A)		957,800
D. Total Construction	**(A+B+C)**		**$ 7,853,990**
E. Site Acquisition/Demolition			300,000
F. Movable Equipment	(8% of A)		510,830
G. Professional Fees	(6% of D)		471,240
H. Contingencies	(10% of D)		785,400
J. Administrative Costs	(1% of D)		78,540
K. Total Budget Required	**(D+E thru J)**		**$10,000,000**

Source: *Problem Seeking: An Architectural Programming Primer* by William M. Peña with William Caudill and John W. Focke. Boston: Cahners Books International, 1977.

nestration, HVAC systems etc.). The most frequently applied unit, however, is a *cost per square foot unit*. It is applied to the total gross area of a facility, or various unit costs are applied to differing functional areas.

Four key factors affect the use of a per-square-foot unit for estimating construction cost: net area or square footage, efficiency ratios, the specific unit cost, and levels of quality of various elements. The total net square footage is determined from the space calculations of the program. If unit costs differ for various functional areas of a facility (the unit cost of a high school gymnasium is likely to be different from the unit cost for classroom areas, for instance), the total area may be broken into separate groupings for calculation.

Net area is converted to gross area to perform the cost calculation. Gross area factors in space other than usable or assignable area; e.g., circulation corridors, mechanical rooms, walls, partitions. An efficiency ratio is used to make the conversion. It is the ratio of net area to gross area and is based on historical evidence for particular building types of particular sizes. Individual architecture firms determine their own efficiency ratios and sig-

nificant differences are often found for the same building type. The conversion calculation usually works like this example:

$$\frac{100,000 \text{ net sq. ft.}}{.50 \text{ efficiency factor}} = 200,000 \text{ gross sq. ft.}$$

Different efficiency ratios also may be applicable to different functional areas within the same facility. An efficiency ratio usually is expressed as a percentage figure, as in 50/50%, 60/40%, 75/25%; the numerator represents the efficiency factor. On the other hand, a gross-to-net ratio, also expressed as a percentage, would be multiplied by the net area to determine the gross area.

A unit cost standard is based on historical evidence gathered from cost performance in actual construction of a particular facility type. Some architecture firms have analyzed the cost history of facilities they have designed to determine unit costs. Others rely on construction indexes that are based on statistical averages on a national scale. Unit price indexes include *Building Construction Cost Data* published by Robert Snow Means Company of Duxbury, Mass.; *Dodge Construction Systems Costs*, published by McGraw-Hill Information Systems Com-

pany of New York; *Building Cost File*, published by Van Nostrand Reinhold Company of New York.

Statistical averages for unit costs (from indexes or by individual firms) have to be adjusted to recognize local market conditions and current economic factors. The base unit price also should be escalated to reflect increases in construction costs expected from the time the estimate is made to a point in the construction period.

The unit cost also varies depending on the level of quality of construction desired for the facility, ranging from no-frills to luxury status. Likewise, the quality level of the spatial/functional plan will vary the efficiency ratio.

Exhibit 4-18 demonstrates the application of per-square-foot units to predict a construction cost estimate. Note that in this case instead of an efficiency ratio, a certain percentage of net area allowing for unassigned space was added to the net area to determine the gross square footage.

Cost Evaluation. One measure of a facility's financial viability is the capital cost of construction. However, it is becoming increasingly important to measure the worth of a facility by criteria that indicate long-term value, return on investment or economic and social benefits compared to expenditure. Techniques such as life cycle cost estimating, value analysis and cost-benefit assessments are frequently applied to assist in making feasibility, program and design decisions.

The necessity of these measures is due primarily to rising costs of both capital investment and operating expenses, with energy costs playing a prominent role in the latter. The expense of building and using a facility has forced owners to use cost evaluation methods that improve the precision of investment decisions for both near and long terms. A brief description of three evaluative methods follows.

Life cycle cost analysis is a means of

ascertaining all recurring and nonrecurring costs of owning a facility during its expected life, from design and construction to accumulated annual operating and maintenance costs at the end of its useful life. Only costs are analyzed. It is used to make decisions or choices among alternatives.

Value analysis considers not only costs but a number of other values as well. It is a means of achieving a best possible balance between worth and cost based on analysis of functional worth. Various criteria are defined and weighted to apply to alternatives, anticipating a choice of one that represents the best balance of values.

Cost-benefit analysis reduces both the costs and the benefits of a facility to monetary values in order to compare them on a common basis. Formulas enable the analyst to determine if the ratio of benefits to costs justifies construction of a facility or if one alternative design is more or less economically advantageous than others.

Resources. *Problem Seeking: An Architectural Programming Primer* (William M. Peña with William Caudill and John W. Focke, Boston: Cahners Books International Inc., 1977) includes an excellent guide to cost estimating principles with clear explanations of efficiency ratios, unit cost determinants and quality variables.

"Construction Cost Control" by James Y. Robinson Jr., AIA, provides an overview of various cost estimating techniques as well as many other aspects of cost planning and control. It is Chapter 12 of *Current Techniques in Architectural Practice* (Robert Allan Class, AIA, and Robert E. Koehler, Hon. AIA, eds., Washington, D.C.: The American Institute of Architects and New York: Architectural Record Books, 1976).

"Life Cycle Costing" is an appendix to C.W. Griffin's book, *Energy Conservation in Buildings: Techniques for Economical Design* (Washington, D.C.:

Construction Specifications Institute, 1974).

Life Cycle Cost Analysis: A Guide for Architects (1977) and *Life Cycle Cost Analysis 2: Using It In Practice* (by David S. Haviland, 1978) are two publications of The American Institute of Architects.

Value Engineering in the Construction Industry (Alphonse J. Dell'Isola, New York: Construction Publishing Company, 2nd edition, 1974) explains value analysis.

Design Cost Analysis for Architects and Engineers by Herbert Swinburne, FAIA, is one of the latest books on the market and includes a chapter on cost analysis in programming and designing (New York: McGraw-Hill Book Company, 1980).

Scheduling. Scheduling is an essential element in any planning effort, from organizing the tasks of programming to projecting the sequence and duration of activities for design and construction of a facility. The factors that affect the time required to complete a project, no matter how uncomplicated it is, must be accounted for and coordinated in order to accomplish its objectives in a timely, efficient manner.

Scheduling is a means of determining the appropriate use of time and resources to accomplish a goal and the various activities involved in pursuing the goal. A schedule includes a list of activities or tasks, time estimates for each and their sum, and a sequence of performance. It enables the programmer, client and designer to visualize the components of work in terms of time and effort required, to project completion dates, to monitor work progress and to evaluate performance and costs.

Although a programmer may develop several different types of schedules for any project, the two most significant and common are the programming schedule

and the overall project schedule. The former is the time plan of the specific tasks to develop the program. It is a pre-programming effort, which is discussed in Chapter 2. The project schedule is the planned sequence of activities involved in developing a facility from its inception to its occupancy or beyond.

At the programming stage of facility development, the project schedule is not expected to define precisely all the task elements and their specific schedules. It is a preliminary estimate that will be reviewed, revised and updated during the course of design and construction as new information becomes available, unforeseen events occur and project changes are made. Nevertheless, the project schedule developed as a result of thorough programming should provide informed approximations of the total time required and projected completion dates; time estimates of routine activities of design, construction and occupancy to accommodate programmatic requirements; and implications of critical events and the special requirements and unusual circumstances that affect project duration.

Products. Of the several types of schedules that may result from programming, most fall into two general categories: those related to accomplishment of a specific goal or objective and those related to performance of routine or continuous activities. In each, however, the schedule must take into account all the factors and events that affect the performance of activities necessary to maintain or complete the project. Among the types of schedules associated with programming are:

—Programming schedule, an organized time plan that coordinates the tasks, resources and assigned responsibilities of developing a program

—Project schedule, the overall plan of effort to initiate and complete a facility project, including planning, programming, design, construction, financing,

EXHIBIT 4-18. EXAMPLE OF CONSTRUCTION COST ESTIMATE BASED ON SPACE PROGRAM

INTERIOR

Net programmed building area	9,650 sq. ft.		
Shared waiting for 40 people at 20 sq. ft./person	800 sq. ft.		
Shared secretarial stations, 3 at 75 sq. ft.	225 sq. ft.		
	10,675 sq. ft. net building area		
+20% for circulation, mechanical, walls, etc.	2,135 sq. ft.		
	12,810 sq. ft. gross	x$34.75/ sq. ft. =	$445,147.00
Budget for furnishing and interior graphics			17,500.00
			$462,647.00

EXTERIOR

Patios (crafts, teen center, social-nutrition)			
3 at 1000 sq. ft.	3,000 sq. ft.	x$1.00/sq. ft. =	3,000.00
Play area (child care and public)			
2 yards	6,000 sq. ft.	x$1.00/sq. ft. =	6,000.00
Walks and landscaping (including kiosk,			
exterior counseling)	12,000 sq. ft.	x$1.00/sq. ft. =	12,000.00
Parking (100 at 320 sq. ft. car)	32,000 sq. ft.		
+20% drives	6,400 sq. ft.		
	38,400 sq. ft.	x$.74/sq. ft. =	28,416.00
Service area	3,000 sq. ft.		
+20% drives	+ 600 sq. ft.		
	3,600 sq. ft.	x$.74/sq. ft. =	2,644.00
			$ 52,080.00

TOTAL	$514,727.00
ALLOWABLE BUDGET	$515,000.00

Source: Program for ''A'' Mountain Neighborhood Center, Tucson, Arizona, prepared by Architecture One
Ltd. of Tucson.

occupancy and other activities

—Design and/or construction schedule, usually a part of the project schedule, detailing the elements and durations for schematic design, design development, construction documents, bidding or negotiation, construction management and construction

—Occupancy schedule, a plan for equipping, furnishing, moving into, operating and maintaining a completed facility

—Projected use schedule, a long-term projection of potential alternative uses or of functional changes due to planned growth, anticipated circumstances and predicted needs

—Master plan or development schedule, a long-term forecast of development or expansion phase accomplishments

—Site development schedule, a plan of work for preparing a site to accommodate a facility

Procedure. Time is a vital element in the success of a project—both for the client and for the programmer and designer. Scheduling must realistically forecast the amount of time necessary to do an effective job while at the same time seeking to minimize the overall duration. Clear identification of the necessary tasks, accurate estimates of their time requirements and well-planned coordination of work performance are the essential ingredients of effective scheduling. These can be translated to the three principal components of a schedule:

—Individual activity or task elements required to achieve an objective or series of objectives

—Time estimates for each element and their sum

—A sequence of performance of activities or tasks that results in achievement of the objectives

There are various techniques for developing effective, efficient schedules for facility development. Several are discussed briefly following this section. The basic procedure for developing a schedule might include the following steps:

—Identify goals. This may seem elemental, but it is important to have a clear and agreed-upon agenda of what the project expects to accomplish. Priorities should be identified also.

—Identify the individual, independent activities or tasks necessary to achieve goals. These may break down into primary and subsidiary tasks.

—Assign responsibilities for performance of activities.

—For each appropriate activity, determine the types of resources needed for performance and appropriate quantities (e.g., professional and technical personnel, computer time usage, labor and materials, equipment).

—Estimate the amount of time necessary to accomplish each activity or task. Estimates may be based on previous experience, standards, consultant advice, or in some cases, formula calculations. A range of estimates for each is often appropriate; i.e., high, low and average.

—Determine an appropriate sequence of activities based on those that can be performed independently and those dependent on the results of others. This functional sequence should consider overlaps in responsibility, simultaneous performance and sequential interdependence.

—Based on time estimates and interdependencies, determine the duration of each activity, taking into consideration potential delays and unforeseen circumstances.

—Identify critical events or dates, both those affected by project work and those outside project control.

—Organize a calendar schedule based on activity durations, critical dates and functional sequence.

—Correlate schedule with other considerations such as products to be de-

livered (e.g., reports, drawings, cost estimates, construction phase completion), inflationary impacts of delays, availability of resources and personnel.

—Reorganize, if appropriate, into phases that represent completion of portions of work or delivery of products. On the other hand, phasing may be the organizing framework for developing the schedule; e.g., predesign, schematic design, design development and construction documents phases.

Bar Chart. A typical means of representing scheduling factors in design and construction is the bar graph or chart. Also called a Gantt Chart after the originator, Henry Gantt, it consists of a list of activities and time line for plotting the amount of time required for each activity by means of a horizontal bar extending an appropriate length opposite each listed item. A simple bar chart is illustrated in Exhibit 4-19. The time line is divided into equal segments, each representing a standard unit of elapsed time (day, week, month). Bars of varying length depict the beginning and end points of individual activities, the amount of elapsed time and the overlaps in performance time of each. A bar chart indicates neither the sequence of activities nor the interdependencies. This information can be inferred by substituting elapsed time units with calendar dates.

The technique is described more fully in Chapter 17 of a book, *Disciplined Creativity for Engineers*, by Robert L. Bailey.

Milestone Chart. Sequencing can be added to the bar chart concept by developing an ordered set of events or achievements and plotting them as points in the time line. On one side of a bar chart are listed the principal activities to be performed (or objectives to be achieved), and the corresponding time bars are installed. Significant events, deliverable products or expected achievements are listed on the opposite side or in a legend

EXHIBIT 4-19. SIMPLE BAR CHART SCHEDULE

	1980								1981											
	MAY	JUNE	JULY	AUG.	SEPT.	OCT.	NOV.	DEC.	JAN.	FEB.	MAR.	APR.	MAY	JUNE	JULY	AUG.	SEPT.	OCT.			
Program	▓	▓	▓	▓	▓																
Schematic Design				▓	▓																
Design Development						▓	▓														
Construction Documents								▓													
Bidding										▓	▓										
Construction												▓	▓	▓	▓	▓	▓	▓			
Evaluations			▓						▓		▓						▓	▓			

with a corresponding symbol (usually a number) representing each. These milestones may be either elements appropriate for several of the primary activities or the sequence of completed activities marking performance of the project work. This method is also discussed and illustrated in *Disciplined Creativity for Engineers*.

Activity Time Chart. This technique is similar to a CPM or PERT network plan (discussed below), but usually is not as sophisticated. As Alvin E. Palmer and M. Susan Lewis explain in *Planning the Office Landscape*, its purpose is to indicate all relevant activities, their starting and com-

pletion dates, interdependencies, and persons or groups responsible for their accomplishment. The chart shown in Exhibit 4-20 illustrates the process of planning explained in *Planning the Office Landscape*. In the chart, boxes represent activities; circles, the starting and completion points of activities; and arrows, the sequence and interdependencies among activities.

Network Charts. The two principal methods of network scheduling are CPM and PERT. They are used in a wide variety of applications, especially where projects or programs (not facility programs) consist of complex interconnections of numerous elements. PERT stands for Pro-

gram Evaluation and Review Technique and was developed as a management tool in the 1950s on the Navy's Polaris submarine project. CPM is the acronym for Critical Path Method, a technique developed specifically for construction scheduling by the DuPont Company.

Both are means of analyzing the performance elements of a project in order to determine its "critical path," the controlling or longest path through the interconnected network of elements necessary for achievement of project objectives. A PERT or CPM network consists of arrows representing activities and direction of progress, circles (usually enclosing a representative numeral) repre-

EXHIBIT 4-20. AN EXAMPLE OF A SIMPLE ACTIVITY TIME CHART

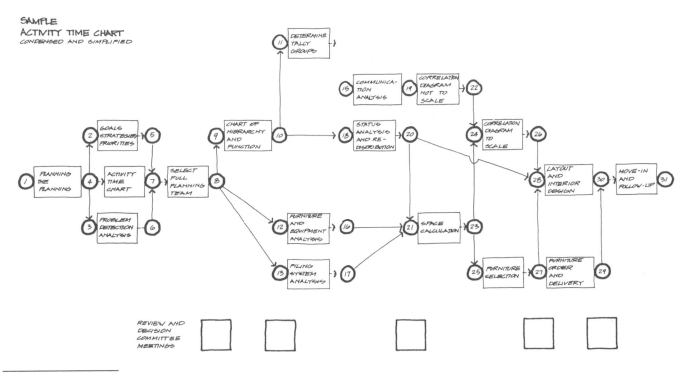

Source: *Planning the Office Landscape* by Alvin E. Palmer and M. Susan Lewis. New York: McGraw-Hill Book Company, 1977.

senting events, goals or end results of activities, and time estimates corresponding to each activity.

The procedure is based on detailing minutely the component activities and their corresponding events. An activity may be broken down into several component activities, for which separate arrows are created and corresponding events identified. Several activities may culminate in a single event, and an event may necessitate several activities. The resulting diagram may appear extremely complex, but it represents a thorough analysis of all the essential tasks involved in performing the project work. (See Exhibit 4-21.)

With a time estimate corresponding to each minute detail of work, it is possible to arrive at a precise total estimate by tracing each activity-event path and summing the times cumulatively. The network diagram also shows which series of activities can be performed simultaneously with others and which are sequentially dependent. It is a useful decision-making tool, since the interconnections indicate significant convergence of factors as well as all the component factors that must be considered at a particular decision point.

When first developed, CPM and PERT were highly sophisticated techniques requiring use of computers. They also had numerous differences in approach and method. Through use, however, the techniques have been simplified and the differences reduced to one or two, and sometimes none. The significant difference between the two in current usage is in the time estimate. While CPM provides a single time estimate for each activity, a PERT network presents three time estimates for each: optimistic, most likely and pessimistic. This range may provide flexibility in determining total project time. On the other hand, it provides an opportunity for improving the realism of an estimate through the use of a statistical calculation to compute a single "expected" time for an activity.

Computer applications for both PERT

EXHIBIT 4-21. A SIMPLIFIED NETWORK SCHEDULE FOR SCHEMATIC DESIGN PHASE

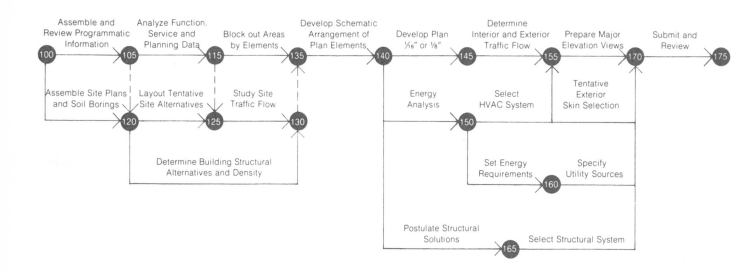

Source: *Planning the Office Landscape* by Alvin E. Palmer and M. Susan Lewis. New York: McGraw-Hill Book Company, 1977.

and CPM as well as other network scheduling systems such as Precedence Diagramming Method (PDM) have been developed. For more complex projects, automated computation is extremely beneficial.

Resources. PERT networks are concisely explained in *Disciplined Creativity for Engineers* (Chapter 17). Detailed discussion of CPM and PERT as well as network scheduling in general is found in "Network Scheduling" by James J. O'Brien, PE, in *Current Techniques in Architectural Practice*. Other references on scheduling include:

—*Scheduling Handbook*, James J. O'Brien. New York: McGraw-Hill Book Company, 1969.

—*Project Management with CPM and PERT*, Joseph J. Moder and Cecil R. Phillips. New York: Reinhold Book Corp., 1970.

—*Critical Path Scheduling*, Joseph Horowitz. New York: Ronald Press, 1967.

DATA ORGANIZATION

"Putting information together" is the simplest way to describe the task of organization. Analysis breaks data into com-

ponents so that they can be visualized, weighed, measured and categorized. Organization recombines information so that it can be evaluated, communicated or reanalyzed.

The first two techniques discussed in this section—relationship matrices and correlation diagrams—are methods of manipulating individual data elements so that a fundamental aspect of information—the relationships among people, parts, ideas, preferences and priorities—can be realized.

Two other methods discussed—analysis cards and worksheets—represent ways to facilitate and structure the col-

EXHIBIT 4-22. TRAIN SCHEDULE MATRIX

Depart/Arrive	Train			
	A	B	C	D
Washington, D.C.	8 am	9 am	10 am	11 am
Baltimore	9 am	10 am	11 am	12 n
Philadelphia	10 am	11 am	12 n	1 pm
New York	11 am	12 n	1 pm	2 pm

lection and analysis of data and the decision-making process.

RELATIONSHIP MATRICES. Establishing the patterns of interaction that exist or are desired within a facility or among its users often begins with a matrix study. A matrix is a relatively simple device that, in its basic form, consists of vertical columns intersecting horizontal rows. Simple matrices can be drawn freehand easily and often are sketched on the spot to work out possible combinations between sets of factors. A train schedule is an example of what a matrix looks like and how it functions, although it does not represent adequately its use for programming, as shown in Exhibit 4-22.

A matrix is one of the most extensively used devices for identifying, defining and/or measuring the relationships among individual items of information. In the train schedule, time is the relationship factor that is demonstrated and it appears at each intersection of a column and a row. Almost any type of relationship between pairs of factors can be demonstrated with a matrix, but only one type can be shown by a single matrix.

The train schedule example also demonstrates clearly the value and the limitation of a matrix. It would be impossible to fix a departure time of a train by simply matching the train to a location. The

schedule of stops of any one train had been figured out before the matrix schedule was created. The matrix serves as a convenient form for *organizing* and *displaying* the information of several schedules in one comprehensive schedule. It enables a traveler to see at a glance all the possible departures and arrivals and traveling periods between any two of several points and to choose the arrangement that best fits traveling needs.

Unlike the train schedule, which displays predetermined data, many matrices are used in the performance of relationship calculations. However, as the train schedule shows, a matrix itself does not perform the calculation nor determine the relationship. It is a means of systematically representing calculations either after they have been enumerated or while the computation is being performed. For example, an adjacency matrix is frequently used in programming to identify which spaces need to be arranged in close proximity to each other and which don't. The matrix provides a structure for organizing the calculations systematically and for visualizing all the possible adjacencies among the list of spaces. One by one, each space is matched to another and a judgment is made as to whether the two need to be adjacent. It would be possible to enumerate a long list of pairs of spaces, but the matrix abbreviates this procedure and dis-

plays the information in a more comprehensible fashion.

Products. Computation of individual relationships between factors is not difficult. It is difficult, however, to visualize the pattern of individual relationships that may exist within a set of several factors. The organizing structure of a matrix makes the computation more convenient and enables the matrix maker to perceive individual interactions in relation to the total set of interactions. The matrix enables a programmer to: organize calculation of relationships among several factors, record them in a systematic order, visualize the total system of relationships, perceive patterns among relationships for further analysis, and display conclusive statements of relationship.

The general uses for which a matrix may be employed include:

—Collect and record data directly about relationships, as in a questionnaire or interview
—Enumerate possible combinations of factors and isolate significant combinations
—Analyze previously determined relationship data
—Summarize optimum relationship data
—Communicate conclusive data
—Describe existing conditions or predict desirable relationships
—Initiate more sophisticated analysis of relationships

As the last item in the above list indicates, the data produced by a matrix may not be sufficient to warrant conclusions about the relationship patterns that are or ought to be. The reason is that matrices are based on "pairwise comparisons"; that is, only two factors are coordinated at one time. A completed matrix provides an organized record of all the possible relationships among a specific number of factors on a one-to-one basis, but it must be examined further to determine how the

EXHIBIT 4-23. BOX MATRIX

FACTOR	A	B	C	D	E
1					
2					
3					
4					

EXHIBIT 4-24. MATRIX COMPARISON OF FACTORS WITHIN A SINGLE SET

FACTOR	A	B	C	D	E
A					
B					
C					
D					
E					

EXHIBIT 4-25. SIMPLE ADJACENCY MATRIX

SPACE	A	B	C	D	E
A	–	1	0	0	1
B	1	–	1	1	0
C	0	1	–	0	1
D	0	1	0	–	0
E	1	0	1	0	–

group of factors are interrelated in total. It is fairly easy to see the total interaction pattern in a simple matrix of only a few factors. When the number of factors is large, however, or when a second dimension of relatedness (such as relative value) is added to the computation, the significant patterns become more difficult to isolate. The matrix data, then, has to be subjected to further or different analysis. Moreover, a matrix cannot be used to determine the relationships among more than two sets of variables or to calculate more than one or two dimensions of relatedness. However, a matrix often provides the initial data for more sophisticated multivariate analysis or multidimensional measurement.

Among the types of information that may be processed by matrix are:
—Functional relationships
—Organizational relationships
—Space relationships (adjacency, proximity)
—Activity relationships
—Activity to context relationships (e.g., adjacency to alley for service, to site edge for views)
—Sensory conflict (environments required vs. stimuli produced)
—Priority ranking of relationships

—Preference measures (see Chapter 3)
—Correlations among variables

Procedure. Several different names are ascribed to matrices, some of which refer to the type of relationship to be identified. Some of the more common descriptors are relationship, interaction, affinity, adjacency and compatibility or incompatibility. The general procedures for constructing and applying matrices are the same for all of them. As mentioned earlier, the basic form of a matrix consists of intersecting columns and rows. Together they form a box that contains a series of smaller boxes where column and row intersect and represent the relationship between each of two factors. This is sometimes referred to as a *box matrix,* like the one in Exhibit 4-23.

Only one type of relationship between factors can be demonstrated in a single matrix, although the relationship may be expressed in terms of two dimensions. For instance, an adjacency matrix may indicate both which rooms in a building should be located near each other and how important the adjacencies are on a scale of priority.

The matrix pictured above is intended

to identify relationships between two different sets of factors. However, a matrix operates at its best efficiency in a comparison of one set of factors among themselves, as pictured in Exhibit 4-24.

In using a matrix, it is important that all the factors or variables to be related are included in the computation. Any number of factors can be related by means of the matrix. However, very large numbers of factors (more than 25) decrease the efficiency of visualizing the patterns of interrelation and increase the possibility of errors in computation. It may be necessary to reduce the number of factors by some means before analyzing them by matrix. Automated data processing reduces these limitations. A computer can be programmed to produce a series of increasingly refined matrices in which the data are reduced to manageable proportions automatically.

The means of recording a relationship calculation are varied. The relationship may be expressed by merely marking the box when a relationship exists and leaving it blank when it doesn't. Frequently a binary form is used in which "1" represents a positive response and "0" represents a negative. The interaction may also be expressed in terms of a value from a range of values, such as +1 to −1. The intersection of column and row may also provide space for inserting appropriate relationship data, as in the train schedule where departure time is the significant relationship factor.

The adjacency or affinity matrix is a type frequently used in facility programming. An example is provided in Exhibit 4-25 to illustrate the matrix procedure. In this case, a list of spaces to be included in a building under design are compared to each other in order to determine which should be located in close proximity. Relationship is expressed in binary form, with "1" indicating a necessary adjacency and "0" representing indifference to adjacency.

Note that it is unnecessary to record the relationship of one factor to itself since that is obvious. Also note that each factor has been compared to each other factor twice so that the computations recorded above the diagonal (from top left to bottom right) are identical to those below it. Where relationships among the same set of factors are mutual one-to-one, as in adjacency, this duplication will always occur. A different relationship measure may not produce a mutual attraction. However, in cases such as adjacency it is possible to eliminate half the matrix computation with a modified form known as a *half-matrix*, which is illustrated in Exhibit 4-26.

The half-matrix example lists the primary functions of a newspaper and shows which functions are interdependent. The degree of interdependence is indicated by a key code. Half the work of completing the matrix has been eliminated, since the interdependence between the editorial function and the production function, for instance, would be a duplicate response of that between the production and the editorial functions.

This matrix may be presented in the final program to guide the designer in determining which operations need to be organized in proximity to each other. Further

EXHIBIT 4-26. A HALF-MATRIX SHOWING ADJACENCY RELATIONSHIPS

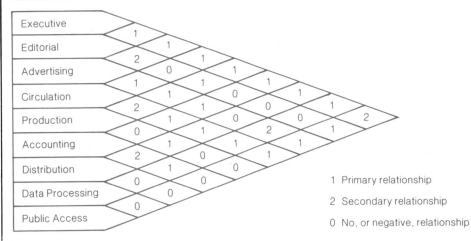

1 Primary relationship

2 Secondary relationship

0 No, or negative, relationship

analysis, however, could provide the designer a clearer picture of how to group functions with primary interdependence, secondary interdependence and no interdependence so that all proximity needs are satisfied adequately.

CORRELATION DIAGRAMS. Another widely used, versatile group of techniques for organizing data to demonstrate relationship is correlation diagrams. They are produced in many varieties and for different purposes. The primary objective, however, is to help visualize the patterns of relationship among large numbers of variables or comprehend the interrelationship of elements in a complex problem, issue or situation. Schematic and detailed design drawings could be said to be complex correlation diagrams. Most working diagrams are less comprehensive, although many are no less sophisticated.

The value of illustrative representations is summarized by J. Christopher Jones in comparing one type, an interaction net, to the interaction matrix. The following quote is from *Design Methods: Seeds of Human Futures.*

The only advantage of a net over a matrix is the ease with which net patterns can be perceived and the problem under-stood. Matrices and nets are complementary ways of expressing a single set of relationships. The matrix enables a pattern that is too complex for the brain to generate all at once to be built up piece-by-piece outside the brain. A net of the same connections permits the assimilation of this pattern, once it has been completed and checked, back into the brain from whence came its constituent parts. Thus the brain can use an external aid to discover patterns among pieces of information that were originally understood only in isolation.

The complementary relationship between interaction matrices and correlation diagrams is especially relevant since the diagram often is based on data obtained from a matrix. Generally, a diagrammatic representation is a new iteration of data which were first identified and isolated by some means, related by matrix and finally recomposed to demonstrate their correlation.

The purpose of correlation diagrams is to organize data into a representative and comprehensible composition for the analysis of data, the evaluation of conclusions or the communication of information. A diagram may express relationships among parts, factors or states of being, or it may

EXHIBIT 4-27. TWO TYPES OF CORRELATION DIAGRAMS FOR THE SAME AREA

(From a new facilities program for an herb tea production company. Program was developed by architects Alan Brown, Roland Hower and Phil Tabb, AIA, who were formerly associated in the firm Joint Ventures Inc. of Boulder, Colorado.)

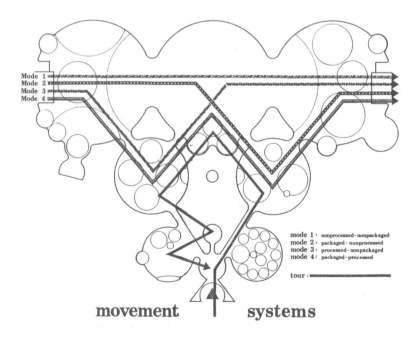

Source: New Facilities Program for Celestial Seasonings of Boulder, Colorado, by Joint Venture Inc. Architects, Environmentalists, Visionaries of Boulder, Colorado.

124   TECHNIQUES AND TOOLS OF PROGRAMMING

express the dynamic interaction among events, activities or processes. Most frequently, it reveals both relationship and interaction. Although not limited to depicting functional and physical space relationships, this is the primary use to which the correlation diagram is put in programming.

Products. There is a great variety of graphic representations used to display and analyze relational patterns. New versions continually appear as programmers and designers attempt to clarify the meaning of relationship and interaction in creative ways. Some of the standard types of correlation diagrams include:

—Bubble diagram, interaction net, link-node diagram, cluster diagram
—Social map, behavior map, sociogram
—Adjacency/proximity diagrams, functional relationship diagram
—Dual graph, point graph
—Block diagram, layout diagram
—Flow pattern diagram
—Organizational chart, chart of hierarchy
—Circuit diagram, Smith diagram

Some of these are discussed later in this section. Examples of two types of correlation diagrams are shown in Exhibit 4-27. They represent different aspects of the same functional area, a proposed new facility for an herb tea producer. One shows functional relation by position among the various functions to be housed in the facility; the other shows the movement patterns of primary processes in herb tea production.

Graphic analysis will show a variety of aspects of a problem, issue or situation. Exhibit 4-28 is a random listing of some relational dimensions that can be shown by correlation diagrams, depending on the various types. More specifically, a correlation diagram may reveal or display the following:

—Connection between individual parts or elements

—Strength or importance of connections
—Relationship pattern of the whole construct
—Grouping or clustering of variables
—Disassociation and/or differentiation among variables
—Dynamic interaction among elements

As already mentioned, the correlation diagram technique is particularly valuable in programming for depicting relationships among functions and/or spaces. Some diagrammatic measures can be used to generate or analyze floor plans. Diagrams also can be adjusted by application of additional criteria, such as rearranging functional areas to group those that need to be in use around the clock or that require continuous cooling.

Procedures. Construction of correlation diagrams varies depending on the type of graphic and the purpose of its use, as well as the type of information available. Most diagrams consist of three basic elements: lines, symbols and space. It is obvious that diagram *space* is essential, but it can be used also to enhance depiction of relative position, distance and value among elements represented. *Symbols* represent the individual factors or elements that are significant to the problem. They may be points, circles, blocks, "bubbles," geometric shapes, pictures or any simple graphic form.

The dynamics of the relationship diagram, however, are found in the *lines*. They demonstrate the quality or the dimensions of the relationship. Most of the dimensions listed in Exhibit 4-28 are expressed by the lines of a diagram, whose principal functions are to connect, enclose and divide symbols. Different line characteristics express different dimensions, specifically:

—Line length; showing functional, social or physical distance from, to and between functional, social or physical elements

—Line width or number of lines between element pairs; showing value, strength, importance of connection
—Line direction; showing direction, source and endpoint, hierarchy
—Line pattern; showing grouping, division, enclosure, overall relational pattern

Exhibit 4-29 presents an example of the use of a series of correlation diagrams to isolate specific elements of major functions, specify interdependences among functions, cluster functional areas, and show relative proximities of each function to each other function. Concentric circles enhance representation of functional distance, measuring relative proximity more precisely than line length.

The procedures for developing various correlation diagrams involve two or three general steps:

—Collect and analyze data to identify

EXHIBIT 4-28. RANDOM LISTING OF RELATIONAL DIMENSIONS

Linkage
Connection
Attraction
Mutual Influence
Selection
Preferential Relation
Interdependence
Exchange
Communication
Dysfunction
Disassociation
Adjacency
Proximity
Social/Physical Distance
Movement
Direction
Grouping
Cluster
Pattern
Arrangement
Organization
Hierarchy

EXHIBIT 4-29. A SERIES OF FUNCTIONAL RELATIONSHIP DIAGRAMS ILLUSTRATE VARIOUS DIMENSIONS

(From the program identified in Exhibit 4-27.)

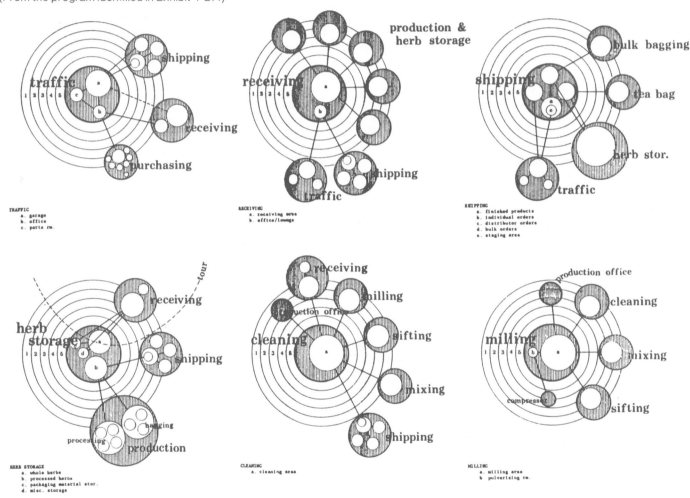

Source: New Facilities Program for Celestial Seasonings of Boulder, Colorado, by Joint Venture Inc. Architects, Environmentalists, Visionaries of Boulder, Colorado.

the significant variables. The relationships among elements of simpler problems or issues may be apparent at once or easily identified through diagramming each related pair of elements one by one until all relations are depicted. More complex situations, however, require an intermediate step.

—Organize the data by rank ordering or relationship matrix, depending on the correlation technique used, so that relationships are identified, fully enumerated and displayed for retrieval.

—The new data on relationships then can be translated into a correlation diagram. It may take two or more attempts

or iterations to produce a diagram that simplifies and clarifies the relational pattern of the elements. In other cases, one type of diagram may be used as a preceding iteration to another type that expresses data differently or more clearly.

Types of Correlation Diagrams. The

numerous types of correlation diagrams (some have been listed previously) vary according to the kind of relationship they demonstrate and according to the general type of representation they employ. The matrix in Exhibit 4-30 indicates that different diagrams can be used best to show one or more of four principal types of relation: functional, physical, social, and relationships among other types of factors. It also categorizes diagrams according to three forms of graphic representation: abstract, pictorial and scaled.

Resources. To present information effectively, correlation diagrams should conform to requirements of proportionality, representativeness and organization. These and other diagram construction standards, as well as many types of diagrams, are examined in a book called *Graphic Problem Solving for Architects and Builders* by Paul Laseau (Boston: Cahners Books International, 1975).

Social Map. This is similar to the behavioral map discussed under observation techniques (in Chapter 3) in that social characteristics are plotted on a scaled drawing such as a floor plan, room layout plan or map. In the case of social maps, however, social attitudes, rather than observed behavior, are recorded. Since attitudes—specifically, preferred social relations among individuals—are not observable directly, data on user preferences must be collected first and then analyzed by other methods. A rank ordering of a group's social preferences can be used to identify preference clusters, which may help organize the map more easily. The individual social preferences are plotted on a layout diagram which shows the stationary positions of individuals within the setting. Preference is indicated by arrow (directional line) leading from one individual's position and pointing to the preferred individual's position.

The technique is useful for showing how

EXHIBIT 4-30. TYPE OF RELATIONSHIP AND FORM OF REPRESENTATION EXHIBITED BY DIFFERENT CORRELATION DIAGRAMS

	RELATIONSHIP				REPRESENTATION		
	FUNCTIONAL	PHYSICAL	SOCIAL	FACTOR	ABSTRACT	PICTORIAL	SCALED
Social Map		●	●		●		●
Sociogram			●		●		
Behavior Map	●	●	●		●		●
Bubble Diagram	●	●		●	●	●	
Link-Node Diagram	●		●	●	●	●	
Block Diagram	●	●			●	●	
Interaction Net	●		●	●	●		●
Dual Graph		●		●	●		●
Adjacency Diagram		●				●	●
Functional Relationship Diagram	●				●	●	
Layout Diagram		●					●
Flow Diagram	●			●	●		
Organizational Chart	●		●			●	

an existing setting might be rearranged to accommodate relational preferences, either in terms of the functional organization or the physical setting. Examples of how it has been applied are given in *Methods of Architectural Programming* by Henry Sanoff.

Exhibit 4-31 is an example of a social map in which individuals in a suite of offices might have been asked which single individual they preferred to work with closely. The pattern of preferences shows how the office setting might be rearranged to match expressed preferences, by either moving individuals or altering the physical layout.

Sociogram. Similar to the social map, and also described in Sanoff's book, the sociogram shows preferred social rela-

EXHIBIT 4-31. SOCIAL MAP INDICATING SOCIAL PREFERENCES OF
INDIVIDUALS

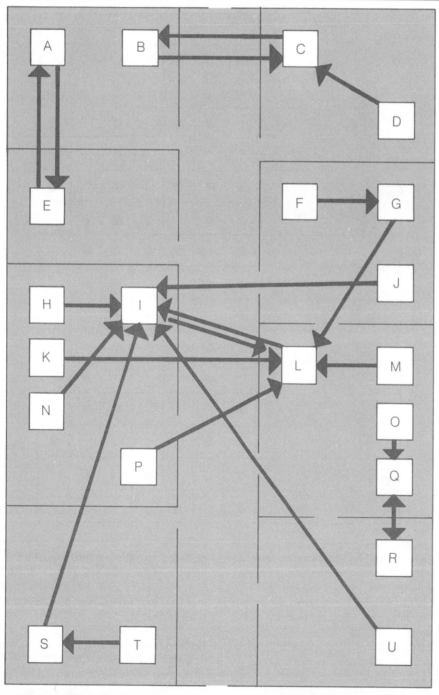

tions between pairs of individuals within a group and the group relational pattern as a sum of the pairings. The analysis is not related directly to a physical setting, but concentrates on the social organization. Relying on previously collected data, the sociogram uses arrows to indicate connection and direction as well as relationship reciprocity. Positioning of symbols (simple graphics such as circles to represent individuals) and arrow direction indicate individual status within the group as perceived by other members and the group as a whole.

Sociograms may be either mutual-choice to show peer relations or hierarchical to show status variations. The sum of individual preferences can reveal cluster associations among various members of a group. These kinds of interpretations depend on the nature of the questions addressed to the investigated group and on the type of analysis performed. Sociologists and other behavioral scientists skilled in social analysis may be helpful or necessary in both the development of proper data and sociogram interpolation.

Sociograms are useful for identifying and defining the underlying social structure of a formal organization. This information can be helpful in organizing an efficient functional structure for a physical setting. Exhibit 4-32 presents a sociogram showing the same data on social relations as indicated by Exhibit 4-31. Note that it shows four distinct clusters of individuals; i.e., those linked together continuously.

Bubble Diagram. A simplistic but effective form of correlation diagram, a bubble diagram consists of "bubbles" or "balloons" that represent factors, functional elements or physical aspects, and lines that indicate connection. Bubbles may be overlapped or joined to show adjacency and interdependence, positioned to show relative proximity or relation significance and/or connected by lines to show specific relationships and the value or inten-

EXHIBIT 4-32. SOCIOGRAM INDICATING SOCIAL PREFERENCES OF INDIVIDUALS

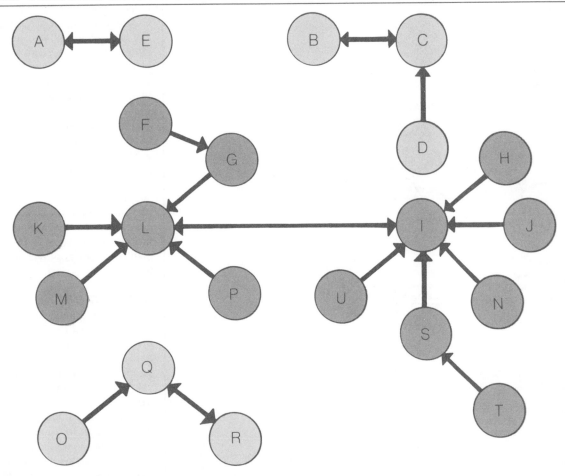

sity of them. Exhibit 4-33 is an example of a bubble diagram.

Preliminary conceptualization of an idea or fact is frequently expressed by free-hand bubble diagram, a method used by programmers at Caudill Rowlett Scott (CRS) of Houston, Texas, to illustrate and record information on analysis cards (a technique described later in this chapter). On the other hand, bubble diagrams have been programmed into computer graphic systems (such as the ARK 2 and PEAC systems employed by Cost, Planning and Management International Inc. of Des Moines, Iowa). The computer generates

bubble diagrams automatically from relationship matrices to identify room relationship patterns and floor plan layouts.

Link-node Diagram. Another relatively simple diagram to show straightforward connections among elements is the link-node. As illustrated in Exhibit 4-34, the diagram consists of nodes that represent connected or unconnected elements and lines that link elements together. The size and position of nodes are insignificant. The connection of elements can be built up one-by-one and the resulting completed pattern will indicate clusters of re-

lated elements. Clustering is a primary objective of simple link-node diagrams. This dimension can be enhanced by the addition of another dimension, the value or intensity of relationship between individual elements, represented by line thickness or number of lines between nodes. The greater the width or plurality of connection, the more significant the relationship.

The source of data on the relative value of relationships in the link-node diagram is a rating or ranking of the individual elements.

Interaction Net. A more complex procedure for analyzing relationship patterns,

EXHIBIT 4-33. BUBBLE DIAGRAM

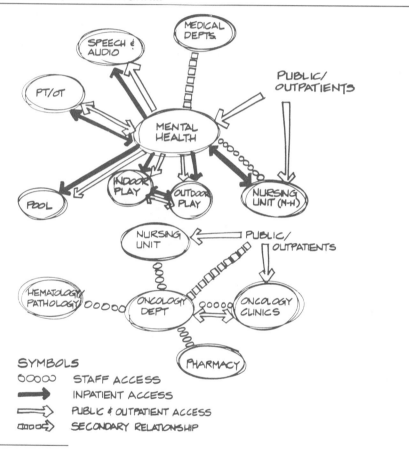

SYMBOLS
- ◦◦◦◦◦ STAFF ACCESS
- ➤ INPATIENT ACCESS
- ⇨ PUBLIC & OUTPATIENT ACCESS
- ▭▭▭⇨ SECONDARY RELATIONSHIP

Source: Development Plan for The Children's Hospital of Denver by Kaplan/McLaughlin Architects/Planners, San Francisco, 1976.

especially among functions and spaces, is the interaction net. Depending on the number and variation of element relations, the interaction net method may require a series of iterations to simplify the relational pattern sufficiently. The source of data for diagram construction is a previously developed interaction matrix.

Development begins by representing all the elements in the set, usually arranged in a circle. The relationship of each element to each other element then is plotted one-by-one by straight line. An intensity dimension may be included by varying the width of lines. A completed graph of an interaction net such as this is shown in Exhibit 4-35.

This first step enumerates by diagram all the interactions previously identified in a matrix. However, the interaction pattern of the whole set may be no clearer than when the individual pairs were listed by matrix. A second graph is necessary. It is created by "unfolding" the graph, or rearranging the elements so that none of the connecting lines cross each other. The second iteration is shown in Exhibit 4-35 also. Other iterations may be necessary or desirable to arrange the elements so that those most closely associated are po-

sitioned near each other or so that alternative layouts can be displayed.

A layout diagram may be created from the interaction net to organize a physical setting such as a room or a single floor plan. The net can be superimposed on an existing layout plan to check the functional efficiency of the plan.

Block Diagram. Similar to, but more geometrically precise than, a bubble diagram, a block diagram may be used to show organization of functional or activity areas. Each area is represented by a square or rectangle that is proportionally sized to the relative amount of space required for the function. Arrangement of the blocks provides a preliminary layout plan for client approval and designer action.

ANALYSIS CARDS. The analysis card technique is based on the use of a collection of index cards to organize and reorganize programming information. Each card carries a single piece of data. As an idea or new item of information is developed, it is condensed to a pithy, graphically descriptive form and presented on an index card (ideally 5″ × 8″, for ease of conversion to 35 mm slides). The purpose of this itemization is to increase the flexibility of data organization in the programming and schematic design phases. As the data are collected and converted to analysis cards, the cards are tacked to a bulletin board for arrangement, consideration, rearrangement and deletion or modification.

The working advantage of the analysis card method centers around the ease of organization and reorganization of data. By keeping information in small, individual bits, the classification process is simplified. Also, the obstacle of the programmer's preconceived notions of information association is reduced when the information is separated physically on two or more cards. As additional cards are included in the program, their relation to the existing information bank of cards can be demonstrated quickly by relative positioning on the display board.

The display of organized analysis cards provides an instant picture of project status and progress. The client can be familiarized quickly with project ideas. The ease of manipulation enables the programmer to test interrelationships among considerations. This flexibility is also an aid to the design team once programming is completed.

For presentation, the analysis cards can be converted to 35 mm slides or can be shown individually by opaque projector. Such a graphic representation reduces the amount of necessary oral explanation, increasing the efficiency of information flow to the audience. Likewise, the cards can be photocopied on 8½″ × 11″ paper and, supplemented with written explanation, can be transformed into a written program report.

Procedure. The technique is described in *Problem Seeking: An Architectural Programming Primer* by William M. Peña with William Caudill and John W. Focke. The book provides eight pointers for constructing analysis cards:

— *Think your message through.* Reduce the information or idea to its simplest terms. If the card is not big enough to hold all of one idea, odds are that the idea can be broken into smaller parts. The goal is to create a card that conveys its intended message at a single glance.

— *Use visual images.* Try to express the concept graphically, with as few words as possible. But do not eliminate words altogether. Label parts of the diagram and give the card a title. To emphasize the magnitude of numbers, draw diagrams to appropriate scale. To maintain the implication of ideas, images must be kept simple and straightforward.

— *Use very few words.* Emphasize the meaning of the drawing with one short

EXHIBIT 4-34. SIMPLE (A) AND COMPLEX (B) LINK-NODE DIAGRAMS

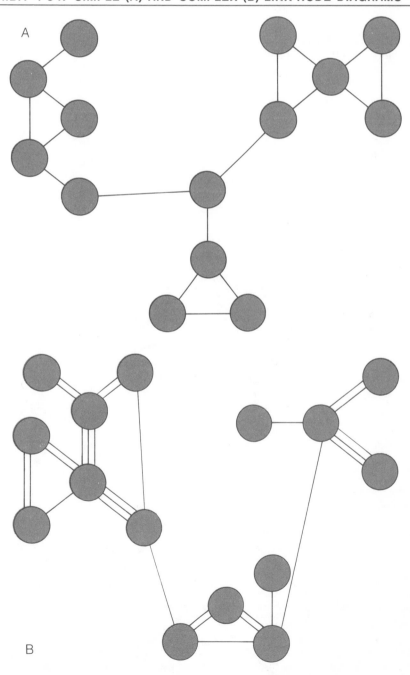

EXHIBIT 4-35. TWO ITERATIONS OF AN INTERACTION NET

(Relationships depicted are from a relationship matrix shown in Exhibit 4-26, which is reproduced here for convenience. In the second iteration, the "Executive" function has been omitted to simplify the diagram.)

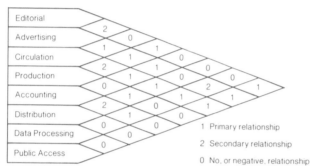

1 Primary relationship

2 Secondary relationship

0 No, or negative, relationship

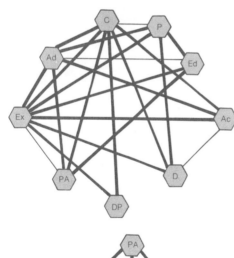

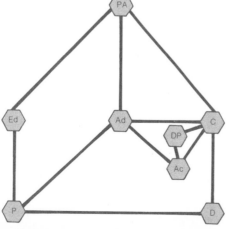

sentence. The objective is speed of comprehension for the person glancing over the analysis card arrangement.

—*Strive for legibility.* Legibility is a function of line width and letter height, according to Peña, who says typewriter print is too small. Minimum letter height should be ⅛", and pen-line width should be #2 or larger.

—*Design for display.* As opposed to book illustrations, analysis cards should be legible enough for a wall display. As in lettering, the size and boldness of the drawings should aid legibility.

—*Plan for cards of different levels of refinement.* Each analysis card will be produced in three forms: "think," "working" and "presentation." Think cards are made at the moment an idea occurs. Done quickly, the purpose is to capture a thought before it is forgotten. Working cards are more carefully thought and drawn out. They must be clear enough to work with, but not so meticulously done as to waste time. The presentation cards are the ultimate product for client review and designer use and are very carefully drawn by one person for consistency.

—*Encourage documentation.* All new thoughts should go down on paper immediately. The purpose of the "think" cards is to relieve the programming team from the stigma of producing presentation-quality work on the first try. After putting the thoughts to paper, they can be reviewed readily and segmented or redrawn as necessary.

—*Plan for "routine" cards.* Order two dozen printed base maps on analysis cards. Routine site information to be considered separately can be then put on separate cards with a minimum of repetitive work. Climate information can be recorded on preprinted gridded analysis cards as well.

Analysis cards are depicted in Exhibit 4-36.

WORKSHEETS. The use of chalkboards

EXHIBIT 4-36. EACH ANALYSIS CARD CONVEYS A SINGLE THOUGHT

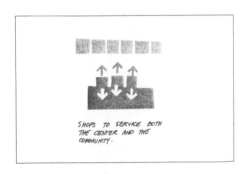

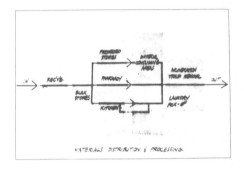

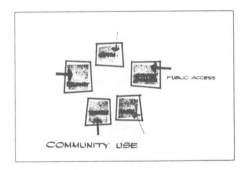

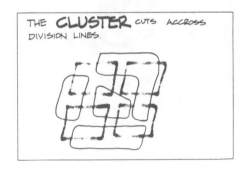

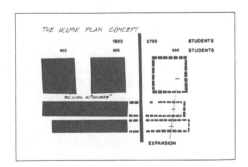

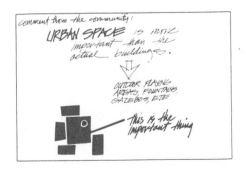

Source: *Problem Seeking: An Architectural Programming Primer*, William M. Peña with William Caudill and John W. Focke. Boston: Cahners Books International Ltd., 1977.

EXHIBIT 4-37. EXAMPLE OF A "BROWN SHEET"

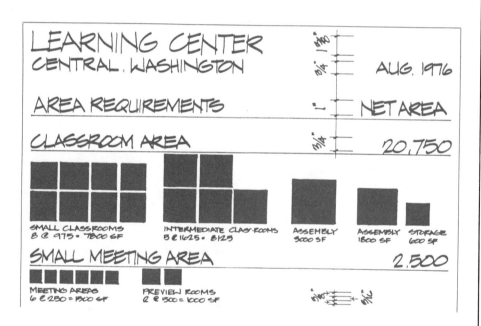

and display-sized worksheets is a common practice in group work sessions. Quick sketches, preliminary outlines, rapid listing of ideas and the interminable revisions, corrections and rearrangements associated with work sessions are easily accommodated by these media. The worksheet has been refined to a sophisticated technique by the firm of Caudill Rowlett Scott (CRS) of Houston, Texas. Their method is to employ sheets of brown wrapping paper and, hence, has earned the title of "brown sheet" technique. It is used primarily for space programming.

Brown sheets serve three functions in the CRS programming systems:

—To present graphically to the client initial information on the number and sizes of spaces (area requirements) of a project

—To be a working tool on which revisions, corrections, additions and reallocation of space needs can be made quickly and conveniently while keeping track of the impact of changes on all parts of the space program

—When the final figures are worked out, to present a graphic and precise numerical accounting of the client's area requirements to the designer

Procedure. A complete description of the method is found in Peña's book, *Problem Seeking: An Architectural Programming Primer*. The brown sheets are intended to convey a comprehensive image of the scope of area requirements for an entire project. Sheets of brown paper (36″ wide) are hung on a wall, where they remain during development of the space program. Each sheet contains information on one or more functional areas. At a glance, the programmer and client can visualize the entire space needs of the project and its individual parts.

Data are recorded on the sheets in two forms. Squares of white contact paper (adhesive-backed and cut to proportionate sizes) represent individual spaces in

Source: *Problem Seeking: An Architectural Programming Primer*, William M. Peña with William Caudill and John W. Focke. Boston: Cahners Books International Ltd., 1977.

size and number. Descriptive data (including functional categories and subcategories, titles of space types, size and number of each space) and area sizes are recorded with felt-tipped markers and pens. In the working stages, alterations are made with white chalk, brown paper patches and replacement of white squares.

The data are organized according to major categories of functions to be accommodated by the facility. Under each category, a row of variously sized white squares is arranged in groups representing the number of spaces in subcategories. Each subarea is titled and identified by size and number of spaces included. The total area of the category in square feet is indicated at the end of each row. These are net areas and a total net area is recorded at the end of the final sheet or the end of the space program summary sheet. A net-to-gross conversion factor is applied to the total to produce the gross area requirement.

The preliminary space program in the form of brown sheets is presented to the client for review and revision. In work sessions, the brown sheets are altered repeatedly. The client may determine, for instance, that more or less space is required for certain functions or that the budget calls for reduction in total area. Allocation of space may have to be revised for any number of reasons. White squares can be removed easily, added, or replaced with appropriate sizes. Figures are crossed out and substituted for new ones. Data are patched over and updated information overlaid.

Changes in one area impact other areas. Whenever an alteration is made, consequent alterations in other areas and in total requirements are made instantly in order to maintain an accurate, up-to-the-moment accounting of space needs. After all compromises, reallocations and corrections are completed, a final version of the brown sheets is prepared. This is photographed in reduced form (standard 8½″ × 11″) and inserted in the program report for presentation to the designer. An example of a thoroughly revised brown sheet is presented in Exhibit 4-37.

ORGANIZED ANALYSIS AND ANALYTICAL ORGANIZATION OF DATA. The heart of information processing combines the interacting counterparts of analysis and organization. The programmer must organize data in order to analyze them. The analysis of data to discover their significance and relation to each other is necessary for effective organization of meaningful program conclusions. Together they produce the design concepts which the programmer communicates to the client and designer for evaluation. However, in order to analyze and organize information, there must be effective communication among all participants in the programming process. The next chapter begins with techniques that foster communication among programmer, client and designer for efficient analysis and organization of data, as well as for effective collection and evaluation.

Chapter 5
Techniques for Communication and Evaluation

Communication is a critical factor in both the effective development and presentation of programmatic information. Many different people, with differing backgrounds and perspectives, are involved in the development and use of a program. Concepts and data must be conveyed among them in a manner that accurately portrays the meanings and purposes.

This chapter first examines several techniques that are useful in the creative production, analysis, organization and evaluation of information by participants in program development. In the second section, methods and procedures for effectively documenting and presenting program information are discussed. The material is intended to provide general guidance to principles of use of written, oral and graphical media.

The chapter also includes a sampling of concepts and techniques of evaluation. These principles may be applied to analysis of data, judgment of conclusions and weighing of alternatives.

PARTICIPANT INTERACTION

The value of group efforts to produce data and decisions in programming is in the old adage "two heads are better than one." If such efforts are well organized and controlled, they can be extremely valuable for programming in terms of saving time, obtaining new ideas and alternative choices, and developing client consensus. On the other hand, poor management of group activities will yield a morass of unnecessary information, may aggravate conflict rather than achieve consensus, and, in general, contradict the main objective of programming, which is to organize useful information into a meaningful program.

Some group communications techniques might be classified as data collecting devices and others as analysis mechanisms, but because they are characterized particularly by interaction and collective decisions, they are grouped to-

gether here. The measures range from relatively brief sessions used primarily to elicit information and generate ideas (discussed first) to group planning sessions aimed at systemized decision making (discussed last).

Many of the techniques are aimed at involving the client in the decision-making process, developing client consensus and educating the client not only to the facts of a project but to the process by which the facts are collected, analyzed and organized into a program.

BRAINSTORMING. Anyone who has had to come up with a creative idea for solving a problem on a tight deadline has probably used brainstorming. It is a fast, inexpensive, versatile technique for tapping the creative resources of a small group. The purpose of brainstorming is to produce as many ideas or suggestions as possible within a limited time period. The theory is that the more ideas generated, the better the chances are of hitting on a good one and that intense, free interaction stimulates creativity.

A brainstorming session can be called on a moment's notice and held almost anywhere. It is useful almost any time during the programming/design process. No special apparatus or materials are needed, nor does it require professional training or administration. Although large group sessions of brainstorming have been reported to be successful, the process works best with groups of 5 to 12 people who have working knowledge of the project or issue. A time limit is not necessary, but may help get the ball rolling a little more quickly. Sessions of 30 to 60 minutes seem to produce the best results.

Products. Ideas, problem solutions, conflict resolution, information discovery and alternative approaches are among the suggestive data, rather than factual or detailed data, that are products of brain-

storming. Evaluation and documentation of ideas follows the creative process. Brainstorming can also be effective in making group members aware of each other's viewpoints.

Procedure. Four rules of order for conducting brainstorming sessions have been postulated by Alex Osborn, who formally developed the concept in 1938:
   —Criticism is prohibited
   —The wilder the ideas, the better
   —The more ideas, the better
   —Combining or building on other ideas is encouraged
"Free association," a term popularized by psychiatry which means uninhibited, spontaneous response to ideas or words, is the key to successful brainstorming. The following guidelines should help in setting up and conducting sessions:

   —A group leader and recorder are necessary. The leader sets a rapid pace, keeps the discussion from lagging, prods members to participate and coordinates responses. The recorder, usually a participant also, writes down each verbal idea on a blackboard or large roll of paper for display to the group.

   —The problem must be clearly and simply stated. If this can't be done, there's no point in trying to solve the problem for the moment.

   —Group members should call out any and all ideas that pop into their heads. Uninhibited thinking is a must. Wild ideas are encouraged.

   —There is no time for criticism or analysis. It inhibits the free flow of ideas from the unconscious mind to the conscious.

   —Building on ideas is the name of the game. Each idea expressed could trigger new, possibly better, ones. The idea display by the recorder is another prompting measure.

   —Words, phrases and other cryptic statements are the proper forms of expression for ideas. Careful phrasing clogs the process.

An alternative brainstorming approach calls for participants to write down individual ideas on cards before the group session begins. Each person reads one idea in turn to the group for discussion and individuals jot down new ideas in response. All the cards are collected at the conclusion, sorted and evaluated.

SYNECTICS. Synectics might be called a technique of the absurd because it purposely employs exaggeration, fantasy and irrationality to unlock problem solutions from the bonds of assumption and presupposition. It is sometimes described as a technique that "makes the strange familiar, and the familiar strange." Through the use of analogies, small group participants are asked to imagine how a specific problem might be approached or solved if *anything* were possible; if, for example, a transportation problem might be solved by "mailing" people; or if one were a skylight, how would one let light into a building but keep heat from escaping? The aim is to temporarily set aside the laws and limits of reality and explore the essence of a problem and the limitless solutions.

Synectics is akin to brainstorming in that free association and wild ideas are necessary. It forbids criticism, encourages novelty and spontaneity, relies on interaction and produces rational solutions to difficult problems. The key is pretending.

Products. The technique was developed by William J.J. Gordon 30 years ago for use in product development. However, it has significant potential for programming and design. It is strictly limited to producing preliminary solutions to specific problems, particularly when problems don't respond readily to conventional, rational analysis.

Procedure. Successful use of synectics depends on strong, experienced leadership and a group with imagination and, preferably, diverse backgrounds. Participants in a synectics group should be selected thoughtfully in order to eliminate rigid personalities and to insure diversity of viewpoints, backgrounds and thinking processes.

At one time, synectics groups were specially trained in the technique and specifically assigned by their organizations to handle difficult problems and innovative solutions. However, the principles of the technique can be applied to a variety of situations and problems. The basic principles of synectics include the following:

—The group should be small: 5 to 10 people.

—Some time should be spent in briefing the group on the nature of the problem and the reasons for it. Practice in use of analogies before tackling the problem is good preparation as well.

—Four types of analogies are used to get the creative thinking process going and to keep it going:

• direct analogy; comparison of problem item with dissimilar item
• personal analogy; the synectics participants imagine themselves as a piece of the problem being discussed
• symbolic analogy; metaphors and similes
• fantasy analogy; wishful thinking or free imagination

—The leader asks the group to think of the problem in terms of a particular analogy. The realm of possibilities within that analogy are then discussed in rapid, stream-of-consciousness manner (like brainstorming) until a correct approach or solution evolves. Once the track of a solution is discovered, the analogy may be set aside and the discussion continue on a realistic plane.

Resources. *Synectics: The Development of Creative Capacity* by William J.J. Gordon. New York: Collier Books, 1961.

Design Methods: Seeds of Human Futures by J. Christopher Jones. New York: Wiley-Interscience, 1972.

BUZZ/RAP SESSIONS. Sometimes referred to as bull sessions, this simple means of examining issues or problems is similar to brainstorming, but usually less intense and often less goal-directed. Like brainstorming, however, it works best with a small group of people familiar with the problem or project. The buzz session may be an informal, spontaneous gathering of client members or a regular meeting of a formally constituted group of key decisionmakers. In any event, the sessions are called to exchange information, discuss ideas or analyze problems associated with a specific topic or project aspect.

Products. The results of such sessions can include ideas, goal identification, problem identification or solution, conflict resolution, client communication and education, information resources, task assignments. The buzz session yields little in the way of hard data on which to accurately base client requirements; it is a beginning point for a more systematic data search. However, it is helpful in telling the programmer what data to look for and where to find it.

Procedure. There are no requirements for buzz or rap sessions except free and open discussion. In a more structured situation, a planning group may be divided into buzz or discussion groups, like committees, with each assigned a discussion task. A group leader is usually appointed to guide interaction and to represent the committee findings or viewpoints when the larger group reconvenes. A recorder to document ideas and information is also necessary. A time limit should be set.

ROLE PLAYING. Hidden in the routine of everyday living are clues to the meaning of certain actions and to the significant features of an environment. Role playing is one way that the programmer can focus a spotlight on the important clues. When people are asked to act out a real or hypothetical situation by playing their own or each other's roles, the significant aspects of their behavior toward their real roles, each other and their environment are accentuated. Because they are only "play acting," it is easier to express feelings that might be repressed in a real situation. Or the actors tend to exaggerate the most important attitudes and actions of the characters, especially when playing unfamiliar roles. The observant role-playing director will be able to pick up on these behavioral "cues." Role playing is especially useful for identifying conflicts among people and for helping people work out solutions to conflicts.

Products. Role playing is a means of extracting the significant from the routine. Behavior patterns or actions and attitudes that go unnoticed by a group in the course of their everyday existence emerge when dramatized on stage in front of an audience. Role playing sessions with client members can help the programmer develop:

—Group awareness of real roles, conflicts and problems

—Identification of conflicts, problems, behavior patterns, interaction patterns, and attitudes

—Conflict resolutions and problem solutions

—Discovery of effects of environment on behavior

—Clues to how members of the group might act in different settings

Procedure. Administering the role-playing technique requires skill in motivating people to "get up on stage" and perform. The programmer may also need the help of a behavioral expert in interpreting the behavior displayed by the role players. Such assistance is especially important when the programmer wants to identify behavior patterns and attitudes toward

the environment, but less important when the objective is to stimulate the members of the group to think about or discuss their situations and problems.

This is generally a small-group method, but it can work with a small core of uninhibited participants dramatizing situations for a larger audience to discuss. In directing a role-playing scene, it is important to clearly identify the situation to be enacted, the roles to be played, and the setting in which the scene occurs. The players may be asked to act out behavior they perceive accompanies the roles in reality or to perform the roles as they imagine individuals in such positions should act.

GAMING. A wide variety of social survey and planning games has been devised to help visualize problems and make decisions. Games are simulations or models of real situations in which choices are simplified and actions must conform to clearly defined rules. That is not to say that such games are easy to play or produce simple solutions. Anyone who has played Monopoly knows that while the real estate development process has been grossly simplified, skillful play involves more than simply buying and selling. Chess is another, but more abstract, model of reality. The rules are straightforward and the basic moves simple, but the combinations of maneuvers that produce the end result are virtually limitless and complex.

Most planning games are designed to yield experimental decisions resulting from choosing among options, assigning values, bargaining and trading, and testing outcomes. Winners are rare, since the objective usually is to produce a common solution rather than a dominant one. Other games are used in survey research to accumulate individual responses to specific situations, which are then analyzed to discover attitude or behavior patterns.

Examples of some games which have

been useful in programming and design include:

—*CLUG* (Community Land Use Game). A kind of combination of chess and Monopoly used in urban planning and design education. It involves buying and selling property with a concern for both investment development and community development.

—*Auction.* A four-stage bidding game based on auction procedures; the objective is to determine personal priorities of group members by having them compete for the same options. In the game, each member chooses several optional solutions to a given problem, ranks them by preference and then competes with other members to "buy" each option.

—*Minipug.* Another priority options game, this one aims to produce a mutually satisfactory solution to a problem in financing. Players are provided a spending limit, price list of design concept options, and continuous background data. Each player selects several options and then begins negotiating and trading with the others to get as many personal options into the final plan as possible. Naturally, many compromises are reached in the course of the game.

Products. Such games may produce information concerning space planning, floor plan layouts, economic decisions, client education, problem simplification and solutions, and design decisions. While games focus on producing a single decision from several options, programmers may use them to observe or test group opinions, attitudes and values, and to identify preferences and behavior patterns. Moreover, since games are simplifications of reality, the decisions they produce tend to be simplifications and should be used as starting points for exploring fact-supported solutions.

Procedure. Some games can be played by small groups, while others are specifically designed to test individual preferences and attitudes. From available games programmers should select the ones that suit specific purposes and groups. The rules and game paraphernalia will vary depending on the game.

Resources. *Serious Games* by C.C. Abt. New York: Viking Press, 1970.

Design Games by Henry Sanoff, AIA. Los Altos, Calif.: William Kaufmann Inc., 1979.

GROUP PLANNING. Most of the techniques under this heading are approaches that require more or less uninterrupted concentration on specific issues or problems with the goal of producing a final proposal, statement, conclusion or decision. These are synthesizing sessions in which the decision-making group of a project, whether it is a large community group or a corporate building committee, comes together with the programmer to weigh alternatives, consider all facets, and take action. Continuous planning sessions can be used to develop, analyze and organize information and to produce program and design decisions. Among these techniques are Workshops, Marathons, "Squatters" and Charrettes. They progress over a specific time period, no more than several days, and are generally intense, goal-directed sessions.

A variation of continuous planning deemphasizes intense concentration and emphasizes continuous, prolonged participation. The key is arranging convenient, long-lasting opportunities for a broad cross-section of a client group to contribute to project development, usually in the form of ideas and suggestions. This variation is useful for sustaining "public" interest in a project, keeping interested parties informed of progress, and soliciting ideas and information from a wide variety of sources. Such a system, called *Bridge*, was developed by a design group at the

UCLA School of Architecture and Urban Planning in connection with design of a new school wing.

In Bridge, organizers established an information station at a main traffic intersection on the campus, where most participants would likely pass during the course of their daily routines. Information on the project was graphically displayed and updated as the project progressed. A volunteer staff was available during heavy traffic periods to discuss the project and answer questions. In addition, spaces were provided on the walls and tables for those who wished to write or sketch suggestions and modifications. The display was continuously altered to reflect acceptable input and explain rejections and revisions.

Broad participation is also an objective of the Workshop technique. *Workshops* can accommodate a large number of people, usually by dividing them up into study groups which report back to the full membership. This technique is effective for community projects. Workshops are well-organized planning sessions which combine a variety of techniques for collecting and analyzing data, solving problems and producing consensus decisions. They are used for generating ideas; identifying preferences, attitudes, problems and conflicts; resolving conflicts and problems; establishing goals; and developing alternative design approaches. A skillful use of the workshop technique is described in the case study of the Commodore Sloat School in Chapter 13.

Marathons, "Squatters" and Charrettes are more intense work sessions. They involve smaller groups of decision-makers or information sources and usually continue until the goal of the meeting is achieved. Other techniques, such as brainstorming, space planning games and the use of wall worksheets are frequently employed during the sessions. The programmer can use these techniques at various times during the programming/design

signing process, but, because of the intensity, they are usually reserved for major decision phases. These concentrated planning meetings are time-savers, enabling the programmer to accomplish several tasks and obtain major decisions in a short period of time, usually one day to one week. They are useful for generating ideas, quickly accumulating data, analyzing and resolving problems and conflicts, and making program and design decisions.

The distinguishing features of *marathoning* are that the sessions take place in a neutral setting away from the distractions of everyday activity and that attention is focused on specific issues continuously for periods of 12 to 16 hours a day for as much as four or five days. The technique is borrowed from the realm of group encounter psychotherapy and is based on the theory that fatigue and conflict can be useful in revealing true feelings and resolving problems. Participants adhere to a strict schedule and work, eat and sleep at the same times. The firm of Kaplan/McLaughlin/Diaz of San Francisco, California, employs marathons in its programming projects.

Squatters, unlike marathons, take place in the client's own backyard, getting the programmer away from office distractions and close to the main sources of information. They are intense day-and-night sessions that last from three to five days and sometimes longer. Developed by the architecture firm Caudill Rowlett Scott (CRS), the technique is used by the firm in a well-defined programming process of its own. At CRS, programming squatters are used early in programming to define problems and issues and later to generate ideas, collect data, analyze information and resolve problems, and finally to develop the program conclusions. The client is continuously and directly involved in the process, which requires thorough preplanning by the programmer, cooperation and effective communication. CRS

EXHIBIT 5-1. A WORKSHOP AGENDA FOR GROUP PARTICIPATION PROBLEM SOLVING

WORKSHOP AGENDA
Day 1—Problem Identification

7 pm Preliminaries

1. Introduction—Project personnel
   Workshop facilitators
   Workbooks

2. Explanation—Project background and scope
   Workshop purpose and goals

3. Instruction —Procedures
   Schedule
   Activities

7:30 pm Self-guided Tour

1. Walk-through of building—follow map in workbook

2. Complete assignments for tour (workbook pp. 5-9)

3. Return to meeting room

8 pm Group Activities

1. Discussion/questions regarding tour

2. Exercise 1—Problem identification (workbook pp. 10-11)

3. Exercise 2—Questionnaire (workbook pp. 12-14)

4. Exercise 3—Problem priorities (workbook p. 15)

5. Discussion

10 pm Closing

1. Summary of workshop conclusions

2. Collect workbooks

3. Announcement of next session

also uses design squatters.

Charrette is an architectural term that means the architect's last minute drive (literally; i.e., by carriage) to complete drawings for a client. Today, it also refers to a brief, intense session in which the programmer or designer, alone or with the client, concentrates on, generally, a single issue or problem with the goal of developing a conclusion by the end of the period. It may last from one to several days. The connotation of last-minute effort also is a current use of the term.

DOCUMENTATION/PRESENTATION

Once the programmer has developed conclusions about a facility's needs, it becomes necessary to organize the concepts in a way that can be used to communicate them effectively to the client, the designer, the public and anyone else who is concerned with the programming effort.

The three basic methods of communicating programming ideas are the printed narrative, an audio-visual presentation and an oral presentation. The *printed narrative* has the advantages of being relatively inexpensive to prepare, permitting careful selection and phrasing of ideas, and being easily targeted at the intended audience. It is the most useful for the designer, providing a worktable reference for design. An *audio/visual presentation*, while often more stimulating and memorable, is comparatively costly and time-consuming to prepare. An *oral presentation* combines many of the advantages of the two, making possible the presentation of selected ideas with some graphic aids. While the oral presentation can be prepared more rapidly than either narrative or audiovisual presentation, it requires careful forethought plus skills in phrasing and delivery to be effective.

Whichever method is used (usually more than one), it will require a clear purpose, consistency of presentation, good graphics and careful attention to language so that it will communicate the desired message to the intended audience. The better the communication effort, the more positive input will be received from those involved in the decision-making process, and the better can be the resulting design.

NARRATIVE. The narrative is a comparatively low-cost method for communicating programming information. It permits the carefully thought-out expression of ideas in written form, which may then be disseminated to a diverse audience for reading at each individual's convenience. However, effective communication in writing requires careful attention to basic principles of language usage, style and logical development of ideas. When a programming study results in a written report to the client, these principles are especially important. In addition, careful attention should be paid to the client's purpose, desired image and intended use of the report—as well as to budget limitations.

Procedure. The first step in constructing a narrative is the development of a detailed outline of the ideas to be communicated, combining ideas from all who are involved in the programming effort. The act of writing a program narrative forces the programmer to refine and sharpen concepts through the rigor of expressing and explaining them to others. The final wording and general editing responsibility may be given to a skilled communicator in the firm or an outside consultant.

Some basic rules of usage and style which the writer should follow include:

—Follow accepted rules of grammar.

—Use the active voice and definite, specific, concrete language.

—Omit needless words.

—Write in a way that comes naturally, avoiding stilted phrasing.

—Revise and rewrite.

—Use orthodox spelling.

—Try to use short, uncomplicated sentences.

—Avoid fancy words and technical jargon; define words unusual to the reader at the first reference.

—Do not take shortcuts at the cost of clarity.

Before writing begins, prepare a schedule for each step in the preparation of the narrative, just as you would for any other client project, and monitor it closely. Prepare a written statement for the narrative, including the nature and character of the intended piece, who will receive it, how long it will be in use, the level of technical understanding it should be written for, and whether it is intended as a working document or a show piece for formal presentation.

Once a draft is ready, the text should be edited for clarity and accomplishment of its purpose. In the initial review, check to see that the narrative contains a message that will enthuse the reader. Once this is achieved, undertake detailed editing, including rearranging text to improve the flow of ideas, removing passages that impede that flow, replacing overly technical passages with understandable terms, checking for overall consistency, and eliminating hackneyed phrases. A final review should be included to make any last changes and to add instructions for the typist or typesetter. At each stage, check spelling.

The final step in the writing/editing phase of a narrative is the preparation of titles, subtitles, decks and scans, which are all devices to help the reader learn, at a glance, what the narrative is all about.

—*Titles* should be brief, catchy invitations to the reader, selected to get the most impact with the least words.

—*Subtitles* should be no longer than one line, include an active verb, if possible, and tell the reader enough about the following text so that it can be skipped if desired. Subtitles help orient the reader through a long text and serve as a visual device to break up long columns of type and rest the reader's eyes.

—*Decks* are short, one-sentence statements that run under the title, telling the reader in more detail what is to follow.

—*Scans* are approximate excerpts from the narrative text, placed in mid-article and set off from the column by rules or placed in normally unused space in the page format. They identify, in a capsule, the gist of the narrative at that point in the text. While not essential, both decks and scans are useful to the reader.

In the final editorial review of a narrative, titles, subtitles, decks and scans should be added or revised for accuracy, impact and brevity.

Publishing the Narrative. For formal reports used to convince a client's constituency as to a course of action, publication of the narrative may require commercial typesetting and printing, use of more than one color, use of fine paper stock and elaborate binding.

For many research and planning reports, however, it is both cost-effective and appropriate to produce the narrative with typewriter type and inexpensive printing and binding performed in an offset reproduction shop. Graphic excitement can be added to the basic typewriter-produced manuscript by including inexpensive, hand-applied devices such as press-type headings; press-on symbols (e.g., circles and squares to mark the beginning and end of sections); and use of capitalization and underscoring to denote varying emphases.

While the camera-ready type is being prepared, the graphic designer for the publication should prepare its preliminary design, making thumbnail sketches of the proposed layout. (See Exhibit 5-2). Factors considered in design include creating the image which the firm or client desires to project, maintaining consistency throughout the publication, assuring the reproducibility of artwork, and retaining sufficient white space for aesthetic appeal. Graphics, typefaces, drawings, photographs and general format should be selected with careful attention to consistency.

When typesetting is required for publication, the graphic designer should choose an appropriate typeface that will be legible and appropriate for the document. The designer should make the necessary specifications for the typesetter, including the design, size and weight of the typeface; leading (spacing) between lines; line width; word spacing; type alignment (justified, flush left, ragged right, etc.); number of proofs; and any special effects or positioning.

Once the camera-ready type is completed, proofread and corrected, final steps include preparation of the final artwork, paste-up of camera-ready mechanicals, and writing of specifications for the printer. Once printed and bound, the publication is distributed to its intended audience. The publication evaluation procedure shown in Exhibit 5-3 includes a list of criteria that may be helpful as a checklist for developing a publication. A looseleaf binder is a very useful format for the designer, if the program is to be a working document.

Resources. *The Art of Plain Talk*, Rudolph Flesch. New York: Collier, 1951.

Creative Communications for a Successful Design Practice, Stephen A. Kliment, AIA. New York: Whitney Library of Design, 1977.

The Elements of Style, William Strunk Jr. and E.B. White. New York: Macmillan Paperbacks, 1962. A classic on how to write readable English. Read once a year to stay in shape.

GRAPHICS. Whether complementing a narrative or providing visual stimulation as part of an oral presentation, graphics assist both programmer and client to "see" the essentials of a problem and improve the clarity of comprehension. Effective visual communications seek to avoid giving too much information—which might obscure the message—or oversimplifying the information to the point that nothing is conveyed.

Products. Graphics include photographs, charts, tables, maps, diagrams, sketches and formal drawings. Drawings should be designed with the reader's needs as the primary consideration. The identity of a drawing's subject must catch the reader's eye and promote rapid assimilation of the whole story. In preparing drawings, factors to consider include standardization of size and format; consistency of scale, lettering, annotation, dimension and detail; suitable grouping of subjects and information; interrelation of drawings with other media; whether the drawing will be used for a few minutes' discussion or long-term reference; whether the drawing is intended for people familiar with drawings and buildings; and what information is relevant to the interests of the intended audience.

When using photographs, either to complement a narrative or as part of an oral presentation, insist on sharpness, clarity and contrast. Careful cropping and sizing often will improve their usefulness.

Graphic Problem Solving. With the growing complexity of programs and building processes, new approaches to building problems are needed so that designers and clients can better understand the relationships between the parts and the whole. Visual problem-solving is a method of abstracting the elements of a problem in order to examine it as a whole, come to understand its underlying structure and then make the judgments required to arrive at a decision. It presents the advantages of creating a high degree of abstraction, conveying complex relationships, allowing direct comparisons, and dealing with the issue of quality. Architect Paul A. Laseau, AIA, has written (and drawn) a thoughtful book on this sub-

EXHIBIT 5-3. FORM AND CRITERIA FOR EVALUATING A PUBLICATION

(Developed by Stephen A. Kliment in collaboration with Evagene Bond and Ivan Chermayeff)

EVALUATION FORM

Subject	Editorial (grade +3 to –3)	Graphics (grade +3 to –3)
1. Planning and structure of publication	+ 2	+ 1
2. Clarity and reader orientation	+ 2	0
3. Style	0	–
4. Illustrations	–	– 1
5. Covers (if any)	+ 2	+ 1
6. Production quality	–	+ 3
7. "Pacing"	+ 1	+ 2
8. Sparkle	+ 1	+ 1
Average:	+ 1.3	+ 1.0

Rating	Description
+ 3	Excellent
+ 2	Superior
+ 1	Good
0	No strong impression
–1	Needs work
–2	Poor
–3	Start over

JUDGMENT CRITERIA

1. Planning and structure of publication

Are contents logically organized?

Is there a clear graphic expression of contents?

2. Clarity and reader orientation

Are charts, graphs, matrices, tables easily comprehended by the layman?

Are titles/headlines clearly worded?

Are visual devices (decks, scans, subheads) used as aids to the reader?

Is there a table of contents?

Are illustrations clearly captioned?

Is the "white space" around text and artwork organized cleanly?

Is color used efficiently?

Are paragraphs limited to a comfortable reading length (15-20 lines)?

If typewritten, is typewriter type used with graphic skill?

Are display (headline) typefaces appropriate to topic?

Are text typefaces appropriate? easy to read?

3. Style

Are words short? sentences short?

Is there consistency in spelling, punctuation, abbreviations?

Is material expressed in simple language appropriate to topic and reader?

4. Illustrations

Are photographs of good quality?

Are photographs cropped to focus on main subject matter?

Are line drawings sharp?

Are plan titles legible even though reduced?

Are illustrations logically related on a page according to scale and subject matter?

5. Covers (if any)

Is all required information included and easy to read?

Is there an appropriate use of the logotype?

6. Production quality

Are paper stock and cover stock appropriate to the purposes of the report?

Is there a pleasant combination of ink and paper color?

Is printing quality good?

Is binding appropriate to the purposes of the report?

7. Pacing

Is the front-to-back movement of the contents a pleasing experience for the reader?

8. Sparkle

Is the overall impact of the publication fresh and lively?

Source: *Creative Communications for a Successful Design Practice*, Stephen A. Kliment, AIA. New York: Whitney Library of Design, 1977.

ject. Some of his ideas from *Graphic Problem Solving for Architects and Builders* are presented here.

Graphic problem solving is based on the recognition of an essential parallel between traditional building design problems and the emerging problems of building processes and building performance, where there is a basic need to see problems in their simplest abstract form. The graphic image makes possible the consideration of the interrelation of many variables, along with common factors such as size, location, identity, relationship and process.

Aside from architectural drawings and sketches, the four basic types of graphic problem-solving devices are bubble diagrams, area diagrams, matrices and networks. Some of these, as well as other diagrams, are discussed in Chapter 4.

Bubble diagrams are the most versatile and basic device for abstractions. They may serve as models of physical space, objects in space, program requirements, activities or existing conditions, which can then be manipulated with relative ease to suggest alternative relationships or arrangements of a set of elements.

Area diagrams are used to summarize information in a way that will allow quick comparison or reference. Intensity mapping, one type of area diagram, can be used to set priorities. Trends, another type, help interpret computer trend analysis into a visual message, providing a prediction of the interaction between people and a building. (See Exhibit 5-4.)

A *matrix* is a simple tool for matching two sets of data to create new combinations for consideration. It is a grid of corresponding rows and columns. The matrix can make visible a pattern of options, opinions or other data, facilitating a comprehensive, qualitative analysis and aiding in communication or evaluation. More detail on matrices is found in Chapter 4.

A *network*, such as a critical path,

PERT or decision tree, can aid analysis through illustrations and perhaps simplification of a process or number of components. For example, a decision tree consists of decisions and possible outcomes, creating a diagram which tends to branch out like a tree as each decision generates two or more possible outcomes. The decision tree is used to project the possible end results of a series of decisions.

A graphic problem-solving technique should be chosen to suit the problem at hand. Some basic tips:

—It is important to be able to see the whole diagram at one glance, so choose a format and size to suit the audience.

—Don't get too formal in sketching diagrams—clarity and speed are most important.

—Once you have a fairly clear abstraction of a problem situation, manipulate or extend the diagram to discover basic relationships and express alternative configurations of those relationships.

—Visual thinking is a process of seeing as well as drawing, so it may take time to develop perceptions about this way of expressing problems.

Graphics play an important role in the problem analysis and solving process for those who are receptive to its possibilities. By making images an integral part of thinking, perceptions can be changed rapidly while retaining a grasp of the total problem. However, problem-solving approaches are of value only if they lead to a point where decisions can be made.

Resources. *Publication Design* by Allen Hurlburt. New York: Van Nostrand Press, 1976. A guide to page layout, typography, format and style.

Creative Communications for a Successful Design Practice by Stephen A. Kliment, AIA. New York: Whitney Library of Design, 1977.

Graphic Problem Solving for Architects and Builders by Paul Laseau,

AIA. Boston: Cahners Publishing Co. Inc., 1975.

Designing for Visual Aids by David Pye. New York: Van Nostrand Reinhold Co., 1970.

Practical Charting Techniques by Mary Eleanor Spear. New York: McGraw-Hill Inc., 1969.

AUDIO/VISUAL AIDS. Audio/visual presentations offer several advantages that help make communications more effective. They help: hold and focus audience attention; compress information; reinforce oral and printed communication; enhance audience interest; present a variety of vantage points; provide otherwise inaccessible information; and deliver a message more quickly, clearly and accurately.

Products. Audio/visual aids include slide shows (from single-screen with live narration to multi-screen, tape-actuated shows); motion pictures, videotapes and filmstrips (with or without sound); display charts; graphs; models and working models; and overhead projector transparencies.

Procedure. Preparation of a 10- to 20-minute slide show can entail two weeks to two months, plus $500 to as much as $5,000 for production. For most applications, therefore, a firm should concentrate on producing a short, simple show that uses existing slides and live narration wherever possible.

Begin by drafting a statement of objectives covering allocated time, type of audience, purpose of the show, format options, type of space in which it is to be shown, and budget. Separate production responsibilities into script and visual chores, although the two should remain in close contact.

With an outline that lists the main points to be covered in the presentation, prepare a preliminary script which will have a dra-

EXHIBIT 5-4. AREA DIAGRAMS (LIKE CHARTS AND GRAPHS) INCLUDE THE DIMENSION OF SCALE FOR MEASURING AND COMPARING

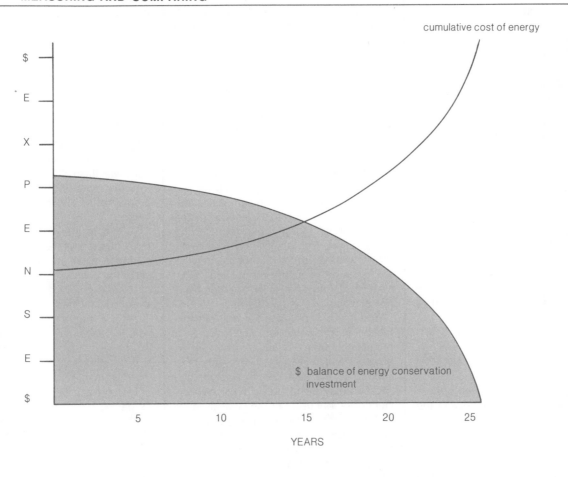

cumulative cost of energy

$
E
X
P
E
N
S
E
$

$ balance of energy conservation investment

5   10   15   20   25

YEARS

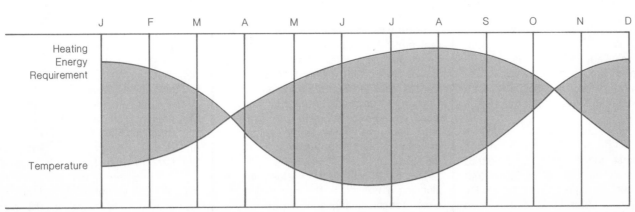

J F M A M J J A S O N D

Heating
Energy
Requirement

Temperature

matic flow and will build toward the desired final impact. Script and visuals must be developed together so they will harmonize.

Visual images, whether simple line drawings, detailed drawings, or photographs of models and completed projects, should be chosen to reinforce the basic objectives of the presentation. Simplicity is generally the key to any good visual—each chart, drawing or slide frame should deal with a single idea that is clearly conveyed.

Use a "storyboard," a series of equal-sized, large cards on which individual visual concepts are developed and captioned, to compile these visual images. Each visual is in large-scale proportion, as in a flip chart, and in finished form represents the artwork that will be photographed for slides. The cards can be rearranged to create the eventual sequence of ideas dovetailing with the narrative script.

Once the appropriate slides and artwork are developed, rehearse tying the whole thing together with live narration that is calculated to unify the presentation and put emphasis where desired. Where the narrator is someone familiar with the project, it is usually much more effective to talk informally or from notes about the subject rather than to read a script.

For any presentation more elaborate than this single-screen, narrated slide show, a media consultant and costly equipment may be required. Extra items which will need to be included in the budget are consultant fees, purchase and development of film and tapes, rental of recording and projection equipment, and rental of a studio for synchronizing visuals with sound.

A special caution in preparing for an audio/visual presentation: When the time for the presentation arrives, be prepared for the many mechanical problems that might occur. Be sure to test the facility and equipment beforehand, and have on hand a spare lamp for the projector.

Resources. *Planning and Producing Slide Programs*, Rochester, New York: Eastman Kodak Co., 1975.

Creative Communications for a Successful Design Practice by Stephen A. Kliment, AIA. New York: Whitney Library of Design, 1977.

Understanding Media by Marshall McLuhan. New York: McGraw-Hill Inc., 1964.

ORAL PRESENTATIONS. At some point in a project, the programmer will find it necessary to talk to an audience, whether it is to report to a client committee or to address a large group representing facility users. The objective of a presentation, whether formal or informal, may be to persuade, convey information, educate, elicit participation or any combination of these.

The major application for oral presentations in programming, however, is a project conference to update the client on progress and to get a decision before proceeding to the next phase. Another application may be to obtain early involvement of facility users or the local citizenry in the project development process. This can help defuse any opposition and may also contribute toward producing more complete programming information and, ultimately, a better design solution.

Procedure. The basic component of an oral presentation is a speech. It should be planned as a series of ideas arranged in a sequence that will produce a buildup toward a desired impact on the audience. One way to do this is to record important ideas on index cards, with one idea per card, then arrange the cards as a series of key-idea cues to be referred to during the speech.

The most important consideration in planning a speech is the intended audience. Technical language, depth of coverage and length of presentation should be determined by the makeup of the audience and their attitude toward the subject. During a presentation, the speaker should try to get some feedback to determine whether the audience is following the points of the speech. If the feedback indicates the audience is responding negatively, the speaker should be prepared to change tack or curtail remarks.

The speaker needs to maintain control throughout the presentation and, if questions are invited, should be prepared to cope with them.

Some important tips to keep in mind in preparing for and giving an oral presentation:

—Plan to insert your lightest material three-quarters of the way through the presentation, since attention will be at its lowest at this point.

—Keep panelists or speakers to their assigned time limits.

—Encourage a discussion/question period. In case questions are not forthcoming, have one or two of your own ready to break the ice.

—Use humor.

—Don't use distracting gestures, such as pacing back and forth; look as many individuals in the eye as you can.

—Use visual aids to increase the understanding, interest and memorability of the presentation.

—Speak reasonably slowly to aid clarity of understanding, but not so slowly or dully as to put the audience to sleep.

—Leave the audience with the point you most want them to absorb. If they remember anything, it will probably be the last thing you say. Make it count.

The most common audio-visual aids for oral presentations are slides and charts. For either medium, it's important to limit one idea or concept to one chart or slide. Don't try to cram too much information on a single slide or chart, and avoid making them too verbal or unreadable. After all, the purpose of the visual aid is to complement, not replace, what you have to say.

If using slides, consolidate their use in one segment of the presentation to avoid continual turning on and off of lights.

If you plan to develop charts during the presentation, prepare a light, penciled outline on each sheet beforehand as a guide. Also test lettering size beforehand to be sure it will be legible.

Analysis cards are an additional visual aid which can help stimulate audience participation. Each card contains a single idea or concept, to be reviewed with the client for instant feedback. The concept can be developed through 5" X 8" cards, an overhead projector or large sheets of wrapping paper tacked to the wall, depending on the size of the audience. Such aids as analysis cards and wall worksheets are also discussed in Chapter 4. With each, the concept is developed orally and notations are added of options in programming or preliminary design solutions.

Resources. "Made, Not Born: A New Slant on Public Speaking" by Andrew Warren Weil in *Consulting Engineer*, December 1978, pp. 40-44.

"The Spoken Word" in *Creative Communications for a Successful Design Practice*, Stephen A. Kliment, AIA. New York: Whitney Library of Design, 1977.

FORUMS. A public meeting, open to all parties affected by a facility project, is not only a means of informing and educating a client group on programmatic issues and decisions, but an effective means of obtaining input to programming from a broad segment of the group. This is particularly important when public acceptance of a project program is vital. A forum is simply an organized meeting, like a stockholders' or town meeting or a public hearing, in which reports may be given and discussion of issues pursued.

The nature of a group which voluntarily convenes for a forum on a project is both an advantage and a disadvantage. On the one hand, participants usually will be genuinely concerned about the issue and put relatively intense effort into discussion. On the other hand, such a group might turn out to be a vocal minority that does not necessarily represent the client's overall views, preferences and values. However, enough people with divergent backgrounds and viewpoints usually participate in such gatherings that the programmer at least gains a sampling that gives direction to further study or evaluation.

Products. The results of a forum could include informed opinion, consensus, problem and conflict identification, identification of groups within the client organization or jurisdiction who are committed to specific viewpoints, or resolution of conflicts through information and interaction. Forums may be used at various points in programming and for various purposes, including:

—At the beginning, to inform the client-users of the procedures and issues involved in the programming project and to gain support and future participation in the activities

—During program investigation, to gather information and identify general issues of concern to users

—During program development, to report on progress and verify preliminary conclusions

—At the end of the project, to report the final results or to receive feedback for evaluation of proposals

Procedure. The forum technique requires no professional training or administration. It is a quick means of disseminating information to a large client membership and of obtaining feedback. Forums can be duplicated easily for several groups in the client organization and may be conducted any place a large group can be accommodated conveniently. Other principles of forum administration include:

—Post and/or publish public announcements of the meeting well in advance and include time, date, location, subject and, if possible, agenda. Since broad participation is desired, the information should be distributed to reach the largest appropriate audience; e.g., through bulletin boards, company or community newspapers, public address or radio/TV announcements. Exhibit 5-5 illustrates a public meeting announcement.

—At the meeting, printed agendas or information sheets should be handed out to participants outlining the subject of the meeting and describing procedures for participation.

—A leader or leader group conducts the forum, making presentations and stimulating and controlling group discussion.

—A recorder (human or electronic) documents all pertinent discussion, data, questions, conflicts, etc. for future reference and review.

—Free, open discussion by all participants and factions should be encouraged.

—The forum may be repeated in order to gain the widest possible participation from the client group.

—The discussion should adhere as closely as possible to the issues that are relevant to the forum's purpose, including those that may have been excluded from the agenda.

PANEL DISCUSSIONS. A variation of the forum technique, this method involves discussion of a relevant issue by a small group for the benefit of a larger audience. The panel members are experts or representatives of the larger group and examine the issue from various points of view or interest. Before making their individual presentations to the audience, the panel members will have studied assigned aspects of the issue and perhaps discussed it among themselves. The panel-

EXHIBIT 5-5. MEETING ANNOUNCEMENT FOR POSTING AND
                CIRCULATION

— NOTICE —

The Library Planning Committee
will hold a public meeting to
discuss plans for the new library.
All interested citizens are
invited to attend and participate.

DATE: Thursday, November 16

TIME: 7:30 pm

LOCATION: Horace Mann Elementary School Auditorium
                8th and School Streets

AGENDA: Opening and introduction by Library Planning Committee

                Presentation by architect

                Open discussion

                Closing and announcements

INFORMATION: Library Planning Committee
                Town Hall
                555-4321

ists make their presentations and then publicly discuss the whole topic, questioning and rebutting each other's remarks. Once the panel has finished this structured portion of the meeting, the audience usually is invited to join the discussion to raise new questions, clarify information and present alternative viewpoints.

Products. The programmer may use panel discussions to inform a broad segment of a client organization about the project or an aspect of it, to stimulate discussion, to involve the client-users in decision making and to obtain background information and feedback. It is a little more efficient than the forum because a good

deal of the debate that usually occurs in wide-open discussion will have been distilled by the panel members who represent the various viewpoints of the larger group.

Procedure. The panel discussion technique focuses attention on the most significant aspects of a problem or issue to insure that these are brought out into the open for the client to examine and discuss. By contrast, identification of important aspects may be one of the objectives of a forum. In preparing for a panel discussion session, the programmer and panelists should discuss the order of presentation so that information is delivered to the audience effectively and efficiently.

Other guidelines for conducting panel discussions include:

—Panelists should represent the divergence of viewpoints and interest that exists among the group for which they are speaking. Panel members also should be articulate and capable of participating in discussion without becoming argumentative.

—The panel is usually small: four to seven members. The actual number depends on the number of parts into which the topic can be divided reasonably and purposefully.

—Each panelist is responsible for researching and analyzing a specific issue and organizing a presentation. The aim is to sort out the significant data and objectively bring it to the attention of the audience.

—A moderator, usually a client member, leads the discussion, introducing, timing and guiding the panelists. At the end of the presentations, the moderator also may summarize the discussion and conduct discussion by the audience.

—In the interests of efficiency and audience attention, a time limit should be set for each presentation and for the whole meeting.

—A recorder keeps notes of the discussion among the panelists and later the audience participation. Prepared statements by panelists will help insure that an accurate record of major points is obtained.

—After formal presentations, the panelists question and comment on each other's remarks and respond to questions and comments from the audience.

WORKBOOKS. Also referred to as "charrette books" or "primer (prime-er) books," workbooks are used to communicate program information needs and to organize programming tasks. Most often, they are directed to client representatives to guide their participation in program development. However, they may be used as a means of communicating the individual programming assignments to the whole programming team, particularly when it is a multidisciplinary group assembled from diverse sources for a specific project.

A workbook is a particularly valuable aid to user participation efforts in programming. It focuses attention on the significant issues and on the areas where users can be of most help to the programmer. It enables the client to comprehend the scope of the project and to identify with the eventual conclusions. It provides specific directions or instructions for participation.

Products. The use of workbooks in programming can help accomplish several things:
—Produce structured evaluation of the issues and/or problems addressed
—Generate ideas and information for the programmer's consideration
—Suggest modifications to the structure of the issue or problem
—Ensure that tasks and assignments are not confused
—Identify potential solutions to problems
—Produce group consensus on program criteria and/or recommendations

Procedure. A workbook is assembled after the issues that need investigation have been clearly identified and the tasks that need to be performed have been defined. The workbook should be neatly composed and consistent, but the format does not need to be formal or rigorously structured. As the name implies, it should be a "work" book. A looseleaf binder provides a good means for constructing a workbook to facilitate insertions and deletions as assignments are completed. However, it can be bound in some inexpensive fashion or simply organized in a portfolio.

Simple graphics help convey concepts, especially to laypersons. Plenty of blank space should be allotted for participant notations and drawings. When the books are intended for use by client participants, the assignments should be realistic and meaningful, not just make-work for token participation. In general, workbooks should contain:
—Identification of the purpose and objectives
—Identification of participants
—Explanation of the procedures
—Definition of the principal issues and problems
—Clear, concise instructions for performing tasks with only as much background explanation as necessary to convey the purpose and procedures of each one

The workbook will be organized by task assignments. These should proceed in some logical order. If the tasks involve observation of various rooms or spaces, for example, the participants should be guided on a convenient route from one to the next. Or, each task may be assigned on the basis of previous tasks, gradually building up the data for evaluation and conclusion.

Resources. See Chapters 8, 13 and 20, where case studies show the use of workbooks in three different projects.

Taking Part: A Workshop Approach to Collective Creativity, Lawrence Halprin and James Burns. Cambridge, Mass.: MIT Press, 1974.

EVALUATION TECHNIQUES

The facility owner and user, designer and programmer make numerous choices and decisions based on available information during the course of programming. The experience and intuition of these participants are important (and sometimes the only) criteria for judging the value, reliability or appropriateness of data, conclusions and options.

Objective measures and criteria can provide a common and consistent basis of judgment among evaluators with differing experiences and perspectives and can help focus the decision process on relevant parameters. The principles and methods explained in this section are intended to aid programming participants in determining the relative importance or priority of conclusions, indicating preferences, weighing benefits of alternatives, assessing impacts of varying combinations of factor dimensions and developing optimum solutions to problems.

RATING AND RATING SCALES. Rating is a measuring method. It is a way of converting feelings or attitudes into quantifiable terms—usually numerical values—for statistical evaluation. The relative value of a variable is the objective of a rating measurement. In other words, a rating can tell a programmer how important, preferred, satisfactory or acceptable a specific variable or set of variables is to an individual or a group. A rating may be a simple choice or a complex ranking. It may address the degree of value of a single variable as in important or unimportant, more or less important, or a range of choices between most important and least important. On the other hand, rating may be used to compare the relative values of two or more factors. More often than not, however, the programmer who uses a rating procedure will be seeking to establish the hierarchy of values among several variables, considering at the same time the range of value of individual variables.

Products. Rating is a very versatile tool that can be applied in a variety of situations. However, it should not be overrated as a technique. It is merely a measure of relative values assigned to the variables in question. Nevertheless, by converting subjective data into quantitative terms, rating enables the programmer to more easily identify significant variables

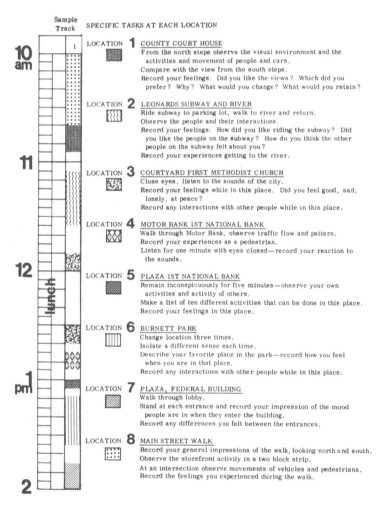

SPECIFIC TASKS AT EACH LOCATION

LOCATION **1** COUNTY COURT HOUSE
From the north steps observe the visual environment and the
activities and movement of people and cars.
Compare with the view from the south steps.
Record your feelings: Did you like the views? Which did you
prefer? Why? What would you change? What would you retain?

LOCATION **2** LEONARDS SUBWAY AND RIVER
Ride subway to parking lot, walk to river and return.
Observe the people and their interactions.
Record your feelings: How did you like riding the subway? Did
you like the people on the subway? How do you think the other
people on the subway felt about you?
Record your experiences getting to the river.

LOCATION **3** COURTYARD FIRST METHODIST CHURCH
Close eyes, listen to the sounds of the city.
Record your feelings while in this place. Did you feel good, sad,
lonely, at peace?
Record any interactions with other people while in this place.

LOCATION **4** MOTOR BANK 1ST NATIONAL BANK
Walk through Motor Bank, observe traffic flow and pattern.
Record your experiences as a pedestrian.
Listen for one minute with eyes closed—record your reaction to
the sounds.

LOCATION **5** PLAZA 1ST NATIONAL BANK
Remain inconspicuously for five minutes—observe your own
activities and activity of others.
Make a list of ten different activities that can be done in this place.
Record your feelings in this place.

LOCATION **6** BURNETT PARK
Change location three times.
Isolate a different sense each time.
Describe your favorite place in the park—record how you feel
when you are in that place.
Record any interactions with other people while in this place.

LOCATION **7** PLAZA, FEDERAL BUILDING
Walk through lobby.
Stand at each entrance and record your impression of the mood
people are in when they enter the building.
Record any differences you felt between the entrances.

LOCATION **8** MAIN STREET WALK
Record your general impressions of the walk, looking north and south.
Observe the storefront activity in a two block strip.
At an intersection observe movements of vehicles and pedestrians.
Record the feelings you experienced during the walk.

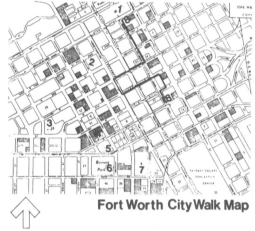

Fort Worth City Walk Map

Source: *Taking Part: A Workshop Approach to Collective Creativity* by Lawrence Halprin and Jim Burns. Cambridge, Mass.: MIT Press, 1974.

and manage the data. Rating can be used at any point in the programming/design/evaluation process. Early in programming, the client may be asked to rate the relative importance of several objectives of a project. At a later point, the programmer may ask client groups to identify the strengths of their preferences among options. For example, a question about alternative transportation methods may be asked of a group of office workers to rate their preferred means of getting to work. This may involve simply ranking in preferential order the options of car, bus, bicycle, train, etc. On the other hand, more precise interpretations might result from posing the question: "If you had your choice, which of the transportation modes would you most prefer to use and which would you least prefer?" or "For each of the transportation modes, please indicate whether you would prefer to use it, not to use it, or neither."

Rating can also be used in making decisions and evaluating choices with regard to programming issues or design proposals. The architect can present alternative solutions to a problem and ask the client to rate them according to which best and which least meet expressed criteria. The architect may also find rating useful in evaluating his or her own decision options, particularly when complex issues are not easily judged individually or when based on detailed criteria. The choice of rating methods depends on the kind of information, nature of the project, client's needs and time available.

Procedure. A cliché often used in conversational inquiries about the merit of a suggestion or a proposal is: "On a scale of 1 to 10, how would you rate this?" The intention of the inquirer is to get a reasonably objective estimate of the value of the proposal; to pin down the opinion by asking for a response expressed in the easily comprehensible terms of numerical value. Scientific inquiries operate in essen-

EXHIBIT 5-7. ILLUSTRATION OF NOMINAL, ORDINAL AND INTERVAL SCALES

7 9	3	1	5 18	10	19 2		12	(nominal)
1 2 3 4 5 6 7 8 9 10 11 12 13 14 15 16 17 18 19 20								(ordinal)

7 9	3	1	5 18	10	19 2	12	(nominal)
0 10 20 30 40 50 60 70 80 90 100							(interval)

tially the same manner. They abstract possible responses into numerical values and ask respondents to choose among them.

The scale in the illustrative inquiry above is an example of a type known as an *ordinal scale*. That is, it is a ranking in order of the set of objects (in that case, only one object) according to an arbitrarily selected ordering range (1 to 10). The range may be 1 to 20, or 60 to 75, etc. because these numbers are insignificant except to identify the relative order of the ranking. Another example is the Top Twenty list of songs on the radio, ranked in order of popularity from the top-rated, the Number One Hit, to the bottom-ranked, number 20.

A statistician wishing to abstract this set of 20 items for ease in handling might assign each one a letter or number, from A to T or from 1 to 20 (since numbers are infinite, they are usually used in large samples that exceed alphabetical limits). This identification or classification system is known as a *nominal scale*, in which the numbers have no value but are assigned merely for convenience.

For purposes of illustration, say the statistician is only interested in ten of these songs and wants to find out where

their popularity falls within the Top Twenty. The ordinal scale that shows the relative order might look something like the first part of Exhibit 5-7 (the top numbers represent the nominal—no value—identifier and the bottom numbers the ordinal rank). Number 7 is ranked the second most popular of the 20 songs and song Number 12 is ranked 19th in popularity; or in terms of the ten songs in question, Number 7 is the most popular, while Number 12 is the least popular.

Now, if the statistician wanted to measure how much *more popular* one of the ten songs is than another, that could be determined by creating an *interval scale*. Such a scale measures relative differences in value among variables, a vital characteristic in examination of complex issues where multiple dimensions of multiple variables are involved.

An interval scale for the song popularity example above might appear as shown in the second part of Exhibit 5-7. Note that the *base interval* is the smallest distance between any of the two objects (the nominal numbers) on the ordinal scale. This interval is used to divide a scale of 0 to 100 into equal parts. In this case, the interval is an arbitrarily assigned value of 5 and is based on the physical distance between 7 and 9, or 5 and 18, or 19 and 2. The numbers of the ordinal scale have been transferred to the interval scale, with each remaining in the same position in relation to the others.

On an interval scale, the statistician can tell not only that song Number 7 is the best liked, but that it is precisely 5 points ahead of Number 9 on the charts, or 70 points more popular than Number 2. In other words, in addition to the rank order, the scale provides a measure of the strength of the popularity of each in relation to all ten songs.

Another type of scale used in assessing

EXHIBIT 5-8. A BLANK LADDER SCALE

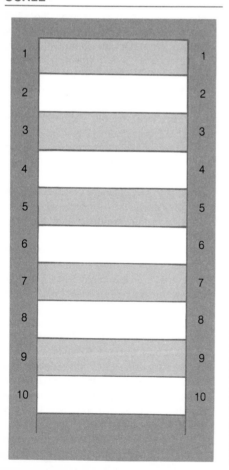

relative value is the *ratio scale*. If a "unique zero" or natural origin point can be fixed, a ratio scale can be created with proportionate ascending or descending increments. A yardstick (soon to become a meter stick) is an example of a ratio scale.

From these basic types of scales, a number of specialized scales and other rating procedures have been developed in the behavioral sciences to aid in measurement of psychological and social variables. Two that have been applied in programming are discussed in the following paragraphs.

Ladder Scale. This ordinal-type scale enables the programmer to identify user-perceived status levels, particularly of circumstances, expectations or performance. Because of its graphic quality—it is shaped like a ladder with equidistant rungs—it is very easy for respondents to understand and use. (See Exhibit 5-8.)

The top rung represents the highest value or most favored level and the lowest rung, the least value. The ladder scale may be presented without rung numbers, but these are often added to aid in identifying the relative positions in the ascending order. As in many statistical scales, the top value will usually be the lowest number. Rarely will a ladder represent more than 10 levels and always they will be in equal increments (just as all risers in any run of stairs should be equal).

Usually presented as part of a questionnaire, the ladder scale will be one of a number of approaches to examining a particular issue. It may be associated with other types of questions on the same data for purposes of comparison, cross-checking or verification of data. The ladder scale question, or questions, will ask the individual to rate an item as to its status by identifying which rung represents the appropriate status level. The question may be repeated to determine past, current and future status, if the programmer

wants to compare perceptions of experience and of expectation. This is a rating of a single item, but the scale may also be used to rate a set of related items by placing them in rank order on the ladder. More frequently, however, the programmer will seek ratings of two or more independent items on the same scale in order to test a possible correlation among them.

All of these laddering functions, most of which relate to user evaluations, can also be performed with other scales.

Rating Charts. Rating doesn't have to be performed on numerically valued scales. As mentioned earlier, a rating can be a simple choice between alternatives; e.g., true-false, agree-disagree, multiple choice. More precisely, the programmer may ask the respondent to rate a series of statements that evaluate an issue, a proposal, criteria, etc. as to whether they are true or false, for instance, in the opinion of the answerer.

For more complex rating choices, a rating chart can be devised. Such a chart might include a list of items to be evaluated against a set of criteria, each of which can be rated by a range of descriptive values. Descriptors could include such ranges as good-indifferent-bad, essential-useful-secondary, strongly agree-agree-no opinion-disagree-strongly disagree, or any other value scale.

A rating chart can be created to evaluate a wide variety of matters in programming and/or designing, from selecting or ordering goals to measuring desirable and undesirable qualities to evaluating existing conditions to assessing the advantages/disadvantages of alternative proposals. The chart's scale of rating choices is used to define the degree of satisfaction or performance of the criteria for each of the items under evaluation. The sample rating chart shown in Exhibit 5-9 illustrates a seven-degree scale for measuring the levels of satisfaction of 10 criteria for 11

EXHIBIT 5-9. A RATING CHART FOR MEASURING USER SATISFACTION WITH HOUSING

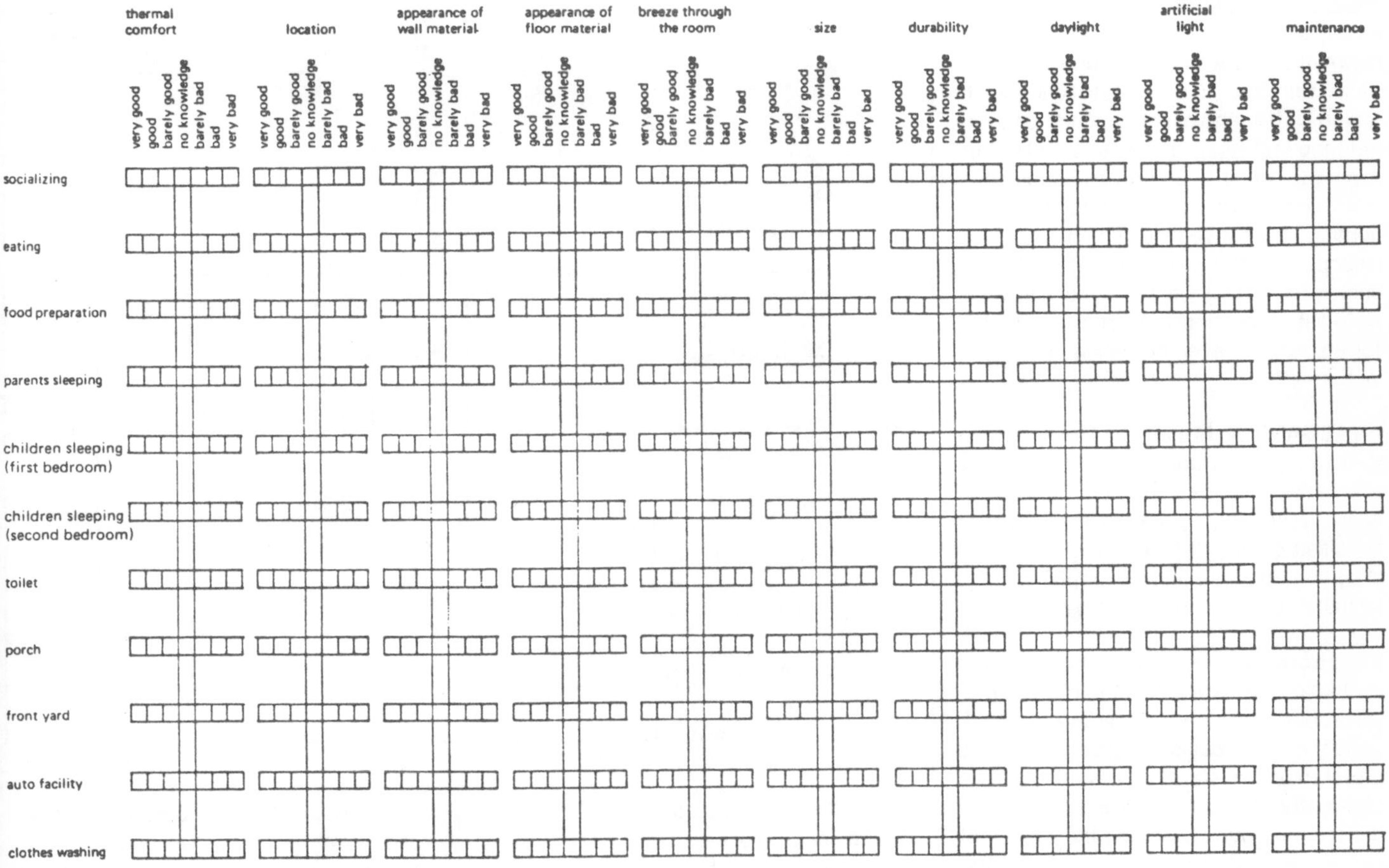

The chart shows rows (activities/spaces) versus columns (attributes), each with a rating scale of: very good, good, barely good, no knowledge, barely bad, bad, very bad.

Column categories (attributes):
- thermal comfort
- location
- appearance of wall material
- appearance of floor material
- breeze through the room
- size
- durability
- daylight
- artificial light
- maintenance

Rating scale (for each column): very good / good / barely good / no knowledge / barely bad / bad / very bad

Row categories:
- socializing
- eating
- food preparation
- parents sleeping
- children sleeping (first bedroom)
- children sleeping (second bedroom)
- toilet
- porch
- front yard
- auto facility
- clothes washing

Source: *Methods of Architectural Programming* by Henry Sanoff, AIA. Stroudsburg, Pa.: Dowden, Hutchinson & Ross Inc., 1977.

functional spaces of a house. Such a chart could be used to evaluate current conditions of a single residence, satisfaction over time by different occupants, or to compare occupant evaluations of several identical structures.

The rating chart is an example of a rather complex evaluation procedure, although, like most rating systems, it is relatively simple to construct and administer. However, obtaining reliable and significant data from any kind of statistical investigation of human values depends on competence in designing scales, selecting appropriate criteria and even determining which issues are pertinent to the investigation. It will save time, money and effort to consult with a professional familiar with survey research techniques, such as a sociologist or opinion research expert, before testing, or even designing, the survey instrument.

EVALUATION MATRIX. This is similar to a rating chart and is used to evaluate alternative proposals, often design options, according to their satisfaction of specified criteria. It is a way of displaying all options in an organized, graphic fashion so that judgments are easier to make.

Products. As a decision-making tool, the evaluation matrix enables the programmer to produce a cumulative score for each option on the basis of such criteria as preference, satisfaction, suitability or acceptability. The scores create a rank order for the options. Among the items that can be evaluated are project objectives, design solutions, site alternatives, or any issue where a decision is called for by the client. The architect will also find it useful in organizing and making programming/design decisions.

Procedure. The evaluation matrix consists of a set of options, listed on one edge of the matrix, and a set of criteria, listed along a perpendicular edge. Inter-

EXHIBIT 5-10. SIMPLE MODEL OF AN EVALUATION MATRIX

	EVALUATION CRITERIA					Total Score	Rank Order
	a	b	c	d	e		
OPTION A	0	+2	+1	−1	0	+2	3
OPTION B	+2	+1	+2	0	+1	+6	1
OPTION C	−1	−1	0	+1	0	−1	4
OPTION D	+1	+2	0	−1	+1	+3	2

secting lines between the two sets create boxed spaces for insertion of scale rates, as shown in Exhibit 5-10.

The scoring scale used to judge satisfaction of the criteria is a range of +2 to −2; more precisely:

    +2 = excellent
    +1 = good
     0 = neutral
    −1 = poor
    −2 = very poor

This type of scale is often used because of the clarity of meaning of the different values. A positive number represents a positive value, a negative number represents a negative value, and a 0 represents no value. However, some consider the use of negative numbers undesirable since a negative score might imply worthlessness when in actuality the rating is only meant to indicate relative value and not absolute value. Note that the score values represent an example of an interval scale, which shows the degree of criteria satisfaction of one option compared with another. The rank order, on the other hand,

EXHIBIT 5-11. WEIGHTED EVALUATION MATRIX

Rating Factors
- +2 Excellent Potential
- +1 Good Potential
- 0 Even
- -1 Poor Potential
- -2 No Potential

Program Development Based on Site Size	COMPARISON AREAS	DEVELOPED	INTERNAL			EXTERNAL						PLAN DEVELOPMENT			SUBTOTALS	
			Modular Development	Full Design Potential	Full Program Potential	Full Accessibility	Potential Parking Facilities	Potential Shared Facilities	Related to Medical School	UCMC Development	Identification	Overall Planning Potential	Phasing Potential	Development of Related Projects		
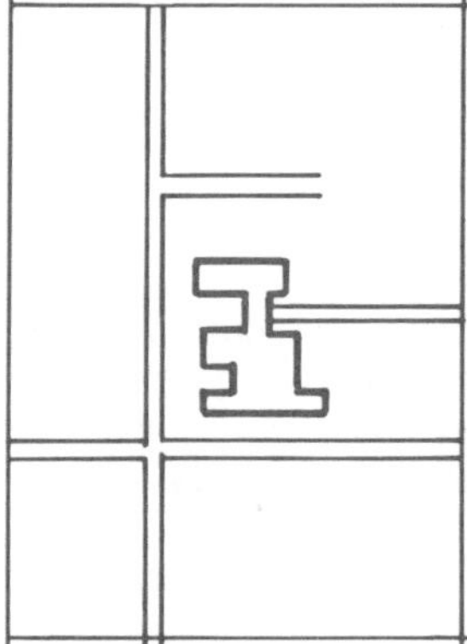 250 B G-3 208,425°	Recommended Program		+2	+2	+2	-1	+1	+1	2	-1	+1	2	+1	+1	+5	+10
	Recommended Effective Size		+2	+2	+2	-1	+1	+1	2	-1	+1	2	+1	-1	+3	
	Ultimate Recommended Effective Size		+2	+2	+2	-1	+1	+1	2	2	+1	2	+1	-1	+2	
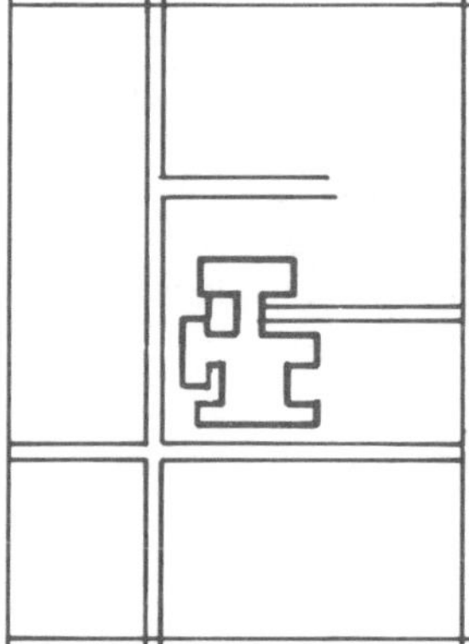 150 B G-2 172,410°	Recommended Program		-1	-1	-1	+1	+1	+2	+2	+1	-1	-1	-2	0	0	-19
	Recommended Effective Size		2	2	2	-1	+1	+1	+1	-1	-1	-1	-1	-1	-9	
	Ultimate Recommended Effective Size		-2	-2	-2	-2	+1	+1	+1	-1	-1	-1	-1	-1	10	
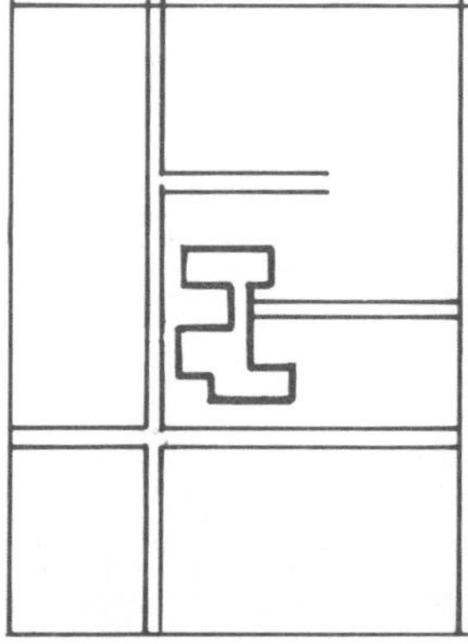 250 B G-3 208,425°	Recommended Program		+2	+2	+2	+1	+1	+1	0	+1	+1	2	+1	+1	15	+45
	Recommended Effective Size		+2	+2	+2	+1	+1	+1	0	+1	+1	2	+1	+1	15	
	Ultimate Recommended Effective Size		+2	+2	+2	+1	+1	+1	0	+1	+1	2	+1	+1	15	

is an example of an ordinal scale and shows only the relative order of option preference.

An example of a more complex evaluation matrix is shown in Exhibit 5-11 and illustrates the variety of factors that can be accommodated with this device at one time.

WEIGHTING. An extra measure of precision can be added to a rating through the use of weight factors. Essentially, a set of weightings is an interval scale which identifies relative levels of importance. These weights are applied to a set of criteria to be used in evaluating items or options. Of course, it is possible and beneficial to rate items according to satisfaction of criteria of equal weight. This can produce a rank order of preference or priority and even measure differentials among the ranked items. Frequently, however, the criteria are of unequal importance; that is, one criterion may have more significance to the judge in deciding which option best meets the criteria in toto. Although weighting factors enjoy wide use in a variety of situations (notably, in architect/engineer selection

procedures of the federal government), some of the weaknesses of the technique (and of ranking) are pointed out in *Design Methods: Seeds of Human Futures* by J. Christopher Jones and are worth examining before using this technique.

Procedure. The simplest method of establishing reliable weights for a set of criteria is to ask those who are going to use the criteria to rate them according to their relative importance. The rater may be either the programmer or the client, depending on who will use the criteria once they have been weighted. It might be useful, however, for both to perform the rating so that agreement is established on the relative importance of the individual criteria before they are applied to a decision-making exercise. An interval scale, such as 0 to 1, 1 to 5, or +2 to –2 is used to rate each one and the resulting numerical values become the weighting factors.

A more complicated procedure for determining weights is explained in *The Design of Social Research* by Russell L. Ackoff. A similar method is outlined by Henry Sanoff in *Methods of Architectural Programming.*

DEVELOPING PROGRAMMING COMPETENCE

Programming opens a variety of new opportunities to the architect and a whole range of new techniques to master. While some techniques described in this and the previous two chapters may be familiar, many others will require practice and trial in new situations. An enterprising programmer will not limit his or her experience to techniques that are familiar and comfortable but will develop skill in new techniques and procedures, judging which are most appropriate and efficient for the task at hand.

New methods for programming and information processing are developing continuously. The use of the computer as a tool for improving efficiency and proficiency in information processing techniques is becoming more widespread. For the architectural programmer, these developments represent opportunities to expand and improve professional practice. The next chapter presents an overview of computer applications and techniques that are or may be useful in programming and expanded architectural practice.

Chapter 6
Computer Aids to
Facility Programming

The computer offers speed, efficiency, precision and reliability to the performance of the procedures and tasks of facility programming. Applied to many of the techniques described in Part Two and to techniques developed specifically for computerization, the computer can vastly improve management and manipulation of large quantities of data. Electronic data processing doesn't do anything that human data processing doesn't. It only enhances human ability to process information. Like any other tool, the computer is an extension of the operator's faculties; specifically, of the faculties of computing, recalling and reporting while sorting out data. (See Exhibit 6-1.)

The capabilities of the computer have been simplistically summarized by Bryan Guttridge and Jonathan R. Wainwright in their book, *Computers in Architectural Practice*. They say: *A digital computer has been described as a high-speed "moron." It has the ability to process information fed into it and to produce an output which is the result of a predetermined sequence of instructions. It cannot learn by its own mistakes and it has no intuition. Its accuracy in processing relies on the skill of the (computer) programmer. A computer will produce rubbish if rubbish is fed into it; conversely, worthwhile results can be formulated from a worthwhile program and its relevant data.* The British architects further simplify this description in noting that the computer can perform five information-processing functions: add, subtract, multiply, divide and re-sort information in a predetermined manner.

This refreshing irreverence for technology has to put the computer in its place as a mere tool. Yet, it can't be forgotten that it is a very handy and versatile tool, the use of which has revolutionized many aspects of society, from grocery check-

EXHIBIT 6-1. THE COMPUTER IS AN EXTENSION OF HUMAN CAPABILITY

out to building construction. The revolution has only just begun in architecture and facility design, which lag behind fields with a history of numerical calculation such as accounting, management and engineering. Although computer programs for processing certain types of design-related information have been around for more than 10 years, they have not enjoyed wide use and many new applications are still in the development and testing stages.

John S. Gero, editor of *Computer Applications in Architecture*, blames the scarcity of such applications on economics, office structure and practice policy. The most pervasive reason cited by Gero, however, is "ignorance of both what is being done (in the field) and what can be done, in addition to a paucity of suitable information on means of achieving objectives using the computer." His book is an attempt to help rectify the situation.

Others, including some who have been on the forefront of developing computer applications for architecture, see the problem more as one of inappropriateness. Vladimir Bazjanac is on the faculty of architecture at the University of California at Berkeley and is a confirmed "nonbeliever" in the promises of computerization for facility design. From his experience as one of the early architectural computer jockeys, he recalls: *I realized that in evaluating the functional performance of buildings, we are dealing largely with unpredictable aspects of human behavior and that we can never simulate (by computer or otherwise) a full range of possible behavioral variations. . . . Since it is questionable whether human behavior in buildings can be controlled, it is also questionable whether functional performance of buildings . . . can be predicted.*

Bazjanac goes on to say: *The promise that computers will improve the efficiency of design is absurd. Even if the use of machines allowed the designer to spend more time designing (and it does not), how can anyone claim that the designer would therefore produce better design solutions? The design process cannot be controlled by the manipulation of resources: Adding resources will not necessarily speed up the design or improve its quality.*

These quotations are taken from Bazjanac's essay in *Reflections on Computer Aids to Design and Architecture*, edited by Nicholas Negroponte. The essay and two others in the book (one by Steve Coons and another by Murray Milne) provide balanced insights into the promises and limitations of computer applications in facility design.

As illustrated in Exhibit 6-2, computer software development is in a growing but still embryonic state. Some of the applications described in this chapter are workable and in current use; others are in the development stage; and still others are dreams of potential application.

COMPUTER CAPABILITIES

The five-function breakdown cited by Guttridge and Wainwright earlier represents only the basic components of the computer's ability. Most of its operations are based on those mathematical functions. In practical, general terms, however, the computer can:

—Store very large quantities of data
—Retrieve stored data very rapidly
—Sort data and isolate requested information
—Calculate at an extremely rapid rate
—Generate numerous options for a particular situation
—Compare these options and select only those appropriate to specified criteria (also programmed into the computer)
—Combine, relate, group and organize data easily, efficiently and to a greater degree of sophistication than manual operations
—Decompose, segregate and transpose data in the same manner

In facility programming and design, the computer procedures most often applied can be summarized under two headings: data management and data manipulation. *Data management* involves straightforward input-output operation and the supporting functions of recording, classification, storage, updating and editing, sorting and retrieval of information in various forms. As a design project proceeds, it continuously generates new and revised data and accumulates a tremendous volume. Just keeping track of the information and keeping it current is a time-consuming, complicated task. The efficiency of computerized data management enables the facility programmer or designer to have available and instantaneously locate and obtain any piece or collection of information required. For example, if a listing of all rooms in a projected building requiring natural light is desired, keyboarding the appropriate code on the computer terminal will produce a printout or screen display of the information. Likewise, a request for a display or a printout of the rooms in that category which are more than 400 net square feet and must have public access will yield the results in a matter of moments.

In order to interpret the implications of programming/design data, it is often necessary to manipulate it in some way. *Data manipulation* ranges from simple calculations to complex analyses and simulations of projected activities. Procedures may involve segregating and recomposing data, representing interactions and relationships, computing values and optimizing objectives. Most of the interpretive procedures possible through computerization are based on some form of interaction analysis, which is discussed in a later section.

At the current level of sophistication of computerized or automated data processing in facility programming, the most reliable and cost-effective uses involve straightforward maintenance and accession of data and the compilation of lists of requirements; e.g., space inventories, area requirements, equipment/furniture lists, code requirements. Nevertheless, considerable experience has been accumulated in performing analytical programming functions such as adjacency analysis, life cycle cost estimating, constraint impact analysis, layout optimization, space standardization and energy conservation projections. A more comprehensive list of computer applications for programming and design that have been implemented was compiled by William J. Mitchell for his book, *Computer-aided Architectural Design*. It is reproduced in Exhibit 6-3.

COMPUTERIZED ANALYSIS TECHNIQUES

The potential applications of computerization to the analytical information-processing procedures and techniques required for programming and feasibility type studies are virtually limitless. A representative sample of some of these is presented here under general categories, although the categorization is not intended to restrict the techniques to only one type of issue or activity.

SYSTEMATIC PROBLEM STRUCTURING. Problem-structuring methods are most appropriate in the initial stages of new and complex problems, where previous experience and existing prototype solutions provide little guidance. Despite limitations, techniques such as Murray Milne's CLUSTR program can produce very useful results. Milne describes his technique in "CLUSTR: A Structure-finding Algorithm," in *Emerging Methods in Environmental Design and Planning*, Gary Moore, editor.

The objective of Milne's and other problem-structuring procedures is to devise an organizing framework out of the elements of a problem itself that enable it to be studied efficiently and logically. Milne's

EXHIBIT 6-2. THREE STAGES OF COMPUTER SOFTWARE DEVELOPMENT

In Dreaming Stage:

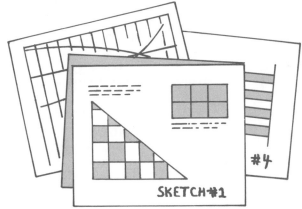

In Development:

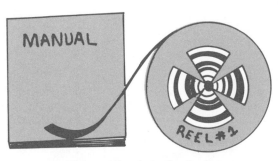

Available and Ready for Application:

EXHIBIT 6-3. COMPUTER APPLICATIONS FOR PROGRAMMING/DESIGNING

BRIEFING PHASE

Feasibility Study
—Economic feasibility analysis
—Housing type mix analysis

Programming
—Problem structuring
—Activity data analysis
—Space need projection
—Accommodation schedule production
—Circulation analysis
—Cluster and bubble diagram generation

SKETCH DESIGN PHASE

Site Planning
—Site mapping
—Slope analysis
—Drainage analysis
—Cut and fill analysis
—View analysis
—Accessibility analysis
—Overlay mapping analyses
—Site plan synthesis

Schematic Design Synthesis
—Floor plan layout
—Three-dimensional spatial synthesis

Performance and Cost Analysis
of Proposals
—Checking for compliance with the brief
—Circulation analysis
—Preliminary structural computations
—Heat gain computations
—Heat loss computations
—Insolation and shadow pattern analyses
—Natural lighting computations
—Artificial lighting computations
—Sound transmission computations
—Reverberation time computations
—Preliminary cost estimation

Presentation
—Plotting sketch plans, elevations, sections
—Plotting perspectives

PRODUCTION DOCUMENTS PHASE

Detail Design
—Building products data retrieval
—Automated detailing
—Structural member selection and sizing

—Mechanical and electrical system detail design
—Duct, pipe, and electrical network layout

Costing
—Generation of bills of quantities
—Pricing of bills of quantities
—Cost analyses

Production
—Generation of schedules
—Generation of specifications
—Plotting of working drawings

CONSTRUCTION SUPERVISION PHASE
Network Analysis
Precedence Diagramming
Project Cost Control

MANAGEMENT FUNCTIONS
Job Costing
Time and Payroll Functions
Invoicing

Source: *Computer-aided Architectural Design* by William J. Mitchell. New York: Petrocelli/Charter, 1977.
NOTE: Comparable phase titles used by AIA are:

MITCHELL	AIA
Briefing	Predesign
Sketch Design	Schematic Design and Design Development
Production Documents	Construction Documents
Construction Supervision	Construction Contract Administration

technique accomplishes this by creating a hierarchy of element relationships or clusters. The four-step procedure is described as follows.

The first step is to identify all the elements of the design problem, usually expressed in the form of problem statements. These are goals, requirements, constraints or performance specifications. All possible issues must be covered in the list of elements.

Next, the elements are "clustered," beginning by pairing individual elements with each other to test for possible interactions. The interactions or relationships of those elements affected are expressed in the form of an interaction matrix (see "Relationship Matrices" in Chapter 4).

The next step in clustering the elements employs the use of the computer. The matrix and elements list are input to a computer program which sorts the elements into clusters, or groups of elements that are directly related to each other. These initial clusters are called "simplexes" in which each element is connected to all other elements of the group. A simplex group has relatively few links to other elements. It represents a discrete subproblem or subsystem.

The computer program, operated by algorithm, continues to identify relationships, in the fourth step, among the simplexes and among the resulting combined simplexes until, eventually, one large cluster is created representing the entire problem. A hierarchy of subproblems, represented by successively larger clusters, has been created out of the individual elements of the problem.

The structure of the problem at each state of clustering can be represented in narrative printout or in graph form. It is often useful to display the complete problem structure in a dendrogram (semilattice or tree structure diagram). Exhibit 6-4 presents a simplified example of a problem-structuring format using the clustering technique. The elements of the problem

EXHIBIT 6-4. PROBLEM STRUCTURING FORMAT EXAMPLE

1. ELEMENTS

a
b
c
d
e
f
g
h
i

2. INTERACTION MATRIX

	a	b	c	d	e	f	g	h	i
a	–		x		x	x			
b		–	x			x	x		x
c	x	x	–		x				
d				–	x	x		x	
e	x		x	x	–				
f	x	x		x		–	x	x	
g		x			x		–		x
h			x		x		–	x	
i		x				x	x	–	

3. SIMPLEXES

a a b b b d d h
c f f g c f e i
e   g i   h

4. DENDROGRAM

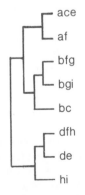

ace
af
bfg
bgi
bc
dfh
de
hi

5. GRAPH

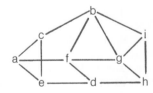

are represented by letters.

Another problem-structuring computer program is described by C.F. Davis in "EPS: A Computer Program for the Evaluation of Problem Structures" in *Emerging Methods in Environmental Design and Planning*.

FEASIBILITY ANALYSIS. At this stage of the programming/design process, the basic parameters, constraints and objectives of a project are established. The multitude of factors which must be considered can be conveniently and efficiently manipulated through the use of computer-based mathematical models. While it doesn't replace accurate information and sound professional judgment, the application of computer techniques to feasibility analysis can help the programmer thoroughly explore the implications of information available.

The basic procedure of feasibility analysis is to first identify and list the variables that define the problem (decision variables, parameters, constraints) and the possible alternatives for each variable. Next, one of a variety of mathematical models that can interrelate the alternative factors to each other is applied. With the model and the computational capacity of the electronic data processor, large and/or complex problems can be manipulated to produce feasible solutions in a variety of ways:

—Enumeration of ranges of feasible solutions

—Evaluation of options against various criteria

—Optimization of an objective

—Analysis of the "sensitivity" of feasible options to variations in the values of decision variables, parameters and constraints

Morphological Analysis. This is one technique for enumerating a range of possible solutions. The objective of morphological analysis is to produce an ex-

haustive list of potential solutions (without judging feasibility) through systematically creating and listing combinations of alternative variables. The computer becomes valuable in this regard when the programmer is confronted with a wide range of variables, each consisting of a number of alternatives. Manually producing all the possible permutations would be extremely laborious and subject to frequent error without the capabilities of the computer.

One disadvantage of morphological analysis is that it produces a significant number of incompatible or infeasible combinations. The technique would be improved if these could be eliminated automatically during computation rather than after the entire list of options is enumerated.

Incompatibility Matrices. One way to achieve the improvement of automatic elimination of infeasible permutations is by the technique of incompatibility matrices. As in morphological analysis, the key decision variables, parameters and constraints must be enumerated and the optional conditions or actions for each one searched out. The objective is to combine individual options into groups that represent feasible solutions accommodating all the variables.

While morphological analysis starts and ends with groups representing all variables, the incompatibility matrices technique begins by matching pairs of variables. The options of one variable are compared with the individual options of another, then a third, variable set; and so on until all options (within their variable sets) have been paired. A series of matrices is used to perform the operation efficiently and conveniently; each matrix represents a pairing.

It is similar to a relationship or interaction matrix, except that instead of comparing the items in one set to each other, items in one variable set are related to items in another set. The matrix is a rep-

resentation of the programmer's judgment of which pairs of items are compatible and which are incompatible in terms of whatever criteria are used to judge compatibility. The key difference between this method and morphological analysis is that feasibility decisions begin as the variables are combined rather than after the morphology is completed.

The efficiency of the matrix method is based on a rule of "pairwise incompatibility"; that is, if two factors are incompatible with each other, neither is the pair compatible in combination with any other variable. Any combination representing all variables that included an incompatible pair would be eliminated automatically from the list of "all possible" permutations.

The computer enhances the efficiency of the operation. Operating on a data base of the incompatibility matrix series and programmed with an appropriate algorithm, the computer can "predict" which combinations contain incompatible pairs and eliminate them from the list of feasible combinations. It does this by simply not computing an infeasible combination, which saves computational effort where there is a large number of possible permutations. Recognizing that any feasibility or programming issue contains dozens or scores of variables to consider, it can be seen that a computerized version of the incompatibility matrices method is invaluable in that it can eliminate automatically the unworkable solutions from the hundreds of permutations that are possible. If weighting factors or performance criteria were added to the feasibility computation (e.g., most or least feasible, order of preference), computerization of the calculations would be even more beneficial.

Optimization. This technique involves a different procedure for ranking feasible solutions in order of value. Optimization is particularly useful in finding optimum feasible solutions in terms of cost or other performance criteria or to measure the "sensitivity" of the optimized solution to variations in design variables (parameters, constraints, decisions). The simplest way to do this is to utilize a computer program which systematically increments values of design variables through the allowable range for each to exhaustively enumerate potential solutions (as in a morphological analysis). Each alternative, as it is computed, is tested against constraints for feasibility. If infeasible, it is eliminated. If feasible, the value of the alternative is computed based on a predetermined constant factor or equation (such as unit cost). The feasible alternative that has the best value would be selected after all computations have been made. However, the optimum solution can be selected by the computer by programming it to measure alternatives against a predetermined objective (such as a "cost-not-to-exceed" figure). This is called the technique of *optimization by enumeration*.

Several computer programs for optimizing feasible alternatives have been implemented. One of the earliest was developed by Caudill Rowlett Scott and is oriented toward high rise office buildings. It analyzes construction cost, cost-per-square-foot of floor area, net income from project, percentage return on investment, etc. The best known is the Building Optimization Program (BOP) developed by Skidmore, Owings & Merrill, which enumerates all possible variable combinations (based on values assigned several key variables) and estimates construction cost and other measures for each combination.

Another technique is *optimization by linear programming*, which is a more appropriate tool when possible combinations of variables are very large. A linear programming problem is characterized by real-number variables, constraints defined by means of linear inequalities (such as $X > 1$), and an objective which is a linear function of the design variables. Computer programs are available which can solve linear programming problems consisting of thousands of variables and constraints with comparative ease.

Other optimization technique computer programs are also available. A survey of programs was produced by J. L. Kuester and J. H. Mize and published as *Optimization Techniques with FORTRAN* by McGraw-Hill (1973). An examination of optimization applications in architecture is found in "Architectural Optimization: A Review" by John S. Gero of the University of Sydney, Australia, in *Engineering Optimization*.

SPACE NEEDS ANALYSIS. Determining the amounts and kinds of spaces required for an architectural project is a fundamental function of programming. Computerization offers numerous opportunities for improving the efficiency, reliability and scope of such analyses. Computer-based mathematical models applied in space analysis techniques are capable of processing vast quantities of data and performing more extensive, sophisticated analysis than is possible by manual calculation.

Simple empirical formulae based on previous experience are a traditional means of estimating accommodation needs such as area, quantity of spaces by type, equipment/furnishing requirements, cost per area, etc. Supplied with data about people, activities and/or equipment, the computer operates through the empirical formula to calculate the objective. Numerous programs of this type have been developed. Simple empirical models can project lists of spaces for a particular type of facility, such as the HPIS (Hospital Planning Information System) developed by Skidmore, Owings & Merrill of New York. The HPIS program produces listings of required spaces together with cost and area summaries.

Limitations of empirical formula models include the lack of a firm basis for optimizing space usage or for performing sensitivity analysis (testing variations in constraints and parameters). Furthermore, since the formula is based on past experience, there is no way of knowing whether past mistakes are perpetuated or that changes in conditions invalidate assumptions.

An alternative approach, which may overcome such difficulties, is to develop a computer-based model of the activity system projected for the project: a mathematical simulation that will accommodate alteration of the variables that comprise the system. A *timetable* is an activity definer around which such a model can be constructed. This has been used successfully in school design, where scheduling is a major determinant of classroom usage. Computer algorithms based on timetable graphs have been used for exploring the effects of different enrollment patterns, curricula schedules and classroom size policies to find optimum distribution of classroom sizes. *Queuing models* have been produced for estimating space needs in facilities that require waiting lines (queues), such as supermarkets, banks, department stores, cafeterias, etc.

Facilities which must accommodate high-volume, complex activity patterns (such as movement of goods, multiple-station circulation, paper flow and communications) require more sophisticated analysis than offered by simple queuing models. One method is *discrete event digital simulation*. This is based on a breakdown of the activity pattern into discrete "events," such as a movement, and "states," such as waiting to move. A discrete event digital simulation model is a computer program that simulates mathematically the occurrence of events and changes of states in a system over time and produces statistics on individual states and the total system. This has been applied in examinations of airport terminals, clinics, parking structures, elevator systems, and other service facilities.

These types of structures involve high-volume traffic, multidirectional movement and multiple states. Exhibit 6-5 presents a flow diagram for simulation that shows the variety of events and states involved in an airport terminal arrivals building, as produced by translation of mathematical simulation into graphic simulation.

Dynamic programming is a computer technique that can be applied to the procedures of *space normalization*. Normalization is a procedure for determining the optimum distribution of activities among a variety of standard space sizes in conjunction with optimization of another variable, such as cost of construction. In small-scale normalizations, dual or multiple optimizations can be worked out by successive enumeration. When the activities to be accommodated by a facility number in the hundreds or thousands, the permutations are virtually impossible to produce. A dynamic programming computerization, however, makes such computations feasible. It is a highly sophisticated and complex technique and the procedures involved require more detailed explanation than can be offered here. E.V. Denardo's book, *Dynamic Programming: Theory and Application* describes the process. Its use in architectural studies is examined by John S. Gero in *Dynamic Programming in Architecture* (1976), one of a series of "computer reports" produced at the University of Sydney, Australia.

INTERACTION AND GROUPING ANALYSIS. Measuring and interpreting interaction and other relationships among variables is a fundamental task in architectural programming. The basic technique for representing interactions is the matrix (interaction, relationship, compatibility, etc.). Although there are numerous types of interaction matrices employed for different measurements and different data, the common operating principle is pairing. A matrix represents a series of pairings that show patterns of functional

EXHIBIT 6-5. COMPUTER-PRODUCED STATE-EVENT FLOW DIAGRAM

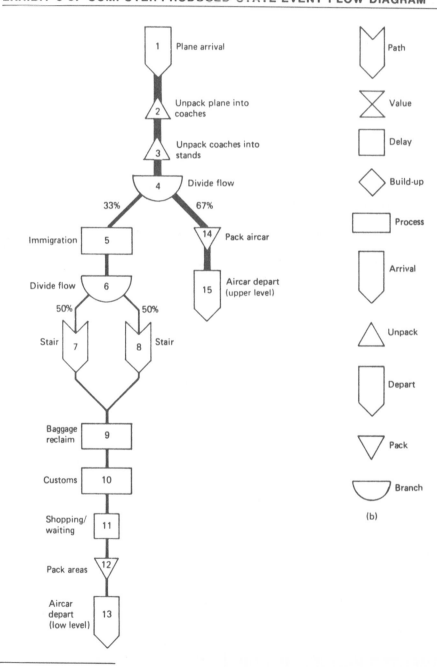

NOTE: Diagram is from *Computer-aided Architectural Design* by William J. Mitchell. According to the book, the source is Applied Research of Cambridge (England), which has developed a general purpose "movement in building simulator" computer program.

association between activities and/or spaces. The implications of these patterns are not easily deciphered from merely "reading" the matrices, particularly when a large number are involved. A further analytical technique is necessary in order to interpret the data. Two techniques for analyzing interaction matrices that have been promoted by the capabilities of the computer are *cluster analysis* and *multidimensional scaling*.

The application of clustering for problem-structuring described at the beginning of this chapter is one procedure for performing cluster analysis. Others include single linkage clustering and average linkage clustering. Although elementary clustering was introduced during the 1930s, it was not until modern, high-speed computers became generally available in the 1960s that sophisticated versions of the type used today began to be developed.

Multidimensional scaling is a technique that measures two or more aspects or dimensions of the relative (rather than absolute) association among variables. It operates on the basis of disassociation among variables—the inverse of specific association—for the purpose of representing matrix data geometrically in terms of "distance" between variables. If the disassociation distance between two variables is long, they are not closely related; if short, there is a strong relationship. A graphic representation of a multidimensionally scaled problem can be produced that is similar to a standard bubble diagram. It will show several relationships among many variables in terms of the relative value of association among all of them at the same time. Except in simple cases, a computer program is necessary to calculate the arrangement with any degree of precision.

COMPUTER PROGRAMS FOR FACILITY PROGRAMMING

Both current and future applications of computer technology for facility programming are examined.

CURRENT APPLICATIONS. A great many computer programs and programming systems have been developed in recent years that can be applied to facility programming. Some have been created specifically to address facility programming activities and issues, especially in the areas of managing space needs inventories and computing space relationships and layout plans. Others incorporate programmatic information processing into comprehensive computer-aided design systems.

Synopses of a number of programs that have been used for feasibility analysis, architectural programming, relational planning and site planning, among other design-related information-processing operations, are included in the first volume of a study report for the Environmental Design and Research Center of Boston. The 1975 report was prepared by Dr. Kaiman Lee, AIA, and is entitled *Performance Specification of Computer-aided Environmental Design* (two volumes). Lee also produced a five-volume report for the Center a year earlier called *Computer Programs in Environmental Design*, which abstracted existing programs.

At the time of publication of the former document, Lee recognized 39 feasibility study, 14 architectural programming, 71 relational planning, and 68 site planning computer programs out of a total of 337. In an overview of the state-of-the-art on computer applications, he referenced the following programs. The status and availability of these are unknown at this time.

Feasibility Study. Those related to cost or economic feasibility of proposed projects. One was Building Optimization Program (BOP), developed by Skidmore, Owings & Merrill of Chicago to evaluate high rise urban office buildings. The program generates alternative geometric configu-

rations and preliminary cost information for the major cost-influencing subsystems of each alternative, as well as data regarding return on investment, cost per square foot, and total project cost.

A similar program, Preliminary Office Building Design (PROB), compares alternative low building designs with largest floor area allowed by zoning requirements to tall buildings with the minimum desired floor area per floor. This program was developed by Alfred P. Swenson of the Illinois Institute of Technology in Chicago.

The Advanced Planning Research Group of Kensington, Maryland, developed Commercial Project Feasibility Analysis, a more general program that evaluates alternative project designs in terms of cost of construction and return on investment.

Still more generic and applicable to a wide variety of building types is the Interactive Site Feasibility Study Model developed by John S. Gero of the Department of Architectural Science of the University of Sydney, Australia. The program permits a great deal of flexibility in applying various parameters to the analysis, and yields a comparison of alternative solutions weighing construction costs, land costs, realization and return.

Architectural Programming. Lee reports that the consensus on use of the computer for architectural programming is that it can record a project's data in terms of a list of rooms with their physical parameters such as sizes, and various requirements such as electrical, HVAC and acoustics. Associated with each room can be a list of the furnishings and equipment within it.

A series of two programs developed by The Architects Collaborative of Cambridge, Massachusetts, are called Facilities Information System and Interiors Facilities Information System. The first deals with the physical characteristics of a list of rooms which is then linked with a furniture data bank in the second system. The program produces area and cost reports, and lists of furnishings, equipment rooms, delivery schedules and delivery labels.

Other two-program series listed include Interior Furnishings Information System and Building Equipment Information Systems by Caudill Rowlett Scott of Houston, Texas; and Hospital Programming Information Systems and Interior Design Information Systems by Skidmore, Owings & Merrill of New York. A similar, but more general, program was developed by Computer Service Inc. of Chicago called Architectural Information Retrieval System with the added ability to generate door schedules and room finish schedules.

The Comprograph program—part of the ARK-2 system developed by Perry Dean & Stewart of Boston, which was acquired by Cost, Management and Planning International Inc. (CPMI) of Des Moines, Iowa, in 1976—is cited by Lee as "probably the most generic and flexible" program for architectural programming. It deals with physical descriptions of rooms and their requirements, furnishings and equipment. It is also linked to two graphic programs, one of which enables information on functional space groupings to be retrieved for use in relational planning with another component, Comproplan.

Relational Planning or Space Allocation. With its large, accurate memory and low computation time, the high speed digital computer can be used to generate as well as evaluate solutions to space allocation problems, according to Lee. He divides this category of programs into five subcategories: interchange, neighboring, random, vector and multiconstrained. Programs listed include:

—Computerized Relative Allocation of Facilities Technique (CRAFT), one of the first applications of computers in architecture, and a later modification, CRAFT 3-D. The original was developed by IBM.

—Computerized Relationship Layout Planning (CORELAP), which was renamed Interactive Computerized Relationship Layout Planning, was initially developed at Northeastern University in Boston. Another version of the program, Computerized Multistory Building Layout (COMSBUL) was developed by Lee.

—Relationship Technique (RELATE), Lester Gorsline Associates of Terra Linda, California.

—Space Organization Method—Interactive (SOMI), developed under a National Science Foundation grant, Columbia University.

—ALOKAT, Allan Bernholtz of Ottawa, Ontario, Canada.

—Automated Layout Design Program (ALDEP), IBM.

—Comproplan (part of ARK-2) developed by Perry, Dean & Stewart.

—LOCAT, by Professor Isao Oishi, College of Architecture, Virginia Polytechnic Institute.

—General Space Planner (GSP), Charles Eastman, Carnegie-Mellon University.

—IMAGE, Massachusetts Institute of Technology.

—Implicit Enumeration Approach to Floor Plan Layout, Robin Segerbloom Liggett, School of Architecture and Urban Planning, University of California at Los Angeles.

Site Planning. Programs listed by Lee in this category include:

—Map Processing System ("the one program that defines almost everything that site planning deals with"), Planning and Transport Research and Computation Co. Ltd. of London, England

—Contour Plotting System-1 (CPS-1), Unitech Inc., Austin, Texas

—VIEWS and SLOPES, Environmental Systems Research Institute of Redlands, California

—CALFORM, Harvard University Graduate School of Design

FUTURE APPLICATIONS. In the field of design, and particularly architecture, the computer has not made a major impact yet. Many architectural offices use computers to handle payroll and billing records, assist in some management tasks, and provide assistance for engineering services. But unfamiliarity with the capabilities of the computer for programming, planning and design services has held back wider application in these areas.

In addition, the cost of operating computerized programs is high, the quantities of data necessary for input are large and the means of obtaining these data are no different nor easier than manual methods.

Nevertheless, the potential for application of computer methods to architectural processes and services, especially programming, appears significant. The trend toward reduced expense of computer hardware and software and the availability of microprocessing technology are combining with the advantages of tremendous data storage capacity, speed and selectivity of data retrieval, and accurate, precise calculation capability to make computer-aided facility programming a promising opportunity. Specific areas where computer usage may become more prevalent or find new application include budget analysis, energy analysis, space management and planning, inventory analysis and statistical manipulations, to name a few.

RESOURCES ON COMPUTER APPLICATIONS

One of the first comprehensive books on computer aids to architecture was published in 1968. Since then, the rapid development of more and more advanced techniques have been followed by release of numerous other publications in the field. Several merit particular attention, both because of their general explanations of how computerization fits into the design process and because of their treatment of applications for facility programming. William J. Mitchell's book, *Computer-aided Architectural Design* (New York: Petrocelli/Charter, 1977), is especially lucid and comprehensive. He devotes an entire chapter to computer use in feasibility analysis and programming and another to automated spatial synthesis, providing guidance for the use of several techniques discussed earlier in this book's chapter. Mitchell's book also includes an extensive bibliography. Other useful references on computers are:

—*Computer Applications in Architecture*, John S. Gero, ed. London: Applied Science Publishers, Ltd., 1977.

—*Computer Programs in Environmental Design* (five volumes), Kaiman Lee, ed. Boston: Environmental Design and Research Center, 1974.

—*Computers in Architectural Practice* by Bryan Guttridge and Jonathan R. Wainwright. New York: John Wiley & Sons, 1973.

—*Performance Specification of Computer-aided Environmental Design* by Kaiman Lee. Boston: Environmental Design and Research Center, 1975.

—*Reflections on Computer Aids to Design and Architecture*, Nicholas Negroponte, ed. New York: Petrocelli/Charter, 1975.

—*Spatial Synthesis in Computer-aided Building Design*, Charles M. Eastman, ed. New York: John Wiley & Sons, 1975.

PART THREE
APPLICATIONS
OF PROGRAMMING

CHAPTERS 7 to 20
PROGRAMMING
CASE STUDIES

CHAPTER 21
PROGRAMMING
IN PRACTICE

The projects examined in the 14 case studies of this part represent a wide range of client organization, facility type and design situation, as well as applications of programming method and information. The case studies discuss many approaches, systems and techniques of processing and producing design information so that the reader may be able to visualize the use of programming principles explained in earlier parts of this book. Each case study examines the roles of client, programmer and designer; the procedures employed for the project; the program results; and the implementation of programmer recommendations.

The concluding chapter, ''Programming in Practice,'' explores some of the management and business aspects of programming, from service agreements and compensation to programming team organization and liability issues. It also forecasts current trends and future opportunities that should be of interest to the design professional who incorporates programming into his or her practice.

Chapter 7
Program for
a Neighborhood
Services Center

FACILITY:

"A" Mountain Neighborhood Center
Tucson, Arizona

CLIENT:

City of Tucson, Arizona

PROGRAMMER:

Architecture One, Ltd.
Tucson, Arizona

Edward T. White III
(Currently on the faculty of the
architecture school, Florida A&M
University, Tallahassee)
Case Study Contributor

CONSULTANT:

Tucson Community Development Design
Center
Tucson, Arizona

DESIGNER:

Architecture One, Ltd.

EXECUTIVE SUMMARY:

A project with a long planning history and
broad community involvement presented
the programmer with the challenge of
managing a large quantity of information
and a diversity of interests and needs.
Systemized information gathering and organizing were the principal functions of
programming, in addition to ensuring client
participation in the decision making. The
project involved identifying project goals,
space needs of 17 different social service
and recreational agencies, and operational needs, as well as effectively communicating the essential information to
both the designer and the client. The program is a guide to the background, issues
and criteria and to the programming process. The neighborhood center has been
constructed.

PROJECT

The impetus for this project came from
community residents who wanted, and

planned for several years to have, a
multipurpose community center built in
their neighborhood. After repeated proposals and finally acceptance of a scaled-
down preliminary program for a first-
phase building of a larger complex, the
"A" Mountain Neighborhood Facility Planning Committee obtained funding to program, design and build its neighborhood
center. The new facility was to be a one-
stop social, health, welfare, educational
and recreational activity center for city
and county residents living primarily within
a three-mile radius of the site. A 40-acre
site adjacent to a high school and a park
provided the location, but site restrictions
permitted only 10 acres to be used.

Although considerable study of space
needs, demographic characteristics and
budget had been performed by resident
groups and public agencies, the project
called for a detailed architectural program.
The charge to the programmer was to respond to two sets of information needs.
The first called for an overview of the
project, including agencies to be housed,
project goals, desired architectural character, space types for each agency, site
development requirements and project
budget. The second, more detailed information set required refinement of available
information, interviews of agencies, investigation of similar facilities, determining
building areas, estimating construction
costs, and producing the program document.

A $600,000 firm budget for the total
project was shared equally by three public

EXHIBIT 7-1. PROGRAMMER'S GOALS AND PROCEDURES AS EXPLAINED IN THE PROGRAM REPORT

ISSUES
—Insure that the programming process and responsibilities are clear to all involved.
—Avoid duplicating effort that has already been made in data gathering.
—Identify and contact all individuals, organizations and agencies that can have
an effect on the project.

PROCESS
—On an administrative level, formulate and agree upon the programming process,
ground rules and responsibilities.
—Collect and organize all the work that has been done to this point.
—Define the total scope of programming participants (users, organizations, agencies,
etc.).
—Identify one representative from each group to be the decision maker and
spokesman for that group.
—Orient representatives to our process, their responsibilities, the schedule and
what we will need from them.
—Submit work done to this point to representatives for verification or change.
—Identify information still needed for programming.
—Hold work sessions with representatives to gather information.
—Document information and submit to representatives for verification or change.
—Test space needs against budget.
—Recycle reduced space allowable back through representatives if required.
—Balance space and budget.
—Distill architectural (form) implications.
—Review planning assumptions with all representatives.
—Produce report.
—Present programming findings to all representatives.

EXHIBIT 7-2. SAMPLE AGENCY "DATA SHEET"

user agency

SOCIALIZATION - NUTRITION

description of activity

SERVICE FOR SENIOR CITIZENS

FULL HOT MEAL (SERVED DAILY)

RECREATIONAL

occupants

staff *2 FULL-TIME · 4 VOLUNTEERS · 6*

public *50 - 75 / DAY (MEALS) 100 - 125 LECTURES AT NIGHT*

duration & frequency of use

FULL-TIME 5 DAYS 7:30 - 3:30

NON-REGULAR EVENINGS

area

SMALL KITCHEN - 36 □' - ACTIVITIES 1000 □' TOTAL - 1586 □'

OFFICE 100 □' - STOR. - 450 □'

parking

staff *6*

public *50 MIN.*

notes

SENIOR CITIZENS CLASSES

LECTURES, MOVIES, SINGING, RECORD PLAYING

COOKING & MEALS - CRAFTS

ACCESS TO OUTSIDE ACTIVITIES - 2300 □

POSSIBLY COVERED

authorities: City of Tucson, Pima County, and the federal Model Cities Program agency. The center would house 17 recreational and social service agencies in a 12,800-square-foot building. Existing conditions for the programming project included the typical space-budget conflict, restrictions on site development, a desert environment and pronounced contours throughout the site, an existing adjacent park and potential functional conflicts due to housing both social service and recreational activities in the same building.

CLIENT

The official client was the city of Tucson. It would operate and maintain the center, in addition to administering the funding and contracting. However, the programmer served several "clients." The other two funding authorities had requirements which had to be met and had also contributed to initiation and research of the project. The agencies which would occupy and offer services in the building were clients, as were the neighborhood residents who would use it.

A programming committee was formed to make major decisions and handle problems that might arise. The committee consisted of representatives from each of the major participating agencies: City of Tucson, Pima County, Neighborhood Facility Planning Committee (residents' group) and the city departments of Human and Community Development and of City Parks and Recreation. The residents' planning group worked especially closely with the programmer, participating throughout the project. It was consulted about the types of agencies to be housed, the extent and type of services to be offered and the beginning concepts for master planning the site at the end of programming. As a result of the long period of planning for the center, the group also had established definite expectations for its design.

EXHIBIT 7-3. SAMPLE SCHEDULE FOR THREE SHARED OFFICES

		MONDAY	TUESDAY	WEDNESDAY	THURSDAY	FRIDAY	SATURDAY	SUNDAY
OFFICE 1	MORNG	YWCA	YWCA	YWCA	YWCA	YWCA		
	AFTERN	YSB	YSB	YSB	YSB	YSB		
	EVENG		NLO		NLO			
OFFICE 2	MORNG		SER		SER			
	AFTERN		PLAN. PAR.		PLAN. PAR.			
	EVENG		NLO		NLO			
OFFICE 3 (ALSO THE CONFERENCE & CULTURE ROOM)	MORNG		LEGAL AID		LEGAL AID			
	AFTERN		CBO					
	EVENG		NLO		NLO			

PROGRAMMER

The programming staff consisted of four people: the project principal in charge of job management; the project programmer responsible for designing the programming procedure, information gathering, analysis, writing and editing, graphics and report format; a graphics coordinator in charge of report production; and a programming consultant from the Community Development Design Center who had worked with the residents from the inception of the center project.

The programmer's contract contained a ''scope of work'' which is summarized in the ''Project'' section of this case study. The contract was for programming services alone and the scope was presented in two sections: Project Description and Additional Services. The first section called for the overview and background data; the second called for specific actions and indicated that the project description was not inclusive.

Total hours spent in programming were 577 over 2½ months, broken down for the following staff:

Project Principal	69 hours
Project Programmer	254 hours
Graphics Coordinator	194 hours
Programming Consultant	60 hours

PROCESS

The programmer's task was essentially to organize existing and new information, ensure that sufficient and essential data were obtained for the designer's needs and translate the information into a form which could be readily used by both the designer and the client. The information management process is summarized in Exhibit 7-1.

The process began with document analysis, the compilation and review of existing data on the project and related issues. Data on the 17 participating agencies were organized and restated in the programmer's format to determine the type and extent of missing information. A previous report on city multiservice neighborhood centers was reviewed. The programming team visited two existing centers and interviewed directors on advantages and disadvantages of differing arrangements and policies.

Each agency was provided information about its needs that had been collected to that point. Interviews were scheduled with representatives to verify the data and collect additional information. Usually no more than two agency representatives participated in each interview. The interviews took place at the agency offices to enable the programmer to observe operations. A data sheet (see Exhibit 7-2) for each agency was used to organize interview topics and record notes from the conversation. The sheet simplified the information-gathering task by arranging previously collected data so that missing pieces could be quickly identified and available data could be verified.

Data collected before and during the interviews included agency program objectives (prepared by the agencies), staffing and scheduling needs, service client characteristics, space needs (area, equipment, environment, etc.), relationships with other agencies and functions, activities, perceptions and problems and other needs. The programmer analyzed, related and organized data into relevant issues and segments such as space use which encompasses the elements of space type and time, as shown in Exhibit 7-3.

The programmer developed a listing of the goals for the center out of the interviews with users and agencies and presented the goal statement to the Project Programming Committee for review and approval. The committee was also instrumental in resolving conflicts. A disagreement between the programmer's recommendation for the best site location and the residents' desire to locate the center elsewhere was settled by a committee vote in favor of the residents.

A conflict which was especially appropriate for the committee (rather than the programmer) to resolve was the competition among agencies for the affordable space. Individual wishes for space exceeded the funds available to provide it. The programming committee performed the space-trimming, primarily by reducing the space requests of the larger occupants. All agencies agreed to the reductions—far more readily than they might have responded to unilateral action by the programmer.

All data collected and documented were submitted to individual agencies for verification, and submitted again once the space-trimming task was completed. Keeping the many client groups and individuals informed and involved in the decision making was an important function of the programmer. Meanwhile, data that did not require such client input, such as land survey and utility information, were obtained independently during the interview period.

PROGRAM

The final activity of the programmer was to synthesize the data accumulated and translate it into design guidelines for presentation in the program report. The guidelines were distilled from a large quantity of information acquired from a wide variety of sometimes competing sources. It was important that they be not only usable by the designer but understandable to the client. The 116-page program was typeset, offset printed and perfect bound and contained numerous illustrations to support data and explain concepts. The program detailed each agency's requirements in a comparable format: goals and philosophy, operations, trends, staffing, schedule, client profile and space needs. Other sections reported conclusions on interagency relationships, parking and service needs, overall project goals and phi-

EXHIBIT 7-4. PROGRAM REPORT CONTENTS

INTRODUCTION
 Participants
 Project Description
 Project History
 Definitions
 Methods

PROJECT ANALYSIS
 Budget
 Schedule
 Philosophy
 Relation to Community
 Agency Analysis
 Parking and Vehicular
 Space Need Summary
 Space-Budget Analysis
 Functional Issues
 Personnel
 Growth and Change
 Site
 Precepts

losophy, functional issues and site analysis. The contents of the program are outlined in Exhibit 7-4.

IMPLEMENTATION

The programmer's report was used at the designer's desk as a reference. A series of directions or design "precepts" concluded the document (see Exhibit 7-5) and demonstrate the clarity of communication with both designer and client. The designer had not participated in the programming but was verbally informed about critical data and issues as they arose. The designer rediagrammed relationships to become familiar with the program contents. At the start of schematics and at intermittent points throughout design, conferences were held between programmer and designer. The center has been designed and constructed.

EXHIBIT 7-5. DESIGN "PRECEPTS" COMMUNICATE WITH BOTH DESIGNER AND CLIENT

● General Exterior Zoning

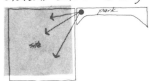

Plan the site for continuity with Vista del Pueblo Park.

Provide access to toilet facilities from exterior recreation areas.

● General Interior Zoning

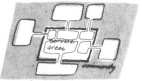

New facility areas can be divided into service areas and community territory.

Service areas are composed of social services and recreational services.

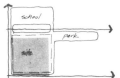

Relate new facility to existing and projected circulation and use patterns.

The building should be at an easily describable address.

Whereas service areas should be controlled, community territory is always open and available at any hour.

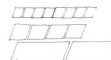

Spaces should be zoned by functional similarity, not by agency labels.

● Atmosphere and Environment

The new center will have a primary target area of one mile and a secondary impact area of two miles.

The facility will receive heavy summer use and afternoon and evening use by youth.

The complex should be designed for easy use by the handicapped and elderly.

The community should feel that it is their center.

Chapter 8
Program for a Middle School

FACILITY:
A Middle School

CLIENT:
An Independent School District, Texas

PROGRAMMER:
Caudill Rowlett Scott (CRS)
Architects, Planners, Engineers
(a CRS Group company)
Houston, Texas

William M. Peña, FAIA
John W. Focke, AIA
Case Study Contributors

DESIGNER:
Caudill Rowlett Scott

PROJECT MANAGEMENT:
CM Associates Inc.
(a CRS Group company)
Houston, Texas

EXECUTIVE SUMMARY:
Operating under a "single-point" project management contract and a "fast-track" timetable, CRS was assigned to program a new school for 1,200 students within two weeks, one-third the usual time allotted for such a project. The firm used its "squatters" technique of continuous intense work sessions to collect and analyze the data rapidly, organizing information according to its standard programming format. Other methods used to process data and stimulate decision making were a client prime-er booklet, analysis cards and "brown sheets." Programming, design and project management tasks overlapped in the time-saving process. The well organized programming methodology was instrumental in completing the project within stringent time limits.

PROJECT

The third middle school for the school district was planned for a 32-acre, flat and partially wooded site adjacent to an ex-

EXHIBIT 8-1. OUTLINE OF PROGRAMMING PROCEDURE

January 22— Awarded Contract
Thursday
School board announced single point contract with CM Associates.

January 23-26— Office Organization
Friday-Monday
Programming group organized; tasks assigned.
Tentative time schedule drafted.
Client prime-er booklet prepared.

January 27— Project Kickoff Meeting
Tuesday
Programming group met with superintendent, business manager and director of secondary education.
Prime-er booklet reviewed; data needs explained.
Programming time schedule reviewed.
Programming/design process explained.
Trial run budget ($5 million) discussed.
Arrangements made for visits to site and to existing schools.

January 28— Site Analysis
Wednesday
Programming group visited new site.
Site conditions documented on "analysis cards."

January 29— School Board Meeting
Thursday
Programming group presented test of preliminary budget to board.
Board indicated desire to reduce enrollment capacity/budget.
Board provided input on goals and policies.
Request made for board to confirm option to buy site.
Visits to existing middle schools made earlier in day.

January 30— Test for Area Parameters
Friday
Programming group reviewed floor plans of existing schools and made area analysis to test area parameters for new school.

February 2-3/4-6— Programming Squatters Sessions
Monday, Tuesday (2-3 p.m.)
Empty classroom near administrative offices converted to work session use.
Programming group documented previously collected data on analysis cards and displayed on wall, organized according to information matrix.
Brown sheets created to display revised space requirements based on new course

enrollment and curriculum data.

New space requirements converted to gross area; cost estimate analysis.

Wednesday-Friday (4-6 p.m.)

Interviews with principals, teachers, service personnel, students conducted during day.

Analysis card and brown sheet displays revised and updated as new information obtained.

Details concerning equipment, etc. documented, but reserved for use in design development.

Work sessions with administrative staff at night involving documentation, evaluation and clarification of new data; tested against cost estimate analysis.

Informal review by school board on night of 6th; school capacity reduced from 1,500 to 1,200 and budget from $5 million to $4.4 million

February 7-8—Program Report
Saturday, Sunday

Space requirements recalculated; brown sheets revised.

Analysis cards supplemented with brief explanatory sentences and reduced by photocopy for use in report format.

Brown sheets also reduced for report and for later use at designer's work table.

New cost estimate analysis prepared.

Program report drafted.

February 9—Program Review
Monday

50-page program report submitted to board through superintendent, three days before regular public meeting of board.

Design team reviewed graphic display of information on functional program, site analysis, cost estimate analysis and time factor.

During remainder of week, design team considered program issues and analyzed building systems and cost.

February 12—Board Approval
Thursday

Board members discussed program report and approved space program and budget with minor modifications.

February 16—Design Squatters
Monday

Design team replaced programming team in same classroom, preparing for week's work on schematic design.

isting elementary school. No educational specifications had been prepared for the project, whose initial scope was a facility to accommodate 1,500 students at a total cost of $5 million. The scope was scaled down as programming progressed to 1,200 students and a $4.4 million budget.

CM Associates Inc. provided project management under a "single-point" (of responsibility) contract. The firm used "fast-track" (or concurrent) scheduling and building systems techniques to compress project delivery time as a hedge against escalating costs. Although the usual programming period alone would have been six weeks, the compressed schedule called for site work to begin within five weeks after the initial meeting. This allowed only two weeks for programming, one week for schematic design and a week in between for the design team to think through the program.

Exhibit 8-1 provides an outline of events during the programming of the middle school, from award of the contract through program completion to its use in preparing the design team for schematics.

CLIENT

The school district was represented by 5 school board members, the superintendent of schools, the business manager, the director of secondary education, 2 principals of existing middle schools, 14 teachers, 3 service staff members (representing the resource center, dietary services and maintenance services) and two groups of 15 students each—a total of 57 people. The programming group had direct access to the school board, meeting in public, informal sessions three times to resolve policy issues such as school size, budget and special education space. The programming group worked closely with the client to develop the project. Client involvement was highly organized and directed by the programmer/manager.

EXHIBIT 8-1. OUTLINE OF PROGRAMMING PROCEDURE (CONT'D)

PROGRAM & DESIGN SCHEDULE

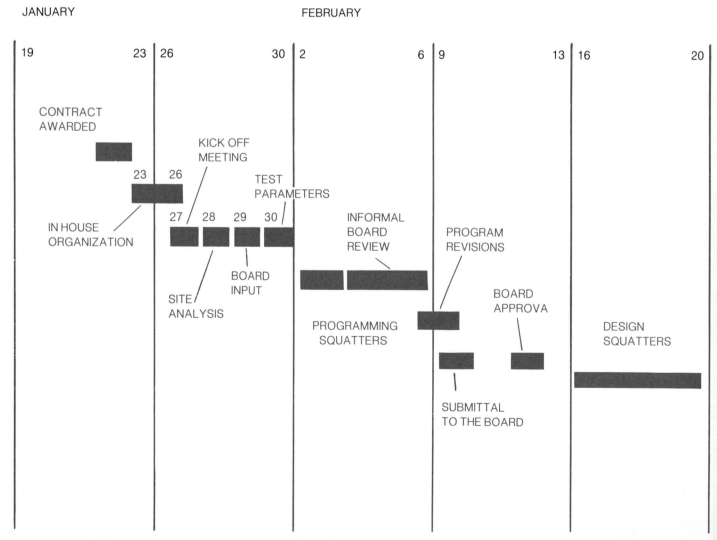

EXHIBIT 8-2. PROGRAMMING MATRIX

	Function	Form	Economy	Time
Establish Goals				
Gather/Analyze Facts				
Uncover/Test Concepts				
Determine Needs				
State the Problem				

PROCESS

The procedure and techniques used to program the school design project are typical of the CRS methodology. The speed and thoroughness with which the programming was accomplished illustrate the advantages of an efficient, well-organized system and an experienced team. The system involves classification of information in a framework which provides a basis for both collecting and documenting data. The organizing framework can be arranged in a checklist matrix that shows five steps of inquiry matched by four elements of data, as shown in Exhibit 8-2.

The "squatters" technique, a CRS method in which the programming group camps in the client's own backyard (in this case, a school classroom) for continuous intense work sessions, was the primary vehicle for gathering data and making decisions. The work sessions included a kickoff meeting with school administrators followed by an informal session with the school board, two days of interview sessions with administrative staff and three days with users (principals, teachers, service personnel and students), two evening work sessions with administrators and an informal review session with the board. The interview schedule shown in Exhibit 8-3 exemplifies the manner in which a large quantity of data was collected in a relatively short period of time.

PROGRAMMER

The programming group consisted of four people: the project manager (representing CM Associates), one CRS programmer, one CRS designer and one CRS project architect. Usually only the programmer and the project architect participate in the programming process. In this case, a designer participated as an observer in order to extend the "incubation period" between programming and design. The designer's role emphasized site analysis and graphic documentation.

The project manager's role was to survey subcontractors for unit prices, providing input to the project cost estimate with data on the level of quality of materials and systems available. The manager was also responsible for the project delivery time schedule. Meanwhile, the project architect dealt with the implications of codes and the availability of systems. This procedure enabled parts of all three project tasks (programming, design and project management) to be accomplished simultaneously.

The total time spent during programming was 260 hours distributed over three calendar weeks. The programming tasks and time required of each programming group member is shown below. Programming was included as part of the basic services of the single-point contract with CM Associates, but was identified as a separate line item cost.

	Preliminary Data Collection	Interviews/ Work Sessions	Revision/ Presentation	
Project Manager (CM)	16	40	20	(cost, schedule)
Programmer (CRS)	24	40	16	(functional program)
Designer (CRS)	8	40	8	(site analysis, documentation)
Project Architect (CRS)	8	40	-	(codes, systems)
TOTAL	56	160	44	

EXHIBIT 8-3. SQUATTERS INTERVIEW WORK SESSION SCHEDULE (FROM CLIENT PRIME-ER)

PRELIMINARY AGENDA FOR THE PROGRAM SQUATTERS

The programming squatters will begin with a thirty-minute briefing to the total group. Following this, we will conduct a series of one-hour interviews. Monday evening the programming team and (superintendent) will meet to review the information collected during the day.

The following day, we will complete the interviews by noon. The team will recap the program and give a preliminary presentation to the total group at 4:30 p.m.

Tuesday evening from 7:30 to 9:30, we will informally review the program with interested board members and selected members of the community and PTA.

MONDAY

8:30 - 9:00	Group Briefing
9:15 - 10:00	Superintendent and Staff to review enrollment projections, general curriculum requirements, administrative and functional organization
10:15 - 11:00	English and Math
11:15 - 12:00	Social Studies, History, Language
12:00 - 1:00	Lunch break
1:15 - 2:00	Science
2:15 - 3:00	Business Education, Industrial Arts
3:15 - 4:00	Home Economics, Art, Music
4:15 - 5:00	Physical Education
5:30 - 7:00	Dinner
7:00 - 10:00	Team Work Session

TUESDAY

8:30 - 9:00	Briefing with Superintendent and Staff
9:15 - 10:00	Food Service
10:15 - 11:00	Librarian
11:15 - 12:00	Student Activities
12:00 - 1:00	Lunch Break
1:00 - 4:00	Team Work Session
4:30 - 5:30	Program Recap—Total Group

Before the initial meeting with administrative staff, the programmer prepared a "prime-er booklet" that was intended to prime the client group for providing the data needed during the work sessions. It included the schedule of meetings, the items to be discussed, a model curriculum, model enrollment distributions and preliminary space program model based on the original 1,500-student goal.

To visually organize information for review and analysis, the programmer used "analysis cards" and "brown sheets." Each analysis card, a 5"×8" plain card, contained a graphic representation of a single piece of information. The cards were organized and displayed according to the matrix framework, to show the data obtained and the data needed. The brown sheets, cut from a roll of ordinary wrapping paper, were used to display statistically and graphically the space requirements calculated from data provided by the client. The inexpensive paper lends itself to and even invites revision of the information displayed.

PROGRAM

The program report contained five main sections, organized according to the programmer's five-step method of inquiry, plus an appendix. The programming and the program are exemplified in Exhibit 8-4, showing extracts from the five parts of the 50-page report.

IMPLEMENTATION

The program was a directive to the designer and a resource for the client. The school board used the program information to decide on the size of the school and the budget for the project. With the program, the board was able to intelligently identify functional and space needs and to balance needs with resources available. The designer, having already participated in the programming process, gained a needed head start in visualizing the existing conditions, the limitations and the resources of the project. The program provided the statistical and conceptual data necessary to produce a design solution that fulfilled the client's needs. The design and construction of the middle school have been completed.

EXHIBIT 8-4. EXTRACTS FROM THE PROGRAM

1. ESTABLISH GOALS

Function

To accommodate a *departmental* organization housing approximately 1200 students in grades 6, 7 and 8.

Form

To provide an educational environment which stresses the *informality* of an elementary school.

Economy

To design the middle school within a maximum budget of *$4,400,000* including land cost.

To minimize long-term *energy* cost within the project budget.

Time

To accommodate *changes* in teaching methods and curriculum.

Operational

To occupy the facility by May 1977.

2. COLLECT AND ANALYZE FACTS

Enrollment Distribution

English	1,200 FTE
Math	1,200
Social Studies	1,200
Science	1,200
Reading	800
Business Education	180
Industrial Arts	300
Homemaking	150
Arts and Crafts	150
Physical Education	1,050
Music	480
Foreign Language	150
Drama / Speech	150
Special Education	25

Utilization

Average Class Size: 25 students

Classroom Design Capacity: 30 students

Teaching Station Use: Six Periods / Day

Teaching Stations Required:

$$\frac{\text{Course Enrollment}}{\text{Average Class Size}} \times \frac{\text{Periods Attended / Week}}{\text{Periods Available / Week}} = \text{T.S.}$$

Example:

$$\frac{1200}{25} \times \frac{5}{30} = \frac{6000}{750} = \begin{array}{l} \text{8 T.S. @ 100\% utilization} \\ \text{9 T.S. @ 90\% utilization} \end{array}$$

Efficiency

Net Area	65%
Circulation, toilets, mechanical, walls and janitor's closets	35%
Gross Area	100%

Site Analysis

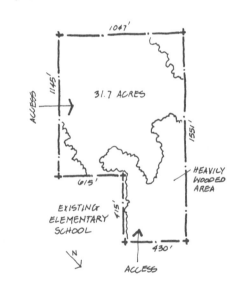

3. UNCOVER AND TEST CONCEPTS

Departmentalization

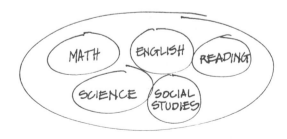

The open instruction areas include five subject groups . . . each managing three grade levels: 6th, 7th and 8th.

EXHIBIT 8-4. EXTRACTS FROM THE PROGRAM (CONT'D)

Team Teaching

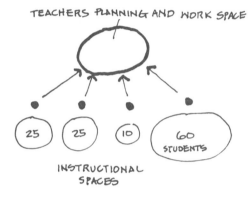

Team teaching will require
a planned and coordinated
effort . . . instructional
space will not be assigned
to teachers.

Adaptability

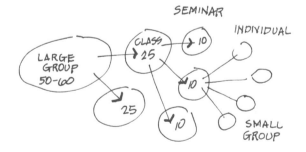

The instructional area must
be adaptable to accommodate
changing group sizes.

Flow

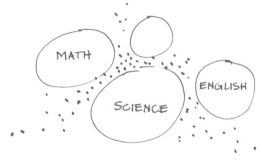

Major traffic flow should
not go through instructional
areas.

Elective Subjects

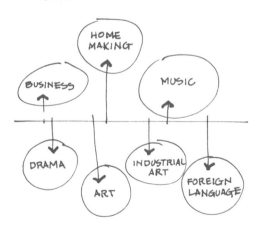

Elective subjects should be
compartmentalized to control
access and to prevent dis-
traction of students in other
instructional areas.

Student Commons

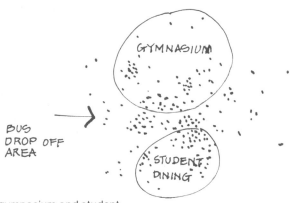

The gymnasium and student dining areas provide space for a student commons . . . a place for students to gather before and after school.

4. DETERMINE NEEDS

Space Requirements Summary

Instructional Space		62,255 Sq. Ft.
Academic Subjects	27,900	
Electives	15,800	
Special Education	1,800	
Physical Education	16,755	
Support Space		14,370
Resource Center	4,750	
Student Dining	5,240	
Administration	2,030	
Teachers' Workrooms	2,350	
Building Service		1,775
Net Area		78,400 Sq. Ft.
65/35% Gross Area		120,615 Sq. Ft.

Cost Estimate Analysis

A.	Building Cost 120,615 Sq. Ft. @ $25.04	$ 3,020,731
B.	Fixed Equipment (7.3% of A)	220,000
C.	Site Development (6.3% of A)	190,000
D.	Total Construction (A + B + C)	3,430,731
E.	Site Acquisition	400,250
F.	Moveable Equipment (6.6% of A)	198,500
G.	Professional Fees (5.5% of D)	187,000
H.	Contingencies (5.0% of D)	171,519
J.	Administrative Costs (.4% of D)	12,000
K.	Total Budget Required	$ 4,400,000

5. STATE THE PROBLEM

Function

Since the organizational structure is departmentalized, *the design should provide departmental identity without establishing fixed boundaries.*

Form

The school should provide for the total needs of the student. *The design should facilitate the unscheduled social interaction of students as well as the scheduled educational activities.*

Economy

The project budget is fixed. *The quality of the building systems and materials must be balanced within the budget without sacrificing durability or maintenance and operation costs.*

Time

The educational needs will change—*the facility must accommodate changes in educational philosophy, teaching methods and techniques.*

Chapter 9
Program for Expansion of an Educational Research Facility

FACILITY:
Lindquist Center for Measurement, Phase 2
College of Education, University of Iowa
Iowa City, Iowa

CLIENT:
Department of Facilities Planning
and Utilization
University of Iowa
Iowa City, Iowa

PROGRAMMER:
Cost, Planning & Management
International Inc. (CPMI)
Programmers/Planners/Project
Managers
Des Moines, Iowa

Mark A. Wilterding, AIA
Herbert K. Enzmann, AIA
Case Study Contributors

DESIGNER:
Skidmore, Owings & Merrill (SOM)
Chicago, Illinois

CAMPUS PLANNERS:
Hodne-Stageberg Partners
Minneapolis, Minnesota

EXECUTIVE SUMMARY:
The purpose of this project was to develop a program and conceptual budget for the Phase 2 expansion of the Lindquist Center for Measurement on the campus of the University of Iowa. The Phase 2 facilities, constructed in 1969, house the University computing center and various research functions of the College of Education. The programmer—Cost, Planning & Management International Inc. (CPMI)—applied advanced computer technology to the techniques of questionnaire interview, space standards, adjacency matrices and diagrams, design simulation and cost management to develop program requirements which would satisfy client needs and conform to preliminary educational specifications and to make cost management projections. The program package was developed over a three-month period and involved 500 hours of personnel time and 130 hours of computer time. The University used the program package to determine the feasibility of the project and the project architect used it to develop schematic design, which was then used with an updated cost management report to secure legislative (state government) authorization for construction funding. Construction began in the fall of 1977 and was scheduled to be completed in 30 months.

PROJECT

The Lindquist Center for Measurement is an educational research center which has pioneered the development of educational testing procedures and services. Part of the University of Iowa's College of Education, the center affords opportunities for direct involvement, particularly at the graduate and research levels, in the research and implementation of innovative testing procedures.

The center houses the computing center for the entire university as well as various research functions of the college. The expansion of the facility was intended to provide space for academic and administrative activities including faculty, special and administrative offices; instructional areas; a learning resource center; and support areas. The programmed area of the project totaled more than 88,000 gross square feet. A functional breakdown of space needs and gross area for the center is shown in Exhibit 9-1. This space program summary is one of the results of the programming effort.

Programming involved defining the exact functional requirements and relationships of the college facility and reconciling differences between projected space needs identified in educational specifications and the university's space allocation standards. The work also included preparation of a complete project budget and a proposed design/construction schedule. The programming and planning effort was the first phase of an extensive project management proposal that included management services and on-site supervision of construction. Site analysis was also performed and, based on optimized functional relationships among departments, several concept massing plans were developed and transmitted to the project architect for use in schematic design.

Automated data processing was a key element at every stage of development and production of program requirements and related cost estimates. Computer use enabled the facility programmer to store and retrieve efficiently the large quantity of detailed data on standard and specialized needs; to quantify and analyze functional relationship data; to select, organize and rearrange data; and to generate alternative configuration concepts of space and functional requirements.

CLIENT

The University of Iowa, located in Iowa City, is one of two major educational institutions in the state. The programmer's contract was with the university, rather than the college of education, through the Department of Facilities Planning and Utilization. The programmer worked closely with the director of this office, the university architect and the dean and associate dean of the college. The facility users (faculty and staff) participated in programming through questionnaires and interviews, which sought detailed specifications on space, equipment and furnishings and functional and adjacency needs.

PROGRAMMER

CPMI is a nonarchitecture firm and a wholly owned subsidiary of an international construction consortium, Green International Inc., which is based in Des Moines, Iowa. The firm does not perform design work, but specializes in professional services for design and construction, including programming and planning, cost management and construction scheduling and management. Its primary market is corporate, professional, institutional and international clients.

The nondesign, specialized services of the firm involve an approach to management of the design and construction process by monitoring and controlling the factors of space, time and cost of specific projects. The firm believes this approach enables it to better define the total framework of individual projects. According to CPMI, the owner benefits from knowing the exact time framework and budget commitments needed. The chosen architect is provided with a predesign package that describes the quality, quantity and functional aspects of the program. The availability of a thoroughly documented and defined program enables a project to be implemented with fewer design errors, budget overruns and construction time delays, according to CPMI.

The agreement between CPMI and the university for this project was a phased contract which specified a guaranteed maximum amount for programming services. Design administration and project management phase services were authorized following the decision to proceed with the project based on the approved program. The programming phase was completed within a three-month period and required 500 hours of personnel time and 130 hours of computer time. The three primary computer systems used in the project are identified in the following breakdown of computer and personnel use.

PERSONNEL
Senior Programming	
Consultant	80 hours
Project Programmers/	
Planners	320 hours

EXHIBIT 9-1. SPACE PROGRAM SUMMARY

		Net	Gross
10.	Faculty Areas		
10.1	Counselor Education	4,317	6,475
10.2	Instructional Design	2,912	4,368
10.3	Elementary Education	3,762	5,643
10.4	Post Secondary Education	1,557	2,335
10.5	Secondary Education	4,137	6,205
10.6	Special Education	2,977	4,465
10.7	Other Faculty Areas:		
	Student/Faculty Lounge		
	College Seminar		
	Research Rooms	4,160	6,240
	Subtotal	23,822	35,731
20.	Special Programs		
20.1	Office of Community College Affairs	932	1,398
20.2	Adolescent Reading Program	360	540
20.3	Clinical Area	1,767	2,650
20.4	North Central Association	522	783
20.5	Student Professional Organization	125	187
	Subtotal	3,706	5,558
30.	Administrative Offices		
30.1	Dean's Office, Collegiate Affairs	2,134	3,201
30.2	Dean's Office, Student Affairs	2,009	3,013
30.3	Educational Placement Office	2,658	3,987
	Subtotal	6,801	10,201
40.	Learning Resource Center		
40.1	Administrative Office	427	640
40.2	Curriculum Lab	8,020	12,030
40.3	Computer Lab	1,000	1,500
40.4	Media Lab/Photo	900	1,350
40.5	Media Lab/Main Studio	5,970	8,955
	Subtotal	16,317	24,475
50.	Class Labs		
50.1	Class Labs/Seminar Rooms/ Discussion Rooms	7,095	10,642
50.2	Regular Class Rooms	1,110	1,665
	Subtotal	8,205	12,307
	LCM TOTALS	58,851	88,272

| Data Technicians and | |
| Technical Support | 100 hours |

COMPUTER SYSTEMS
Computer-aided	
Design/Interactive	
Graphics System	100 hours
Cost Management	
Reporting System	20 hours
Design and Construction	
Scheduling System	10 hours

PROCESS

CPMI's work on the Lindquist Center involved a number of predesign tasks and continuous updating of information throughout the life of the design/construction project. The programmer's function as data manager was distributed among three primary components of project development: design (architectural and engineering) plus construction cost management and project scheduling. The computer greatly enhanced the programmer's ability to not only develop programmatic data but to update information and allocate it among the components and project phases. These roles are outlined and summarized in the process/data flow diagram shown in Exhibit 9-2.

The process interfaces use of questionnaire/interview data collection techniques with advanced computer processing, modeling and interactive graphic simulation systems. Since acquiring the rights to the ARK-2 computer program system (developed by the former firm of Perry, Dean & Stewart Architects and Planners) in 1976, CPMI has been developing advanced state-of-the-art computer-aided design techniques, computer cost management methods and management information control systems. The firm has developed a systems approach which enables programmers/planners to process, modify and distribute pertinent pieces of data among appropriate components.

EXHIBIT 9-2. PROCESS/DATA FLOW DIAGRAM

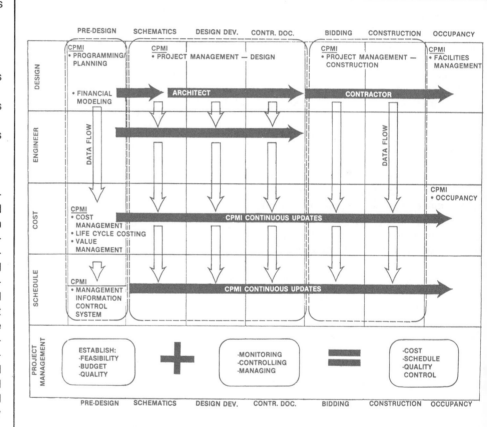

The data base for the Lindquist Center Project was established through questionnaires completed by faculty and staff users of the facility and follow-up interviews. The detailed, 14-page questionnaire yielded data on space requirements; existing and projected personnel levels; special electrical, mechanical and plumbing, environmental quality, communications and audio-visual needs; and equipment and furnishing requirements. Questionnaire results also identified primary and secondary functions of spaces, functional flexibility, adjacency needs and aesthetic considerations.

The data were sorted, categorized and stored in the computer for retrieval as needed. The programmatic requirements of the facility were organized into five broad functional categories: faculty area, special program, administrative offices, learning resource center and classrooms. Each category was further divided into functional areas and these, in turn, into specific task areas or rooms.

Based on analyzed data from the questionnaire, the computer was able to generate a listing of optimum systems requirements for each room, functional area and general functional area. For example, the

EXHIBIT 9-3. SAMPLE PRINTOUT OF FUNCTIONAL REQUIREMENTS FOR DARKROOM

SEQUENCE NO 106   PAGE   1
                                                             DATE 12/27/76

FUNCTION TITLE: STUDENT B & W DARKROOM

DIVISION: LEARNING RESOURCE CENTER
DEPARTMENT: MEDIA LABORATORY
QUANTITY: 1

*** QUANTITY * ********** SPECIAL NOTES *************************
IDENTIFICATION
BUILDING TYPE: NONE
PHASING STATUS: PRECISION SAL

*** QUANTITY * ********** SPECIAL NOTES *************************
DIMENSIONS
PRECISION CODES: FLEXIBLE
                                      NET AREA ALLOCATION: 400.00
                                      CRITICAL LENGTH: 20.00
                                      CRITICAL WIDTH: 20.00
                                      CRITICAL HEIGHT: NONE
                                      COMMENTS: YES
                                      PROTOTYPE: YES

*** QUANTITY * ********** SPECIAL NOTES *************************
FUNCTION
PRIMARY FUNCTION: MEDIA-PHOTOGRAPHIC
SECONDARY FUNCTION: INSTRUCTION-INDIVIDUAL
                                      INSTRUCTION-GROUP
                                      OBSERVATION
FLEXIBILITY: TOTAL FLEXIBILITY

*** QUANTITY * ********** SPECIAL NOTES *************************
OCCUPANCY - CODE
ASSIGNED PERSONNEL: NONE
SPACE ALLOCATION: NONE
OCCUPANCY RANGE: NONE
                                      PLANNED OCCUPANCY: 6.00
                                      MAXIMUM OCCUPANCY: 10.00

*** QUANTITY * ********** SPECIAL NOTES *************************
ADJACENCY
VERTICAL ADJACENCY: PLUMBING CHASE
HORIZONTAL ADJACENCY: MINOR CORRIDOR

*** QUANTITY * ********** SPECIAL NOTES *************************
ENVIRONMENTAL
VISUAL CONTACT: OPEN/SEMI-PRIVATE WITH PARTITIONS
NATURAL LIGHT: INTERIOR - NO NATURAL NECESSARY

EXHIBIT 9-3. SAMPLE PRINTOUT OF FUNCTIONAL REQUIREMENTS FOR DARKROOM (CONT'D)

```
**************************************************************** QUANTITY * ********* SPECIAL NOTES *************************
COMMUNICATIONS
TELEPHONE:                                                                   NONE
AUDIO/VIDEO:                        AUDIO/VIDEO:
T. V. :                             NONE
COMPUTER:                           NONE
CLOCKS:                             SPECIAL


**************************************************************** QUANTITY * ********* SPECIAL NOTES *************************
ELECTRICAL
OPTIMUM FOOT CANDLES:               NORMAL
LIGHT FIXTURES:                     FLOURESCENT/CEILING
LIGHTING DISTRIBUTION:              WALL WASH
ELECTRICAL CONTROL:                 LOCK SWITCH
ELECTRICAL EMERGENCY:               NONE
POWER:                              110 VOLTS
WIRE:                               NONE
PLUGS:                              MULTIPLE PLUGS @ DESKS


**************************************************************** QUANTITY * ********* SPECIAL NOTES *************************
PLUMBING
SINK & DRAIN:                       ACID RESISTANT SINK AND DRAIN
PLUMBING FIXTURES:                  EYE WASH
FIRE SAFETY:                        NONE
WATER SUPPLY:                       HOT AND COLD WATER

                                    CONSTANT WATER TEMPERATURE:     68.00
GAS AND VACUUM:                     NONE


**************************************************************** QUANTITY * ********* SPECIAL NOTES *************************
HEATING/VENTILATING/AIR COND
                                    AIR TEMPERATURE:                72.00
HEATING/COOLING REQUIREMENTS:       NORMAL
HUMIDITY:                           CLOSE TOLERANCE
FILTRATION:                         FILTERED
THERMOSTATIC CONTROL:               AUTOMATIC-REMOTE CONTROL
HVAC EXHAUST:                       EXHAUST - HIGH VELOCITY CONTROLLED


**************************************************************** QUANTITY * ********* SPECIAL NOTES *************************
EQUIPMENT/FURNISHING
SPECIAL EQUIPMENT:                  PHOTO LAB EQUIPMENT             2.00
SPECIAL EQUIPMENT:                  PHOTO LAB EQUIPMENT             1.00
SPECIAL EQUIPMENT:                  PHOTO LAB EQUIPMENT             1.00
SPECIAL EQUIPMENT:                  PHOTO LAB EQUIPMENT             16.00
SPECIAL EQUIPMENT:                  PHOTO LAB EQUIPMENT             6.00
SPECIAL EQUIPMENT:                  PHOTO LAB EQUIPMENT             3.00
SPECIAL EQUIPMENT:                  PHOTO LAB EQUIPMENT             6.00
SPECIAL EQUIPMENT:                  PHOTO LAB EQUIPMENT             3.00
SPECIAL EQUIPMENT:                  PHOTO LAB EQUIPMENT             1.00
SPECIAL EQUIPMENT:                  PHOTO LAB EQUIPMENT             30.00
SPECIAL EQUIPMENT:                  PHOTO LAB EQUIPMENT             2.00
SPECIAL EQUIPMENT:                  PHOTO LAB EQUIPMENT             3.00
SPECIAL EQUIPMENT:                  PHOTO LAB EQUIPMENT             10.00
SPECIAL EQUIPMENT:                  PHOTO LAB EQUIPMENT             5.00
SPECIAL EQUIPMENT:                  AUDIO/VISUAL EQUIPMENT          4.00
SPECIAL EQUIPMENT:                  WASTE BASKET                    4.00
```

EXHIBIT 9-4. RELATIONSHIP MATRIX AND CORRELATION DIAGRAM

COMPUTER AIDED FUNCTIONAL GRAPHIC ANALYSIS

RELATIONSHIP MATRIX

```
        -    106-  113-  114-  118-  121-  108-  109-  111-  117-  120-
122-    6    6     6     6     6     6     1     3     5     2
        -    106-  113-  114-  118-  121-  108-  109-  111-  117-
120-    3    3     6     3     5     5     1     3     5
        -    106-  113-  114-  118-  121-  108-  109-  111-
117-    6    6     6     6     4     4     4     6
        -    106-  113-  114-  118-  121-  108-  109-
111-    6    6     6     6     6     6     4
        -    106-  113-  114-  118-  121-  108-
109-    2    4     1     1     3     3
        -    106-  113-  114-  118-  121-
108-    6    6     6     5     4
        -    106-  113-  114-  118-
121-    2    2     2     1
        -    106-  113-  114-
118-    1    1     2
        -    106-  113-
114-    1    1
        -    106-
113-    2
```

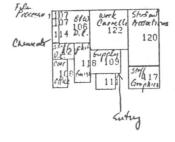

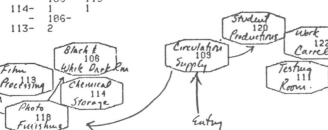

MEDIA LAB PHOTO

		NUM	LEN	WID	UNIT AREA	ITEM AREA
404	106 BLACK & WITE DK	1	20	20	400	400
404	108 COORDINATORS OF	1	25	7	175	175
404	109 CIRCUL & SUPPLY	1	20	15	300	300
404	111 TEST ROOM	1	10	13	130	130
404	113 FILM PROCESSING	2	5	5	25	50
404	114 CHEMICAL STO	1	5	10	50	50
404	117 STAFF GRAPHICS	1	20	14	280	280
404	118 PHOTO FINISHING	1	25	10	250	250
404	120 STUDENT PRO.	1	35	20	700	700
404	121 STAFF DARK ROOM	1	15	10	150	150
404	122 WORK CARRELL	1	25	25	625	625
CIRCULATION		50%			1555.	

	AREA
NET	3110
CIRC	1555.
TOTL	4665.

requirements for a photographic darkroom in a media laboratory of the learning resource center can be generated by computer within minutes, as shown in the illustration of a computer printout (Exhibit 9-3). The printout identifies the area requirements (dimensions), primary and secondary functions, adjacencies, systems needs and equipment/furnishing needs.

Once the computer has quantified and specified individual functional requirements, the programmer then examines data on adjacency requirements and, with the computer, groups individual rooms within an area, and areas within major space categories. Finally, all functional areas are interrelated. At the same time, effort must be made to accommodate similarities and differences of requirements among the various unit types. Without the computer, correlating all these data and their implications would be long and laborious, if not impossible at the scale accomplished by the ARK-2 system.

The proximity grouping begins by pairing each unit with others through a relationship matrix. The completed matrix demonstrates the total relationship among all units within a group. Clustered units are then expressed in the form of correlation (bubble) diagrams, graphically showing not only which units are adjacent but the degree of proximity as well. Finally, the units are massed in a rough sketch according to the arrangement revealed in the bubble diagram. Exhibit 9-4 shows the adjacency computations (matrix, bubble diagram, sketch) and the accompanying

EXHIBIT 9-5. STANDARDIZED SPACE UNITS

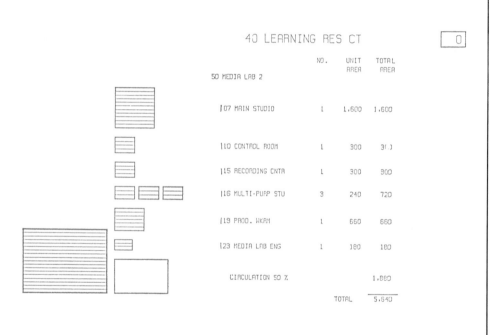

40 LEARNING RES CT   ☐ O

50 MEDIA LAB 2	NO.	UNIT AREA	TOTAL AREA
107 MAIN STUDIO	1	1,600	1,600
110 CONTROL ROOM	1	300	300
115 RECORDING CNTR	1	300	300
116 MULTI-PURP STU	3	240	720
119 PROD. WKRM	1	660	660
123 MEDIA LAB ENG	1	180	180
CIRCULATION 50 %			1,880
TOTAL			5,640

01 LINDQUIST CNTR   RECTANGLE SCALE   50   PAGE   21

space dimensions for the units of a media laboratory in the learning resource center.

The sketch provides an approximation of space sizes, but another computer iteration incorporates exact dimensions and produces a graphic representation of the area mass for general design manipulation and alternative arrangements of functional spaces within and among areas. Alternative massing plans for the entire facility are generated by computer graphic simulation incorporating vertical and horizontal space relationships and circulating and ancillary spaces.

This stage of program development em-ploys space standards or standardized space units for each type of work station or smallest functional unit. The various types of spaces and their accompanying scaled graphic representations for a media laboratory are shown in Exhibit 9-5.

PROGRAM

The concept plans were the culmination of the program development that also incorporated site analysis information. Along with a program summary and the complete functional analysis, the final re-port to the client also included a concep-tual project budget, accompanied by a cost management report and code analysis and conceptual project schedule (design/construction). The contents of the cost management report, which was based on programmatic requirements, are outlined below:

  Basic Assumptions
  Markup, Design Contingencies
    and Escalation
  Cost Comparison
  Historical Parameter Estimates
  Zoning and Code Analysis
  Alternative Cost Comparison
    for 2 Selected Options

Project-related costs identified by the pro-grammer included site development, equipment and furnishings, general construction, professional fees and contingency construction costs.

IMPLEMENTATION

The approved program package was used by the University as the basis for determining the feasibility of proceeding with the project. The project architect was required to use these reports as the control document for developing all schematic design presentations. Within four weeks of receiving the program package, the architect developed schematic designs corresponding with the program data, functional planning concepts and site analysis reports. The programmer revised the project budget to reflect the architect's plans and outline specifications. The schematic design and updated cost management report were used by the University to secure legislative approval of construction appropriations. Bids were received on the project construction in September 1977 and the final award was six percent below the project budget. The schedule called for completion of construction by the spring of 1980. CPMI monitored design and construction of the project with the data of the program package.

Chapter 10
Feasibility Study and Program for a Health Clinic

FACILITY:
South Broadway Clinic
Albuquerque, New Mexico

CLIENT:
Family Health Center
Albuquerque, New Mexico

PROGRAMMER:
Design and Planning Assistance Center
(DPAC)
Albuquerque, New Mexico

John P. Petronis
Lawrence S. Kline
Edith A. Cherry
Case Study Contributors

(These three DPAC staff involved in programming the project have since associated with Wolfgang F.E. Preiser in the firm Architectural Research Consultants Inc. of Albuquerque.)

DESIGNER:
Pacheco and Graham Architects
Albuquerque, New Mexico

EXECUTIVE SUMMARY:
The program for a 4,300-square-foot neighborhood medical clinic was presented in the form of "performance standards" for design that reflected the needs of the various users. Prior to developing these standards, the programmer conducted a feasibility study of several building options and then investigated the attitudes, activities, problems and interests of the clinic users (staff and patients). In both feasibility study and programming, the techniques used included observation, literature search and open-ended interviews. The 11-week project produced a 100-page report translating user requirements into design performance specifications that could be intelligently judged by the client and used by the designer. The project has been completed and the program used for three other designs.

PROJECT

The Family Health Center, a local nonprofit health-care agency, was faced with the difficulty of planning the relocation of one of its five clinics when the church building it occupied was found in violation of state health regulations. With limited monetary resources, the center requested the services of Design and Planning Assistance Center (DPAC) to develop a facility plan that it could use to raise funds.

Both time and money were project constraints. The clinic had to be situated in an approved structure within six months or it would lose its license. As a nonprofit agency, it was short of capital for construction and moving, which had to be raised before the deadline.

DPAC recommended and undertook a comprehensive programming process. It involved two phases: a feasibility study of the various building options open to the client and a "performance specifications" program of the most feasible option. The program was to serve as a guide to the designer and a vehicle for communication between designer and client users. The 4,300-square-foot facility was to house services for residents of a low-income neighborhood.

CLIENT

The Family Health Center (FHC) is a nonprofit corporation providing primary health care to low-income residents in neighborhoods of the Albuquerque area through five small clinics of 3,000 to 4,000 square feet in size.

In addition to the FHC administrators, the client included the various facility user groups: professional staff, nonprofessional staff and the patients. During programming, a distinct dichotomy of interest was discovered between the first group and the latter two groups.

PROGRAMMER

The Design and Planning Assistance Cen-

ter is a community service agency sponsored by the School of Architecture and Planning at the University of New Mexico. It provides, at no cost except direct expenses, architectural and planning services to people of New Mexico who cannot afford regular professional fees. A staff consisting of VISTA volunteers and students carries out the projects with consultation from practicing professionals and under the guidance of a faculty member who is also a licensed architect.

The total services rendered by DPAC for the feasibility study and programming was performed over an 11-week period and required more than 650 person-hours. The work was performed by three DPAC staff members: a project director responsible for project management, client contact, scheduling, interviews and presentation; an assistant whose primary responsibilities were interviewing and graphic presentation; and a project reviewer who participated at the inception, midpoint and conclusion of the project.

PROCESS

The client had identified four options for opening a new clinic to replace the one being closed: rehabilitation of the existing facility, relocation to an unused supermarket, renovation of surplus military housing or new construction. The client's initial expectation was that DPAC would select the best option and develop floor plans which could then be used in soliciting funds to implement the project. The programmer recommended instead a process of systematically investigating all the options and then identifying the specific architectural needs of the client-selected option. The programmer suggested this approach would provide a better fund raising tool and a more useful basis for design after funds were acquired.

The programming project consisted of two phases: a feasibility study and a performance specifications program. The procedure employed is outlined in Exhibit 10-1. DPAC approached the feasibility study as a technical task of providing information that could enable the client to make its own choice among the various options. After initial meetings with clinic administrators and visits to existing clinics to define the problem, the programmer began the data-gathering task. Information concerning clinic operations and space needs was collected by research and interviews with clinic staff. The data were recorded on preorganized "data sheets." A completed data sheet is shown in Exhibit 10-4, which illustrates its other use as part of the performance specifications program.

From the accumulated data, the programmer identified specific goals and criteria for the new clinic. The various options were compared with these criteria in a matrix (see Exhibit 10-2) which revealed conflicts. A ranking of these problems according to cost and time necessary to solve them enabled the client to identify the most feasible options. The client's first choice was the military housing option since it met most of the overall criteria and required the least acquisition capital. The client decided to pursue renovation of the housing units with construction of a new addition.

Once a choice of building type was made, the programmer then addressed the more specific requirements for the design of the facility that would respond to the needs of the users; in other words, how this particular facility "ought to" perform for the providers and recipients of health care. Initially, group interaction to deal with the major issues was suggested as a way of ensuring that all parties would communicate with each other and the programmer. The FHC administration preferred a less direct approach, however, and the programmer devised a three-stage procedure for identifying and testing client user requirements before design. See Exhibit 10-3.

EXHIBIT 10-1. OUTLINE OF PROGRAMMING PROCEDURES

ANALYSIS OF FEASIBILITY OF VARIOUS BUILDING OPTIONS (3 WEEKS)

Defined the problem through:
- —Meetings with clinic administrators
- —Site visits to existing FHC clinics

Collected data on clinic operations and space needs by:
- —Researching literature
- —Interviewing clinic staff
- —Recording interview information on "data sheets"

Established goals and criteria for facility from obvious dysfunctions in existing facilities and operations and from interview data

Selected alternative approaches by:
- —Identifying mismatches between established criteria and characteristics of the various options available
- —Ranking mismatch problems according to cost and time to resolve

Presented findings for client evaluation and option choice:
- —Client choice: convert military housing by renovation, new addition

DEVELOPMENT OF PERFORMANCE SPECIFICATIONS (8 WEEKS)

Defined procedure (group interaction sessions ruled out) for identifying and testing client requirements for design; three steps:
- —Observations, interviews, research
- —Draft performance standards
- —Test client response to standards

Collected data by observation, interviews with clinic staff and 50 patients, and literature search (1 week):
- —Used 15-question, open-ended interview on user attitudes, design issues
- —Identified discrepancy between attitudes of professional staff and those of nonprofessional staff and patients
- —Conducted literature search on clinic planning/design approaches

Organized information into format that communicated with both client and designer to test issues identified—performance standards consisting of graphic and narrative display of:
- —Performance variable statements
- —Design variables
- —Constraint variables

Program reviewed by client:
- —Compilation of performance standards reproduced and displayed in clinic for staff and patient review (10 days)
- —Meeting with staff: revised program
- —Revised program distributed to wider audience

Data collection in the programming phase was accomplished through the use of interviews, observation and a literature search. While a search of resource materials on planning and design of small-scale clinics was conducted, the programmer observed and questioned clinic users in an effort to discover attitude and behavior patterns. The interviews of both staff and patients used the same 15-item questionnaire. The open-ended questions ranged from queries on feelings about the physical appearance of the existing building to key word response questions testing attitudes toward such issues as "professionalism" and "efficiency." Responses were recorded by hand.

The survey revealed a definite difference in attitude between the professional staff and the patients and nonprofessional staff. The priority concerns of the first group were the management aspects; i.e., cleanliness, efficiency, proper installation of equipment and supplies. The patients and nonprofessional staff, on the other hand, were more concerned with the social nature of the clinic; i.e., the psychological and social comfort of the clinic. These differing perceptions of how the facility ought to perform led to an ordering of the kinds of spaces that ranged from "convivial" to "professional." An examining room is an example of a professional-oriented space, while the waiting area of the clinic is an example of a space which requires more attention to the conviviality of the design.

The programmer compiled the information into a format which was explicit enough for the users to understand and judge and which would provide the designer with usable guidelines (see Exhibit 10-4). Thus, the client's requirements for design were expressed in terms of a series of "performance standards" for the various activities, aspects, areas and functions of the clinic. The standards consisted of performance variables or statements of what the design ought to

EXHIBIT 10-2. A COMPARISON MATRIX LISTING FEASIBLE BUILDING OPTIONS IN RELATION TO DESIRED CRITERIA

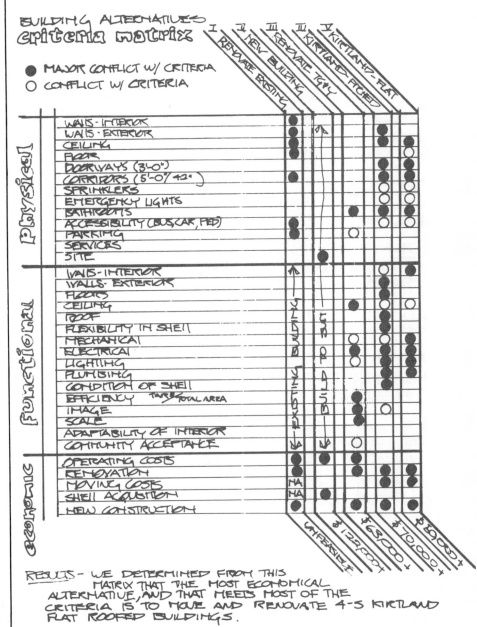

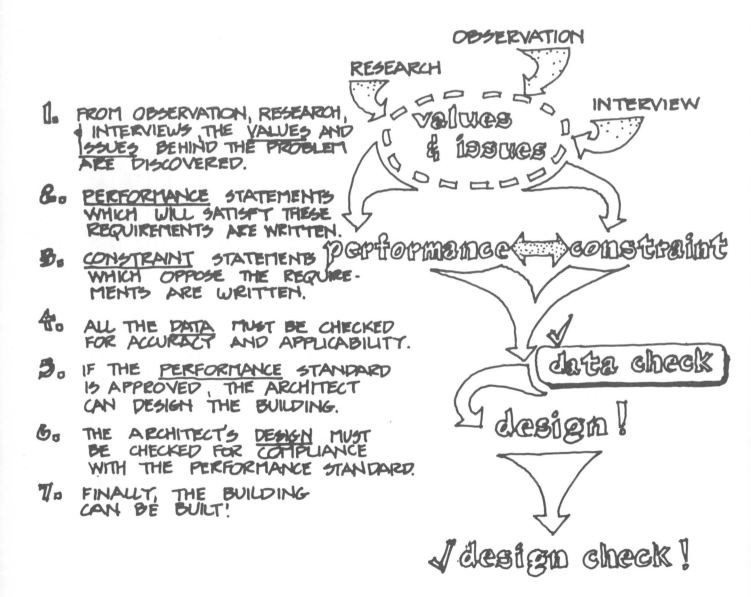

1. FROM OBSERVATION, RESEARCH, & INTERVIEWS THE VALUES AND ISSUES BEHIND THE PROBLEM ARE DISCOVERED.

2. PERFORMANCE STATEMENTS WHICH WILL SATISFY THESE REQUIREMENTS ARE WRITTEN.

3. CONSTRAINT STATEMENTS WHICH OPPOSE THE REQUIRE-MENTS ARE WRITTEN.

4. ALL THE DATA MUST BE CHECKED FOR ACCURACY AND APPLICABILITY.

5. IF THE PERFORMANCE STANDARD IS APPROVED, THE ARCHITECT CAN DESIGN THE BUILDING.

6. THE ARCHITECT'S DESIGN MUST BE CHECKED FOR COMPLIANCE WITH THE PERFORMANCE STANDARD.

7. FINALLY, THE BUILDING CAN BE BUILT!

context: reception

A RECEPTIONIST OFTEN SETS THE TONE FOR THE ENTIRE CLINIC. IN OUR TALKS WITH THE PATIENTS MOST MENTIONED HOW FRIENDLY THE RECEPTIONIST WAS. A CAREFULLY DESIGNED RECEPTION AREA CAN HELP THIS INITIAL CONTACT BETWEEN STAFF & PATIENT BE A GOOD ONE.

performance: reception

problem: MEETING THE RECEPTIONIST

point of view: THE INITIAL CONTACT WITH THE RECEPTIONIST IS VITAL TO THE USER'S TOTAL PERCEPTION OF THE BUILDING AND THE SERVICES PROVIDED. AS IT IS THE FIRST STEP IN THE ACTUAL USE OF THE BUILDING, THE RECEPTION AREA SHOULD OFFER CLUES TO OTHER FUNCTIONS OF THE BUILDING.

performance:

a. CONVERSATION WITH THE RECEPTIONIST SHOULD BE COMFORTABLE FOR BOTH PARTIES; THE RECEPTIONIST SHOULD NOT BE FORCED TO STAND THROUGH-OUT THE DAY.

b. THE USER SHOULD BE AWARE OF THE LOCATION OF OTHER BUILDING FUNCTIONS, SO THAT DIRECTIONS NEED NOT BE SPECIFICALLY GIVEN.

c. THE RECEPTION AREA SHOULD BE DISTINCTLY SEPARATE FROM THE WAITING ROOM, ESPECIALLY WITH REGARD TO THE SOUND LEVEL OF THE AREA. CONVERSATION SHOULD NOT BE DIFFICULT.

d. THE RECEPTIONIST SHOULD BE ABLE TO MAINTAIN MINIMAL VISUAL CONTROL OVER OTHER BUILDING AREAS.

e. ACCOMODATIONS FOR THE RECEPTION OF THE HANDICAPPED ARE REQUIRED.

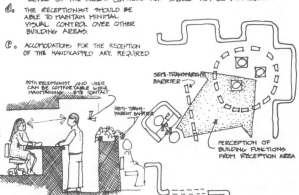

notes

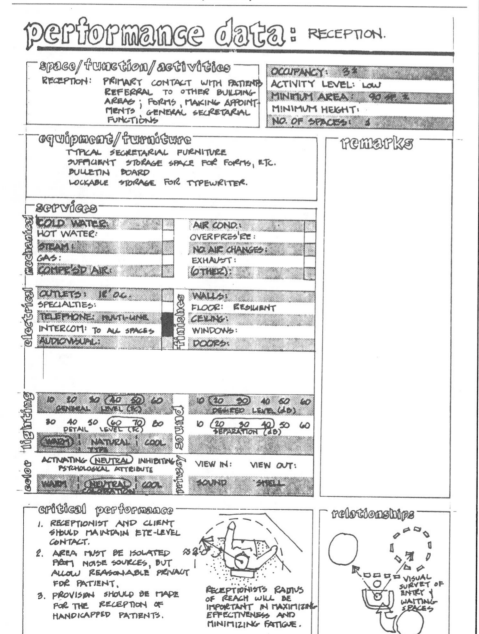

performance data: RECEPTION.

space/function/activities

RECEPTION: PRIMARY CONTACT WITH PATIENTS REFERRAL TO OTHER BUILDING AREAS; FORMS, MAKING APPOINTMENTS GENERAL SECRETARIAL FUNCTIONS

OCCUPANCY: 3
ACTIVITY LEVEL: LOW
MINIMUM AREA: 90 ft²
MINIMUM HEIGHT:
NO. OF SPACES: 1

equipment/furniture

TYPICAL SECRETARIAL FURNITURE
SUFFICIENT STORAGE SPACE FOR FORMS, ETC.
BULLETIN BOARD
LOCKABLE STORAGE FOR TYPEWRITER.

remarks

services

mechanical:
COLD WATER:
HOT WATER:
STEAM:
GAS:
COMPR'SD AIR:
AIR COND.:
OVERPRES'RE:
NO. AIR CHANGES:
EXHAUST:
(OTHER):

electrical:
OUTLETS: 18' O.C.
SPECIALTIES:
TELEPHONE: MULTI-LINE
INTERCOM: TO ALL SPACES
AUDIOVISUAL:

finishes:
WALLS:
FLOOR: RESILIENT
CEILING:
WINDOWS:
DOORS:

lighting:
GENERAL LEVEL (fc): 10 20 30 (40 50) 60
DETAIL LEVEL (fc): 30 40 50 (60 70) 80
(WARM) NATURAL COOL

sound:
DESIRED LEVEL (dB): 10 (20 30) 40 50 60
SEPARATION (dB): 10 (20 30 40) 50 60

color:
ACTIVATING (NEUTRAL) INHIBITING
PSYCHOLOGICAL ATTRIBUTE
WARM (NEUTRAL) COOL
COLOR TEMPERATURE

privacy:
VIEW IN: VIEW OUT:
SOUND   SMELL

critical performance

1. RECEPTIONIST AND CLIENT SHOULD MAINTAIN EYE-LEVEL CONTACT.
2. AREA MUST BE ISOLATED FROM NOISE SOURCES, BUT ALLOW REASONABLE PRIVACY FOR PATIENT.
3. PROVISION SHOULD BE MADE FOR THE RECEPTION OF HANDICAPPED PATIENTS.

RECEPTIONISTS RADIUS OF REACH WILL BE IMPORTANT IN MAXIMIZING EFFECTIVENESS AND MINIMIZING FATIGUE.

relationships

VISUAL SURVEY OF ENTRY & WAITING SPACES

RECORDS

do, performance data or technical information for implementing the performance statements, and constraint variables describing the factors which tend to limit design options (time, money, site conditions, codes, etc.).

Copies of the performance standards were left in the clinic for review and comment by staff and patients. After 10 days, the programmer met with the staff to make any necessary revisions in the program which was then distributed to a wider audience.

PROGRAM

The performance standards or specifications addressed not only individual spaces, but activities, related issues and center programs as well—such as reception area, support services, treatment, children, community health and other programs. Each aspect was examined in the facility program with a context page (diagram and terse background statement); a performance page explaining the problem, the programmer's point of view and the performance statements; and a performance data page presenting the quantitative information necessary for design action. The 100-page program document (see Exhibit 10-5 for contents outline) also included an introduction to programming, discussion of the performance concept, a "vocabulary" of graphic illustrations used in the program, and the constraints sections detailing the various factors which were preconditions of design.

IMPLEMENTATION

The client or designer could use the program by checking the "performances" and the "constraints" for accuracy and validity and then generating design alternatives that satisfied the performance requirement within the existing constraints. The final program was also used by the client to solicit federal funds for the

EXHIBIT 10-5. CONTENTS OF PROGRAM

guide to the contents

indroduction

BACKGROUND OF THE PROBLEM
PROCESS WE USED
ISSUES INVOLVED

performances

THESE ARE PERFORMANCE SPECIFICATIONS THAT TELL WHAT THE BUILDING SHOULD DO BASED UPON THE ISSUES INVOLVED AND THE PARTICULAR CONTEXT. FOR MOST OF THE SPACES OF THE BUILDING IT INCLUDES:

- A CONTEXT WHICH GIVES A BACKGROUND
- A PERFORMANCE A PAGE THAT TELLS WHAT THE SPACE SHOULD DO BASED UPON THE ISSUES INVOLVED
- A DATA PERFORMANCE A PAGE THAT PROVIDES THE TECHNICAL SPECIFICATIONS FOR EACH SPACE

THESE PERFORMANCES ARE SUMMARIZED IN A CRITICAL PERFORMANCE DIAGRAM

AUXILLARY SPACES HAVE PERFORMANCE SPECIFICATIONS IN THE SUPPORT SECTION

constraints

CONSTRAINTS ARE THOSE FACTORS WHICH TEND TO OPPOSE THE FREEDOM OF THE PERFORMANCES DESIRED
- ASSIGNABLE AREAS
- FLOWS
- CODES
- SITE
- CLIMATE
- TIME
- MONEY

problem review

THIS IS A REVIEW OF THE PROGRAM AND INCLUDES A FLOOR PLAN TO ILLUSTRATE HOW THE SPECIFICATIONS WORK IN DESIGN

appendix

THIS INCLUDES THE INITIAL FEASIBILITY STUDY WE UNDERTOOK

project. When funds were obtained, DPAC's involvement ended and the project architects used the program as the basis for design. However, after securing federal funding, the client learned that the grant could only be used for renovation or purchase of a new building. Therefore, the renovation-new construction option selected was ineligible and the client decided to renovate the former supermarket building for the new clinic.

Although the constraints of the project changed, the performance variables remained the same and the program was still used as a basis for a new design. Since then, the program has also been used, with minor alterations, for the design of three other clinics in the Family Health Center system.

Chapter 11
Feasibility Program for a Cultural Arts Center

FACILITY:
Bergen County Cultural Arts Center
Bergen County, New Jersey

CLIENT:
County of Bergen
Cultural Arts Commission

PROGRAMMER:
The Eggers Group P.C.
Architects and Planners
New York, New York

Case and Company Inc.
Consultants to Management
New York, New York

Bryant P. Gould, AIA
C. Daniel Bergfeld
Case Study Contributors

EXECUTIVE SUMMARY:
Anticipating the need for centralized cultural arts facilities to accommodate the varied needs and interests of both county residents and cultural arts groups, the county government commissioned a study of the feasibility of such a project. The Eggers Group and Case and Company were retained to jointly develop the study, which included determining the need and potential for establishing a center, the scope of such a facility, its costs and a recommended site. The study project was divided into two phases: Survey of Need and Facilities Program/Site Selection. Phase A involved a telephone opinion survey in the community, interviews with potential facility users (cultural arts groups), statistical analysis and recommendations for project organization and schedule. The second stage (Phase B) involved a questionnaire, extensive interviews with users, statistical analysis, site evaluations, detailed facility program and construction and operation cost estimates. The programming and site selection phase required 600 person-hours to complete. The program called for a $17.7-million new centralized facility of approximately 154,-000 gross square feet. However, the

county chose to divide the center between two sites: a smaller new facility at the recommended site to contain a portion of the functions and renovation of existing facilities at another location to house the remaining functions. Both phases of the feasibility program have been approved by the county.

PROJECT

The purpose of this project was to determine the feasibility of constructing and operating a government-sponsored cultural arts center. The Bergen County Board of Chosen Freeholders, the local legislative government, had found interest in cultural affairs was growing among both arts groups and county residents, but that facilities to support cultural activities appeared to be inadequate. Two previous studies of the cultural arts in northern New Jersey substantiated these assumptions. The Freeholders decided to investigate the extent of interest in and scope of need for a major cultural arts center in their community that could accommodate a variety of artistic activities and events.

The Board established a temporary Cultural Arts Commission and retained a team of architects and management consultants to jointly perform the investigation. The two professional firms—The Eggers Group P.C., Architects and Planners, and Case and Company Inc., Consultants to Management—divided the study tasks into two parts: Phase A, Survey of Need, and Phase B, Facilities Program/Site Selection. A third phase would involve the presentation of some form of conceptual plan for the proposed center if it was determined to be feasible. This arrangement was followed by the county in its approval procedures and its contracts with the team.

The use of programming in this project demonstrates the variation of its applicability. A feasibility program is a decision-making tool that permits a client to judge

whether or not a project is possible or worthwhile and to visualize the scope of a potential project. The data and conclusions are tentative and flexible, allowing the client as much latitude as is reasonable to plan the scope of the project. Eventually, the feasibility program is refined in detail and precision until it becomes the final program of requirements for design that is transmitted to the project designer.

In determining the feasibility of a Bergen County Cultural Arts Center, the programmer lacked a foundation on which to build a program that reflected the client's needs. While there was evidence of need for a center, there was no substantiation of it, nor any measure of its extent. It was necessary, therefore, to investigate the need for the project in order to determine what physical elements could satisfy it.

The objectives of the Survey of Need were to determine:
—The level of interest within the county in having a cultural arts center
—The level of interest in supporting a center
—The demographics of potential users
—The types of uses that were needed and the extent of potential use
—The potential for satisfying needs through existing facilities
—The type of organization and schedule necessary to develop and run a cultural arts center

The programmer translated this information into an identification of the physical elements that could satisfy these needs by:
—Measuring more precisely the extent of potential utilization of a center
—Defining the types and amounts of space that would be needed for various uses
—Identifying the relationships among various spaces
—Identifying performance requirements of spaces

In addition, the programmer added to

this interpretation of user needs design information available from knowledge and experience such as need for access to facilities, support services, circulation and conversion of net to gross area. The programmer was responsible also for determining site feasibility and, therefore, had to investigate and evaluate potential sites. Another task, estimating the costs of constructing and operating a center, was particularly pertinent to the feasibility of the project.

The facilities envisioned for the project were to include areas for presentations of performing and visual arts, for cultural education and information and for a museum, as well as working areas for artists, organizations and administration.

CLIENT

The County of Bergen was the client for this project, but it comprised several clients to whom the programming team was responsible to one degree or another. The contract for the feasibility study was between the programmer and the county government, represented first by the County Board of Chosen Freeholders and second by the County Cultural Arts Commission. The Commission was responsible for making recommendations on the feasibility of a cultural arts center; the Freeholders, for authorizing the study, reviewing the recommendations and authorizing continuation of the project. They represented another larger group, the voters and taxpayers of the county, whose wishes and needs had to be considered by the programmer also.

The primary client groups with whom the programmer worked were the Cultural Arts Commission and the potential users and supporters of a cultural arts center. The latter groups included county residents, the major audience for the artistic events the center should accommodate;

various organizations such as schools, public recreation organizations and arts support groups, who could make use of the facilities in one way or another; and the artists and artist groups. Each of these groups provided input, in one form or another, to the data collection efforts of the programmer.

PROGRAMMER

Although the contract for the feasibility study was assigned to The Eggers Group, the study was carried out as a joint venture between the architects and Case and Company. The latter took primary responsibility for developing the Survey of Need, while the Facilities Program / Site Selection phase was executed, in large part, by The Eggers Group. Compensation was established as a lump sum of $18,300 for Phase A and $16,700 for Phase B. The programming team consisted of four personnel: a project administrator and facilities planner from The Eggers Group and a survey administrator and survey coordinator from Case and Company. Volunteer county residents participated in the execution of the survey. The study took approximately six months; programming and site selection work required 600 hours of personnel time.

PROCESS

It is not always convenient or practical to program a project from direct knowledge of its users' needs, although the programming process is intended to enhance efficient, effective access to this type of information. To a greater or lesser degree, the programmer may rely on the owner's interpretation of those needs, on previous experience and predilection, on knowledge of similar projects, on research information and on standardized data to figure out design requirements. When the programmer has the opportunity to develop firsthand project-specific user data, it enhances the ability to respond knowledgeably and efficiently with a viable plan of requirements to meet those needs.

In determining the feasibility of a cultural arts center for Bergen County, the programmer had the opportunity to investigate the specific needs of the project users because the client was willing to pay for it. In actuality, there was little choice. First of all, the client had limited information on the interest and willingness of county residents to support the project. Second, the information that would be used to program requirements was necessary in order to justify the project. Finally, the diversity of potential uses inherent in a community-supported facility mandated original research.

A survey of need, therefore, was a logical first step in determining 1) the feasibility of having a cultural arts center at all, 2) the feasible nature and scope of such a center, 3) a feasible site and 4) the feasible costs of constructing and operating a center. The Phase A Survey of Need focused on the first of these goals and, to a lesser degree, on the second. It identified the potential user groups (both audience and artists) and their specific needs in terms of utilization of facilities, types of activities and spaces, and preliminary definitions of space requirements.

The second phase of the project, Facilities Program / Site Selection, focused on the latter three goals. Based on needs defined in Phase A, the program refined and detailed information on user groups, particularly those that would rehearse, perform, create and exhibit in the facilities. After cataloging the users' space needs, annotated by functional criteria and utilization estimates, the programmer added space for centralized services and identified functional relationship and area requirements.

The development of the feasibility study allowed a classic progression from the general to the specific, as depicted below.

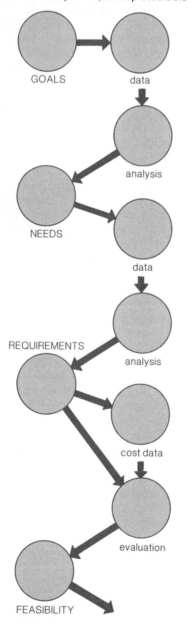

The specific procedures involved in the study project are outlined in Exhibit 11-1.

EXHIBIT 11-1. OUTLINE OF PROGRAMMING PROCEDURES

PREPARATION
County Board identified need for feasibility study
County Board created Cultural Arts Commission to administer study; retained consultant team
County Board mandated study charge to Commission
Consultants organized study project; two phases

SURVEY OF NEED: Phase A
Conducted field survey of 122 cultural arts groups in county:
—Identified mission, size, finances, number of events, space needs
—Asked opinions on need for and support of a center
—Interviewed 90 of the groups
Interviewed 34 directors of community groups, arts support organizations, school systems, libraries, municipal recreation programs on interest in having a center and possible utilization of facilities
Conducted telephone opinion survey of county residents:
—1098 contacts; 537 refused participation, 51 did not complete interview
—510 households responded
—Used 15- to 20-minute interview questionnaire
—Used volunteer citizens for interviewing
Obtained general demographic data on county and other areas from literature
Surveyed 23 existing buildings to ascertain potential use as cultural arts center
Performed demographic statistical analysis of:
—County in general
—Cultural arts groups
—Potential audience market
Assessed need for cultural arts center perceived by consumers and artists; identified needs and problems; analyzed current space utilization
Estimated space requirements:
—Measured interest in having and using center
—Identified kinds of spaces and facilities required
—Classified activities and space types
—Defined space types
—Analyzed utilization of spaces
Evaluated potential existing buildings for use as center
Projected organization and schedule for project development
Commission approved Phase A report

FACILITIES PROGRAM: Phase B

Identified list of 57 cultural arts groups which had expressed interest in using facilities during Phase A survey; refined list to 44 which had expressed quantifiable demand for space

Submitted "checklist" questionnaire to 44 groups in order to confirm previously collected data, add and detail new data on:
— Activities involved in use of facilities
— Types of spaces and utilization
— Support facilities and equipment

Interviewed 22 of these groups based on questionnaire

Organized activity and use information into description of physical requirements:
— Identified space types needed
— Established functional criteria for each space
— Prepared utilization matrix by space type and groups showing extent of use
— Allocated area dimensions to functions (net square footage)
— Determined gross square footage conversion
— Identified functional relationships and produced conceptual diagram

Compared space requirements of proposed center with 17 existing similar facilities

SITE SELECTION: Phase B

Identified potential sites through proposal invitations to 70 county municipalities

Inspected 9 sites, conducting interviews with appropriate officials and representatives

Prepared analytical reports of each site

Commission visited four selected sites; heard presentations by sponsors

Performed objective evaluation of three sites; investigated fourth site further:
— Identified evaluation factors
— Identified site selection criteria
— Weighted each factor on scale of 1 to 3 of importance
— Rated each factor (scale of 1 to 5) on its satisfaction of each selection criterion
— Scored each factor and site for comparative analysis

PROJECT COST: Phase B

Established construction cost estimate for each program element using unit cost method (Total, $11.5 million)

Established site development cost estimate of recommended site (Total, $1.4 million)

Established total project development cost including professional fees, furnishings and other costs (Total, $17.75 million)

Projected operating costs of proposed center including fixed, program and production costs:
— Surveyed 27 existing similar cultural arts centers to collect data on financial statements, operating cost breakouts, floor plans and space tabulations, staffing patterns, schedules and activities
— Selected those closest in size and use to proposed center for analysis and produced generalized model for cost estimate

Drafted fund-raising guidelines for client use in project development

USER DATA COLLECTION. There were two primary categories of users that were explored in the project: artistic supporters (audiences, community groups, taxpayers) and artistic producers (artists, exhibitors, arts groups, managers). The types of techniques employed to identify user needs in both phases of the feasibility study were structured and open-ended interviews, questionnaires and literature search. Opinions of both groups were solicited through structured interviews, such as the telephone survey described in Exhibit 11-2. General and specific background data were obtained from literature resources on demographics and from questionnaires. These aided in the statistical analysis of perceived user needs, especially in the first phase of the study.

In the second phase, a detailed "checklist" questionnaire was used to elicit specific factual data on space needs, utilization of space, and activities. These data were verified and expanded through follow-up interviews with selected groups. A sample of the type of information requested in the questionnaire-interview is shown in Exhibit 11-3.

USER DATA ANALYSIS. The objective of the analysis was to quantify, sort and organize and arrange information into a system and order which would yield meaningful conclusions about physical requirements of facility use. Statistical analysis was applied, particularly in the survey of need, to determine percentage figures and identify pertinent patterns of information. Data were organized into useful categories and related to themselves and data from other sources. For example, data collected on projected use of facilities were categorized and tabulated in a utilization chart as shown in Exhibit 11-4.

The programmer organized translated collected information into a set of functional criteria for the various types of spaces that had been identified in Phase A interviews and Phase B questionnaire-

EXHIBIT 11-2. TELEPHONE SURVEY METHODOLOGY

A forced-choice interview questionnaire was used for all interviews requiring between 15 and 20 minutes for completion.

The interviewers were residents of Bergen County who identified themselves as volunteers from the Bergen County Cultural Arts Commission, and indicated that the purpose of the survey was to assess the need for a cultural arts center serving the County.

The households surveyed were selected randomly from the telephone directory.

Households were called between the hours of 7:00 and 10:00 p.m. during 15 weekday evenings in the time period from November 7-30, 1977.

A total of 510 interviews were fully completed (all 14 questions answered):

—Partially completed questionnaires totalled 51 and were not included in the tabulation of survey results.

—A total of 1098 households were called, and 537 refused to participate in the survey.

This sample size permits generalizations to be made about the total population at a 95 percent confidence level.

EXHIBIT 11-3. SAMPLE ITEMS FROM "CHECKLIST" QUESTIONNAIRE

Please insert numbers in the schedules below.

A	NUMBER OF PERFORMANCES	Number in Each Month (1)													TOTAL
		J	F	M	A	M	J	JY	A	S	O	N	D		

B	ANNUAL HOURS OF PERFORMANCE & REHEARSAL	HOURS EACH PERFORMANCE (2)	NO. REHEARSALS EACH PERFORMANCE	HOURS EACH REHEARSAL

C.	NUMBER OF PARTICIPANTS IN PERFORMANCE	AUDIENCE	PERFORMING STAFF	ORCHESTRA (in pit)	PERFORMERS

a. Scope of Group Activities

Activity	Number of People in Group	Frequency of Sessions	Length of Sessions (Hrs.)	Time of Use (Check)		
				Day	Eve.	Weekend
Painting						
Drawing						
Print making						
Photography						
Sculpture						
Ceramics						
Arts & Crafts						
Other:						

interviews. The programmer also applied knowledge of general physical requirements of spaces to the specific perceived needs of users in order to determine space allocations and define other types of spaces not specifically referenced by users. Finally, using user data and general architectural expertise, the programmer identified functional relationships among activities and spaces and developed a conceptual diagram of an integrated cultural arts facility, as shown in Exhibit 11-5.

SITE EVALUATION. A large number of proposed sites and competing interests prompted the county to ask for development of an objective evaluation method for determining the most appropriate location for the new facility. After narrowing the field of sites to three that were considered best by the Commission, the programmer used a weighted factor rating system to perform the evaluation. Each factor to be considered in selection was assigned an importance weight of from 1 to 3. Satisfaction of each of a list of selection criteria was expressed by a rating on a scale of 1 to 5. This produced a weighted rating for each criterion satisfied by a site and the total indicated the "score" for each site. Comparison of the scores of the three sites led to selection of a recommended site. The matrix in Exhibit 11-6 shows the results of the site evaluation.

PROGRAM

Two reports were produced for the feasibility study, one from each phase of the work. The program was contained in the Phase B report. It called for a central complex that included four main areas totaling about 154,000 gross square feet at a cost of approximately $11.5 million. Included would be a concert hall, theater, flexible theater, backstage services, rehearsal

EXHIBIT 11-4. SHEET FROM FACILITY UTILIZATION CHART

	Performing Group	Estimated Audience	Number of Performers	Number Musicians in pit	Number Performances per year	Total days Facility in use
CONCERT HALL	ORCHESTRAL					
	New Jersey Symphony	1500-2200	82-100	-	14	16
	Bergen Youth Orch.	800-1200	85-90	-	5	10
	OPERA					
	New Jersey Opera Co.	1800-2000	60	75	9	36
	Opera Classics	1200-2000	85	45	5	10
	DANCE					
	N. J. Ballet Co.	1500-2000	30-40	20-60	18	20
	Garden State B llet	1800-2200	20	32	6	12
	Joan Wolf School	1100-1500	25-40	-	4	6
	CHORAL					
	Pro Arte Chorale	1500	up to 200	-	2	4
	Newark Boys Chorus	2000	35	-	4	4
	TOTAL DAYS PER YEAR					118
	NEW OUTSIDE GROUPS (PHASE A REPORT) *					110
	ALLOWANCE FOR GROUPS NOT RESPONDING TO SURVEY					50
					TOTAL	278

* Also includes usage by Bergen Community College and Bergen County Museum.

EXHIBIT 11-5. FUNCTIONAL RELATIONSHIP DIAGRAM

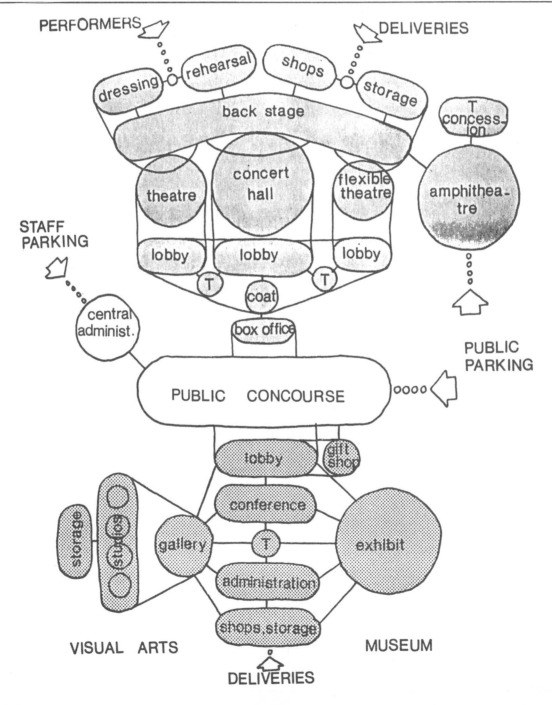

space, box office, visual arts area, museum, visual arts/museum services area, public concourse and central services.

The program report included a narrative description of the functional criteria for each type of space, categorized under the four main headings: museum, performing arts facilities, visual arts facilities, and central services/public concourses. The program also included tables identifying estimated utilization of the spaces by various artistic activities. These data were followed by a net-area space allocation by function and subfunction and summary of the functional relationships among all parts of the complex, including a diagrammatic rendering.

The Phase B report also identified the potential sites for the complex, explained the selection procedure and presented a comparative evaluation of three primary sites. A cost estimate for site development was added to the cost estimate for construction in a summary presentation. (See Exhibit 11-7). Finally, the report presented operating cost estimates and a set of fund-raising guidelines for the county to use in seeking development monies.

Three-fifths of the 176-page report was devoted to appendices which included backup data, procedures used in programming the facility and site analysis reports.

The first phase report (79 pages) presented the findings of the survey of need. It included a demographic analysis of the county, assessment of the need for a cultural arts center based on evaluation of artists' and county residents' needs, preliminary estimates of space requirements and evaluation of user needs, and a projection of the schedule and type of organization needed to develop the project. Appendices identified arts groups and arts support organizations, documented the survey methodology, and listed the existing facilities for potential utilization.

The listing of contents of both reports is presented in Exhibit 11-8.

EXHIBIT 11-6. SITE EVALUATION MATRIX

FACTOR	Weight	Site A Raw	Site A Weighted	Site B Raw	Site B Weighted	Site C Raw	Site C Weighted
A. LOCATION							
1. Near Population Center	2	5	10	3	6	3	6
2. Near Geographic Center	1	3	3	5	5	2	2
3. Near Center of Major Highway System	3	4	12	4	12	3	9
B. SERVICE TO COMMUNITY							
1. Cultural Opportunities for Disadvantaged	2	4	8	3	6	4	8
2. Direct Contribution to Urban Redevelopment Plans	2	5	10	0	0	4	8
C. PHYSICAL CHARACTERISTICS							
1. Size Adequate for Proposed Facilities	3	3	9	5	15	2	6
2. Buildable Shape and Topography	3	3	9	5	15	1	3
3. Good Subsoil Conditions	2	-	-	-	-	-	-
4. Vegetation and Landscaping	1	0	0	5	5	2	2
5. General Environment of Neighborhood	2	3	6	5	10	2	4
D. SITE UTILITIES							
1. Adequate Capacities to Serve Arts Center	3	(Assumed to be equal)					
2. Connections available at or near Site	2	(Assumed to be equal)					
E. STATUTORY REQUIREMENTS		Raw	Weighted	Raw	Weighted	Raw	Weighted
1. Zoning Compatible with Intended Use	2	(Assumed to be equal)					
2. Easement or other Legal Constraints	2	(Assumed to be equal)					
F. ACCESS							
1. General Access							
– Main highway interchange near the Site	3	4	12	3	9	1	3
2. Local Access							
– Direct route from main highway to Site (good orientation for strangers)	2	2	4	3	6	1	2
– Local road system handles (or could handle) peak loadings w/no significant delays	3	2	6	1	3	1	3
3. Public Transportation Serves Site	2	4	8	1	2	2	4
G. PARKING							
Adequate land available on/or near site for surface parking	3	3	9	5	15	2	6
H. EXISTING SERVICES							
1. Buildings suitable for conversion and/or expansion	3	0	0	4	12	3	9
2. Maintenance & Security	2	2	4	4	8	2	4
I. IMAGE		Raw	Weighted	Raw	Weighted	Raw	Weighted
1. Site capable of containing Major Cultural Arts Centers	2	3	6	5	10	2	4
2. Site identifies with County rather than local community	2	4	8	4	8	2	4
J. EXISTING ARTS PROGRAMS (arts groups now active at site)	2	1	2	2	4	3	6
K. EASE OF FULFILLMENT (absence of legal complications, organizational complexities, etc.)	3	1	3	3	9	2	6
L. LAND AQUISITION* COST	2	land free					
M. BUILDING & SITE DEVELOPMENT* COST	2	50% cost paid by State					
WEIGHTED TOTALS			129		160		99

*Data to be developed following response from site owners

IMPLEMENTATION

The initial program was revised after the Cultural Arts Commission decided to divide the center between a new facility and renovated existing facilities. The theater, flexible theater and visual arts area were eliminated from the proposed new building and the size of the museum was increased. Although the cost estimate was slightly higher in this version, the cost to the county was reduced as a result of anticipated contributions from the state government and other sources.

The feasibility study was used by the Cultural Arts Commission to determine the scope of the project and select a site for the new facility. As indicated, the Commission decided to divide the center between two locations. The program provides the basis for conceptual studies, financial planning and organization. The Board of Chosen Freeholders approved both Phase A and Phase B reports, after their acceptance and endorsement by the Cultural Arts Commission. The Freeholders have committed the county to financial support for improvements to buildings at one of the sites. Studies were to be made for administrative organization and financing of new construction at the other site. It was expected that "Phase C," the conceptual studies, would be authorized at the completion of the county's study.

EXHIBIT 11-7. PROJECT DEVELOPMENT COST ESTIMATE

Building Construction Cost Estimate
Building costs were derived by a unit cost method applied to the various program elements, and break down as follows:

FUNCTION	GROSS SQ. FT.	COST/SQ. FT.	COST
Performing Arts			
A. Concert Hall	42.966	$ 90	$ 3,866,940
B. Theatre	15,554	90	1,399,860
C. Flexible Theatre	8,008	65	520,520
D. Backstage Services	14,353	40	574,112
E. Rehearsal Space	6,160	50	308,000
F. Box Office	770	50	38,500
Visual Arts	18,018	65	1,171,170
Museum	23,870	90	2,140,300
Visual Arts/			
Museum Services	8,085	55	444,675
Public Concourse	10,000	75	750,000
Central Services	6,083	50	304,150
	153,877		11,518,227
Total Building Cost		Say	$11,500,000

Site Development Cost Estimate
The following assumptions were made to arrive at a reasonable site development cost:

Site is at Bergen Community College
25 acres of land will be designated as the Cultural Arts Center of which 14 acres will be cleared for building, parking, etc.
Parking for 1,000 cars will be provided
Outdoor amphitheatre will be included with some wood risers, lawn seating and lighting

Clear 14 acres		$ 14,000
Parking lots to include lighting and drainage		750,000
Amphitheatre		150,000
Paving and Walks		100,000
Landscaping and Planting		250,000
Bring Utilities to Building		100,000
		1,364,000
Total Site Development Cost	Say	$1,400,000

Project Cost
A figure of 25% should be added to the sum of Building Construction and Site Development Costs to cover professional fees, furniture (including site furniture), furnishings, legal fees and administrative costs such as insurance.

Total Site Development and Building Construction Cost	$12,900,000
25%	3,225,000
	$16,125,000

Contingency
At this stage of project development a 10% contingency should be added to the project cost to allow for minor adjustments in program, variables in square foot price and unusual construction conditions not foreseen at this time, such as rock excavation or severe water conditions.

Project Cost		$16,125,000
10% Contingency		1,612,500
Total		17,737,500
Estimated, Probable Construction Cost	Say	$17,750,000

EXHIBIT 11-8. CONTENTS OF FEASIBILITY PROGRAM REPORTS

SURVEY OF NEED (Phase A)

I. INTRODUCTION

II. THE PERFORMING AND VISUAL ARTS IN BERGEN COUNTY

III. ASSESSMENT OF THE NEED FOR A CULTURAL ARTS CENTER IN BERGEN COUNTY

IV. PRELIMINARY ESTIMATE OF SPACE AND FACILITIES

V. NEXT STEPS IN THE BERGEN COUNTY CULTURAL ARTS CENTER PROJECT

VI. APPENDICES
   A. Telephone Survey Methodology
   B. Arts Groups and Organizations Contacted
   C. Buildings Surveyed
   D. Arts Groups Interested in Participating in a Cultural Arts Center
   E. Directory of Performing and Visual Arts Groups in Bergen County

FACILITIES PROGRAM/SITE SELECTION (Phase B)

CONCLUSIONS

BODY OF REPORT
   Part A—Introduction
      1. Background
      2. Purpose and Scope
   Part B—Facilities Program
      1. Need for the Program
      2. Collection of Data
      3. General Observations
      4. Assumptions Used in Programming
      5. Performing Arts Facilities
      6. Visual Arts Facilities
      7. Bergen County Museum
      8. Central Services
      9. Space Allocations
      10. Additional Space Allowances
      11. Functional Relationships
      12. Comparison with Similar Arts Centers
   Part C—Site Selection Study
      1. Steps in Development of Study
      2. Comparative Evaluation, Three Sites
      3. Recommendation
   Part D—Total Project Cost
   Part E—Operating Costs
   Part F—Fund-Raising Guidelines

APPENDIX
   A. Facilities Program Checklist
   B. Comparison with Similar Arts Centers
   C. Site Selection
      1. Reports of Site Visits
      2. Site Visit Itinerary
      3. Fact Sheets for Sites
      4. Supplementary Report— Meadowlands Site
   D. Englewood Proposal
   E. Bergen Community College Proposal

Chapter 12
Feasibility Study and Program for Hospital Facilities

FACILITY:

Grossmont Hospital Additions
Mental Health and Physical Rehabilitation Centers
La Mesa, California

CLIENT:

Grossmont Hospital
La Mesa, California

PROGRAMMER:

Kaplan/McLaughlin, Architects/Planners
(now Kaplan/McLaughlin/Diaz)
San Francisco, California

John Boerger
Herbert McLaughlin, AIA
Case Study Contributors

DESIGNER:

Kaplan/McLaughlin, Architects/Planners
San Francisco, California

EXECUTIVE SUMMARY:

The client, a 400-bed, growing general hospital wished to add facilities for two new departments to its existing building. The client desired that a separate program be developed. The architect was selected partially on the basis of experience in programming, in general, and in the design of one of the two facility types, in particular. The firm provided complete architectural services for the project, including the programming. Client participation in program development was a key feature of the project. Chief among the techniques employed was the "marathon" work session—a continuous, intense meeting of architect and client to evaluate information and make program decisions. The six-week programming phase was completed ahead of schedule. The facilities have been constructed. The contributor of information for this case study feels that the architect should program any design project undertaken and should not be referred to as a "programmer" and a "designer" but as an "architect." Although the term programmer is used in other case studies to identify the programming roles of architects in design projects, the preference of the architect has been accommodated in this instance.

PROJECT

The client wished to build a 30-bed mental health center and a 30-bed physical rehabilitation center as additions to an existing general hospital. The 27-acre site had only 15 acres of usable area.

The programming project consisted of two parts: a feasibility study and an architectural program. The goal of the first was to analyze the "market" for the services proposed, the patterns of cost reimbursement, building and staffing costs and potential profitability. This study would also include an outline master plan for the hospital. The architectural program was to be a detailed amplification of the master plan. It would identify design objectives, functional relationships, space requirements, principles of design and typical design models of these types of buildings, types of construction available and costs.

Together, these parts of the program would provide the client and the architect a complete guide to the financial feasibility, constraints and detailed criteria for effectively collaborating in the development and evaluation of designs. Programming was to be completed within six weeks.

CLIENT

Grossmont Hospital was a rapidly growing, 400-bed general hospital in suburban San Diego. The client was represented by a diverse group of administrators, technical staff, medical personnel, members of the hospital board and community mental health board and a consumer representative. These representatives worked closely with the architect, particularly during the intensive work sessions called marathons.

A previous master plan, prepared by a hospital consultant firm, led the client into programming with two preconceptions: The two facilities should be combined, and one new multistory building should be a direct expansion of existing buildings near the existing physical therapy department. However, the client was open, enthusiastic about the programming process and sympathetic to exploring new directions.

ARCHITECT

Kaplan/McLaughlin, an architecture and planning firm, had developed programming as a specialty of its office. The capability to provide programming services and the firm's experience with mental health facility projects (one of the two facility types of this project) were major factors in its selection by the client.

The programming team consisted of a partner-in-charge and project architects for the rehabilitation center and for the mental health center. The firm views programming as a distinct, but integral, part of architectural design. Its approach includes the marathon sessions and a great deal of client participation in programming and design.

Programming was provided under a contract for total architectural services, but identified and paid for as a separate phase of the project. The amount of time required for programming, over nearly a six-week period, totaled 500 person-hours, plus drafting services. This included the services of:

Partner-in-charge	100 hours
Project architects (2)	400 hours

PROCESS

Client participation was a key element in the programming phase of the facility design. Architect and client worked together

EXHIBIT 12-1. PROGRAMMING PROCEDURES OUTLINE

Orientation meeting
- —Architect discussed history of building type, principles of hospital planning and process of programming to be used
- —Architect provided client a reading list to prepare for programming participation

Brief survey of existing hospital and plans by architect to ascertain:
- —Department sizes
- —Physical patterns of development (potential)
- —Desirable relationships among present functions and activities

Survey of other facilities by architect and key client staff
- —Six facilities housing rehabilitation programs visited (varying designs)
- —Altered client preconceptions
- —Client educated to designer's vocabulary of spaces, solutions and relationships

Survey of competing services; study of market/financial feasibility
- —Identified services available in market and those with potential for development by client
- —Interviewed directors of local mental health and physical rehabilitation programs and county mental health program
- —Questionnaire used by interviewers
- —Data collected included patient admission rates, lengths of stays and age and sex; occupancy; inpatient and outpatient programs; emergency services and diagnostic operations; patient origins and referrals; community services; staffing, revenue sources and expenditures

Marathon sessions
- —Client and programming team met at neutral, distant location for one- or two-day continuous work sessions
- —Client decision makers involved in meetings
- —Set general directions for programming and design
- —Set specific criteria for master plan to meet
- —Evaluated and voted approval of specific conceptual schemes

Detailed architectural program of two hospital centers

Final report for approval of board of directors of hospital

in collecting information, analyzing it and developing guidelines for the eventual design. Programming, in this instance, was not only a matter of processing information, but of "educating" the client and developing a basis for confident, competent decision making by the client.

The work was conducted in two stages. The first involved the collection of the background data which would be used in the second stage when the architect-client work sessions took place. Stage 1 was accomplished in three weeks. Exhibit 12-1 provides an outline of the programming procedure. The steps are roughly sequential, although some overlapped in the interest of saving time.

While each step of the programming involved the client to one degree or another, the most intense client participation occurred during the "marathons," or continuous, intense work sessions typical of the Kaplan/McLaughlin operation. The purpose of these meetings was to make the major decisions which would form the basis of the program. It was essential, therefore, that they involve client representatives who had authority to make the decisions.

The programming team and client group gathered at a resort a reasonable distance away from the distractions of daily activities. Several marathons of one or two days each were held, with some devoted to each of the two facilities being programmed. Some participants attended all sessions, while others joined the activity as their special knowledge or interest was called for. The programming team was present at all marathons. Hospital personnel participating in all sessions included the administrator, the assistant administrator in charge of the project, the director of plant operations and maintenance, the assistant director of nursing, the director of hospital social services and an occupational therapy consultant.

In marathon sessions, the programming group met continuously, breaking only for meals, refreshment or, in the case of overnight sessions, for sleep. The purpose of uninterrupted, unrelenting attention to the issues and problems was to foster a sense of urgency and intensity which improved concentration and productivity. To sustain interest and perseverance required leadership that provided motivation, sympathy and encouragement. The setting was also an important factor and was relaxed, comfortable and group-oriented, fostering maximum communication.

During the course of programming, the architect produced a variety of concepts for consideration by the client (see Exhibit 12-2). From background data on health-care needs and trends in the Grossmont service area, two statistical scenarios for its growth were created. These projected modest and substantial development, and, from these data, alternative physical patterns of development were outlined and displayed on site drawings (see Exhibit 12-3).

While the development alternatives were reviewed, the architect was drafting the space program and alternative conceptual schemes. Five alternative schemes (presented in drawings and narrative description) were reviewed by the client and two selected for further evaluation (see Exhibit 12-4).

Final selection was based on evaluation of the schemes using a value-rating system devised by the client groups representing the two centers (see Exhibit 12-5) and on consideration of costs of construction and operation. The architect had also provided construction cost and scheduling estimates of alternative building types. Finally, a detailed program of treatment, design and space needs was prepared for each new department.

PROGRAM

The product of the programming effort consisted of several components. Independent reports, in addition to the feasibility/architectural program document, were presented on workloads, staffing, depreciation, expenses and financial feasibility of the centers, and there was also a report on recommended changes in the construction which was under contract at the time.

The master plan component (feasibility/architectural program) of the final report reviewed the objectives and roles of the hospital in the community, projected 25-year growth patterns and identified departmental expansion needs.

The final report (a 62-page document) was also broken into several parts, providing background on the programming process, the hospital's objectives, development plans and alternative schemes, budget and scheduling, and parking program. The architectural program reports on each of the two departments contained

EXHIBIT 12-2. ALTERNATIVE GROWTH SCENARIOS

GROSSMONT HOSPITAL DEVELOPMENT PLANS

YEAR	PLAN I – MODEST		PLAN II – SUBSTANTIAL		PLAN III – MODEST	
1977	400 BEDS	LOBBY & ADMIN ADDITION	400 BEDS	LOBBY & ADMIN ADDITION	400 BEDS	LOBBY & ADMIN ADDITION
1980	400 BEDS	ADD TO ADMINISTRATION OUTPATIENT SERVICES	480 BEDS	NEW 6 FLOOR ADDITION: 2 FLOORS-80 NEW BEDS 2 FLOORS-80 REPLACEMENT BEDS 1 FLOOR-OUTPATIENT SERVICES 1 FLOOR-NEW EMERG/OUTPAT. REMODEL: CONVERT 80 BED WEST TOWER INTO ADMIN. EXPANSION: LABORATORY	400 BEDS	MINOR REMODELING ADD TO MENTAL HEALTH
1985	480 BEDS	NEW 6 FLOOR ADDITION 2 FLOORS-120 NEW BEDS 2 FLOORS-80 REPLACEM'T BEDS 1 FLOOR-OUTPATIENT SERVICES 1 FLOOR-NEW EMERG/OUTPAT. REMODEL: CONVERT 80 BED WEST TOWER INTO ADMIN. EXPANSION: LABORATORY REHABILITATION MENTAL HEALTH RADIOLOGY	600 BEDS	NEW 6 FLOOR ADDITION: 3 FLOORS-120 NEW BEDS 1 FLOOR-SPECIALTY CARE UNITS 1 FLOOR-OUTPATIENT SERVICES 1 FLOOR-ADMINISTRATIVE SERVICES EXPANSION: RADIOLOGY LABORATORY MENTAL HEALTH REHABILITATION SURGERY ADDITION: MEDICAL OFFICE/ SERVICE BUILDING	500 BEDS	NEW 6 FLOOR ADDITION 3 FLOORS-100 REPLACEMENT BEDS 1 FLOOR-NEW EMERGENCY & OUTPATIENT ADDITION: PARKING BLDG EXPANSION: POWER PLANT RADIOLOGY LABORATORY ADMINISTRATION 20 PSYCH BEDS
1990	480 BEDS	ADDITION: MEDICAL OFFICE/SERVICE BUILDING W/ OUTPATIENT SERVICES ADD TO & REMODEL RADIOLOGY, SURGERY & CENTRAL SERVICES	680 BEDS	NEW 6 FLOOR ADDITION 2 FLOORS-80 NEW BEDS 1 FLOOR-80 I.C.U. REPLACEM'T BEDS 1 FLOOR-OUTPATIENT/ADMIN. 1 FLOOR-OUTPATIENT(OPTIONAL USES) CHANGE I.C.U.s TO ANCILLARY FUNCTIONS	500 BEDS	NEW 6 FLOOR ADDITION NEW MEDICAL OFFICE/SERVICE BUILDING ADD TO & REMODEL RADIOLOGY, SURGERY & CENTRAL SERVICES
1995	600 BEDS	NEW 6 FLOOR ADDITION 3 FLOORS-120 NEW BEDS 1 FLOOR-SPECIALTY CARE UNITS 1 FLOOR-OUTPATIENT SERVICES 1 FLOOR-ADMIN. SERVICES EXPANSION: RADIOLOGY LABORATORY MENTAL HEALTH REHABILITATION SURGERY	800 BEDS	NEW 5 FLOOR ADDITION 3 FLOORS-120 NEW BEDS EXPANSION SURGERY RADIOLOGY ANCILLARY SERVICES ADDITION: MEDICAL OFFICE/SERVICE BUILDING	600 BEDS	NEW 7 FLOOR ADDITION 2 FLOORS-80 INPATIENT BEDS 1 FLOOR-20 ICU BEDS 1 FLOOR-80 ICU REPLACEMENT BEDS 1 FLOOR-20 SPECIALTY BEDS - REPLACEMENT 2 FLOORS ANCILLARY & ADMIN. EXP. REMODEL: ICU INTO ANCILLARY
2000	600 BEDS	REPLACE AT LEAST 120 OBSOLETE BEDS IN PRESENT SOUTH WING W/ NEW TOWER ALTERNATE SOLUTION: ADD 3 FLOORS TO ANY TOWER	800 BEDS	REPLACE AT LEAST 120 OBSOLETE BEDS IN PRESENT SOUTH WING W/ NEW TOWER ALTERNATE SOLUTION: ADD 3 FLOORS TO ANY TOWER	600 BEDS	NEW 7 FLOOR ADDITION 5 FLOORS-REPLACE 200 1975-1980 23 YEARS OLD NEW MEDICAL OFFICE/SERVICE BUILDING CONVERT OLD BEDS TO ANCILLARY ADD 2 FLOORS OF OUTPATIENT AND ANCILLARY PARKING STRUCTURE
2005	600 BEDS	EXPAND & REMODEL ANCILLARY SERVICES	800 BEDS	EXPAND & REMODEL ANCILLARY SERVICES	600 BEDS	EXPAND & REMODEL ANCILLARY SERVICES
2010	600 BEDS	NEW 6 FLOOR ADDITION 3 FLOORS-REPLACE 80 1975 BEDS 23 YEARS OLD	800 BEDS	NEW 6 FLOOR ADDITION 3 FLOORS-REPLACE 80 1975 BEDS 23 YEARS OLD	600 BEDS	NEW 6 FLOOR ADDITION 3 FLOORS-REPLACE 80 1975 BEDS 23 YEARS OLD
2015	600 BEDS	DEMOLITION OF SOUTH OR WEST WING - EXTENSIVE REMODELING	800 BEDS	DEMOLITION OF SOUTH OR WEST WING - EXTENSIVE REMODELING	600 BEDS	DEMOLITION OF SOUTH OR WEST WING - EXTENSIVE REMODELING

EXHIBIT 12-3. ALTERNATIVE DEVELOPMENT PATTERNS (2 OF 5)

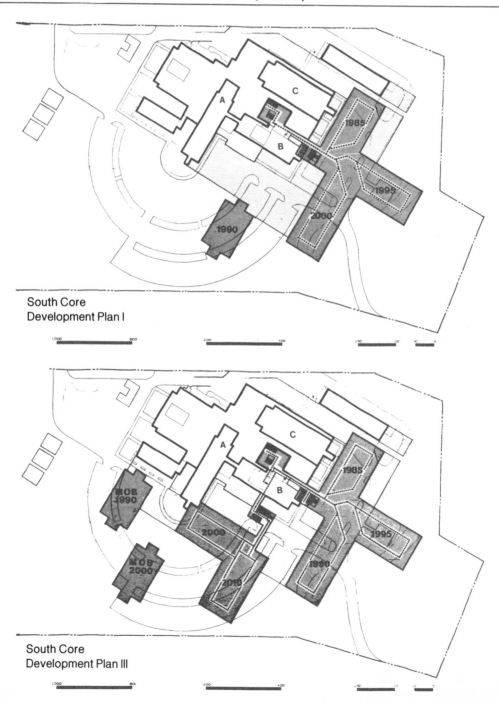

South Core
Development Plan I

South Core
Development Plan III

EXHIBIT 12-4. ONE OF TWO SELECTED CONCEPTUAL SCHEMES

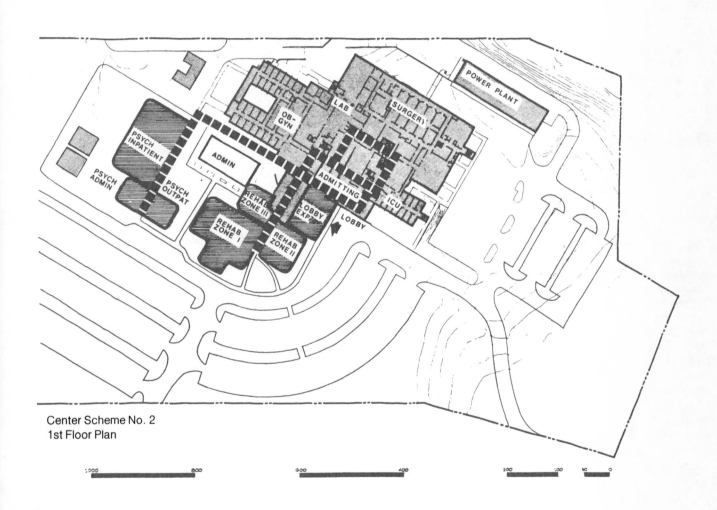

Center Scheme No. 2
1st Floor Plan

a description of the treatment program required, reference to staff/economic reports, design guidelines, and a comprehensive list of space requirements. Exhibit 12-7 illustrates the cumulative requirements of the "Space Lists."

The full program was completed and approved by the hospital board ahead of schedule for the programming phase. See Exhibit 12-6 for an outline of the program's contents.

IMPLEMENTATION

The program was closely followed in the schematic design and design development phases. The buildings were sited according to the master plan recommendations. One significant deviation from the program was that closer review of rehabilitation bedroom requirements led to a larger design. The process of marathon sessions and client participation continued into the later phases of the design project.

EXHIBIT 12-5. VALUE-RATING SYSTEM FOR EVALUATING EXISTING FACILITIES

("1" is least important and "5" is most important)

PHYSICAL REHABILITATION	Value
Access to the main Hospital (elevator core)	5
Horizontal expansion to add a 15-bed module	5
Vertical expansion for additional facilities other than rehabilitation	4
Horizontal expansion into the exisiting Hospital	1.25
Physician access from the main Hospital for daily visits to rehab patients	3
Identity of the rehab center as a recognizable building	2
Openness and space around the building	4
Natural light on the interior through skylights or courtyards	5
Horizontal access to natural grade; access to rooftops is not desirable	4
Saving and using existing landscaping features around the Hospital	2

PSYCHIATRY	Value
Access to the main Hospital (elevator core)	1
Horizontal expansion to add a 15-bed module	4
Vertical expansion for additional psychiatric facilities	4
Horizontal expansion into the existing Hospital	4
Physician access from the main Hospital	2
Identity/anonymity	2
Openness	5
Horizontal access to natural grade	5
Natural light on the interior through a skylight	3

EXHIBIT 12-6. PROGRAM REPORT CONTENTS

INTRODUCTION/CREDITS

OBJECTIVES OF GROSSMONT
 Role of the Hospital
 Likely Developments of the Hospital District and Region
 Likely Developments of the Hospital

DEVELOPMENT PLAN
 Development Trends
 Growth Plans
 Physical Patterns

EXAMINATION OF SITES AND SCHEMES FOR THE CENTER
 Scheme Description
 Scheme Evaluation
 Notes on Evaluation

BUDGET/SCHEDULE
 Construction Costs
 Schedule
 Parking Facilities
 Construction Description

MENTAL HEALTH CENTER
 Treatment Program
 Design Guidelines
 Space List

PHYSICAL REHABILITATION CENTER
 Treatment Program
 Staffing/Economics
 Patient Character
 Design Guidelines
 Space List

EXHIBIT 12-7. SPACE LISTS FROM PROGRAM DOCUMENT

SUMMARY OF PROGRAMMED AREAS

Open Inpatient Unit	7,275 sq. ft.
Closed (Intensive Care) Inpatient Unit	1,185 sq. ft.
Inpatient Therapy Area	1,280 sq. ft.
Outpatient Day/Evening Care and Expansion	2,290 sq. ft.
Administration	760 sq. ft.
NET AREA	12,790 sq. ft.
Add allowance for circulation, partitions and mechanical equipment @ 0.67 of the net area	8,570 sq. ft.
GROSS BUILDING AREA	21,360 sq. ft.
Outdoor Space not included in Gross Building Area	10,000 sq. ft.

Physical Rehabilitation Center

SUMMARY OF PROGRAMMED AREAS

Zone I: Inpatient Care Unit	12,560 sq. ft.
Zone II: Outpatient/Entrance Area	2,370 sq. ft.
Zone III: Therapy Areas	3,400 sq. ft.
Subtotal of Net Areas	18,330 sq. ft.
Add allowance for circulation, partitions and mechanical equipment @ 0.60 of the net area	11,000 sq. ft.
GROSS BUILDING AREA	29,330 sq. ft.
Outdoor Spaces not included in Gross Building Area	2,800 sq. ft.
Alternate for building a Hydrotherapy Pool, not included in the Gross Building Area	
Net Area	2,000 sq. ft.
Add 0.50 of net area	1,000 sq. ft.
GROSS AREA FOR POOL	3,000 sq. ft.

Chapter 13
Feasibility Study for Redesign of an Elementary School

FACILITY:
Commodore Sloat Elementary School
San Francisco, California

CLIENT:
San Francisco Unified School District

PROGRAMMER:
Marquis Associates
Architecture/Planning/Interior Design
San Francisco, California

Robert Marquis, FAIA
Cathy Simon, AIA
Case Study Contributors

CONSULTANT:
Lawrence Halprin & Associates
San Francisco, California

DESIGNER:
Marquis Associates

EXECUTIVE SUMMARY:

Faced with an antiquated school building, limited budget, short time schedule for upgrading the facility to government earthquake-resistant standards and a school community which opposed the original renovation plan, the city school board called in Marquis Associates (formerly Marquis & Stoller) to conduct a feasibility study of alternative designs. The programming task was to identify community concerns and to develop consensus on needs and priorities within severe budget and time constraints. With the aid of a group dynamics consultant, the programmer used a customized workshop technique to achieve these goals. Provided a clear direction by the various elements of the school community, Marquis Associates was able to quickly and effectively produce three alternative conceptual plans and, eventually, a final scheme that satisfied both the community needs and the school board's administrative concerns. From initial workshop planning through schematics, the project was conducted over a three-month period, requiring 405

person-hours by the programmer and consultant team to complete. The same firm also designed the school renovation, which is now constructed and in use.

PROJECT

Commodore Sloat Elementary School was a 50-year-old building which needed to be upgraded structurally in order to meet the requirements of California's earthquake-resistant building law known as the Field Act. The Board of Education of the San Francisco Unified School District budgeted about $1 million to make the necessary improvements. Its initial renovation plan, however, made little change in the aesthetic and functional design of the building. Members of the school community opposed the plan, objecting that the two stories, long corridors and inflexible classrooms were not suitable for educating the kindergarten–through–third-grade pupils who would attend the school.

The school board called on Marquis Associates to conduct a feasibility study of design alternatives for meeting educational, community and Field Act requirements within the $1 million budget. The architect believed it was imperative to involve the parents, teachers, neighbors and school officials in the planning process. The objective was to ascertain their requirements for a satisfactory building and to develop community consensus on suitable design approaches. The results would give the architect a basis for developing the alternative feasible design schemes.

The existing school was located on a 4.5-acre site bounded on two adjacent sides by narrow, residential streets and on the other sides by noisy, heavily traveled commercial streets. The school was easily accessible by foot or automobile for school children, and the community made heavy use of the facility and its grounds. The size of the site afforded flexibility for developing alternative configuration and

positioning schemes and ample space for future community service buildings.

In addition to the budgetary constraints, the architect/programmer was restricted by a short time frame. The Field Act required that working drawings for a project be completed within seven months of its inception.

CLIENT

The elected school board of the city and county of San Francisco, as a political entity, was sensitive to the school community's needs and interests. Uncertain of the proper direction to take after community opposition to its plan, the school board turned to a firm which not only had a proven architectural record in the district, but could also organize citizen participation in planning. Thus the community itself was also the programmer's client. While the school board's needs were essentially political and economic, the community's interests were in ensuring that the eventual design reflected the character of the neighborhood, enhanced the education of its children and served other community needs. The community included parents, teachers, administrators, neighbors and students. Forty-two people, representing all parties except the pupils, participated in the workshop program. Had the pupils been older, the programmer would have insisted on their inclusion.

PROGRAMMER

Marquis Associates is an established, medium-sized architecture firm in San Francisco engaged in a multiservice practice. Its client list is varied, but emphasis is on housing, educational and other institutional projects. The firm's interest and experience in the workshop planning technique was a major consideration in its selection for the Commodore Sloat project.

The programmer retained a consultant,

Lawrence Halprin & Associates of San Francisco, to help design and administer the "Take Part Workshop" (described in the book, *Taking Part*, by Lawrence Halprin and James Burns published by M.I.T. Press) that was used to establish client user requirements for the project. James Burns of that firm was the workshop leader.

Separate contracts were signed with the school district for the workshop, which went beyond routine programming services, and for the feasibility study. However, the firm credited a portion of its programming fee toward schematic design services because programming enabled the design staff to begin schematics with sophisticated knowledge of the project, program and constraints, and with a clear direction for design.

The person-hours required to complete the total project are summarized below:

Workshop Preparation   140 hours
Workshop Participation   105 hours
(15 staff for 7 hours
during 2 sessions)
Feasibility Study   160 hours

In addition, community participants spent a total of 280 person-hours in the workshop (40 people at two 3½-hour sessions).

PROCESS

The programmer devised a two-session community-participation workshop, conducted with the aid of its consultant, to establish the user requirements for the school. In addition to the user-needs program, the project also produced a site analysis, a conventional space program, a series of alternative schematic plans and a final conceptual scheme. Exhibit 13-1 outlines the procedure followed in programming the school project.

Successful involvement in the project by the community (including the many groups affected by the school) and accurate interpretation of its needs in the

EXHIBIT 13-1. PROGRAMMING PROCEDURE OUTLINE

Preparation
—Study problem
—Examine original rehabilitation plan
—Invite community participants to workshop
—Prepare workshop agenda and materials

Workshop
First Evening
—Introduce program and conduct warm-up exercise
—Send participants on "awareness walk" in and around facility
—Divide participants into small groups for planning sessions
—Present group's plans of approaches to different scenarios
Second Evening
—Recap previous session's work with slide show
—Conduct verbal survey (30 prepared questions, plus spontaneous remarks)
—Divide participants into small groups to devise "designs"
—Ask groups to determine priorities in designs
—Present group plans
—Summarize results of workshop
—Send workshop report to all participants

Feasibility Study
—Perform site analysis
—Prepare alternative siting plans (four)
—Develop space program (interim and ultimate plans)
—Devise schematic plans (three alternatives for both interim and ultimate needs) showing: site plan, floor plans, cost estimate data, optional cutbacks to meet budget limit, phasing plan and the pros and cons of each
—Present three alternatives to school Field Act Committee (same group as workshop participants)
—Committee selects one of the three
—Publish feasibility study

Design
—Devise final schematic plan
—Present to school board for approval
—Design new school, retaining portion of old building

EXHIBIT 13-2. WORKSHOP STUDY ISSUES

ISSUES FOR WORKSHOP
COMMODORE SLOAT SCHOOL

SPACES
What kinds of spaces do we need in our school?
Should our classrooms be open? Self-contained? Or a combination of both?
What kind of flexibility do we need? (ESEA, ECE, Gifted, etc.)
Do we want preschool facilities?
How many students do we want to provide for?

OUR BUILDING
Do we want to keep our old building?
Should we save some of it?
What do we like about it?
What don't we like about it?

OUR GROUNDS
What kinds of play spaces do we need?
Should we use some space for other activities?
What do our neighbors use it for?

OUR NEIGHBORHOOD
How should we relate to our neighbors?
How does the community use our school?
What is the community involvement in school activities?

MONEY
How much would it cost to reconstruct our old building to meet Field Act requirements?
Should we build a new, but smaller school?
Should we build some new, reconstruct some old?

SCHEDULES
How can we help to meet deadlines for Field Act work?
Can we use the school while construction is going on?
How can the work be phased?
Should we provide for the possibility of future additions?

---

feasibility proposal led to a contract for design of the facility. The discussion of the programming process focuses on the use of the Take Part Workshop technique to identify user needs and develop community consensus on design needs.

PROJECT PREPARATION. After examining the background on the school, the school board's rehabilitation proposal and the community's resistance, the programming firm and consultant identified the major issues for exploration at the workshop. The issues were drafted in presentation form, along with an agenda, for distribution at the workshop (see Exhibit 13-2). Invitations to attend the workshop sessions were sent out to members of the various groups affected by the project (parents, neighbors, teachers, administrators and school board members). Inducements to attend—including babysitting, transportation and refreshments—were offered in the invitations, which were followed up with telephone calls.

WORKSHOPS. The first evening session started with an introduction of the workshop leaders and an explanation of the objectives and process of the workshop. Each participant received a workbook that included assignments to be completed that night. After a warm-up exercise in which everyone imagined he or she was a second-grader coming to Commodore Sloat the first day of a new school year, the group moved off through the building, grounds and neighborhood for an "awareness walk" (see Exhibit 13-3). The workbooks instructed individuals to record impressions of certain locations and aspects of the school within specified time limits. Reactions to this exercise showed that it was a very enlightening experience for group members and aided their judgments on what needed to be done to the school (see Exhibit 13-4).

Returning from the awareness walk, participants were divided into six small groups and each was requested to "design" the school under a different fictional scenario or set of conditions. One group was told, for example, that Commodore Sloat had been declared a national historic landmark and must be preserved. Other scenarios ranged from designing a school with unlimited funds to rebuilding it after demolition by an earthquake. Paper, markers, glue, collage materials such as cereal boxes and old magazines and other materials were provided for the group planning activity. At the conclusion of the first session, each group made a presentation of its plan for discussion and the workshop leader summarized the common elements and the conflicts among the various schemes.

EXHIBIT 13-3. MAP OF "AWARENESS WALK" FOR WORKSHOP PARTICIPANTS

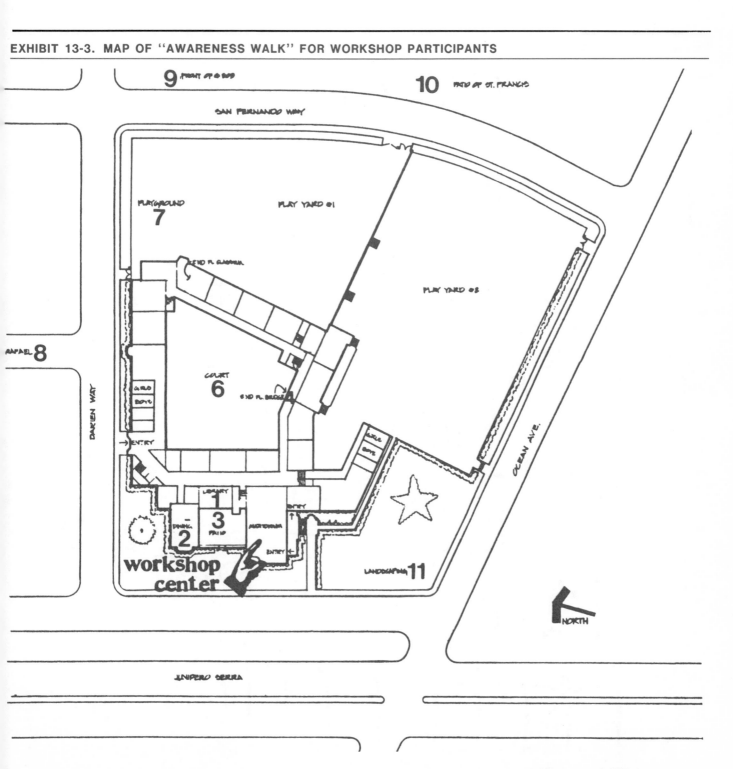

LOCATION 9

IN FRONT OF 309 SAN FERNANDO WAY

5 min .

SIT DOWN ON THE STEPS, FACING THE SCHOOL GROUNDS.

MAKE A SKETCH OF WHAT YOU SEE ON THIS PAGE. NOTE ON THE SKETCH WHAT YOU LIKE
AND WHAT YOU DISLIKE IN WHAT YOU SEE.

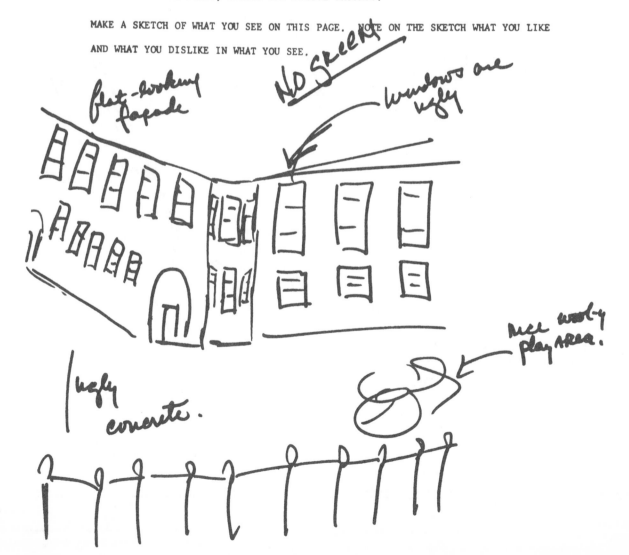

On the night of the second session, a slide show replayed the highlights of the first session's activities and conclusions. The leader then surveyed the group on its attitudes toward the school and its redesign. This was done by oral questionnaire, with the leader reading out 30 statements and the audience responding with a show of hands as to whether they believed each was "true" or "false" or "so-so." Additional comments were also taken (see Exhibit 13-5).

A second group planning session was conducted. This time, each of the five groups was given the same assignment: to organize and plan graphically a school for the site, including or excluding any elements of the existing facility, to accommodate normal education activities. Near the end of the planning period, the workshop leader reminded everyone that the budget was limited to less than $1 million and asked them to establish priorities for implementing their plans. The second session concluded with plan presentations.

FEASIBILITY STUDY. The results of the workshop revealed the priority concerns of all the parties affected by the school as well as the group's preferences for its redesign. They identified which elements were most important, how the group would like them organized, what portions of the existing building should be preserved and what would constitute a satisfactory character and configuration. With this information as a guide, the programming firm produced three alternative conceptual plans. However, the plans were preceded by detailed analysis of existing site conditions and siting options, and by development of a program of space requirements and functional relationships to accommodate the enrollment. Tentative space programs for short-term (interim) and long-term (ultimate) enrollment projections were drafted (see Exhibit 13-6).

With the development of the three al-

EXHIBIT 13-5. SURVEY STATEMENTS

1. When I look at Commodore Sloat it pleases me.
2. Commodore Sloat is antiquated and should be demolished.
3. C.S. should use all its property for school uses only.
4. We do not need any more facilities for play at C.S.
5. We need facilities for child care and senior citizens.
6. Neighbors of C.S. are happy to have it as a neighbor.
7. I want a new smaller school for 300.
8. I want a renovated and expanded school for 700.
9. C.S. should not change from a K-3 school.
10. C.S. should become a K-6 school again.
11. C.S. should sell part of its property and put the school on the rest.
12. We should keep open during construction.
13. We should close C.S. for a year during construction.
14. C.S. faculty and the neighborhood churches plan a lot for their common interests.
15. Our athletic fields are the right use for the area.
16. Community use of C.S. is very important in our planning.
17. C.S., as it is, was designed with children in mind.
18. C.S., as it is, was designed with teachers in mind.
19. If I were designing a school, I would design it for kids.
20. If I were designing a school, I would design it for teachers.
21. I would like C.S. to be like a little village of buildings.
22. I would like C.S. to be contained in one or two major buildings.
23. I think outdoor space use is as important as what happens indoors.
24. The parents and the teachers of C.S. frequently have different values and objectives.
25. The people of the neighborhood have a strong interest in the welfare of C.S.
26. More money will eventually be needed for what I want for C.S.
27. There is strong agreement among parents, teachers and the school district about what is needed here.
28. The school and the community relate very well.
29. We use the facilities of the city as much as we should for learning.
30. I would like to keep involved like this in helping decide on the future of C.S.

ternative plans, the community group was again called in, this time constituted as the local Field Act Committee, to review the proposals and to indicate its preference. Each alternative included several features intended to aid judgments. It included site plans (interim and ultimate), floor plans, space requirement and cost estimate data, graphic rendering of what the budget figure would buy, a phasing plan for construction and a discussion of relative advantages and disadvantages.

As a result of the review and expressed

preference, a fourth and final concept plan was developed and presented to the Field Act Committee and to the school board for approval.

PROGRAM

The program document was delivered in two reports: one on the process and results of the workshop, and the other on the background and proposals of the feasibility study. The 56-page Workshop Report documented the techniques used to

EXHIBIT 13-6. SAMPLE SPACE PROGRAM

TENTATIVE PROGRAM 1

K-3 school for 300-360 students @ 75-90 per grade

Office		850 sq. ft.
Clerk	200	
Principal	150	
Conference / Vice Principal	200	
Workroom	150	
Nurse	150	
Multipurpose (seating for 300)		2,250
Stage and table storage		800
Teachers' lunch and toilets		400
Media Center		1,800
13 classrooms		13,950
1 special classroom	900	
3 teaching clusters, each with		
3 classrooms and a common		
media-resource area @ 3,150	9,450	
3 kindergartens @ 1200	3,600	
Ancillary spaces		
Kitchen		150
Storage + maintenance		300
Toilets		400
Park + rec office		150
Sub-total		21,050
(× 1.25 for circulation)		26,313 sq. ft.

identify community preferences and consensus and presented the conclusions developed by the group. The Feasibility Report, a 47-page document, presented the site analysis; siting option analysis with drawings; space program; and the three alternative conceptual plans with drawings depicting ultimate and interim site plans, ultimate and interim floor plans, budget-limited plan and construction sequence. The content of each report is outlined in Exhibit 13-7.

IMPLEMENTATION

The final concept plan combined the best of the two alternatives selected by the community group. It saved and remodeled the much regarded cafeteria / auditorium element of the existing building and added a centrally located media center and one-story clusters of classrooms surrounding individual courtyards. All these elements were derived from the workshop preferences.

The process of intensive client and building committee involvement continued on a frequent basis throughout schematic design and design development, and to a lesser extent during development of working drawings. The school has been completed.

EXHIBIT 13-7. PROGRAM REPORT OUTLINES

Workshop Report
TABLE OF CONTENTS

INTRODUCTION

SUMMARY

THE FUTURE

CONCLUSION

DOCUMENTATION: THE FIRST EVENING
  Introductions and Objectives
  Through a Student's Eyes
  Awareness Walk
  Group Planning: Six Scenarios
  Summary of First Evening

DOCUMENTATION: THE SECOND EVENING
  Introductions and Slide Show
  Attitudes about Commodore Sloat
  Group Planning: Activity Score
  Group Presentation of Plans

PEOPLE
  Workshop Participants
  Workshop Team

Feasibility Report
TABLE OF CONTENTS

INTRODUCTION

SITE ANALYSIS

SCHEMATIC PROGRAM

THREE APPROACHES TO THE PROBLEM
  Scheme 1
  Scheme 2
  Scheme 3
  Original Rehabilitation Scheme

CONCLUSION

Chapter 14
Design Criteria for a Single Family Residence

FACILITY:
Residence
Fairfax County, Virginia

CLIENT:
Anonymous

PROGRAMMER:
MLTW/Turnbull Associates
Architects and Planners
San Francisco, California

William Turnbull Jr., FAIA
Case Study Contributor

DESIGNER:
MLTW/Turnbull Associates
Architects and Planners
San Francisco, California

EXECUTIVE SUMMARY:
Programming was an unidentified, but important service in the design of a new residence for a five-member diplomatic family. The architect served as both programmer and designer for the project and the "program" consisted of the initial schematic design which incorporated the identified client's needs and design constraints. Programming was a matter of identifying and documenting the specific requirements of the client (through informal, conversational interviews), as well as the factors (such as site conditions, code restrictions, budget and schedule) which limited the opportunities of both client and designer. The 7,210-square-foot house, including both enclosed space and exterior porches and decks, was constructed in 1975.

PROJECT

A State Department official and his family wished to have a new, permanent residence designed for a suburban Washington, D.C. site. Because the family was posted overseas every two years or so, their house was a symbol of permanence in their lives. Although the house was to be located in the Washington area, the client requested the services of MLTW/ Turnbull Associates which is located in San Francisco.

Programming, which is a standard but not formally distinguished feature of the firm's residential design services, was a matter of identifying and documenting the specific factors which would influence the design of the particular building. In a project of such individuality, the paramount factor to discover was the client's personal needs. As the architect stated, the goal was to "try and determine those idiosyncracies which set [the family] apart from other clients and provide the key for making a special, individual, single-family house for them to inhabit and enjoy."

Aside from identifying the personal goals, wishes, attitudes and behavior of the client, programming involved identifying external factors which constrain the design, such as site conditions, code restrictions, budget and schedule.

CLIENT

The client was a family of five consisting of a foreign-service officer, his wife (who was active in community affairs), two teenagers and a preteenager. The family was sharply aware of the world around them and able to articulate clearly their living patterns, preferences and specific wants. All participated in informal programming interviews and the wife accompanied the architect on a tour of the existing home, explaining the family's lifestyle.

The family had no preconceptions in terms of "style," but specifically requested that the house be maintenance free, very comfortable and informal. They were conscious of the amount of money they wished to spend and their initial requirements simply called for a living room, dining room, kitchen, sleeping areas for three children, a master bedroom and a place to house and use their large library of books.

PROGRAMMER

Programmer and designer were a single architect, the principal of MLTW/Turnbull Associates. The small architecture and planning firm has a nationwide practice concentrating in residential design. Much of the programmer's task for this project involved a series of informal, conversational interviews with the client, observation of the existing home and the new site, and examination of regulatory codes and covenants. The work involved three or four meetings of four to six hours apiece. There was no separate contract for programming, which was part of the design services rendered, nor was it even formalized by the title of programming.

PROCESS

The programming process, specifically for a single-family dwelling, was one of compilation of data from various sources: interviews, field observations, code checks and the architect's own insights on the information as it was collected. In a project as small and uncomplicated as this, the programmer carried much of the data in his head in terms of priorities, needs, desires and the distillation of critical factors such as the budget and conflicts in individual desires.

Programming evolved into a series of informal meetings and discussions in the family's existing home, sitting over coffee or at the dining table. The interviews were conversational, with the programmer simply chatting, catching insights to the family's needs from their responses and taking it all down in shorthand notes on a pad (see Exhibit 14-1). The discussion included the client's goals, hopes and dreams and historical images that had appealed to them. It also included specific requirements of space, budget, schedule.

There were two or three such meetings with the family, and the programmer returned to the home office in San Francisco

EXHIBIT 14-1. PROGRAMMER'S NOTES RECORD CLIENT'S NEEDS

STUDY - SMALL -
BOOKS - USED
FIREPLACE.
COZY TO TALK

WR - TERRIE'S ESCAPE.
TO BE LIVED - IN - NOT PARLOR.

DINING - (FIT W KITCHEN) - ? RAISED   (CHESTER ○ . 48'
EXISTING.   seat 10 comfortably)
WARREN - SITS/DRINKS : TERRIE COOKS

KITCHEN : MUST FUNCTION.
GALLEY -
STORAGE : SHELVES OR CLOSET -
          CLEANING CLOSET.
          POTS/PANS HANG - OUT.
STOVE WORKING SPACE.
DISH STORAGE CLOSE TO DW
STORAGE FOR DISHES IN DINING.

2ND FL.
DUMB WAITER : TRASH DOWN STAIRS - HOW GARBAGE CAN -
DISPOSAL
non mechanical   DRAWERS + SHELVES.

NO BASEMENT.
LAUNDRY : NEXT TO BED ROOMS
BOOKCASES IN ALL BED ROOMS.
→ TERRIE LEFTHANDED

LINEN CLOSET.
ATTIC : STORAGE   (STORAGE RM) PACK RAT . 8X8 +
                                      ONE WALL CLOSET.

+ BOOKS - BUILT - IN
+ DESK WORKTOP.   CLOSETS   SHELVES NOT DRAWERS

SUNNY : BED RM - RADIO - (WANTS WINDOW SEAT)
FAMILY DOESN'T REALLY USE BED ROOMS
GUEST ROOM.
WARREN SHOWER STALL / TERRIE BATH TUB .
? BATHS.
MBR - MOST LIGHT CORNER / OF HOUSE.

to transcribe, elaborate on and file them. These data served as the primary basis for the design work. A secondary source of data was the limitations placed on the project by local codes and requirements (see Exhibit 14-2). The zoning and building codes were checked, as were any specific restraints placed on the site by the developer (e.g., bulk, size or style, or review rights on final design). The master plan of the development was also reviewed.

A parallel step to the code check was a site visit in which opportunities and problems were noted or photographed. The site was analyzed for views, wind, solar orientation, proximity to neighboring houses, privacy, and vegetation patterns. (See Exhibit 14-3 for site plan). Soil qualities were identified by surface inspection. The architect's site inspection was augmented by topographic surveys and technical soil reports by consultants.

After the interviews with the family on their requirements, the architect examined the existing house, again noting on a pad comments about its living patterns. Possible building organization and general character were left to the architect's schematics, and specific character was only discussed in terms of space and light. The distribution of spaces, their sizes and characteristics, equipment and finishes had been identified in the previous discussions.

No special studies on energy, environmental impact, life cycle costs, etc., were performed. The only special work was an evaluation with the local power company to determine if the house could be electrically heated and with a local civil engineering firm to determine if the ground would accept water percolation.

PROGRAM

The information collected by the programmer was combined with his knowledge and insights into a set of conclusions about

CODE CHECK

FIRE ZONE : ASSUMED OUTSIDE OF FIRE ZONE"
OCCUPANCY GROUP : L-3
TYPE OF CONSTRUCTION : TYPE 4 UNPROTECTED
LOCATION ON PROPERTY : 30' FROM SIDE LOT LINE
FLOOR AREA : 4800/FLOOR ← ALLOWABLE
HEIGHT AND NUMBER OF STORIES : 35', 2½ STORIES
OCCUPANT LOAD :

  MIN : STAIR WIDTH 36" ←
  MIN : HEADROOM 6'-8"
  HANDRAILS 30 - 33"
  RISER MAX : 8¼"
  TREAD MIN : 9" + 1¼"
  — MAY REQ 2ND MEANS OF EXIT FROM
     UPPER ROOF DECK
  NON-RATED ROOF COVERING OK FOR TYPE 4-B
                              CONST.

BLDG CODE ORDINANCE
FAIRFAX COUNTY
  MIN SILL HT OF 24" OR REQ GUARDRAIL
  36" GUARDRAIL FOR L-3   8" SPS. BUT
  GUARDRAIL NOT REQ IF WINDOW HAS AN
  EXT BALCONY / DECK PORCH ETC.

BLDG HEIGHT : 2½ STORIES
               35' ABOVE GRADE

HEIGHT MEASURED FROM AVERAGE GRADE
TO MEAN (AVERAGE) HEIGHT OF SLOPING
ROOF

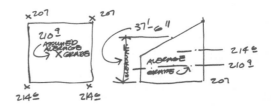

       207   207
       5   37'-6"
              244 5
              210 9
              ─────────
              339 ← AVERAGE HEIGHT

design requirements. These were not formalized nor passed back to the client for review, however. Instead, they were incorporated into the first schematic design which was then submitted to the client for review and comment. This schematic and the notes from the client-designer review meeting (see Exhibit 14-4) formed the basis for the final design.

IMPLEMENTATION

The program served as a yardstick during design to check and verify the concepts developed and also as a reference to help clarify issues and conflicts which arose. The house that was designed and completed in 1975 accommodated the individual and collective needs of the family, closely following needs and patterns first expressed.

EXHIBIT 14-3. SITE PLAN

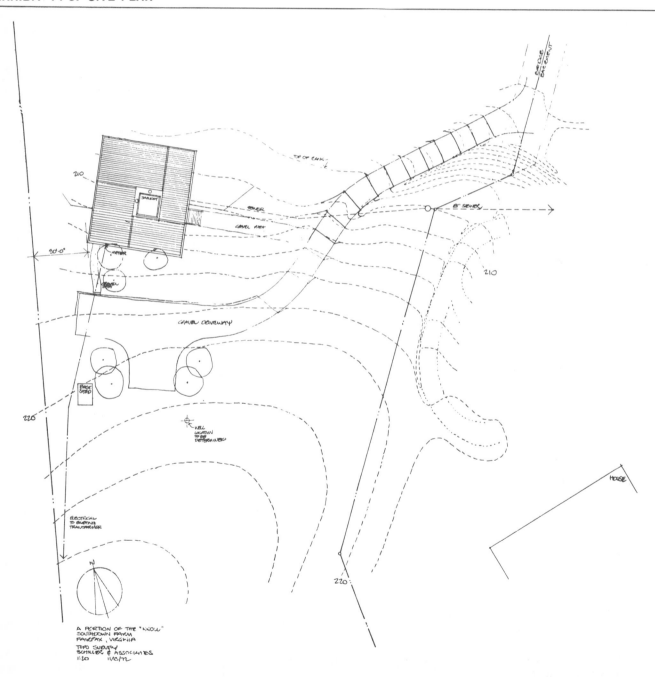

EXHIBIT 14-4. SAMPLE SKETCHES FROM THE INITIAL SCHEMATIC DESIGN

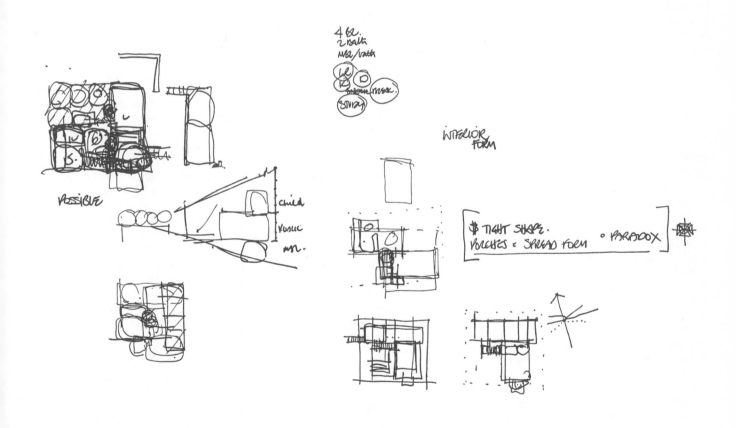

Chapter 15
Master Plan Program for a Riverfront Development

FACILITY:
Penn's Landing Riverfront Development
Philadelphia, Pennsylvania

CLIENT:
Old Philadelphia Development Corp.
(OPDC)
Penn's Landing Committee
(subsequently known as OPDC Penn's
Landing Corp.)

PROGRAMMER:
Murphy Levy Wurman
Architecture and Urban Planning
Philadelphia, Pennsylvania

Alan Levy, FAIA
(now principal of Alan Levy / Architecture
and Urban Planning, Philadelphia,
Pennsylvania)
Case Study Contributor

CONSULTANT:
Gladstone & Associates
Economic and Market Consultants
Washington, D.C.

EXECUTIVE SUMMARY:
In 1970, the city of Philadelphia, through
the quasi-public Old Philadelphia Development Corp. (OPDC), wanted to prepare
a master development program for a 28-
acre waterfront redevelopment project
that could be partially implemented in time
for the 1976 Bicentennial Celebration. The
architecture and urban planning firm of
Murphy Levy Wurman was selected to
master plan the project through a five-
stage process that required active participation of many public and private interests in the decision making. Programming involved defining project objectives,
developing a program of uses, identifying
design performance criteria and propos-
ing feasible development options. The
program was adopted in its entirety by
the client in 1971. Thirteen million dollars
in public improvements have been completed from the resulting design, in addition to $13 million spent originally.

PROJECT

The Waterfront Redevelopment Project,
conceived as part of a 1961 master plan
for revitalizing Philadelphia's central city,
had been studied and designed by a succession of architects, engineers and planners before 1970. The firm of Geddes
Brecher Qualls Cunningham (GBQC) developed the first master plan for the project in 1963, and its 1968 revised plan was
the basis for the configuration of the landfill area. In 1970, the city directed the Old
Philadelphia Development Corp. (OPDC)
to devise a plan for developing the 28-
acre site, part of which needed to be
complete in time for the 1976 Bicentennial
Celebration. Although a program of uses
for the site had evolved primarily for promotional efforts, there was no definitive
development program that specified feasible uses, identified their functional relationships, scheduled the development and
future expansion, and integrated the plans
with other nearby development work.

Murphy Levy Wurman was one of a
limited number of firms invited to submit
proposals for this task to a selection
committee consisting of business people,
planners and government officials. The
committee awarded the firm a $60,000
contract for programming and urban design services to develop the waterfront
master plan in five phases over a nine-
month period.

The Penn's Landing site was a 28-acre
landfill and 10-acre boat basin that had
been created (based on the 1968 revised
master plan) by clearing a half-mile-long
section of old piers. The narrow strip ran
north and south along the west bank of
the Delaware River and was bounded on
the west by Delaware Avenue and the partially completed interstate highway section. Points of access to the site were restricted by highway designers, and the
grades at the boundaries were firmly established. Private and public developments were anticipated, but no budget

had been determined.

CLIENT

A Penn's Landing Advisory Committee
represented the Old Philadelphia Development Corp. (OPDC), a quasi-public organization responsible for overseeing central
city development. Because of the high
public interest in the project, the committee included many other representatives
of government, business and neighborhood interests who wished to be directly
involved in program development and decision making. The programmer made numerous presentations during the course
of the work, both to inform the various
publics of progress and to gain consensus
and support. There were three major client
groups involved in the programming:
   —Representatives of city and state
   agencies including the city's managing
   director, finance director, director of
   development, head of physical planning
   for the planning commission, commerce
   department director and officials of the
   state departments of commerce, planning and transportation
   —Members of neighboring community
   organizations
   —Staff and board members of OPDC
   which included representatives of the
   private business and financial sector

Since the site was created from aban-
doned riverfront piers, there were no residents or businesses directly affected by
development. The primary concerns of
community representatives were obstruc-
tion of riverfront views and generation of
traffic in the area.

PROGRAMMER

Murphy Levy Wurman (since disbanded)
was a relatively small (12-person) architecture and urban planning firm with experience in large scale urban design projects. For this project, a team was organ-

ized consisting of five architects, trained and experienced in planning, redevelopment and programming, and a consulting economist who specialized in urban development and was familiar with local conditions. Engineering services were made available through the firm which engineered the landfill area and from the city's port authority. The city planning commission provided liaison staff for coordination of zoning matters and other related plans and projects.

The programming required 3,600 person-hours to complete over a ten-month period. Subsequent to completion of the master plan program, the firm was retained for several other services related to the project including preparation of the developer's package, technical advice in developer selection, activity programming for the boat basin, corporate graphics and project coordination for Bicentennial activities, preliminary design of project improvements, and services as coordinating architect through final construction of project improvements.

PROCESS

Defining the client's needs and specific requirements started from ground zero with a site and the client's interest in developing it. The programmer had to help the client define project objectives before identifying the possible uses that could accommodate those goals. Programming was a progressive process of integrating the functional requirements of the project with the varied interests of the client group, the design parameters, the regulatory restrictions and the physical limitations, all of which had to be identified in the process. The success of the programming effort relied heavily on the client's active participation in providing information and making decisions for a development which would have a broad impact on the city's aesthetic, social and economic vitality. The outline of the program-

EXHIBIT 15-1. OUTLINE OF THE PROGRAMMING PROCESS

Analysis of previous planning and existing constraints
—compared five previous alternative plans in terms of response to such factors as circulation, parking, open space, use distribution, massing and relation to the interstate highway
—studied site constraints and opportunities in terms of areas restricted to construction, zones required for access and movement, dimension limitations and utility easements
—report presented to committee for review and modification

Definition of project objectives and program goals
—presented alternative development scenarios to client in the form of "polarities," or extremes (such as single use development) in order to elicit strong positive or negative reactions
—developed relationship matrix to identify possible relationships between functional aspects and user aspects and compare these factors with project goals
—presented descriptions of similar local and familiar developments to help committee visualize scope and problems of the project
—with failure to generate definite goal statements from the committee through the above approach, programmer submitted alternative statements for committee debate and modifications
—report presented identifying project objectives and outlining the decision-making process
—established program of uses, or functions

Integration of use program with design considerations
—identified space relationships
—examined impact of architectural factors such as building massing, sight lines, orientation, unifying roof lines, arcades, plazas
—identified design performance issues

Establishment of use and design controls
—formalized an itemized set of use and design controls, specifying development criteria and restrictions
—client committee, city agencies and community groups reviewed and commented
—second draft, incorporating comments, modified to reflect language and scope of city zoning and planning regulations
—final draft used in developer's package for selection competition

Presentation of final report
—cost estimates prepared, economic impact analyzed
—critical path schedules prepared
—devised space budgeting system for integrating economic factors with space factors
—analyzed impacts of alternative program component combinations
—accompanied by promotional graphics and models for committee presentations

EXHIBIT 15-2. ALTERNATIVE DEVELOPMENT PLANS, 1963-1969

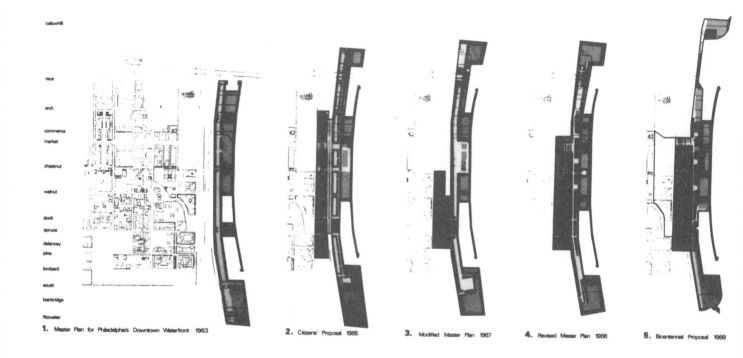

callowhill

race

arch

commerce

market

chestnut

walnut

dock

spruce

delancey

pine

lombard

south

bainbridge

fitzwater

1. Master Plan for Philadelphia's Downtown Waterfront 1963   **2.** Citizens' Proposal 1965   **3.** Modified Master Plan 1967   **4.** Revised Master Plan 1968   **5.** Bicentennial Proposal 1969

mer's activities shown in Exhibit 15-1 reveals the progressive nature of the process.

The programming project was organized according to the five stages described in the outline. The first step was to identify the relevance of previous work in planning the waterfront redevelopment to the current effort. The programmer made a comparative analysis of the five major alternative development plans which had been proposed since 1963, showing their impacts on primary factors such as circulation, open space, parking, use distribution, massing and relation to

the interstate highway (see Exhibit 15-2).

In the first stage, the programmer also studied the existing site conditions in terms of restrictions and opportunities. This provided a clear definition of which areas of the site could be developed. These preliminary investigations were summarized in the initial report to the Penn's Landing Committee.

With this as background, the programmer then sought to elicit from the client group the specific project objectives and program goals for developing the waterfront. An interactive process between the programmer and the OPDC Penn's Land-

ing Advisory Committee, which represented the city, the state, the business sector and nearby communities, was designed and carried out in a series of presentations. The programmer described similar projects that were familiar to the client; for example, local shopping centers, other central city developments, etc. A report on San Francisco's waterfront development was particularly helpful for the client in visualizing the scope, nature and problems of such an urban renewal project.

Other presentations emphasized relationships among development factors, including the interaction potential between functions and users of the project and between space allocation and space organization. To aid in identifying the relative significance of some of these variable relationships, the programmer developed a relationship matrix matching user aspects with functional aspects. Exhibit 15-3 shows one matrix which has been expanded to incorporate an additional dimension: the relationship of these factors to project goals.

The interactive approach was unsuccessful in generating a complete definition of the client's project objectives, and the programmer turned to presenting a series of prepared statements based on results of the interactive sessions for review and modification by the group. The presentations also included alternative development scenarios in the form of extreme cases, or "polarities," such as restricting development to a single use (e.g., commercial, institutional, residential) or focusing development on a single goal (e.g., public accessibility or profit maximization). The outcome of this stage of the project was general consensus on the specific project goals and a comprehensive program of uses (or functions) which should be incorporated in the project. The resulting report also summarized the process by which the programming decisions had been reached.

It was now possible for the programmer to focus on the physical implications of the functional needs of the project. Studies were conducted of space requirements, space organization and the primary architectural factors which would constrain design. Although the programmer examined design aspects such as building massing, sight lines, orientation, unifying roof lines, arcades and plazas, the constraints which evolved stressed performance rather than prescriptive criteria. Performance issues identified in this third stage of the project included such factors as guaranteeing corridors for river

EXHIBIT 15-3. USER/FUNCTION/GOAL MATRIX

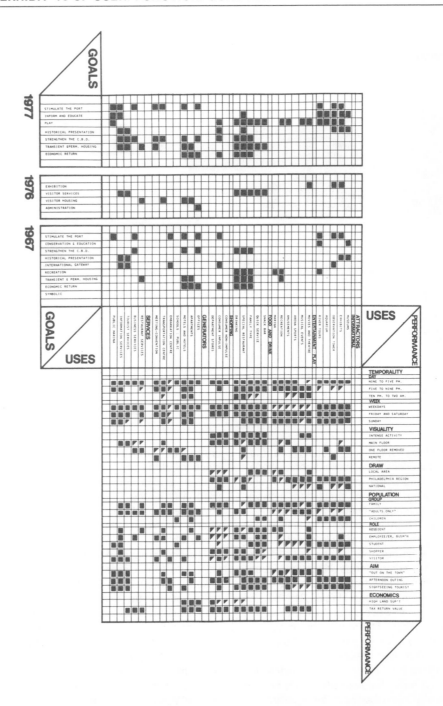

VISUAL PENETRATION

THEORETICAL MASS

PENETRATION AT CITY STREET VIEWPOINTS

WIDENED TO INCREASE VISIBILITY

VISUAL PENETRATION MAXIMISED

views (see Exhibit 15-4), locating "attractor" functions (i.e., restaurants, shops, etc.) along points of public access, and mandating a public circulation network through creation of public easements.

The fourth stage of programming involved the formal establishment of use and design controls, or the specific performance criteria for development. Essentially, this involved cataloguing the issues identified in previous stages. The bulk of the work, however, was in the client review process. The report was presented to the committee, various city agencies and community groups. A second draft incorporating their comments was then reworked through consultation with the city planning commission to incorporate the

appropriate language and regulatory restrictions of the city zoning ordinance. The final set of use and design controls was used later in the OPDC Penn's Landing developer's package as a guide to developer/architect teams for submitting proposals.

The final programming task was to develop pro forma economic analyses and critical path schedules which would enable the client and the selected developer to determine the most feasible development alternatives. A space budgeting system also was devised to integrate economic factors with space factors and enable program users to evaluate the impacts of various combinations. However, this tool was not used by the client.

PROGRAM

The program consisted of five major documents delivered at various stages of the project. These progressive reports provided the principal opportunities for interactions with the client, resulting in continual refinement of the program and the final recommendations for alternative development actions. The five reports are summarized below:

—Analysis of existing plan alternatives and site conditions and opportunities

—A program of uses identifying the types of uses that could be accommodated by the site and reflecting a variety of interests, day and night use, yearround activities, and permanent and

transient functions; also established de-velopment objectives and program goals and summarized the process of decision making to that point
—A study of space relationships and organization taking into consideration general architectural factors and design constraints
—A program of use and design controls expressing development criteria (see Exhibit 15-5)
—The final report presenting cost es-timates, economic impacts and critical path schedules

The final program, developed in close cooperation with the client, was intended to enable the client to assess the various possible program combinations and to af-ford the project designer a clear definition of client requirements and project limita-tions, with maximum flexibility to arrange the functions and forms of development.

IMPLEMENTATION

The client adopted the program in its en-tirety in late 1971 as the joint effort of programmer and client committee and used it fully in subsequent stages, includ-ing preparation of a developer's package and the conduct of a competition for de-veloper/architect teams in 1973.

The public improvements called for by the program and design were completed in 1976 at a cost of $13 million. A state museum was constructed on the site, and a changing program of activities at the boat basin has drawn tourists and city res-idents to the waterfront. However, private development (which was to include an of-fice building, a hotel, apartment buildings, retail and other attractor facilities, and parking) experienced difficulties in getting started. The developer originally selected in 1974 was dismissed by the Penn's Landing Corp. in 1977. Efforts to resume private development were revived in 1979.

EXHIBIT 15-5. PAGE FROM PROGRAM REPORT #4 EXEMPLIFIES USE AND DESIGN CONTROLS

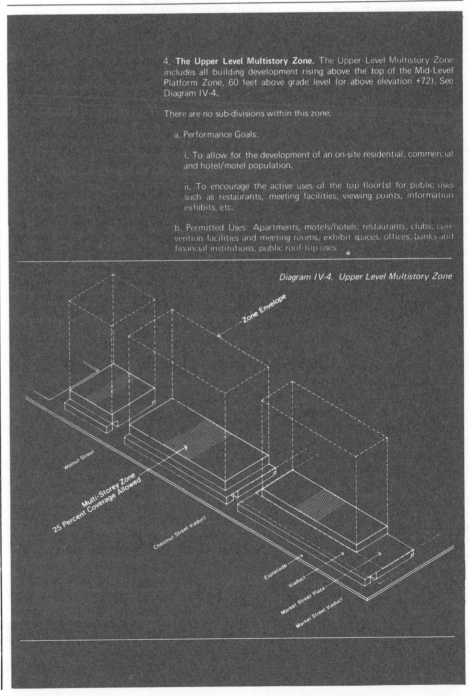

4. **The Upper Level Multistory Zone.** The Upper Level Multistory Zone includes all building development rising above the top of the Mid-Level Platform Zone, 60 feet above grade level (or above elevation +72). See Diagram IV-4.

There are no sub-divisions within this zone.

a. Performance Goals:

i. To allow for the development of an on-site residential, commercial and hotel/motel population.

ii. To encourage the active uses of the top floor(s) for public uses such as restaurants, meeting facilities, viewing points, information exhibits, etc.

b. Permitted Uses: Apartments, motels/hotels; restaurants; clubs; con-vention facilities and meeting rooms; exhibit spaces; offices; banks and financial institutions; public roof-top uses.

Diagram IV-4. Upper Level Multistory Zone

Chapter 16:
User Needs Program
for a Research
Facility

FACILITY:
Engineering Research Building
Research Triangle Institute
Research Triangle Park, North Carolina

CLIENT:
Research Triangle Institute (RTI)

PROGRAMMER:
School of Design
North Carolina State University
Raleigh, North Carolina

Henry Sanoff, AIA
Graham Adams
Ann Smith
Case Study Contributors

EXECUTIVE SUMMARY:
The results of this study of user needs were intended to provide the initial information for a more complete program for a new engineering research building. The 44,000-square-foot facility, to be located on the campus of a multidiscipline research complex, was to house a variety of research operations which relied heavily on computer applications. The objectives of the programming were to identify activities and activity relationships, organizational and functional relationships and user perceptions of and preferences for office settings. A variety of data collection and analysis techniques were employed by the programming team from the North Carolina State University School of Design, including standardized programming sheets, relationship matrices, correlation diagrams, and questionnaires containing semantic differential tests and open-ended questions. The program represented the user-related space requirements for the building and was intended as a guide for the designer and a model for the client in continuing development of program information and dialogue with the designer.

PROJECT

The objective of the project was to develop an initial program of space requirements for a specialized facility based on individual and group functions, activities and user preferences. The project involved three elements which were related to physical space needs: activity analysis, functional and organizational relationship analysis, and evaluation of the perceived adequacy of office environments. This user-needs study was intended to provide the design architect behavior-related information with which to form a facility that would respond directly to the client needs.

In addition, the programmer approached the project with two other objectives in mind: to sensitize prospective facility users to their working environments and to provide the client a programming model with which to continue the user-needs dialogue with the designer.

The facility was to be a new building of approximately 44,000 square feet which would become a part of the existing research institute campus. The building had been selected by the U.S. Department of Energy as a solar demonstration project.

CLIENT

The Research Triangle Institute (RTI) is a private organization engaged in research and development in four main areas: social sciences; statistical sciences; chemistry and life sciences; and energy, engineering and environmental sciences. The primary purpose of the organization is to organize research teams to conduct contract research which generally is heavily reliant on computer applications. Research engineers and project coordinators are the main users of this particular facility.

The client was actively involved in the programming; first, to provide data and, second, to gain a better understanding of user-environment relationships. A facility study committee was established by the Institute to project space needs, and the programmer involved the client, both management and research staff, through individual interviews, group workshops and questionnaires. Forty-one members of the engineering research staff, representing three levels of organizational positions, participated in the office setting evaluation survey.

EXHIBIT 16-1. OUTLINE OF PROGRAMMING PROCEDURES

1) Programmer devised standardized programming sheet.
2) Department managers, during interviews, filled in programming sheet, cataloguing activities, personnel, space needs and equipment/storage needs.
3) Programmer compared secondary activities (necessary to accomplish primary activities) with each other in relationship matrix for each division or department.
4) Activities were grouped from matrix into correlation diagrams of principal functions within each division or department.
5) Programmer prepared department/division/function interaction matrix for use in interviews with department managers.
6) Department managers identified relationships by matrix among functions/divisions/departments.
7) Programmer mapped relationship patterns from matrix in an interaction net.
8) Programmer administered "perception survey" to obtain user evaluations of office environments.
9) Programmer analyzed results of survey.
10) Programmer documented findings and presented program to designer and client.

EXHIBIT 16-2. SAMPLE OF COMPLETED PROGRAMMING SHEET

primary activity **1**
Data Collection
A statement identifing the primary activity.

division
Technology
Applications Center

department
Technology and
Resource Management

School of Design, North Carolina State University

**primary
activity description** **2**
A statement defining the objectives of the
primary activity.

Obtain the material
necessary to execute
the analysis required
to document/prepare
contract study

Notes:

spatial requirements **4**
Statements and projections of space needs to
accomplish the primary activity.

1. 144 square feet
    Computer terminal
    HVAC control
    Medium privacy
2. 144 square feet
    Medium privacy
    Library for department
    Medium privacy
3. 144 square feet
    High privacy
    Telephone conversation area
4. 288 square feet
    Low privacy

secondary activities **5**
The activities that are necessary to accomplish the primary activity.

1. Computer search
2. Library search (department library)
3. Telephone survey
4. Mail survey

participants **3**
The people involved in the activity at any
one time.

1. 2 Senior Professionals
    2 Professionals
2. 2 Senior Professionals
    2 Professionals
3. 2 Senior Professionals
    2 Professionals
4. 2 Professionals

equipment– storage needs **6**

1. Computer terminal
    Tape storage
2. Shelves to store printed material
3. Desk/telephone
4. Layout for materials

PROGRAMMER

A programming team was organized from the School of Design of North Carolina State University. Working under the direction of a professor of architecture, two graduate assistants collected and analyzed the program information. Additional advice was obtained from an assistant professor. The work was performed over a period of three months and required a total of 515 person-hours. A breakdown of individual effort follows:

Professor	20	hours
Graduate Assistant	450	hours
Graduate Assistant	40	hours
Assistant Professor	5	hours

PROCESS

Programming was a process of problem identification, information collection and information organization resulting in "a communicable statement of intent," according to the program author. The program report explains that programming "is an operating procedure for systematizing the design process" and the program "provides an organizational structure for the design team and a clear, communicable set of conditions for review by those affected by its implementation."

In this case, development of the program involved three principal tasks: identification of user activities and activity relationships, identification of functional and organizational relationships, and evaluation of user perceptions of office environments. Techniques employed included standardized programming sheets, interviews, relationship matrices, correlation diagrams and questionnaires that included semantic differential scales and open-ended questions. An outline of the programming procedures is presented in Exhibit 16-1.

The forms, data collected and findings developed in programming were intended

EXHIBIT 16-3. ACTIVITY RELATIONSHIP MATRIX

to be used by the client in adding and refining information throughout the programming/design process.

Many operations are involved in the performance of research and there are numerous variations in operations among the various functions, divisions and departments of the engineering research program. An activity analysis was performed to enable the programmer, and ultimately the client and designer, to understand the exact nature of the research functions and their relationship. The initial step was the preparation of a programming sheet which could be used by all departments to collect standardized information on their activities and needs. See example in Exhibit 16-2.

In interviews with department managers, the programming sheets were filled out, identifying organizational elements (division/department), primary activities, participants (personnel), space requirements for those activities (size, support requirements, level of privacy needed), the secondary activities necessary to accomplish the primary activities, and the equipment/storage needs. Since the last four categories of data (numbers 3 through 6 of the programming sheet) were related, each item was keyed by corresponding numerals among these categories. For example, two Senior Professionals and two Professionals required 144 square feet of space to perform computer searches for which a computer terminal was needed. All of these are keyed with the numeral "1."

When all the programming sheets were completed, the secondary activities of each division or department were listed in a relationship (or affinity) matrix. This was used to identify the proximity relationships of the activities performed by comparing each activity to each other one. Three criteria were considered in completing the matrix: Did the activity occur in the same space as another activity, in close proximity to it, or independent of

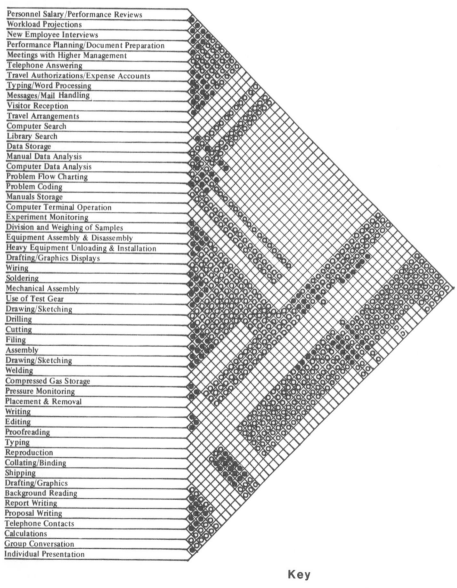

Personnel Salary/Performance Reviews
Workload Projections
New Employee Interviews
Performance Planning/Document Preparation
Meetings with Higher Management
Telephone Answering
Travel Authorizations/Expense Accounts
Typing/Word Processing
Messages/Mail Handling
Visitor Reception
Travel Arrangements
Computer Search
Library Search
Data Storage
Manual Data Analysis
Computer Data Analysis
Problem Flow Charting
Problem Coding
Manuals Storage
Computer Terminal Operation
Experiment Monitoring
Division and Weighing of Samples
Equipment Assembly & Disassembly
Heavy Equipment Unloading & Installation
Drafting/Graphics Displays
Wiring
Soldering
Mechanical Assembly
Use of Test Gear
Drawing/Sketching
Drilling
Cutting
Filing
Assembly
Drawing/Sketching
Welding
Compressed Gas Storage
Pressure Monitoring
Placement & Removal
Writing
Editing
Proofreading
Typing
Reproduction
Collating/Binding
Shipping
Drafting/Graphics
Background Reading
Report Writing
Proposal Writing
Telephone Contacts
Calculations
Group Conversation
Individual Presentation

Key

● (solid) = high interaction

○ (open) = medium interaction

(vacant) = no interaction

the other activity? The proximity relationships of activities of the Process Engineering Department are shown in Exhibit 16-3.

From the matrix it was possible for the programmer to identify groups of activities that occurred within the same space and the activity groupings that related to each other. To clarify and illustrate these functional-space relationships, the programmer created a correlation diagram identifying the specialized functionspaces and their connections to each other. In Exhibit 16-4, for example, the activities of the secretarial function occur within the same physical area and have a functional relationship with the activities occurring in the department office and the conference area.

Since the activities of any one department within the engineering research group are often connected with the activities of other departments, the programmer then turned to identifying those relationships. Another matrix, listing each department and its divisions and functions, was created and the department managers asked to identify the working relationships with other departments by filling in the matrix. In this case, the level of interdependence among departments was measured in terms of high relation (solid bullet), medium relation (hollow bullet) and no relation (blank). The factors involved the occasional sharing of professional staff and equipment and the interactions of management. When interviews and matrices were completed for each department, a composite matrix was created and conflicting information was resolved in review sessions with managers. An interaction matrix is shown in Exhibit 16-5.

These data were further reduced to clarify relationships by, once again, drawing a correlation diagram or interaction net. Those departmental functions, regardless of oganizational position, which maintained a higher degree of interaction were grouped together and their lesser relationships with other groups were iden-

EXHIBIT 16-4. FUNCTIONAL CORRELATION DIAGRAM

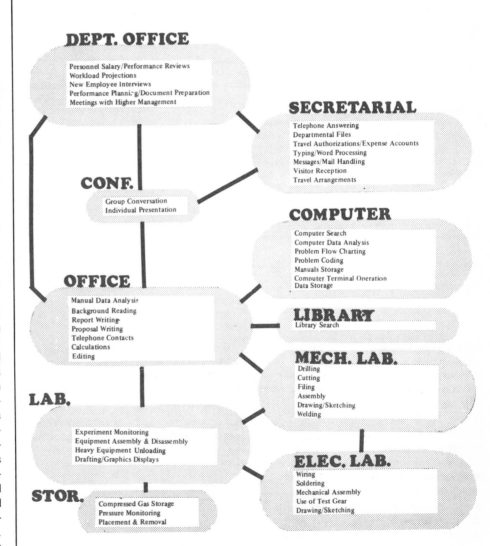

DEPT. OFFICE
Personnel Salary/Performance Reviews
Workload Projections
New Employee Interviews
Performance Planning/Document Preparation
Meetings with Higher Management

SECRETARIAL
Telephone Answering
Departmental Files
Travel Authorizations/Expense Accounts
Typing/Word Processing
Messages/Mail Handling
Visitor Reception
Travel Arrangements

CONF.
Group Conversation
Individual Presentation

COMPUTER
Computer Search
Computer Data Analysis
Problem Flow Charting
Problem Coding
Manuals Storage
Computer Terminal Operation
Data Storage

OFFICE
Manual Data Analysis
Background Reading
Report Writing
Proposal Writing
Telephone Contacts
Calculations
Editing

LIBRARY
Library Search

MECH. LAB.
Drilling
Cutting
Filing
Assembly
Drawing/Sketching
Welding

LAB.
Experiment Monitoring
Equipment Assembly & Disassembly
Heavy Equipment Unloading
Drafting/Graphics Displays

ELEC. LAB.
Wiring
Soldering
Mechanical Assembly
Use of Test Gear
Drawing/Sketching

STOR.
Compressed Gas Storage
Pressure Monitoring
Placement & Removal

EXHIBIT 16-5. DEPARTMENTAL RELATIONSHIP MATRIX

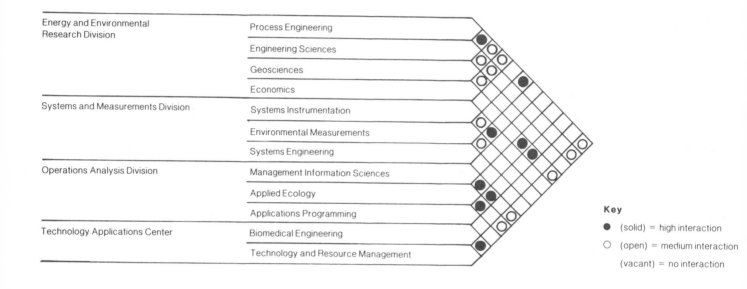

Key
- ● (solid) = high interaction
- ○ (open) = medium interaction
- (vacant) = no interaction

tified by connecting lines. Exhibit 16-6 illustrates the resulting interaction net.

Modeling of the correlation diagrams would enable the designer to visualize the possible arrangements of various types of spaces within departments and the locations of the different department functions in relation to each other.

Finally, the programmer surveyed the prospective facility users to obtain their analyses as individuals and as groups (senior professionals, professionals and junior professionals) of the quality of their working environments. Two different approaches were used to collect their evaluations of present offices and preferences for "ideal" office settings: semantic differential scales and open-ended questions. Both of these were included in a questionnaire distributed to 45 engineering research staff; 41 were completed and returned.

In the semantic differential test, the individuals were asked to rate both their present office and four photographs of different office settings according to a list of 20 antonym or bipolar adjective pairs. The procedure was to mark the adjective within a five-interval range that described

the particular office, as in the example below.

When the questionnaire results were tabulated, a composite profile of the three groups' responses (based on mean values) was charted on a blank semantic scale list. The profile of the group evalu-

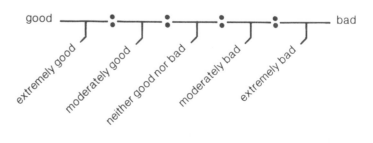

EXHIBIT 16-6. DEPARTMENTAL INTERACTION NET

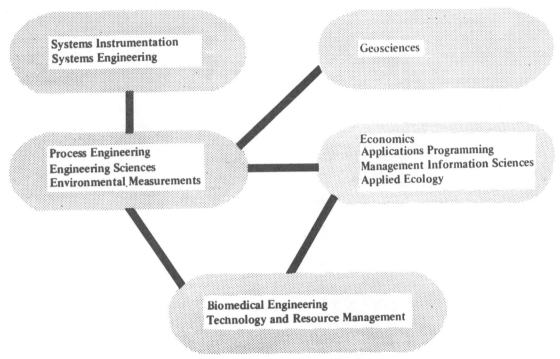

ations is shown in Exhibit 16-7.

Semantic scale analysis enabled the programmer to quantitatively describe user perceptions and preferences, identifying general tendencies for each of the three groups and for the whole sample of research professionals. The programmer also sought to qualitatively analyze the comments and opinions of the group reflected in their collective responses to open-ended questions. The questions requested information from individuals on:

—What aspects of their present office they liked

—What aspects they disliked

—Their preferences for the "ideal" office

—Their reasons for their ratings of the four photographed offices in the semantic differential test

The programmer then derived analytical conclusions about the group's feelings to-ward office work environments from the collected responses, particularly identifying differences and similarities among the three professional group levels.

PROGRAM

The collected and analyzed data were organized into a program report of 214 pages. As stated in the report, a program "is a prescription for a desired set of events influenced by local constraints, and it states a set of desired conditions and the methods for achieving those conditions." The program is also "the first step in a sequence of phases in the design process, the results of which will ultimately effect some type of change in the environment."

The report was organized in four specific areas of programming activity. The first section is a systematic description of activities and activity requirements within the various departments to be housed in the engineering research facility. The second section outlines the departmental interactions, describing the critical links of professional and departmental interactions. The third section reports the results of the user perception survey on office environments. A final section contains specific recommendations for client and designer derived from interviews, observations and research of the departments and divisions of the engineering research group.

IMPLEMENTATION

The information in the report, according to the author, provides the initial steps in establishing the program for the new building. The program of user needs was turned over to the design architect who

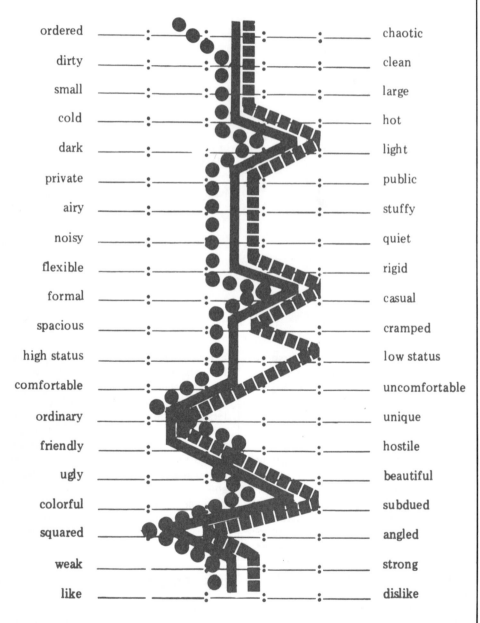

		chaotic
ordered		chaotic
dirty		clean
small		large
cold		hot
dark		light
private		public
airy		stuffy
noisy		quiet
flexible		rigid
formal		casual
spacious		cramped
high status		low status
comfortable		uncomfortable
ordinary		unique
friendly		hostile
ugly		beautiful
colorful		subdued
squared		angled
weak		strong
like		dislike

had been selected by the time the study was concluded. It was intended to be used by the designer as a guide to behavior-related space requirements and by the client as a model for continuing collection, analysis and refinement of program data in cooperation with the designer. Furthermore, the involvement of the client in the programming process itself was intended to sensitize the users of the facility to their behavior, their working environments and the relationships between them.

Chapter 17
Program for a County Government Office Building

FACILITY:
Arundel Center at Broad Creek
Anne Arundel County, Maryland

CLIENT:
Anne Arundel County, Maryland

PROGRAMMER:
RTKL Associates Inc.
Architecture/Planning-Urban Design/
Engineering
Baltimore, Maryland

David R. Beard, AIA
Case Study Contributor

EXECUTIVE SUMMARY:
The purpose of the project was to devise a program that would be a guide for design of a new central office building, anticipating a relocation of the legislative and executive operations of the Anne Arundel County government as well as expansion needs through 1990. The programmer, RTKL Associates Inc., used the techniques of literature search, questionnaire-interview, space standards, adjacency matrices and adjacency diagrams to develop design requirements that would satisfy client needs. The building program identified space requirements by department and for the total facility and functional adjacency requirements among and within departments. The program requirements were used, together with a site analysis, to develop conceptual plans of the facility and to estimate construction costs. The program was prepared over a four-month period and required 780 person-hours to complete. The county has accepted, but not implemented, the program.

PROJECT

The Anne Arundel County government retained RTKL Associates Inc. to study the feasibility of constructing a new central office building and relocating 18 legislative and executive offices and support services from its old headquarters in Annap-

EXHIBIT 17-1. PROGRAMMING PROCEDURES OUTLINE

PROGRAM PLANNING
—Identify programming objectives
—Identify primary information sources
—Identify and schedule programming tasks
—Assign responsibilities

DATA COLLECTION
—Review client data/conduct literature search on similar facilities
—Draft and send questionnaire to department heads
—Interview department heads based on questionnaire
—Observe activities and existing facilities through guided tours
—Review data and obtain missing information

DATA ANALYSIS AND ORGANIZATION
—Compare departmental space requests with inventory of existing space and previous allocation projections
—Develop workstation space standards
—Identify similar functional spaces and common space needs
—Apply space standards and assign department space requirements
—Identify interaction patterns among departments
—Compare and collate interdepartmental adjacency needs (matrices)
—Identify interaction patterns within departments
—Diagram space arrangements within departments
—Compare total space requirements with county projections and budget limitations

DOCUMENTATION
—Tabulate departmental space requirements (current/future) by function
—Diagram standard space units
—Display interdepartmental adjacency requirements in matrices for each department and master matrix for total building
—Write descriptions of departmental purpose and organization and of functional areas
—Diagram internal space adjacencies and interactions by departments
—Combine into individual departmental programs

REVIEW AND REVISION
—Review and adjust departmental space requirements
—Monitor summary review by administration
—Monitor final review of departmental programs by department heads, and adjust material to suit
—Revise space projections to conform with cost constraints

SITE EVALUATION/BUILDING DIAGRAMMATICS

CONSTRUCTION COST ESTIMATE

PROGRAM PUBLICATION

olis to the new facility at its Broad Creek government complex. Under a contract for programming services, the architecture/engineering/planning firm was to deliver a three-part report consisting of a detailed building program, site analysis, and construction cost estimates.

The study was a preliminary step in deciding whether to sell the old Arundel Center to the State of Maryland. Regardless of its decision, the county intended to use the program to develop expansion and reorganization plans for either the old or the new facility. The building program was to determine the county's long-range space needs and recommend functional space organization. Site analysis would involve evaluation of two alternative locations at Broad Creek and selection justification. Program requirements and site evaluation would form a basis for estimating capital construction costs.

The county had estimated, based on simple population and government growth projections, that expansion over the ensuing 14 years would require a building size of about 95,000 square feet. This was also in line with a preliminary cost estimate. In addition, a master plan of the Broad Creek property called for a building of six to eight stories with relatively small floor areas.

CLIENT

Anne Arundel County government provides public services for 350,000 residents of a growing, urban area adjacent to the city of Baltimore and the Chesapeake Bay. Although the programmer's immediate client was the government, the program addressed three levels of client needs: the public, who would pay for the project and use the county services and the new facility; their legislative and executive representatives, who were concerned with cost and operating efficiencies; and the government employees who worked in and operated the facility. The

EXHIBIT 17-2. QUESTIONNAIRE FOR DATA COLLECTION

I. METHOD OF OPERATION
1. A brief description of your department's responsibilities and required tasks.
2. How does your department fit within the county government organization?
3. How is your department subdivided? Describe the activities of each section.
4. What information or material is received by your department and how is it processed?
5. How many staff and work positions are necessary in order that your department functions properly? This is for the present and future operations.
6. Which work positions can be open, and which require privacy?
7. What are the filing requirements for your department and how often do you purge your files? What are the legal requirements for maintaining records for your department?
8. What are your department's requirements for conference or meeting space? What is the frequency of the meetings and the average number of attendees?
9. What special equipment or furnishings are required for your department, if any?
10. Provide a rough plan showing how your department could best function.
11. What changes, if any, are expected in operations, organization or staffing over the next 5 to 10 years?

II. LOCATION REQUIREMENTS
1. Describe where information and/or material come from and where it goes after leaving your department.
2. What is the volume and frequency for the movement of information and material?
3. What automation, if any, is required or desired for movement of information or material (computers, pneumatic tube, etc.)?
4. What departmental contact with the public is necessary or desired?
5. Does the department now, or will it in the future, share space, equipment or personnel with other departments?
6. Provide a rough diagram showing your department's relationship with other departments.

III. EXISTING FACILITIES
1. Discuss present functional problems with your facilities.
2. Tour the department (with interviewer).
3. Other questions and/or comments.

EXHIBIT 17-3. STANDARD SPACE UNITS (EXAMPLES)

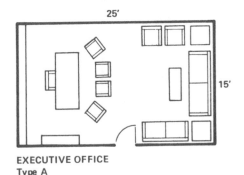

25'

15'

EXECUTIVE OFFICE
Type A
375 Sq. Ft.

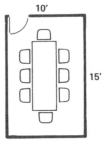

7'-6"

10'

PLANNER/ENGINEER
Type F.1
75 Sq. Ft.

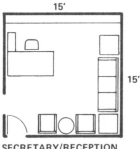

15'

15'

SECRETARY/RECEPTION
Type C.1
225 Sq. Ft.

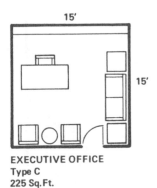

15'

15'

EXECUTIVE OFFICE
Type C
225 Sq. Ft.

10'

15'

SMALL CONFERENCE
Type SC
Seats 6 - 8
150 Sq. Ft.

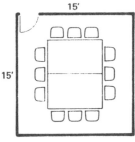

15'

15'

MEDIUM CONFERENCE
Type MC
Seats 10 - 12
225 Sq. Ft.

---

client was directly involved in the programming process at every stage.

PROGRAMMER

RTKL, a large multiservice firm serving primarily corporate and institutional clients, assigned a principal-in-charge and four architects and programmers to the project. Services rendered by RTKL were development of programs for the legislative and administrative operations, support services, and parking facilities; site analysis; preparation of building diagrammatics (conceptual plans) for visualizing program requirements; and construction cost estimating.

RTKL agreed to a staged contract allowing award of a lump sum fee for programming services alone. A contract for complete architectural services was to be awarded following a decision to proceed with the project. Programming time, over four months, amounted to 780 hours, which are itemized here:

Principal-in-charge	120 hours
Project architects/ programmers	500 hours
Technical support (drafting/typing)	160 hours

PROCESS

Progressive review and revision enabled the programmer to adjust the program as it was developed, saving time and ensuring client acceptance by the time it was complete. Although programming tasks frequently overlapped, the procedure followed the general sequence shown in Exhibit 17-1.

PROGRAM/PLANNING. Programming tasks were organized around three objectives: establish space requirements for each department and operation; identify

EXHIBIT 17-4. EXTERNAL ADJACENCY MATRIX

From \ To	County Executive[1]	Law Office	Planning & Zoning	Zoning Hearings	Inspections & Permits	Recreation & Parks	Finance Office	Budget Office	Personnel Office	Central Services	Buildings & Grounds	Purchasing Office	Data Processing	Civil Defense	County Council	County Auditor	Board of Appeals	Extension Service	Public	Evening Use	Service
County Executive[1]		○						○				○							◐		
Law Office	○							○											◐		
Planning & Zoning	○	○			●	○													●		
Zoning Hearings		○	◐														●		○	○	
Inspections & Permits		○	●				○												●		
Recreation & Parks																			●	○	
Finance Office					○								●						●		
Budget Office	●												○						◐		
Personnel Office							○												●	○	
Central Services	○						○				○	○									
Buildings & Grounds							○					○							○		●
Purchasing Office		○					●	○													
Data Processing							○												◐		◐
Civil Defense																					
County Council																			●	◐	
County Auditor							◐						●						◐		
Board of Appeals				◐			○												○	○	
Extension Service																			●	○	

● Strong Adjacency   ○ Moderate Adjacency   ◐ Negative Adjacency

economical, effective adjacency patterns among the various functions; and synthesize this information with a site "program" into a feasible building concept. A programming team, consisting of RTKL personnel and representatives of the county Department of Public Works (DPW), administered the project.

DATA COLLECTION. Interviews of department heads were conducted by two teams, each consisting of one DPW and two RTKL representatives. The interviews were based on a questionnaire distributed two weeks earlier, although the sessions did not follow the intended structured format. The questions (see Exhibit 17-2) were tailored to the programming objectives. An observational tour of existing facilities and activities followed each department interview. Observation provided new information and enabled the programmer to clarify and verify data obtained in the interview.

DATA ANALYSIS AND ORGANIZATION. The assembled information was sorted and categorized for analysis in three groups: functional area requirements (space needs), external adjacencies (interdepartmental interactions), and internal adjacencies (intradepartmental interactions). Area requirements were determined using the space standard technique. A space size was calculated for each type of function performed by the county, establishing a standard space unit for each workstation. The space standards were developed, through agreement with department administrators, and diagrammed as illustrated in Exhibit 17-3. As space requirements for each department function were tabulated, the appropriate standard was applied and net area assigned to the workstation. Stan-

EXHIBIT 17-5. INTERNAL ADJACENCY DIAGRAM

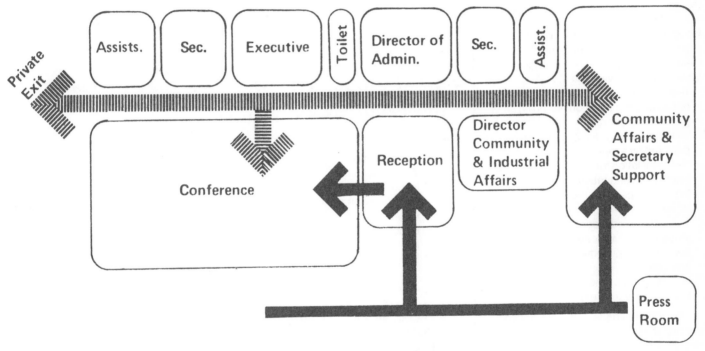

MANAGEMENT GROUP & COMMUNITY AFFAIRS

dardization of workstation spaces reduced the overall space requested by departments, fostered client consensus on program requirements, and provided the programmer flexibility for organizing spaces.

The programmer made space organization decisions with the aid of two display techniques: adjacency matrices and adjacency diagrams. To identify external adjacencies, or proximity needs, among offices, the programmer created a matrix for each department. It revealed the other departments with which it should be physically associated, as well as the need for public access and for support service access. The master matrix shown in Exhibit 17-4 defined the network of adjacencies for the entire county operation, produced by combining the individual matrices.

The internal adjacencies of each office were identified by arranging workstation diagrams in patterns that expressed functional relationships as well as public and controlled access. An example of an adjacency diagram is reproduced in Exhibit 17-5.

SITE ANALYSIS/BUILDING DIAGRAMMATICS. One of the two sites was recommended for development based on relative satisfaction of specific criteria including size, natural features, development costs, energy conservation. Building diagrammatics enabled the programmer to display for the client conceptual plans for arranging functional groups based on area requirements and adjacency requirements.

PROGRAM

The final program document consisted of a series of ''programs'' of varying detail for: workstations (space standards), departments, support services, parking facilities, site, and conceptual plans. The document was organized into six sections according to these categories, plus an introduction and a reprint of the questionnaire. The departmental programs provided the client, and the potential designer, a detailed accounting of requirements for design. Each department program contained five elements:

—A narrative description of responsibilities and organization, including an organizational chart
—The external adjacency requirements depicted by a matrix
—A tabulation of space requirements listed by workstation (function) showing the space standard code, net square footage, number of personnel
—A narrative description of each workstation unit indicating use, special equipment requirements, and desirable adjacencies
—A diagram of the space organization (internal adjacencies)

The contents page of the program document, shown as Exhibit 17-6, lists the elements of the program for the Arundel Center at Broad Creek.

IMPLEMENTATION

The Anne Arundel County Council accepted the program for use as a guide to designing the new facility or planning expansion and reorganization at the old Arundel Center in Annapolis. To date, the program has not been implemented.

EXHIBIT 17-6. PROGRAM REPORT CONTENTS

1. INTRODUCTION
   1.1 Statement of Tasks
   1.2 Program Summary
   1.3 Site Analysis
   1.4 Diagrammatics
   1.5 Desired Functional Adjacencies
   1.6 Program Methodology
   1.7 Definition of Terms

2. UNIT SPACE STANDARDS

3. DEPARTMENTAL PROGRAM
   3.1 County Executive
   3.2 Law Office
   3.3 Planning and Zoning
   3.4 Zoning Hearings
   3.5 Inspections and Permits
   3.6 Recreation and Parks
   3.7 Finance Office
   3.8 Budget Office
   3.9 Personnel Office
   3.10 Central Services
   3.11 Building and Grounds Office
   3.12 Purchasing Office
   3.13 Data Processing
   3.14 Civil Defense
   3.15 County Council
   3.16 County Auditor
   3.17 Board of Appeals
   3.18 Extension Service

4. BUILDING SUPPORT PROGRAM
   4.1 Additional Program Elements—Direction Office
   4.2 Additional Program Elements—Building and Grounds Office
   4.3 Additional Program Elements—Purchasing Office
   4.4 Vehicle Maintenance

5. PARKING
   5.1 Data Sources
   5.2 Employee Parking
   5.3 County Owned Vehicles
   5.4 Visitors
   5.5 Existing Parking Resources at Broad Creek
   5.6 Parking Requirements Summary
   5.7 Parking Facility Operation

6. SITE ANALYSIS
   6.1 Introduction/Summary
   6.2 Master Plan
   6.3 Site Size
   6.4 Natural Features
   6.5 Utilities and Site Drainage
   6.6 Accessibility
   6.7 Views
   6.8 Energy Conservation
   6.9 Noise
   6.10 Cost of Site Development
   6.11 Site Options for Future Development

7. DIAGRAMMATICS
   7.1 Introduction
   7.2 Program Options
   7.3 The Diagrammatic Plan
   7.4 Parking Structure

APPENDIX
   Interview Questionnaire

Chapter 18
Design Criteria for Medical Research Laboratories

FACILITY:
Prototype Laboratory for 200 Modules
Ambulatory Care and Research Facility
   (ACRF)
National Institutes of Health (NIH)
Bethesda, Maryland

CLIENT:
National Institutes of Health (NIH)
Bethesda, Maryland

PROGRAMMER:
Space for Social Systems (SPACE4)
Alexandria, Virginia

Pamela Clayton, AIA
Liz Macklin
Carolyn Raeke
Case Study Contributors

DESIGNER:
Space for Social Systems (SPACE4)

EXECUTIVE SUMMARY:
This project, the development of design criteria for a group of 200 medical research laboratories, went beyond traditional programming, although that task was an essential element in the process of "programming" the laboratory prototype. Programming, in this instance, was a research/design/evaluation process. It produced a set of criteria which would not only guide the ACRF project architect/engineer and the client's in-house architectural/engineering staff in designing the individual laboratory modules, but would enable the laboratory users to manipulate components in creating their own "designs." The project involved identifying functional and behavioral needs, translating those needs into performance criteria for design, and documenting the programming/design/evaluation process. A variety of behavioral research and other data collection, analysis and evaluation techniques were used including observation mapping, annotated photography, open-ended interviews, group planning sessions, activity relationship matrices, space relationship diagramming, working model manipulation, and user evaluation. A prototype full scale model was designed and was to be constructed for user evaluation before finalizing the design criteria.

PROJECT

Dissatisfied with the work environments of existing laboratory rooms at its vast medical research complex, the National Institutes of Health (NIH) wished to investigate alternatives to the "standard" laboratory design before building 200 modules in its new Ambulatory Care and Research Facility (ACRF) which was under construction. The project would involve not only design of a new prototype, but an examination of the typical laboratory environment to discover its inefficiencies and the characteristics which affected user productivity. The design criteria produced from the study would provide guidance for design and construction of the new laboratory modules and for remodeling existing laboratories. The process by which this was accomplished was also to be documented for use by NIH and other government and private sector research operations.

CLIENT

The client was a government-sponsored agency, the nation's center for medical research activities. The programmer worked directly with the Engineering Design Branch of NIH, its architectural and engineering services office. It was this office which had identified the working environment problem. The efforts of the Branch and of other designers had created alterations in the standard laboratory, but traditional architectural approaches had not produced satisfactory results. Typical laboratories were still unstimulating and inefficient places to work. The Engineering Design Branch decided that the solution might lie in a more systematic and approach to the problem.

A project manager was assigned by the Branch to administer the study with the programmer. Information input to programming from the client was provided by three groups: managers, designers and users. The managers and designers were engineers and architects from the Engineering Design Branch. The users were some occupants of existing laboratories examined by the programmer, but mostly members of an ACRF Design Committee which included representatives from laboratory buildings other than those in the programmer's study sample.

PROGRAMMER

SPACE4 is an architectural research firm specializing in development of design criteria. Its stated approach to architecture is through research-oriented design, using behavioral research techniques to identify human needs in relation to environment and to produce design studies and solutions which respond to those needs.

Programming and prototype design (including construction documents) were accomplished within 50 calendar days, requiring approximately 800 person-hours. Of this time, about 400 person-hours were attributable to program research and development, the first phase of the project. Personnel time breakdown for this phase is as follows:

Project Director	120 hours
2 Research Associates	280 hours

Tasks of the project director included contract and project administration, project design and scheduling, research analysis, program reviews and technical direction. One research associate was responsible for information collection; design, execution and analysis; and program development. The second research associate prepared program information and later was responsible for writing and editing the report.

The project was developed under a fixed-fee contract. The firm's fee for this

EXHIBIT 18-1. PROGRAMMING/DESIGN/EVALUATION PROCESS

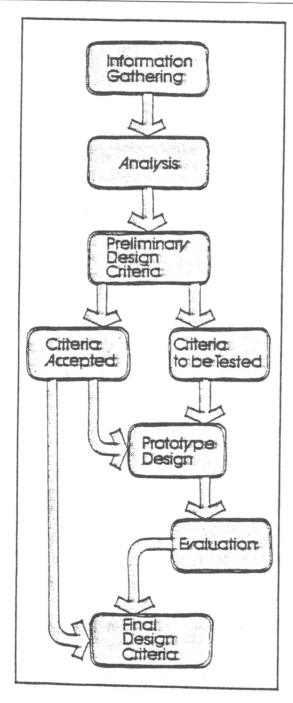

type of work averaged $35 per hour at that time. Additional time and compensation were involved in subsequent user evaluation studies employing a full-scale model of the prototype laboratory.

PROCESS

The procedures of programming—i.e., the process of systematically gathering and analyzing information on client needs—were not restricted to a particular phase of the project called programming. In a sense, the proramming process extended throughout the entire project. Information was continuously collected, analyzed, tested, revised and tested again in order to produce a realistic "program" of client needs and needs fulfillment. Although this project included a phase called "programming," the processes of programming and design were integrated, together with the process of evaluation (see Exhibit 18-1).

The project had begun with the goal of increasing user satisfaction while achieving management objectives. To accomplish this, both groups needed to understand and participate in the research design process. What the programmer discovered through this participation was the distinction between the goals (needs) of the two groups (see Exhibit 18-2). Understanding and accommodating both was important to the success of the project.

The programmer devised a participatory process for all phases of the work, using a project management strategy which overlapped the goal-setting and the data-gathering activities. Group work sessions were conducted with both user and manager groups, while baseline data on existing conditions of laboratories in three buildings of different design were collected.

In the goal-setting sessions, the programmer used a simple technique which was not only easy for clients to complete, but a quick and effective means of ac-

EXHIBIT 18-2: VISUALIZING DIFFERENT GOALS OF DIFFERENT CLIENT GROUPS

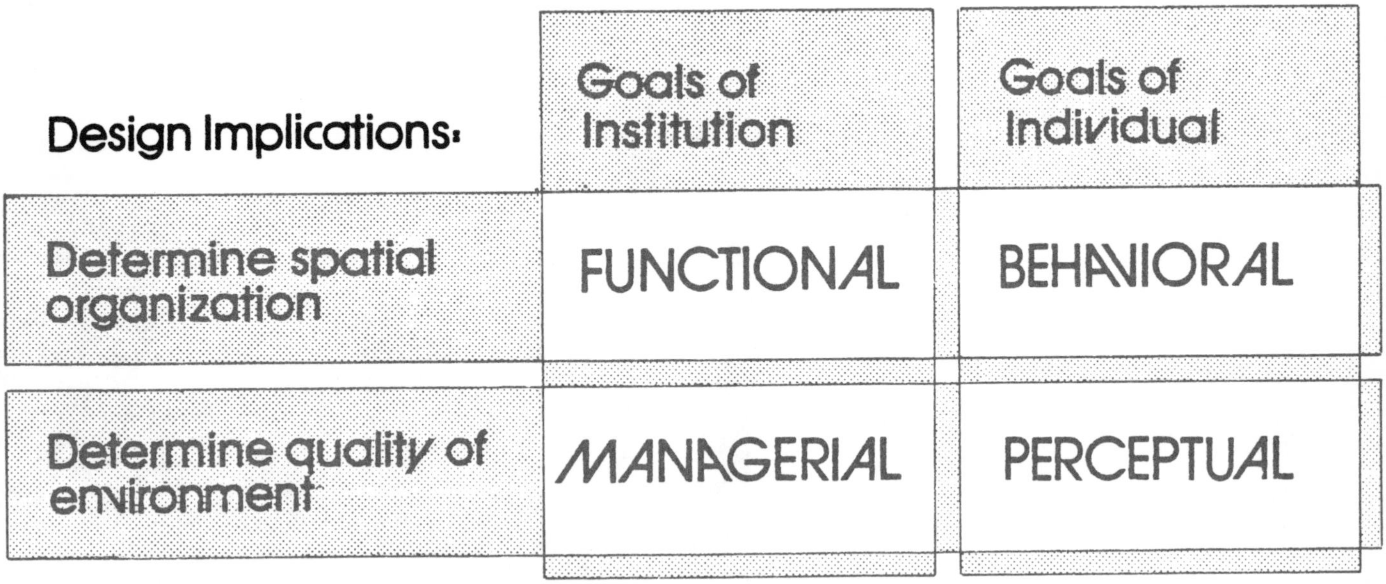

Design Implications:	Goals of Institution	Goals of Individual
Determine spatial organization	FUNCTIONAL	BEHAVIORAL
Determine quality of environment	MANAGERIAL	PERCEPTUAL

quiring the information needed. Individual participants listed three goals, each on a separate index card. The collected cards were sorted and arranged into categories. From this point, the group discussion of goals began with a clear idea of what members believed was important for the design to achieve.

Gathering quantitative data on the existing conditions of laboratories in the NIH complex was necessary before the programmer could identify what the problems were and what possible solutions could be devised. Two main techniques were employed: observation and open-ended in-terviews with laboratory personnel. However, a variety of techniques were used to record, classify, organize and analyze the information obtained by observation and questioning. Some of these are illus-trated in Exhibits 18-3 and 18-4. In ad-dition, the programmer conducted a litera-ture search of state-of-the-art laboratory design (programmer reports little informa-tion available in this regard) and document analysis of previous design drawings.

From the information accumulated and analyzed, the programmer produced pre-liminary design criteria for individual lab-oratory activities. But this was far from the end of the project. Before final design criteria were developed, these "first thoughts" would undergo evaluation, re-finement and testing. The first evaluation came from another round of group work sessions with the two client committees. For this purpose, a series of wall-sized analysis sheets were prepared (Exhibit 18-5). Each sheet identified a specific ac-tivity and described it in diagrams and words. One column listed the preliminary design criteria, while corresponding col-umns provided space for user committee comments, manager committee com-ments and designer comments.

EXHIBIT 18-3. DATA COLLECTION TECHNIQUES

(Examination and illustration of "physical traces" of use of space through annotated photographs provides programmer, designer and client with information and focus on pertinent design issues. A space use inventory provides a detailed record not only of architectural features and equipment, but of how occupants use and alter space.)

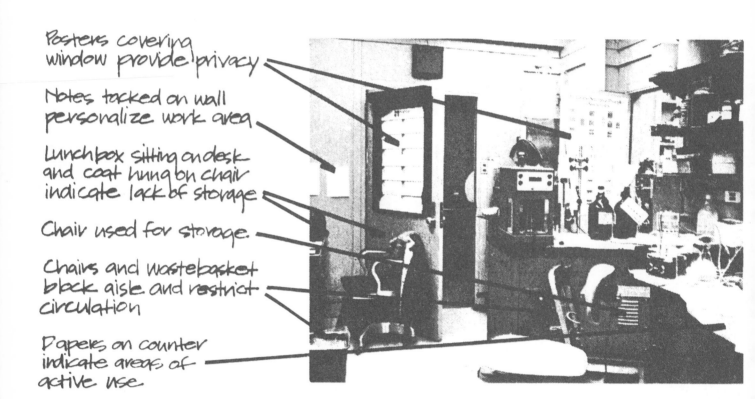

Posters covering window provide privacy

Notes tacked on wall personalize work area

Lunchbox sitting on desk and coat hung on chair indicate lack of storage

Chair used for storage.

Chairs and wastebasket block aisle and restrict circulation

Papers on counter indicate areas of active use

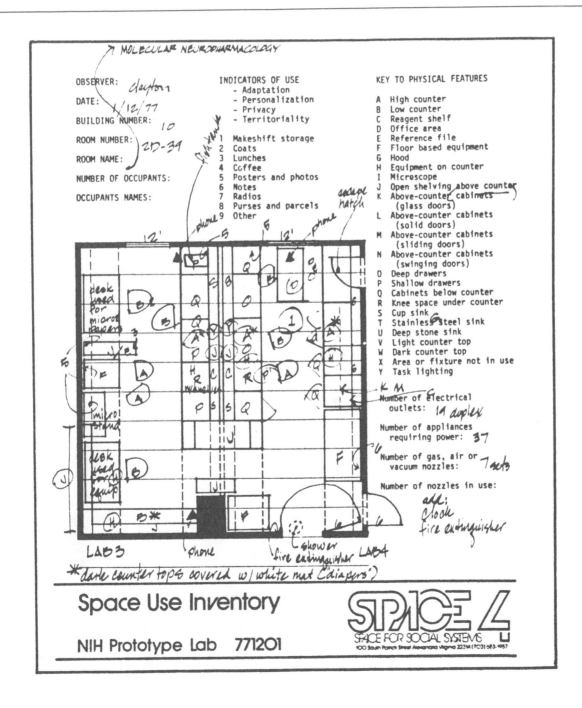

Space Use Inventory

NIH Prototype Lab   771201

SPACE4
SPACE FOR SOCIAL SYSTEMS
100 South Patrick Street Alexandria Virginia 22314 (703) 683-1957

EXHIBIT 18-4. DATA ANALYSIS TECHNIQUES

(Simplified diagrams of existing elements in a space enable the programmer to focus on relationships between activities and components and to identify necessary adjacencies and ideal arrangements. Adjacencies, perhaps in more detail, can also be expressed in the form of a matrix of relationships. Knowledge of what exists can be translated into what should be in the form of a more simplified matrix of element location relationships.)

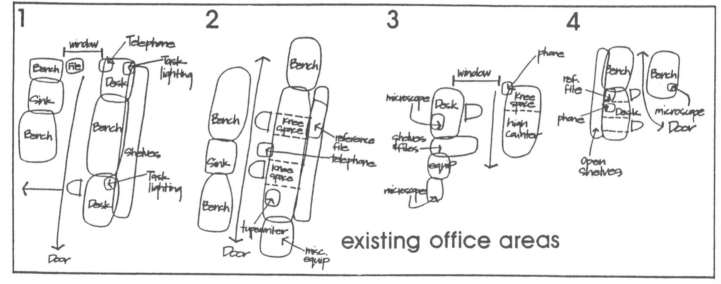

existing office areas

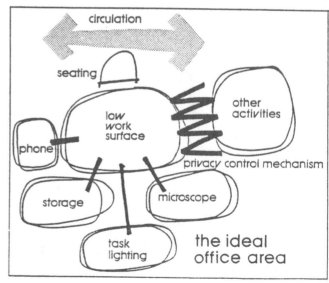

the ideal office area

Adjacencies

Column headers (left to right):
TASK LIGHTING · POWER · BACK COUNTER TOP · LIGHT COUNTER TOP · DEEP STONE SINK · STAINLESS STEEL SINK · CUP SINK · KNEE SPACE BELOW · CABINETS BELOW · SHALLOW DRAWERS · DEEP DRAWERS · CABINETS ABOVE (SOLID) · CABINETS ABOVE (GLASS) · OPEN SHELVING ABOVE · MICROSCOPE · EQUIP ON COUNTER · HOOD · FLOOR BASED EQUIP · OFFICE AREA · DESK FILE · REAGENT SHELF · HIGH COUNTER · LOW COUNTER · WINDOW

	TASK LIGHTING	POWER	BACK COUNTER TOP	LIGHT COUNTER TOP	DEEP STONE SINK	STAINLESS STEEL SINK	CUP SINK	KNEE SPACE BELOW	CABINETS BELOW	SHALLOW DRAWERS	DEEP DRAWERS	CABINETS ABOVE (SOLID)	CABINETS ABOVE (GLASS)	OPEN SHELVING ABOVE	MICROSCOPE	EQUIP ON COUNTER	HOOD	FLOOR BASED EQUIP	OFFICE AREA	DESK FILE	REAGENT SHELF	HIGH COUNTER	LOW COUNTER	WINDOW
PHONE	1							3					3	2		1	1		4	4	2	3	2	5
DOOR				1					1		1	1	3		3	1	4	1	1			7	2	
WINDOW								1	1	1			1	2		1		5	2		2	1		
HIGH COUNTER		3		a			1	3	7	3	8		3	1		2	6	1						
LOW COUNTER							3		5	5					1	1	1	8						
REAGENT SHELF			5									2	5	3	5	3	3							
DESK FILE	2			1			1	1	1			3	2				1	3						
OFFICE AREA									4	4			2		2	1	1	1						
FLOOR BASED EQUIP		3		3				2	1	3	4		5	1		1	1							
HOOD								3					4	1	1	1								
EQUIP ON COUNTER	1			a		3	2		1	3		3	2											
MICROSCOPE							1	1			1	1		2										
OPEN SHELVING (ABOVE)		1		7			2			3	2	2												
CABINETS ABOVE (GLASS)				2																				
CABINETS ABOVE (SOLID)				2																				
DEEP DRAWERS		1		2			5	4	1															
SHALLOW DRAWERS				3			4	3																
CABINETS BELOW		1		4			2																	
KNEE SPACE BELOW																								
CUP SINK		1		3																				
STAINLESS STEEL SINK		1																						
DEEP STONE SINK																								
LIGHT COUNTER TOP		1																						
BACK COUNTER TOP		1																						
POWER	1																							
TASK LIGHTING	1																							

Number indicates frequency of adjacent relationship in space inventory plan

Existing Design: Items found next to one another

Locational Relationships between Laboratory Elements

+ proximity desirable
O proximity not necessary
− proximity undesirable

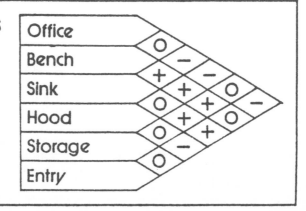

Office · Bench · Sink · Hood · Storage · Entry

EXHIBIT 18-5. PRELIMINARY DESIGN CRITERIA WERE PRESENTED ON WALL-SIZED ANALYSIS SHEETS FOR CLIENT/DESIGNER REVIEW AND COMMENT

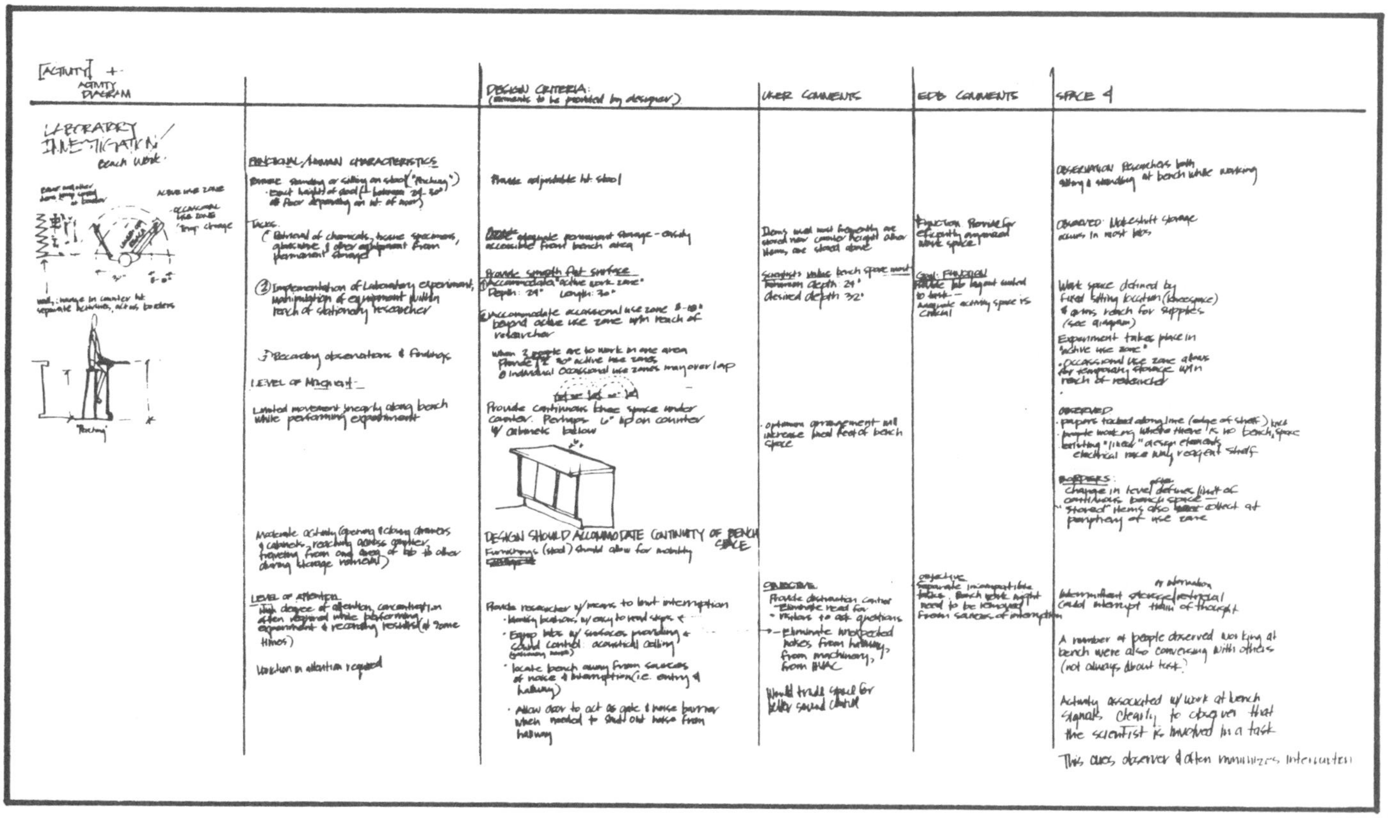

Although testing of design criteria would continue, the preliminary criteria evaluation essentially concluded the programming phase of the project.

PROGRAM

The program document was not completed until after all elements of the project were finished. However, a partial program was given to the engineering and design team before completion. It included a design concept for a prototype laboratory along with diagrams of space use, communications patterns, work flow, noise generation, functional compatibilities and environmental quality statements. These were used in design of the working model of the prototype and of the full-scale mockup.

The full program was presented in the form of a final report. This was a working document which included presentation of the programming/design process, the evaluation of the demonstration process, photographs of the working models and prototype mockup, and designer/user guidelines for laboratory design. The contents of the program report are listed in Exhibit 18-6. The report contained 105 pages plus an appendix.

EXHIBIT 18-6. PROGRAM REPORT CONTENTS

1_____The Project Scope

9_____Introducing Research into Design

_____Programming

13_____A Systematic Process

43_____A Design Response

_____Simulation

91_____and Evaluation

105_____ Appendix

IMPLEMENTATION

From the program and prototype design, a full-scale mockup was to be built along with a mockup of a "standard" NIH laboratory in the next stage of the project. These would be placed side-by-side and used for evaluation of design response to the criteria developed in programming. Prior to this, a smaller scale working model of the prototype was constructed. Laboratory users could examine the design criteria by manipulating and observing the miniature elements in the dollhouse-like model. Again, the programmer/designer would collect and analyze user reactions to the prototype for refinement of the design criteria.

Chapter 19
Light and Color Study
for Psychiatric
Residence Units

FACILITY:
Nursing Units of The Clinical Center
National Institute of Mental Health
Bethesda, Maryland

CLIENT:
National Institute of Mental Health (NIMH)
National Institutes of Health (NIH)
Bethesda, Maryland

PROGRAMMER:
Spivack Associates Inc.
Environmental Designers and Programmers
Newtonville, Massachusetts

Mayer Spivack, MCP
Joanna Tamer
Case Study Contributors

EXECUTIVE SUMMARY:
The purpose of this project was to provide performance and materials specifications for lighting and color design in a resident psychiatric research and treatment facility. Through behavioral research, the objective was to discover, document and optimize the effects of light and color on the facility users (patients and attendant staff in four wings of the Clinical Center which house schizophrenics, manic depressives and depressives) and to determine how these effects influenced both the treatment program and the psychiatric disease processes. The project also involved an evaluation of the resulting design solutions once implemented and communication of the programming/evaluation methodology for future use by the client. The program was developed using the Design Log Method, a creation of Spivack Associates involving a systemized procedure for data collection and translation of behavioral information into design performance requirements. In addition to behavioral research, the programming involved literature search, photographic documentation and physical tests of light sources and paint pigments for compatibility. The programming phase of the project was conducted over a four-month period and involved 1,316 person-hours. Implementation of the program was expected to be completed by the end of 1980 with the evaluation phase to be conducted within one year of implementation. In contrast to most of the case studies in this book, this project employed a rather unique methodology and concentrated intensely on a comparatively small portion of a total facility. It is a focused example of an indepth user needs study.

PROJECT

Spivack Associates was contracted jointly by the National Institutes of Health (NIH) and the National Institute of Mental Health (NIMH) to conduct behavioral research and to design the light and color environment in the four residential psychiatric wings of the NIMH facility. No structural changes were allowed under the contract.

The objectives of the project were to discover and document the psychological, perceptual and social effects of the existing lighting and color in the facility and to optimize effects that supported the treatment program and staff goals. Of particular concern was the elimination of environmental conditions that supported the specific disease processes, such as the absence of visual clarity in the environment which promotes gross misinterpretation of person/environment boundaries, environmental scale and shape and color.

The research and design were limited to light and color and texture. Thus, the architectural elements of concern were surface colors and textures (walls, ceilings and floors), light source type, lamp output characteristics and color, fixture type and natural light (window and window treatment, including safety barriers and light control). One wing was carpeted as a test, and the study evolved to include specifications for carpeting of all four wings. In both programming activities and design solutions, the programmer was cautious to avoid interfering with the medical research conducted in the facility.

The NIMH nursing units (wings) were typical double-loaded corridors as found in most hospitals. The corridors were extremely long and dark. Many bedrooms on the sunny side of the building had been converted to staff offices and interview rooms. Dayrooms and nurses' stations were adjacent and located in the center of the corridors. Bedrooms were often too dark for reading, even with the lights on. Window design and detention screens shut out 50 percent of the daylight in bedrooms and ceiling-mounted fluorescent fixtures produced intense glare. Most floor surfaces were vinyl asbestos tile; the dominant corridor floor color was aquamarine green. Other surfaces were government standard pastels which appeared "dirty," and the varying colors, under existing light conditions, often could not be distinguished from each other.

CLIENT

The National Institute of Mental Health is part of the National Institutes of Health, the federally sponsored medical research organization. The programmer worked closely with the project architect from the Engineering Design Branch of NIH and with the staff and patients of the Clinical Center at NIMH. At the Clinical Center, research is conducted to determine the biological causes and possible cures of selected mental illnesses. Of the four nursing units under investigation in the project, one was devoted to treatment of depressives, two to treatment of manic depressives and one to treatment of schizophrenics.

The programming effort addressed the needs of the following groups:
—Patient population in residence (current and future) and their visitors
—The staff of nurses, assistants and doctors who conduct the medical re-

search and treatment programs in the units

PROGRAMMER

Spivack Associates is a small consulting firm specializing in behavior-based environmental design for corporate, public and institutional settings. The firm president, Mayer Spivack, has directed the Unit of Environmental Analysis and Design at Harvard Medical School's Laboratory of Community Psychiatry since 1966. He and Joanna Tamer, the firm's Director of Design Systems, developed the programming methodology, the Design Log Method, used in this project. The programming phase of the project was completed in four months and involved three professionals for a total of 1,316 person-hours. The breakdown for the three is as follows:

Principal designer	376 hours
Project manager/ assistant designer	752 hours
Research assistant	188 hours

All additional support services were included in the overhead multiplier of the firm.

PROCESS

Spivack Associates applied the procedures of the Design Log Method, the programming system developed by Spivack and Tamer, to the NIMH project. The method is a system of organizing and interpreting behavioral data so that it is relevant and useful to the designer. It also involves systematic recording of significant design data, all design decisions and their rationales for later use in evaluating the design.

A Design Log is simply sheets of paper clipped into a binder for recording information according to a preorganized format. Each type of setting in a project is afforded a section in the binder and information on each is developed and recorded according to the following sequence of procedures:

—*Observation.* Observations about a setting (e.g., room type) are combined with external data from similar experiences and knowledge. This is essentially a data collection task that might include literature search, observation studies, interviews, questionnaires, etc.

—*Performance requirements.* The interplay between environment and behavior that was observed is addressed in terms of what actions are needed to resolve a problem, improve or change conditions, or enhance desired behavior. This section is identification of the requirements and objectives for the settings in terms of the activities and behavior that occur within them.

—*Generic and/or materials specifications.* Specifications for design actions, general enough to allow the architect creative latitude, are proposed that would satisfy the performance requirements of the setting. Materials and workmanship specifications are generally left to the architect.

In the NIMH project, the focus was on the light and color aspects of the facility only and the log was limited to the behavioral effects of these aspects on the users (patients and staff) of the four nursing units. The Design Log Method refers primarily to the content and organization of the information necessary for design, but it also involved other procedures and techniques for collection and analysis of

---

EXHIBIT 19-1. PROGRAMMING/EVALUATION PROCEDURES

PROJECT ORGANIZATION
—Organize and schedule tasks and project delivery timetable

DATA COLLECTION
—Conduct literature search using computerized lists from medical libraries and other resources
—Photodocumentation of all surfaces of sample nursing wing accompanied by notation of differences among four wings
—Observe settings and behavior in each wing, including programmer's own behavior
—Interview staff and patients, by individual and group, regarding their observations and attitudes about the environments

DATA ANALYSIS AND ORGANIZATION
—Collate research and observation data and write "observation" section of Design Log
—Derive conclusions and specify performance requirements in "performance requirements" section of Design Log
—Develop preliminary design and test samples

DESIGN AND DOCUMENTATION
—Write "design and materials specifications" section of DESIGN LOG

IMPLEMENTATION

EVALUATION
—Develop "protocol" for conducting evaluation based on original design intentions formed in Design Log
—Develop questionnaire evaluating user response to environment after design changes are implemented, and conduct interviews of patients and staff
—Analyze and document findings
—Recommend alterations to initial design

EXHIBIT 19-2. INTERVIEW QUESTIONS FOR PATIENTS AND STAFF

QUESTIONS TO PATIENTS RE: LIGHTING

Introduction—We are trying to learn about how to make the lighting better in this part of the hospital.

We could use some advice. People who are living or working here can help us by telling us what they know and feel about the lighting.

Will you talk with us and tell us your opinions and feelings about the lighting?

PQL: 1—How do you feel about the lighting in your room?
a) How do you use your room and its lights?
b) Do you have to make any special arrangements to do what you want?
c) Let's look at it, show us how it is.
d) Let's look at the corridor: What's right about it? What's wrong about it?

PQL: 2—In a small group meeting, how do people who live here use:
a) the dayroom
b) their bedrooms
c) the recreation room

PQL: 3—Where else in the Clinical Center do you go when you leave this floor and why do you like it there?

QUESTIONS TO PATIENTS RE: COLOR

PQC: 1—How do you feel about the colors of the:

walls:	room/corridor	Why?
floor:	room/corridor	Why?
ceiling:	room/corridor	Why?

QUESTIONS TO STAFF RE: LIGHTING

SQL: 1—How do you feel about the lighting in the:
a) corridor
b) office
c) dining area
d) dayroom
e) recreation room

SQL: 2—How do the patients react to the lighting?
a) Where do loners go?
b) Where do patients go when depressed? Why? Lighting? Where do patients go when hallucinating? Why? Lighting?

SQL: 3—What special understanding and knowledge do you have about the effects of light:
a) on patient in general
b) on your patients specifically
Do you intentionally use the lighting as a therapeutic control or modality?
a) If so, how?
b) How would you *like* to use it?

SQL: 4—Have patients ever damaged lights or themselves with lights?
a) Do patients bring lamps from home?
b) Do patients move lamps from one place to another?

SQL: 5—What departments and what administrative procedures and limitations are responsible for lamp design and maintenance?

QUESTIONS TO STAFF RE: COLOR

SQC: 1—How do you feel about your own color environment here?

SQC: 2—How does it affect the patients?
Can you tell us about the effects of:
a) color on patients in general
b) on your patients in particular

SQC: 3—Do you use color as a treatment modality? If so, how?

SQC: 4—How would you *like* to use color?

SQC: 5—What are the likely color associations for these patients?

data. The execution of the project, including the programming and evaluation phases, is outlined in Exhibit 19-1.

DATA COLLECTION. After organizing the project tasks and schedule, the first step in the study was an extensive literature search. The programmer, using the MEDLARS computerized medical information bank, obtained a list of documents related to two categories of information: 1) psychiatric treatment space: light/color, and 2) psychiatric treatment space: behavior and design. Selecting from the computer printout list, the programmer obtained and reviewed relevant materials. In addition, a supplementary list of documents on photobiological research was developed from contacts with leading specialists in this field. Pertinent references were incorporated into the Design Log and used as criteria for design.

Another task was to photograph all surfaces to be designed in one of the wings and all surfaces to be designed in the other wings which differed from the base unit. Notations were made of the differences in color, structure and light. In addition, light meter readings were taken and recorded for relevant areas in all four units. The color slides were coded and ordered; a master list identified all the slides in sequence.

Since colors reproduced in the slides differed greatly from actual colors on site, paint chips were collected from the federal government supply standards book and from walls of the actual site. This information was used in designing the color schemata for the settings.

The investigation of the settings also included direct observation and interviews (see Exhibit 19-2) with both patients and staff in all four nursing units. The programmer spent many hours in each wing, observing settings, body positions, individual and group movements, and interactions between the users and their environments. The observation activity included the pro-

grammer's own attitudes and behavior in reaction to the environment. The programmer recorded these observations on audio tapes which were transcribed later in the office.

Interviews included both individual and group sessions with staff and patients. Although the client doubted the reliability of information provided by psychotic patients, the programmer found that they were able to describe vividly their interactions with the environment, their own disease processes and the perceptual distortions caused by the afflictions. Condensed data from the interviews were recorded (using microcassettes) and later transcribed.

DATA ANALYSIS AND ORGANIZATION. Observation and interview data on

---

EXHIBIT 19-3. A SAMPLE OF PERFORMANCE REQUIREMENTS FOR LIGHTING

PR#15   DOORWAYS AND COMMUNICATION AREAS SHOULD RECEIVE SPECIAL TREATMENT

High quality lighting designed to support non-verbal communication (by means of three-dimensional modeling, full sunlight balanced visual spectrum, figure ground clarity, lack of glare) should be installed wherever people are most likely to gather and talk. This requirement applies particularly to bedroom doorways, the nursing stations and their doorways, the patient lounges, dining rooms, and all corridor zones immediately adjacent to these areas. (See PR#31.)

PR#16   NO DARK ZONES SHOULD EXIST

Illumination designs should leave no areas dark or dim enough to be considered depressing, forgotten, off the path or, simply, dark or dim. Maintaining these perceptual minimum levels will prevent hallucinating patients from retreating to these areas and worsening their condition through negative environmental effects.

PR#17   LIGHT FIXTURES SHOULD PRODUCE NO GLARE

No light fixture should become a source of glare under foreseeable operating conditions Fixtures should not have a high visual attention demand value when compared with the rest of the environment. Their perceived brightness when viewed from a distance should be low. When standing or sitting with the head in a normal, erect position within the lighting zone of a direct downlight, one should not have a direct line of sight to the light source.

PR#18   LIGHT FIXTURES SHOULD BE INNOCUOUS

Light fixtures should not demand attention. They should blend into the background. Neither fixture, form, shape, mechanical details, the radiating light, their mass or glare should draw interest.

PR#19   LIGHTING SHOULD REVEAL MEANINGFULNESS

Lighting should be chosen and arranged to illuminate and reveal the characteristics of the features and details of and in the environment which are meaningful for patients by virtue of expectation and prior association.

EXHIBIT 19-4. DESIGN LOG SPECIFICATION ILLUSTRATION FOR ONE TYPE OF LIGHTING FIXTURE

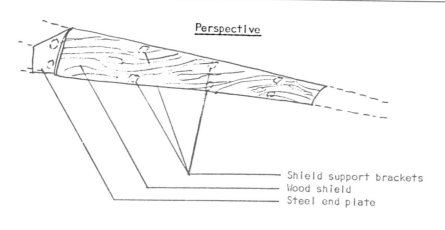

Perspective

- Shield support brackets
- Wood shield
- Steel end plate

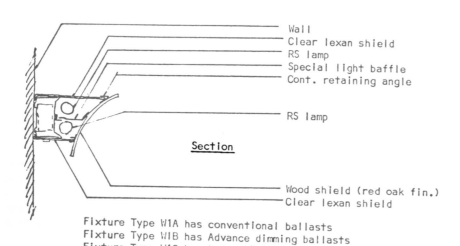

- Wall
- Clear lexan shield
- RS lamp
- Special light baffle
- Cont. retaining angle

- RS lamp

Section

- Wood shield (red oak fin.)
- Clear lexan shield

Fixture Type W1A has conventional ballasts
Fixture Type W1B has Advance dimming ballasts
Fixture Type W1C has Lutron "HiLume" Fixture Packs

LIGHTING FIXTURE TYPE W1   NIH CLINICAL CENTER

Manufacturer: Lam Inc.
Catalog #: DL-0151
Sketch #: W1
25 February 1979

This sketch is intended only to clarify the design concepts for this fixture. Manufacturer shall submit shop drawings to Spivack Associates for approval at least five days prior to bidding.

the effects of light and color on users were analyzed and categorized. This information was then reorganized into performance requirement categories. The programmer's conclusions were produced in the Design Log format under the "observation" section. These conclusions and the supporting data were then translated into performance requirements for each setting, drawing from performance requirement categories that included, for example, "behavioral responses to light and color," "biological responses to light and color," and "recommendations by interviewees." The performance requirement section of the Design Log was drafted, identifying design decisions and their rationales. A sample of performance requirements is shown in Exhibit 19-3.

From the performance requirements, the programmer selected preliminary materials and design schemata for testing. The programmer specified to the NIH architect the areas and materials to be included in the "test patch" evaluation. The sample surface patches were prepared and evaluated under the specified lighting systems (using portable fixtures and selected lamps). Satisfactory performance of the preliminary materials and lighting enabled the programmer to choose the final material specifications.

DESIGN AND DOCUMENTATION. An optimum setting was designed for each of the four wings based on the behavioral criteria developed out of the literature research and user needs research. Each addressed the specific needs of the individual populations of the wings. The programmer then wrote specifications for:
- The materials to be applied or installed
- The methods of application
- Installations
- Lighting fixture modifications

One fixture specification illustration is shown in Exhibit 19-4.

EXHIBIT 19-5. DESIGN LOG CONTENTS

INTRODUCTION TO THE DESIGN LOG

PART I   OBSERVATIONS
          Observations: Section I (Color)
          Observations: Section II (Light)

PART II   PATIENT AND STAFF RESPONSES TO INTERVIEW
          PROTOCOLS ON LIGHT AND COLOR
          Introduction
          Patient and staff interview responses to
              color (based on 10 categories)
                  Index
                  Text
          Patient and staff interview responses to
              light (based on 32 categories)
                  Index
                  Text

PART III PERFORMANCE REQUIREMENTS
          Index to performance requirements
          Text: 48 performance requirements

PART IV   DESIGN AND MATERIALS SPECIFICATIONS
          Index (A-F)
          Text: A. Demolition in preparation for
                   renovations
                B. Lighting
                C. Ceiling treatment
                D. Window treatment
                E. Wall covering and paint
                   Schedule A
                F. Carpeting and coving

PART V   APPENDICES
          Index
          Appendix A: Protocol for observations
          Appendix B: Protocol for staff and patient
                      interviews
          Appendix C: Fluorescent lamp spectral data
          Appendix D: Bibliography on the design of
                      hospital environments: effects
                      on human perception and behavior
          Appendix E: Bibliography on photobiological
                      research
          Appendix F: Reprints

PROGRAM

The Design Log for the NIMH nursing units constituted the program. Data was reorganized and drafted in report form. As indicated earlier, the format included sections on observations, performance requirements, and design and material specifications. All design decisions and their rationales were recorded in the report, with supporting data included as appendices. An outline of the contents of the 378-page report (including appendices) is presented in Exhibit 19-5.

IMPLEMENTATION AND EVALUATION

The report was presented to the NIH Engineering Design Branch for implementation of the program/design. Some 6 to 12 months after recommendations were carried out, the programmer was to return to the site to perform an evaluation of the effectiveness of the new design. In this phase of the project, the programmer compares the effects of the altered environment on the users with the design intentions identified in the performance requirements and material specifications sections of the Design Log. The programmer will write an evaluation questionnaire based on the Design Log Method specifications and rationale, converting the language of the rationale for the specifications into questions regarding the environment. This conversion will assure that the evaluation of the environment and its effects on its users will parallel the design intentions stated in the materials specifications. Both observation and interview sessions are employed in the evaluation. These sessions investigate the assumptions, rationale, specifications and implementation of the design.

Chapter 20
Design Criteria for a
Zoo Exhibit Complex

FACILITY:
Discovering Apes Complex
Topeka Zoological Park
Topeka, Kansas

CLIENT:
Topeka Zoological Park
Topeka, Kansas

PROGRAMMER:
Zooplan Associates Inc.
Wichita, Kansas

Jack Jones, AIA
Case Study Contributor

CONSULTANT:
Saul L. Kitchener, Director
San Francisco Zoological Gardens
San Francisco, California

DESIGNER:
Phil W. Coolidge, AIA
Topeka, Kansas

EXECUTIVE SUMMARY:
User needs are an important consideration in programming modern facilities. But users are not homogeneous and their individual needs for comfort, safety and health—to name a few—diverge and often conflict. The programmer's task is not only to identify the specific needs of distinct user groups, but to seek out ways in which disparate needs can be harmonized and conflicts resolved. This project illustrates the issue in an extreme case, where the programmer sought to accommodate the divergent needs of three very different user groups: exhibited animals, exhibit viewers and exhibit keepers. It also illustrates the manner in which specialized knowledge can be blended with design information both in a unique kind of practice and in this particular case. Zooplan Associates is a consulting firm specializing in programming/planning/designing services for zoos and aquariums. For the Discovering Apes Complex of the Topeka Zoological Park, the firm engaged the services of an expert on apes to assure the

EXHIBIT 20-1.   OUTLINE OF PROGRAMMING PROCEDURE

Programmer reviews project concept and theme, and zoo master plan

Programmer establishes project team consisting of:
- —Coordinator and technical staff
- —Staff and special consultants
- —Client representatives
- —Local architect

Client coordinator (zoo director) compiles and sends background data, including information on:
- —Existing conditions and constraints
- —Current operations and procedures
- —Other zoo facilities
- —Project goals and needs
- —Animals to be exhibited

Programmer compiles charrette workbook and sends to project team

Project team members read workbook and other materials in preparation for charrette

Project coordinator conducts charrette involving:
- —Exchange of information and ideas
- —Theme development
- —Identification of design issues, all technical requirements and problems

Technical staff drafts report of data produced by charrette and sends to all participants

Project team submits additional comments and data

Technical staff conducts detailed research on technical requirements and problems and collates with information from consultants/other project team members

Programmer drafts design criteria and presents to client for approval

---

well-being of the project's permanent inhabitants, while it provided general expertise in zoo planning and the process of identifying the particular design needs of the client. Techniques employed for the project included the programming charrette and charrette workbooks. Zoo personnel, ape consultant, programmer and architect cooperated in the team venture. The results were a set of design criteria for meeting the facility use needs of apes, keepers and visiting public. The complex is currently under construction.

PROJECT

The Topeka Zoological Park was an existing facility operated by the city of Topeka, Kansas. A master plan, previously prepared by Zooplan Associates, called for additional exhibits based on a theme of public education and recreation. The Discovering Apes Complex was to be the first exhibit in the expansion envisioned by the master plan. It would set the pace for future facilities in terms of educational experience and architecture.

The goal of the exhibit project was to provide a unique learning experience for the occasional and periodic visitors to the zoo. Based on the master plan, apes had been selected as the type of exhibit resource that could enable the zoo to achieve this objective; in particular, that could provide the visitor a direct sensory experience with the animals and their natural environments, stopping short of interaction.

At the time the programmer was retained to develop the design criteria for the exhibit complex, the client had not determined which of the four ape species were suitable for the exhibit and the planned facility. The programmer's task was to develop the basic exhibit theme into a set of specific action goals—from selecting the exhibit species to specifying sight and safety barriers—that would express and support the theme. The architecture itself was to be subservient to the theme objectives, enhancing the educational experience of the exhibit rather than showcasing the complex.

A sum of $550,000 was established

prior to programming as a preliminary budget for construction of the single building, adjacent walks and necessary adjacent sitework. This figure did not include exhibit furnishings, graphics, animals, equipment and professional fees. Subsequent to programming, the budget was increased to $1 million.

CLIENT

The owner of the project is the city of Topeka, while the programmer's paying client was the Topeka Friends of the Zoo Inc., a nonprofit organization of zoo supporters. Neither city officials nor Friends participated directly in the programming. The principal client was the zoo itself and the programmer worked closely with its personnel, who represented one of the three principal user groups the project would accommodate.

The other two user groups were the zoo-visiting public and the animals to be exhibited. No special studies were performed to ascertain directly the needs of the zoo's visitors. Zooplan Associates re-

EXHIBIT 20-2.   GORILLA EXHIBIT WITH TUNNEL VIEWING AREA

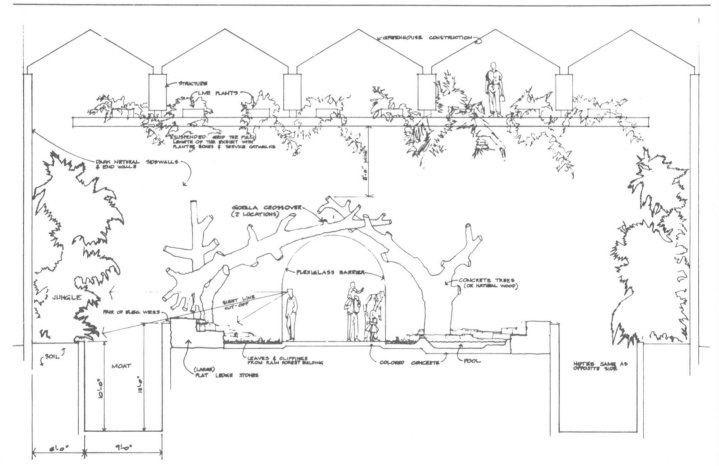

lied on its own broad experience in planning public spaces of this nature and on the input of Topeka zoo personnel to determine visitor needs. The health, safety and welfare needs of the apes were identified and addressed through consultation with an authority on the primate species.

PROGRAMMER

Zooplan Associates is a consulting firm that specializes in planning, development and operation of facilities for the keeping and exhibition of live animals. It is composed of zoo directors (active and retired)

and zoo architects and has provided services for more than 50 zoos since it was incorporated in 1972. The senior consulting staff is headed by Dr. R. Marlin Perkins, director emeritus of the St. Louis Zoological Park and best known as the originator and narrator of the long-running television program, Wild Kingdom. An architect, Jack Jones, AIA, is the firm's general manager.

Although the firm combines zoo and architectural expertise in its consulting services, its general procedure is to provide only those services that are not available from local professionals.

For the Discovering Apes Complex, the programming team consisted of a project coordinator, two senior consulting staff members, an outside special consultant on primates, and an architecturally trained technical staff person. A local architect, who would eventually develop the design, was also involved in the programming.

PROCESS

The programmer's function was primarily to coordinate information and information sources. The process consisted of identifying information needs, eliciting expert

EXHIBIT 20-3. ORANGUTAN EXHIBIT AND VIEWING GALLERY

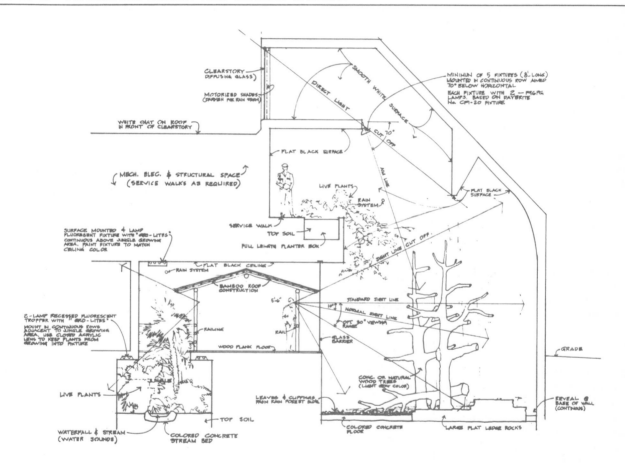

knowledge, collating it with available client data, refining user need information and translating conclusions into requirements for design. Rather than performing original research to determine user needs, the programmer relied on the availability of expert knowledge in both zoological and architectural disciplines. This technical information was combined with client goals and background data through a repetitive review/feedback/proposal procedure to produce the detailed design requirements. Exhibit 20-1 illustrates the programming procedure.

During the charrette, two species of

apes were selected for the exhibits: gorillas and orangutans. Charrette interaction also produced the basic concepts for enabling exhibit visitors to observe as closely as possible the natural habitat and behavior of the apes. Two separate exhibits within a single complex were recommended. The gorilla exhibit would be observed by means of a tunnel through the exhibit, providing views of ground-level as well as tree-swinging activities. This afforded the zoo the opportunity to accommodate the behavioral needs of the gorillas—who spend part of their lives on the ground and part in the trees—at the

same time allowing visitors access to a realistic simulation of the natural setting and behavior of the gorillas. Exhibit 20-2 shows the programmatic treatment of these user needs.

The coordination of viewing area and exhibit area for the orangutan section of the complex is another example of how the user needs conflicts indigenous to this type of facility were resolved through programming. As Exhibit 20-3 illustrates, the orangutans, who are tree-dwellers, could be observed by means of an elevated, simulated-treehouse platform that would put visitors at eye level with the apes' habitat. The exhibit and viewing gallery arrangement provides for both the needs of the ground-dwelling humans to have a full view of the animals and the need of the arboreal primates to dwell in their natural habitat.

Always the programmer had the task of accommodating multiple needs. Specification of resilient, transparent barriers between apes and humans, for instance, would protect each from interference with the other, prevent transmission of diseases and provide clear views for the public into the exhibit.

Likewise, the need to provide apes with settings as similar as possible to their natural environments was as important to the apes' psychological well-being as it was to the success of the educational experience. At the same time, zookeepers needed landscape elements which would resist rapid deterioration due to animal behavior: Frequent replacement would be costly, time-consuming and disruptive to the exhibit operation.

These divergent requirements were handled in one way by instructing that the design should include sturdy materials in areas used by the apes and placement of live plants that foster a jungle atmosphere out of the reach of the animals.

Programming the apes complex involved integrating knowledge of user needs—the physical and psychological welfare of the apes, the educational and recreational expectations of the exhibit viewers, and the operation and maintenance requirements of the zoo—with architectural expertise on materials, building elements and space organization.

PROGRAM

The program consisted of a collection of design criteria. The criteria were expressed as requirements and instructions to the design architect, who had a hand in developing them. The 34-page program report included requirements for site work,

design character, and the exhibit, public and support facilities. The contents of the complete program are outlined in Exhibit 20-4. To illustrate the number and extent of design criteria which were established in the program, the individual items—each of which was followed by detailed explanation in the actual report—are listed below for the gorilla exhibit area.

GENERAL
EXHIBIT ENCLOSURE
   Spatial Requirements
   Barriers
   Surfaces
   Furnishings
   Animal Welfare and Breeding Factors
   Environmental Factors
   Service Access and Facilities
PUBLIC VIEWING FACILITIES
   Arrangement
   Spatial Requirements
   Safety
   Convenience
OFF-EXHIBIT HOLDING FACILITIES
   Location
   Spatial Requirements
   Barriers
   Surfaces
   Furnishings
   Animal Welfare and Breeding Factors
   Environmental Factors
   Service Access and Facilities

IMPLEMENTATION

The program of design criteria, together with concept drawings illustrating major design elements, were prepared by the programmer and presented to zoo officials for approval. Upon approval, schematics were prepared, followed by design development and working drawings. The Discovering Apes Complex was scheduled for completion in the summer of 1980.

EXHIBIT 20-4. PROGRAM CONTENTS OUTLINE

  I. INTRODUCTION

 II. DISCOVERING APES: AN OVERVIEW

III. THE SITE

IV. DESIGN CHARACTER

 V. GORILLA FACILITIES
   A. Exhibit Enclosure
   B. Public Viewing Facilities
   C. Off-Exhibit Holding Facilities

VI. ORANGUTAN FACILITIES
   A. Exhibit Enclosure
   B. Public Viewing Facilities
   C. Off-Exhibit Holding Facilities

VII. PUBLIC FACILITIES
   A. Graphics
   B. Circulation

VIII. SERVICE FACILITIES

Chapter 21
Programming in Practice

Programming has been explained in terms of its process, procedures, techniques and products, and examples of applications have been given in the case studies of the previous chapters. From a business standpoint, programming may be called a practice or, at least, part of a practice. In architectural practice, it is a service—a design or design-related service. Traditional agreement forms most often identify it as an "additional" service beyond "basic" services while the newer, cost-based agreement forms include it as a "predesign phase" service. What is a programming practice and what constitutes a programming service? Is it a single service or a series? Is it marketable? Should an architect be compensated for programming or use it as a means of organizing design information for his or her own purposes? Does programming apply exclusively to design projects or are there other opportunities for programming in architectural practice?

The answer to all these questions is that "it depends." It depends on the individual's perception of the design process, of programming in particular and of the relationship of program to design. It depends on the nature and scope of a project, an intended program and the information required. Finally, it depends on the interest of an owner in obtaining and of an architect in offering specified services for an individual project.

CHANGES IN NATURE AND SCOPE OF PROGRAMMING

The business aspects of programming have changed because the nature and scope of programming have become more complex and comprehensive. A program is still an essential part of the project process and its purpose remains to identify the requirements of the client for facility design.

Twenty-five years ago, the traditional program in architecture wasn't much more than a list of requirements or stated needs of the client. It might have included such items of information as number and dimensions of spaces, site limitations, functions to be housed in the facility, number of occupants, special needs and, perhaps, budgetary considerations. Typically, the client was responsible for providing this "shopping list," sometimes with the help of an architect or programming specialist. The architect often had to perform the task of interpreting and reorganizing the information in a form most useful to the design professional and at no additional cost to the client.

For a variety of reasons—the changing nature of clients, increasing complexity of building functions and construction, greater recognition of social responsibilities, more demands on the capabilities of architects and changes in considerations of economy and liability exposure, for instance—this simplistic approach to programming has been undergoing considerable modification. Not only has traditional program information become more extensive and precise, but the types and nature of information required for programs has expanded. Both clients and architects have come to recognize that factors such as user behavior and perception, energy use, economic conditions, public interest, environmental impact and land use significantly influence facility use and design.

Clients who recognize the multiplicity and complexity of factors affecting design want to be sure they are adequately considered before design decisions are made. Those with the resources may acquire in-house programming expertise, creating facility planning and programming departments within their organizations. Others without the continuous need or financial resources to support staff programmers turn either to their architects or to the growing field of programming specialists to develop programs on a project-by-project basis.

In the architectural profession, client need for more extensive and precise predesign information and designer interest in relevant, reliable, comprehensible program data have influenced the nature and scope of programming services. Architects with programming expertise no longer merely evaluate owner-supplied programs and organize data into an appropriate format for design, but also research and develop the program information as well. The amount of time, the types of resources and the techniques required to accommodate more definitive, comprehensive program information have altered the range and level of services the architect can offer and the compensation arrangements between owner and architect.

CONTRACTS AND COMPENSATION

It is obvious not all facilities are the same. Just as the design will vary in complexity, detail and accommodations, as well as the amount of time and effort to produce it, so will the program. The facility type and the needs of the individual project determine the form of agreement, scope of services and level of compensation for programming services. Other determinants might include:

—Client interest in and willingness to pay for specific services
—Availability and adequacy of owner-supplied program information
—Type of information that must be developed and the means of developing it
—Need of specialized consultants
—Architect's ability to provide specified services

FORMS OF AGREEMENT. There are two current approaches to provision of programming services by architects who use standard AIA agreement forms. The first and older is that of AIA Document B141, Standard Form of Agreement Between Owner and Architect. According to

EXHIBIT 21-1. SELECTED PARAGRAPHS FROM AIA DOCUMENT B141 (July 1977 edition)

ARTICLE 2, The Owner's Responsibilities

2.1 The Owner shall provide full information regarding requirements for the Project including a program, which shall set forth the Owner's design objectives, constraints and criteria, including space requirements and relationships, flexibility and expandability, special equipment and systems and site requirements.

ARTICLE 1, Architect's Services and Responsibilities

1.7 ADDITIONAL SERVICES

The following Services are not included in Basic Services unless so identified in Article 15. They shall be provided if authorized or confirmed in writing by the Owner, and they shall be paid for by the Owner as provided in this Agreement, in addition to the compensation for Basic Services.

1.7.1 Providing analyses of the Owner's needs, and programming the requirements of the Project.

EXHIBIT 21-2. PROVISIONS OF DESIGNATED SERVICES AGREEMENT (B161—November 1977 edition)

ARTICLE 1

1.1 DESIGNATED SERVICES

The Architect's Designated Services consist of those services agreed to be performed directly by the Architect, through the Architect by utilization of Outside Services, and by Coordination Services performed by the Architect on services provided by the Owner, for and necessary to the Project, as identified and described in the Scope of Designated Services attached to and made a part of this Agreement.

ARTICLE 2, The Owner's Responsibilities

The following responsibilities will be undertaken by the Owner, in addition to those Services designated to be performed by the Owner and described in the Scope of Designated Services attached to and made a part of the Agreement.

2.1 The Owner shall provide full information regarding requirements for the Project.

this approach, programming is considered an "additional" service beyond the "basic" services of schematic design, design development, construction documents, bidding or negotiation and construction administration. The program is the owner's "responsibility" under the B141 contract, but its preparation may be delegated to the architect by the owner. Exhibit 21-1 indicates the basis for this type of arrangement.

However, the architect has at least a minimal obligation to participate in programming a facility, even if it is only to the extent of reviewing, evaluating and agreeing to a program provided by the owner. Under the section on architect services and responsibilities (Article 1, B141), the agreement indicates the architect is obligated to "review the program furnished by the Owner to ascertain the requirements of the Project and shall review the understanding of such requirements with the Owner." This is considered a part of schematic design phase services, and that subsection also notes the architect shall "provide a preliminary evaluation of the program and the Project budget requirements, each in terms of the other. . . ." Finally, another provision says that schematic design documents shall be based on "the mutually agreed upon program and Project budget requirements."

All too often the architect finds an owner-supplied program deficient or inappropriate for design, leaving only three options after a contract has been signed: accept the program as is, modify or redo it, or terminate the agreement. It's unlikely a responsible architect will choose the first alternative and unwise to take the last resort. Consequently, architects have been forced, in some cases, to provide programming services without compensation in order to insure the adequacy of design programs and keep their contracts.

Although it is possible to absorb the cost of programming in some situations, in many others it is totally unfeasible. As programming information has become more complex and extensive, the amount of time, specialized knowledge and original investigation required to produce it have increased substantially. In a growing number of instances, particularly for complex building types such as hospitals, absorbing the cost of programming may mean not only lowering compensation, but losing money.

On the other hand, some architects believe programming should be an obligation of the architect and included in basic services. Their view is that it provides the best means of collecting proper information and making predesign decisions, which is in the best interests of both client and architect. Establishing an adequate base fee (perhaps as part of schematic design services) in the contract at the beginning compensates for the additional time and expense of programming.

The newer approach using AIA agreement forms is for programming to be assigned to the architect by mutual agreement with the owner on a "scope of designated services." This is the arrangement defined in the complementary AIA Documents B161, Standard Form of Agreement Between Owner and Architect for Designated Services, and B162, Scope of Designated Services. In the B161/162 nine-phase categorization of design services, programming is classified as one of several "predesign" services. No specific reference is made to programming in the agreement form (B161), except under the owner's responsibility it indicates "the Owner shall provide full information regarding requirements for the Project." (See Exhibit 21-2.)

The B161/162 documents more clearly establish responsibility for the program by simply "designating" it to either the owner or the architect in the wording of the agreement. This doesn't get around the problem of inadequate owner-supplied programs, but it does provide the archi-

EXHIBIT 21-3. PROGRAMMING AND RELATED SERVICES (EXCERPTS FROM B162)

PREDESIGN

Programming:
—Design objectives, limitations and criteria
—Space requirements
—Space relations
—Number and functional responsibility of personnel
—Flexibility and expansibility
—Special equipment and systems
—Site requirements

Space Schematics/Flow Diagrams for:
—Internal functions
—Human, vehicular and material flow patterns
—General space allocations
—Analysis of operating functions
—Adjacency
—Special facilities and equipment
—Materials handling
—Flexibility and expansibility

Existing Facilities Surveys: Researching, assembling, reviewing and supplementing information for projects involving alterations and additions to existing facilities or determining new space usage in conjunction with new building program

Marketing Studies: Determining social, economic and political need and acceptability of the project

Economic Feasibility Studies, estimates of:
—Total project costs
—Operating and owning costs
—Financing requirements
—Cash flow for design, construction and operation
—Return on investment
—Equity requirements

Project Development Scheduling: Establishing tentative schedule for predesign services, decision making, design, documentation, contracting and construction

Project Budgeting:
—Conversion of programmed requirements to net area requirements
—Development of initial approximate gross facility areas
—Evaluation of construction market conditions
—Application of unit cost data to gross areas
—Estimates of related costs such as site development, landscaping, utilities, services, furniture, equipment, and design services

Presentations to:
- —Owner
- —Building committee/staff committee
- —User groups
- —Financing entities
- —Owner's consultants

SITE ANALYSIS

Site Analysis and Selection, including:
- —Identification of potential sites
- —On-site investigations
- —Movement systems, traffic and parking studies
- —Topography analysis
- —Analysis of deed, zoning and other legal restrictions
- —Studies of available construction materials, equipment, labor
- —Studies of construction market
- —Overall site analysis and evaluation
- —Comparative site studies

Site Development Planning: Preliminary site analysis; comparative evaluation of conceptual site development designs

On-Site Utility Studies: Establishing requirements and preparing initial designs for on-site utility services

Off-Site Utility Studies:
- —Confirmation of location, size and adequacy of utilities serving site
- —Determination of requirements for connections to utilities
- —Planning for off-site utility extensions and facilities

Environmental Studies and Reports:
- —Determination of need or requirements for environmental monitoring, assessment and/or impact statements
- —Ecological studies
- —Preparation of environmental assessment reports
- —Preparation of environmental impact reports

Project Budgeting: Development of statement of probable construction cost for site-related work based on programming and scheduling of site work and consisting of application of unit cost data

tect greater opportunity to assume the responsibility and clearly specify that it is subject to compensation before a contract is signed.

The approach of designated services is fully explained in the AIA book, *Compensation Guidelines for Architectural and Engineering Services.*

SCOPE OF SERVICES. The contents of a program will be reflected in the types of services called for in the agreement between owner and architect. Both AIA Documents B141 and B162 identify the basic elements of a program as including information on:
- —Design objectives
- —Space requirements
- —Space relationships
- —Flexibility
- —Expandability (or expansibility)
- —Special equipment and systems
- —Site requirements

The B162 document adds "number and functional responsibility of personnel" to the list, as well as "design limitations and criteria."

In determining the scope of services to provide these and other types of information related to the program, it should be remembered that considerably more work may be involved than organizing and documenting readily available data. Detailed investigations, facility user surveys, observational studies and complex analytical procedures may be necessary to develop the information needed for the basic elements of a program. The range and extent of activities necessary to perform programming should be carefully considered before deciding which should be included in standard programming service or under different additional or designated services.

Both the B141 and B162 documents leave room for expansion of the basic scope of programming services. In B141, "additional" services might include:
- —Analysis of owner's needs

—Programming the requirements of the project

—Providing financial feasibility or other special studies

—Providing planning surveys, other site investigations and environmental studies

—Providing other services that might be considered part of programming

A much wider variety of services the architect may offer the owner is identified in the nine phases of design services included in B162. Many of the services categorized under Predesign (where programming is placed), Site Analysis, and Supplemental Services could be considered parts of a programming project. Several of the service types and their particular considerations have been excerpted for Exhibit 21-3 to demonstrate both the possible extent of programming and of data that might be suitable for a program.

COMPENSATION. Equitable fees for programming services can be determined by using the cost-based compensation approach espoused in AIA's 1978 *Compensation Guidelines for Architectural and Engineering Services*. This approach segregates design and design-related services into discrete areas where each may be priced individually. AIA Documents B161 and B162 provide for contracting for professional services in this manner. The cost-based approach relates proper compensation to the level of effort required for tasks.

Other approaches may be used. If programming is lumped in with traditional basic services, the architect should be cognizant of its value separately so that an adequate overall fee can be calculated. The alternative is to determine a separate fee for programming as an "additional service"; i.e., an approach of AIA Document B141. Nevertheless, an architect may consider programming to be a professional obligation or an operational efficiency in practice, rather than a service

EXHIBIT 21-3. PROGRAMMING AND RELATED SERVICES (EXCERPTS FROM B162)(CONT'D)

SUPPLEMENTAL SERVICES

Special Studies: Investigations, research and analysis of owner's special requirements related to master planning

Life Cycle Cost Analysis

Value Analysis

Energy Studies

Tenant-related Services

Computer Applications

Materials and Systems/Testing

justifying a charge to the client. If that is the case, the architect should be aware of the possibility of reduced profit on any particular project through this approach.

It is not possible to recommend rules-of-thumb for determining compensation levels. Each project should be examined based on its specific requirements. One procedure for estimating compensation involves creating a detailed task matrix in which a task listing is matched with personnel assignments. Hours or days can be allocated for each task to arrive at estimated total time and labor costs. Programmers might be advised to include adequate time estimates for such items as extra interviews, meetings and presentations, establishment of standards and midstream changes by the client. These might appear innocuous enough when estimating, but can eat up considerable time when actually carried out.

THE PROGRAMMING PRACTICE

There are a variety of ways to incorporate programming services into an architectural practice. The choice depends on several variables including preference, size of firm and practice, degree of pro-

gramming expertise within firm, availability of programming and related consultants within the geographic area of primary practice, market for programming services and competition for programming projects. The four chief means of organizing for programming practice are:

—Facility programming specialist firm

—Architecture firm with a programming department or staff

—Associations or joint ventures with programming firms

—Architect retaining programming consultants

The first two of these arrangements represent permanent availability of programming expertise, while the second two represent the use of programming assistance on a project-by-project basis. Whether or not a firm has programmers on staff or on call, the level and kinds of programming expertise required for each project may vary. In determining the suitable composition of a programming staff or a programming project team, it will be helpful to understand the different types of programming expertise that may be necessary and the workings of multidisciplinary teams.

MULTIDISCIPLINARY TEAMS. Design

EXHIBIT 21-4. BASIC PROGRAMMING TEAM

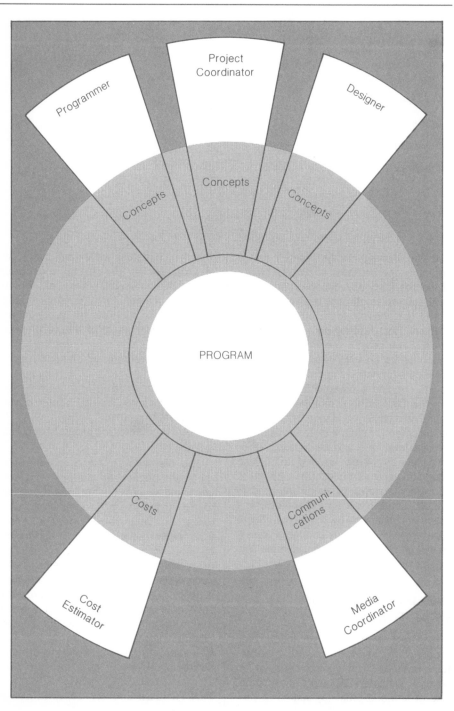

projects are increasingly carried out by teams of professionals representing various disciplines. The same is true for programming. The kinds of expertise necessary for a given project will depend on its purpose and goals, size and complexity, the types of information necessary, the means for developing data, the client's interests and the resources available. Each of these variables also will affect the number of personnel needed for particular tasks and the size of the whole programming team. The three levels of programming team composition discussed below represent types of expertise or functions rather than number of personnel. In addition to professional team members, there may be need for technicians and nontechnical workers to perform certain routine tasks.

Basic Team. The essential functions of a programming team usually include the following: project coordinator, architect programmer, cost estimator and media coordinator (graphic artist and/or editor/writer). Conceivably, one person, moderately skilled in all areas, could constitute the programming ''team.'' However, for any project beyond the simplest type of facility, there is usually too much work involved to expect a single person to complete programming with reasonable speed and efficiency. At least two people, each doubling up for various functions, should be involved, and often it may be more, depending on the scope of the project.

If the design architect for the project has been selected, or if the same firm is providing both program and design services for a project, a representative from the design team should participate in the programming. This is mutually advantageous to both the programming and designing functions and the same type of exchange is often extended into the design phases of a project. The typical components of the basic team are illustrated in Exhibit 21-4.

Comprehensive Team. Programming may involve provision of more comprehensive services to prepare a project adequately for design or to uncover basic program information. The addition of specialized consultants to the programming team for the duration of a project may be necessary in order to address all the physical, human and environmental aspects of a facility. The composition of a comprehensive programming team (see Exhibit 21-5) may include some or all of the following:

—Project coordinator
—Programmer/architect
—Designer/architect
—Engineer
—Economist/cost analyst
—Social scientist
—Environmental planner
—Management consultant
—Energy analyst
—Media coordinator

Larger, more complex projects involving intensity and variety of activity and function, complicated systems, substantial and long-range economic and environmental implications, and need for energy conservation (as most facilities do) require greater depth in investigation of design implications. The role of specialized consultants on the programming team is twofold: to contribute their expert knowledge and skill to the program and to interact with each other in program development. Just as a facility is an integrated whole, the development of meaningful program information requires not only accumulation of various kinds of information but integration and synthesis of it as well. The interaction among the various members of the programming team during the entire course of program development helps the programmer take all design-influencing factors into account concurrently and make reliable, efficient decisions.

Any of the categories identified earlier can be broken down to more specific

EXHIBIT 21-5. COMPREHENSIVE PROGRAMMING TEAM

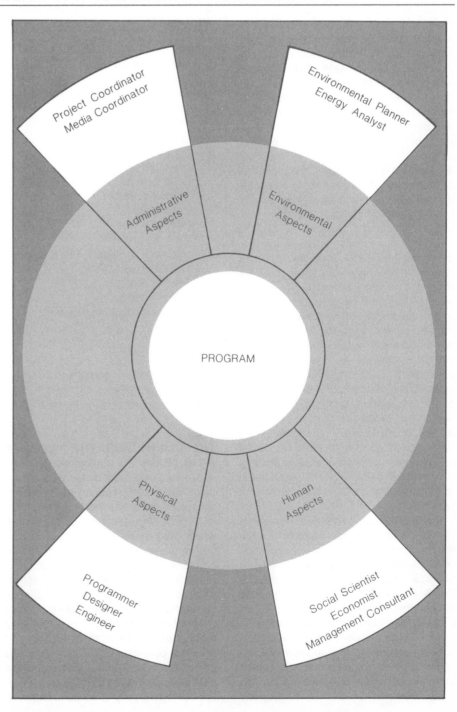

types of specialties, but two in particular should be clarified. Environmental planners (both natural and built environments) would include site planners, land use planners, ecologists, urban planners and others that might provide comprehensive viewpoints to programming issues. The social scientist category, likewise, might include sociologists, social psychologists and others concerned with behavioral aspects of social activity.

Expanded Team. During the course of programming, or preferably at inception, the programmer may identify certain information needs that require short term use of specialists. Consultants may be called on at particular points in the programming to perform specified tasks or to advise on specialized aspects of the project. They may be needed to provide expert information, to prepare information or to employ specific techniques. Special consultants added to the team on an ad hoc basis might include facility type specialists (architects or other disciplines), engineering specialists, financial analysts, space planners, computer programmers/operators, market analysts, survey researchers, facility/equipment specialists and group dynamics consultants. Many other disciplines may be used to provide information and services for programming. Exhibit 21-6 briefs a list of fields from which programmers occasionally draw resources.

The categorization of three levels of team composition is not hierarchical. Consultants and programming staff should be retained on an as-needed basis—for practice in general and/or for projects. If only one type of consultant is needed for an otherwise relatively simple project, it is not necessary to organize a comprehensive team in order to retain an expert. A basic programming team, with the addition of the single necessary consultant at the appropriate time, will do the job nicely. However, as mentioned, relatively

EXHIBIT 21-6. SOME SOURCES OF SPECIALIZED PROGRAMMING INFORMATION

—Acoustics
—Architectural graphics
—Communications
—Criminology and law
—Demographics
—Education/library science
—Geography
—Health care
—Fire protection
—Food service
—Political science
—Real estate
—Security
—Systems analysis
—Materials/systems testing
—Operations research
—Theater design
—Traffic analysis
—Zoning and building regulation

complex facilities or broad and long range programming studies will benefit from the use of comprehensive multidisciplinary teams.

THE CLIENT AND THE PROGRAMMING TEAM. The participation of clients in programming modern facilities has become at once more difficult and more necessary. In the past, their role was either to provide the program or to turn the whole thing over to an architect or other programming consultant. Both clients and programmers, however, have come to recognize that the extent and complexity of program information is too great for non-design-oriented client representatives to produce without professional assistance. Nor can they make reliable, cost-effective decisions about programs after completion based on lay understanding of data and conclusions alone.

The tendency, by choice and necessity,

is for client decisionmakers to take a participatory role in program development. The manner in which the client participates and, to an extent, is allowed to participate by the programmer, affects the speed and efficiency with which the program and budget are approved and the amount of revision in the program that inevitably will be made. Some programmers, for instance, make periodic reports or presentations to clients on the progress of program development. Others may develop a series of increasingly refined and detailed programs, each of which is reviewed and approved in joint working sessions between programmer and client to provide direction for succeeding program iterations.

As indicated by Exhibit 21-7, program development should be viewed as a joint effort between programmer and client. Not only does this approach improve efficiency in data collection and help avoid inappropriate decisions along the way, it also enables the client to more readily comprehend and identify with the completed program.

Client representation in programming is often in the form of a team or committee. Usually, it includes key staff concerned with fiscal and operations management as well as executives responsible for primary functions of the organization. The policy board of the organization may have a standing or ad hoc building committee which will participate in programming. Even large institutions with facility planning staff may assign appropriate administrators to the team working with the consultant programming team.

The participation of facility users in program decision making is less prevalent, but in many cases they have become important contributors, at least in developing information that shapes program decisions. Even if not part of the program development team, users can be involved for their own awareness and for program input in many ways. Public hearings, informal

EXHIBIT 21-7. PROGRAM DEVELOPMENT TEAM

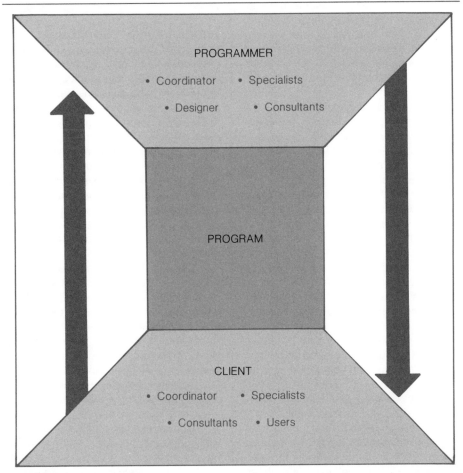

PROGRAMMER
- Coordinator
- Specialists
- Designer
- Consultants

PROGRAM

CLIENT
- Coordinator
- Specialists
- Consultants
- Users

group meetings, surveys and individual interviews are some means by which facility occupants and operators gain access and input to program development.

LIABILITY IMPLICATIONS. Design errors and omissions leading to liability claims frequently result from lack of knowledge of client needs, according to insurance companies. The basic objective of programming is to provide the designer with information on client needs. Both the information produced by programming and the information-producing methods help insure the designer obtains not only adequate information but appropriate and reliable information. Better design data reduces the possibility of design error and, consequently, the potential of liability claims. If claims can be decreased on a broad enough scale in a geographic area as a result of better-informed design solutions, it could lower the liability insurance premiums for the area.

The potential for reduced liability exposure is more practically attainable in another way. A firm which concentrates on sedentary work that doesn't result in construction—such as programming, feasibility analysis, planning, report preparation, etc.—is less exposed to liability claims than a firm which primarily works in design projects. Liability insurance premiums are much lower for this type of practice than for a regular design practice.

OPPORTUNITIES. Programming can improve the efficiency and effectiveness of producing information for design. Once a firm has built up experience, resources and staff to provide full programming services, this expertise opens opportunities for additional applications besides those directly related to design projects. Proficiency in the methodology and techniques of information processing (collecting, analyzing, organizing, communicating and evaluating data), coupled with architectural knowledge, enables the programmer to extend his or her services to other areas; for instance:

—Economic feasibility analysis
—Facility use market analysis
—Environmental behavior research
—Energy audits and analysis
—Community development planning
—Organizational and management planning
—Activity program development
—Environmental and social impact assessment
—Facility and land-use planning

In addition to providing compensation directly, such a scope of service offerings broadens a firm's exposure to potential clients and to potential design projects. Programming and other predesign services for a facility also may boost a firm's chances of obtaining a design services contract for the facility. In fact, a firm may be willing to sustain a small loss on predesign services in order to obtain a design project or improve the efficiency of its design services for a project.

Similarly, providing programming services for facility types with which a firm has minimal design experience increases the potential for design projects.

TRENDS IN PROGRAMMING

Facility programming and related pre-design analyses appear destined to play an increasingly important role in design decision making. Economic and social conditions have forced facility owners and developers to be more conscientious about investments in new facilities and in rehabilitation of existing ones. They need thorough and precisely defined data in order to judge not only the feasibility of projects but the economic and functional implications of potential designs. And, they are increasingly willing to make relatively small investments in useful predesign information in order to improve the viability of design and construction investments, which are more substantial.

On the other side of facility development, designers, too, are recognizing the benefits of systematic programming. It helps them better serve their clients' interests in economical, efficient and user-responsive designs. At the same time, it can improve the efficiency of their own design decisions, providing a means to obtain, analyze and manage the large quantity and diversity of data involved in accommodating complex building technology, proliferating standards and regulations, user requirements, long-range planning, economic conditions and many other variables. Programming also offers the opportunity for expanding architectural services.

Programming is in transition. It is being redefined by increased and varied applications. The traditional program of client requirements—based on an owner's assumptions about size and function—is being replaced by feasibility analysis, original investigation of user needs, space planning, behavioral research studies, demographic and economic forecasts, statistical evaluations and functional performance criteria, among others.

The emphasis of programming has shifted away from its end product, the program, to the process of developing the program information. The shift to more design analysis has fostered development of methodologies, techniques and professional expertise to perform programming applications. As a result, three different, but not necessarily divergent, trends have become evident:

—Programming is becoming more prevalent as a predesign activity or service performed by architects in design projects, for the purposes of data management, task administration and defining project needs clearly and precisely.

—It is developing as a distinct process—as opposed to a design phase—that is applicable to various stages and tasks of the design process. Wherever information must be analyzed or processed, the methods of programming may be applied; i.e., a programmer may program information for predesign work, schematic design and design development. Furthermore, programming also may involve evaluation of design in relation to satisfaction of program requirements and in relation to construction and operation performance.

—Improved data management, information processing and decision making are not the only trends and advantages of programming. It is also a marketable service. This fact has been slow to catch on among architects, although a program traditionally has been an integral part of most architectural projects. In other fields, however, programming has been developing as a specialty practice. Management consultants, environmental design researchers and facility type specialists are meeting client demand for predesign information with functional programming and facility planning services. Other clients—in particular, large institutions, government agencies and corporate organizations—have filled the need for these services by creating programming and planning staffs for in-house projects.

Exhibit 21-8 depicts the implications of these three trends in relation to the design process.

PROCESS AND PROCEDURES. The process of programming is useful for facility design not only in developing preliminary concepts and predesign data but in producing and analyzing necessary information for various stages of design. Thus, while programming is becoming more distinguishable as a specialized activity, it also will become a more necessary and integral element of the whole design process. This fact is relevant whether programming is practiced as a segregated, integrated or interactive activity with designing. Other trends in the development of the programming process and procedures include:

—Social conditions and the consumer advocacy movement, as well as heightened social awareness among designers, will increase attention to user needs. This trend will be manifested by more program investigations of human factors influencing design and by more research by social scientists on environmental behavior. Consequently, more and better user-needs data will be available to programmers from research findings.

—Correspondingly, user participation will increase in providing first-hand data for programming studies and in decision making for program conclusions and concepts.

—The increasing emphasis on user needs will foster greater use by programmers of behavioral research procedures and techniques and behavioral consultants.

—This is an indication of the trend toward greater use of multidisciplinary teams for both programming and designing and of the wider scope of professional expertise that can be expected to be included in programming teams.

—As postdesign, postconstruction and postoccupancy evaluation become established as part of the facility development

EXHIBIT 21-8. PROGRAMMING IN THE DESIGN PROCESS

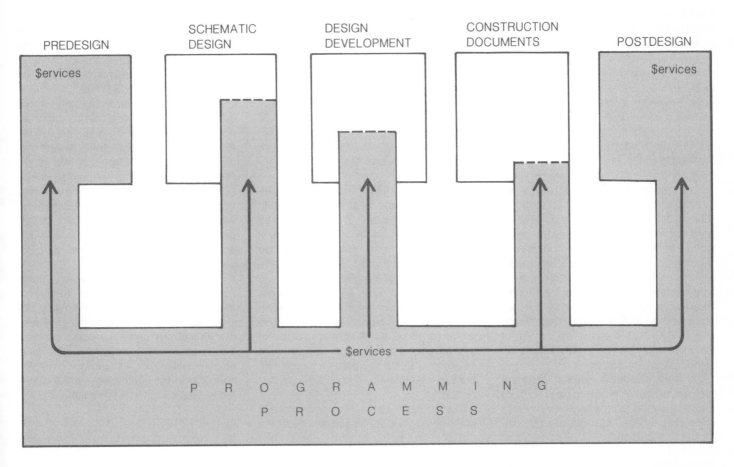

PREDESIGN   SCHEMATIC DESIGN   DESIGN DEVELOPMENT   CONSTRUCTION DOCUMENTS   POSTDESIGN

$ervices

$ervices

$ervices

P R O G R A M M I N G

P R O C E S S

process, the program will become a valuable evaluation instrument and programming techniques will be used for data collection and analysis.

—The growing importance of energy conservation in design and of the need for predesign information on energy resource and use implications point to greater opportunities for energy analysis studies in programming and related areas. It is another indication of the pattern of more interprofessional cooperation, as architects, engineers and others combine their different perspectives on and concepts of energy conservation to more

economical, efficient designs.

—Computer applications in programming will continue to increase. The advantages of speed and efficiency in data management and manipulation are only outweighed by costs and lack of competence by design programmers. Increased experience in the use of computer techniques and operation of equipment will overcome the latter problem, while development of microprocessors and mini-computer units are making computer-aided programming and design both affordable and convenient to a broader market.

—At the same time, the demand by cli-

ents for more sophisticated data analysis will lead to greater use of existing computer methods and development of new applications and less use of time-consuming and costly techniques and operating procedures. The areas most likely to see greater computerization are those involving recording, retention and recall of masses of numerical data and statistical manipulations. Cost evaluations, space management, energy use analysis and user attitude survey analysis, as well as various business records management, appear to present the greatest opportunities for such electronic data processing applications by programmers.

PROGRAMMING IN ARCHITECTURAL PRACTICE.

The trend toward broadened architectural services will include more programming. It is a natural extension of design activities and coincides with architects' holistic approach to design problems. However, in order to perform programming successfully, architects need to develop analytical approaches and analytical skills, in contrast to their traditional synthesis-solution orientation.

Development of the analysis perspective for design problems has been aided by increases in the number of professional schools that offer programming and related courses. At least two dozen architecture schools now teach programming in some form or other. Also, educators have been alerted to the need for graduate courses in programming by the professional examination guide of the National Council of Architectural Registration Boards (NCARB). Twenty-five percent of the guide and example test has been devoted to programming since 1973.

As more architects develop programming expertise, it will be applied to more design projects and a wider variety of nondesign services such as energy analyses, environmental and social impact assessments, feasibility studies, long-range plans and management studies.

The appeal of nondesign architectural services is enhanced by the reduced liability exposure. Architects turned off by trends in the jurisprudence system toward more scattergun lawsuits and bigger awards and by higher liability insurance premiums, but who still wish to contribute toward betterment of the environment, will find programming and related services increasingly attractive for specialty practices.

Programming has the potential of becoming a separate discipline. It is nearing that status in the way it is practiced by many nondesign specialists. What remains is for it to be formalized by recognition of shared values and basic principles among programmers. Already there are small meetings of programmers at the annual conference of the Environmental Design Research Association (EDRA). This group could be the potential nucleus of a professional association, which could establish practice standards and promote broader acceptance of programmers' expertise.

In architectural practice, competence in programming is more frequently one of the criteria used by clients in selection of firms for design projects. From another perspective, there is a trend toward greater legal responsibility on architects to fulfill program requirements established by the architect or another programmer. As a result, there also has been a corresponding tightening of program definition.

As facilities become more complex and influences on their form and function become more diverse, numerous and critical, the need for adequate, reliable and appropriate design information will grow. Programming provides a systemized methodology for accommodating the information needs of both clients and designers. And, it represents an opportunity for improved and expanded practice and the consequent increase in sources of compensation.

The success of an architectural practice depends on the ability to deliver needed services. Through improved skill in programming methods, better programs of client requirements will result in better design responses to requirements. Clear, precise definitions of design problems cannot help but contribute to efficient, effective and creative design solutions.

Bibliography

CHAPTER REFERENCES

(See ''General References'' for complete citations for books.)

CHAPTER ONE

''Architectural Analysis—Prelude to Good Design,'' William M. Peña and William Caudill in *Architectural Record*, Vol. 125, No. 5 (New York: Dodge Corp., May 1959)
Current Techniques in Architectural Practice
Facility Programming
Introduction to Architectural Programming
Methods of Architectural Programming
Problem Seeking: An Architectural Programming Primer
''Programming,'' *Current Techniques in Architectural Practice*
''Programming: Demanding Specialty in a Complex World,'' *Architectural Record*, Vol. 144, No. 3 (New York: McGraw-Hill, September 1968)
Royal Institute of British Architects Handbook of Architectural Practice and Management

CHAPTER TWO

Facility Programming
Introduction to Architectural Programming
Problem Seeking: An Architectural Programming Primer

CHAPTER THREE

Architectural Psychology: Proceedings of the Lund Conference
Behavioral Research Methods in Environmental Design
Design Methods: Seeds of Human Futures
Designing for Human Behavior
''The Development of a Usable Lexicon of Environmental Descriptors,'' *Environment and Behavior*, Vol. 2, No. 2 (New York: McGraw-Hill, September 1970)
Direct Observation and Measurement of Behavior
The Dynamics of Interviewing
Environmental Design Research (EDRA 4)
Environmental Psychology
The Handbook of Social Psychology
Interviewing in Social Research
Introduction to Environmental Psychology
Man-Environment Interactions Part II (EDRA 5)
The Measurement of Meaning
Methodology of Social Impact Assessment
Methods of Architectural Programming
Neighborhood Space: User Needs and Design Responsibility
The Participant Observer
Planning the Research Interview
Proceedings of the First EDRA Conference
Proceedings of the Third EDRA Conference
Questionnaire Design and Attitude Measurement
Recording and Analyzing Child Behavior
Research Methods in the Behavioral Sciences
Survey Sampling
Visual Anthropology: Photography as a Research Tool

CHAPTER FOUR

Architectural Psychology: Proceedings of the Lund Conference
Basic Statistical Methods
Behavioral Research Methods in Environmental Design
Critical Path Scheduling
Current Techniques in Architectural Practice
Design Cost Analysis for Architects and Engineers
Design in Architecture: Architecture and the Human Sciences
Design Methods: Seeds of Human Futures
Designing for Human Behavior
Disciplined Creativity for Engineers
Ecological Psychology
Enclosing Behavior
Energy Audits
Energy Conservation in Buildings
Energy Conservation Through Building Design
Energy Estimate Analysis
Energy Planning for Buildings
Factor Analysis of Data Matrices
Graphic Problem Solving for Architects and Builders
Introduction to Statistical Analysis
Life Cycle Cost Analysis: A Guide for Architects
Life Cycle Cost Analysis 2: Using It in Practice
Methods of Architectural Programming
Multidimensional Scaling and Related Techniques in Marketing Analysis
Nonparametric Statistics
Nonparametric Statistics for the Behavioral Sciences
The Oregon Experiment
A Pattern Language
Planning the Office Landscape
Problem Seeking: An Architectural Programming Primer
Proceedings of the First EDRA Conference
Project Management with CPM and PERT
Scheduling Handbook
Statistics for Psychology
Statistics Made Simple
Time Budgets of Human Behavior
The Timeless Way of Building
Value Engineering in the Construction Industry

CHAPTER FIVE

The Art of Plain Talk
Creative Communications for a Successful Design Practice
Design Methods: Seeds of Human Futures
The Design of Social Research
Designing for Visual Aids
The Elements of Style
Environmental Design Evaluation
''Made, Not Born: A New Slant on Public Speaking,'' Andrew Warren Weil in

Consulting Engineer, December 1978
Methods of Architectural Programming
Planning and Producing Slide Programs
Practical Charting Techniques
Publication Design
Serious Games
Synectics: The Development of Creative Capacity
Taking Part: A Workshop Approach to Collective Creativity
Understanding Media

CHAPTER SIX

"Architectural Optimization: A Review," John S. Gero, in *Engineering Optimization*, Vol. 1, No. 3 (London: Gordon & Breach Science Pub., 1974)
Computer-aided Architectural Design
Computer Applications in Architecture
Computer Programs in Environmental Design
Computers in Architectural Practice
Dynamic Programming in Architecture
Dynamic Programming: Theory and Application
Emerging Methods in Environmental Design and Planning
Optimization Techniques with FORTRAN
Performance Specification of Computer-aided Environmental Design
Reflections on Computer Aids to Design and Architecture
Spatial Synthesis in Computer-aided Building Design

CHAPTER THIRTEEN

Taking Part: A Workshop Approach to Collective Creativity

CHAPTER TWENTY-ONE

Compensation Guidelines for Architectural and Engineering Services

GENERAL REFERENCES

Applied Imagination: Principles and Procedures of Creative Problem Solving. Alexander F. Osborn. New York: Scribners, 1957.

Describes creative thinking as a method for problem solving and outlines physical and psychological criteria for optimizing creative thought.

Architectural Design and the Social Sciences. Donald Conway, ed. Washington, DC: AIA, 1975.

A collection of theory and research papers to "foster and make clear the process of collaboration between architects and social scientists and to identify some of the problems inherent in this collaboration."

Architectural Psychology: Proceedings of the Lund Conference. Rikard Kueller, ed. Stroudsburg, Pa.: Dowden, Hutchinson & Ross, 1973.

From a 4-day conference. Topics include the psychological aspects of lighting, theory and applied research in architectural psychology, and architectural psychology's role in future planning.

Architecture, Problems, and Purposes: Architectural Design as a Basic Problem-Solving Process. John W. Wade. New York: John Wiley & Sons, 1977.

Programming is discussed throughout the book as a primary step in the problem seeking-problem solving phase of design. Subsections are summarized with margin notes for quick reference.

The Art of Plain Talk. Rudolph Flesch. New York: Collier, 1951.

Basic Statistical Methods (4th ed.). N.M. Downie and R.W. Heath. New York: Harper & Row, 1974.

Behavioral Architecture: Toward an Accountable Design Process. Clovis B. Heimsath. New York: McGraw-Hill, 1977.

Discusses the need for considering building use and human behavior patterns when synthesizing design. One chapter is devoted to techniques for relating these patterns directly to design.

Behavioral Research Methods in Environmental Design. William M. Michelson, ed. Stroudsburg, Pa.: Dowden, Hutchinson & Ross, 1975.

Seven social science methodological approaches are explained in terms of relevance to research in environmental design, with specific guidelines for application. They are: research design; paper-and-pencil tests; option trade-off games; survey research; time budgeting; photographic recording of environmental behavior; and direct observation of environmental behavior.

Buildings for People: Behavioral Research—Approaches and Directions. Arthur I. Rubin and Jacqueline Elder. Washington, D.C.: National Bureau of Standards Special Publication 474, Government Printing Office, 1980.

Directed toward the practicing architect and the architectural student, this book describes the use of social science techniques in design problem solving for enhancing the relationship between man and the built environment. The book is divided into seven parts: problem definition; the scientific research approach; man-environment research methods; the senses of hearing and vision; the less explored senses; a summary and discussion of future directions; and an extensive collection of reference material.

Color & Human Response: Aspects of Light and Color Bearing on the Reactions of Living Things and the Welfare of Human Beings. Faber Birren. New York: Van Nostrand Reinhold, 1978.

A theoretic guide to efficient use of color and light in design for maintenance of good visual, physical and emotional well-being of proposed users. Author's experience rests mainly in application of color to industrial and institutional work environments, however observations made are applicable to human-use programming in general.

Compensation Guidelines for Architectural and Engineering Services, (2nd ed., rev.). Washington, D.C.: American Institute of Architects, 1978.

Management guide to cost-based compensation. A component of the AIA Financial Management System. Detailed procedures for determining scope of services and compensation based on costs of providing professional services.

Computer-aided Architectural Design. William J. Mitchell. New York: Petrocelli/Charter, 1977.

Directed toward the practical aspects of computer use in the architectural office. Divided into four parts: Fundamental Concepts of computer-aided architectural design; Data Bases applicable to architecture; Interfaces—the hands-on operation of the computers; and the Problem Solving capabilities of computers in design formulation. Includes chapter on programming and feasibility analysis.

Computer Applications in Architecture. John S. Gero, ed. London: Applied Sciences Publishers Ltd., 1977.

Design and documentation applications, including discussion of computerized space planning techniques. Written for those unfamiliar with computers.

Computer Programs in Environmental Design (five volumes). Kaiman Lee, ed. Boston: Environmental Design and Research Center, 1974.

An explanation of computer use in de-

sign, written for the typical design professional, followed by 4½ volumes of computer program abstracts. Abstracts describe the uses and limitations of each program, and provide resource addresses for further information.

Computers in Architectural Practice. Bryan Guttridge and Jonathan R. Wainwright. New York: John Wiley & Sons, 1973.

A basic guide to the design professional interested in using computers but unfamiliar with the computer-aided design process. The book describes the many uses to which architects can put the computer.

Creative Communications for a Successful Design Practice. Stephen A. Kliment. New York: Whitney Library of Design, 1977.

Explains the use of various communications media in creating an optimum impression on clients and business associates. The book describes different media (such as newsletters, audiovisual presentations, the spoken word and photography) with specific advantages and requirements of each medium. Includes a section on ways to reach the public media.

Critical Path Scheduling. Joseph Horowitz. New York: Ronald Press, 1967.

Current Techniques in Architectural Practice. Robert Allan Class and Robert E. Koehler, eds. Washington, D.C.: American Institute of Architects and New York: Architectural Record Books, 1976.

Overview of architectural practice, with emphasis on management. Includes graphics to complement the text and annotated bibliographies. Chapter 11, by Herbert P. McLaughlin, specifically addresses architectural programming.

Design Cost Analysis for Architects and

Engineers. Herbert Swinburne, FAIA. New York: McGraw-Hill Book Co., 1980.

The basic premise of this succinct, readable book is that cost analysis is based on both the program and the design.

Design for Human Affairs. C.M. Deasy. Cambridge, Mass.: Schenkman, 1974.

Design Games: Playing for Keeps with Personal and Environmental Design Decisions. Henry Sanoff. Los Altos, Calif.: William Kaufmann Inc., 1979.

Collection of 18 games engaging practical approaches to making personal, group and community planning and design decisions. Games simulate situations including making personal housing choices, helping plan for schools and recreation areas, and community development.

Design in Architecture: Architecture and the Human Sciences. Geoffrey Broadbent. New York: John Wiley & Sons Ltd., 1973.

Design Methods in Architecture. Geoffrey Broadbent and Anthony Ward. New York: George Wittenborn Inc., 1969.

Design Methods: Seeds of Human Futures. J. Christopher Jones. New York: John Wiley & Sons Ltd., 1970.

Analysis of "traditional" and "modern" design methods. New methods are discussed in terms of problem-solving flexibility. Part 2 of the book presents 35 design problem solving strategies.

The Design of Social Research. Russell L. Ackoff. Chicago: University of Chicago Press, 1953.

Designing for Human Behavior. Jon Lang, Charles Burnette, Walter Moleski and David Vachon, eds. Stroudsburg, Pa:

Dowden, Hutchinson & Ross, Inc., 1974.

A collection of essays describing the social, behavioral and psychological factors of design. The book is divided into three subsections, two theoretical and one practical. Many social science research techniques are explained in terms of their application to programming and design.

Designing for the Disabled, (3rd ed.). Selwyn Goldsmith. London: RIBA Publications, 1976.

A detailed overview of the psychological and physical factors affecting planning and designing for the handicapped. Government regulations referenced are British.

Designing for Visual Aids. David Pye. New York: Van Nostrand Reinhold Co., 1970.

Designing the Open Nursing Home. Joseph A. Koncelik. Stroudsburg, Pa.: Dowden, Hutchinson & Ross, Inc., 1976.

The open nursing home is a concept which concentrates on designing with the social and physical needs of the infirm elderly in mind. Some concrete suggestions are made regarding space use and furnishing needs.

Designing with Community Participation. Henry Sanoff, ed. New York: McGraw-Hill, 1978.

Multiple examples of successful projects including ideas, methods, concepts and start-up strategies that stress the need for a sharing of expertise among designers and those affected by environmental change.

Direct Observation and Measurement of Behavior. S.J. Hutt and C. Hutt. Springfield, Ill.: Charles C. Thomas, 1970.

Disciplined Creativity for Engineers. Robert L. Bailey. Ann Arbor, Mich.: Ann Arbor Science Publishers Inc., 1978.

The Dynamics of Interviewing. R.L. Kahn and C.F. Cannell. New York: John Wiley & Sons Ltd., 1957.

Dynamic Programming in Architecture. John S. Gero. Sydney, Australia: University of Sydney, Dept. of Architectural Science, 1976.

Dynamic Programming: Theory and Application. E.V. Denardo. Englewood Cliffs, N.J.: Prentice-Hall, 1975.

Ecological Psychology: Concepts and Methods for Studying the Environment of Human Behavior. Roger Barker. Palo Alto, Calif.: Stanford University Press, 1968.

Educational Specifications and User Requirements for Intermediate Schools. Toronto: Ryerson Press, 1969.

User-needs study for Toronto school system. Covers seven main areas, concerning student needs and motivations, school board requirements, user requirements and availability of educational facilities, administrative and ancillary needs in the public schools.

The Elements of Style. William Strunk Jr. and E.B. White. New York: Macmillan Paperbacks, 1962.

Emerging Methods in Environmental Design and Planning. Gary T. Moore, ed. Cambridge, Mass.: MIT Press, 1970.

Compiled articles concerned with differing user-needs studies and design methods for solving problems of the physical environment. Some emphasis is put on the computer's role in programming and design. Written for the working architect as well as architectural researcher.

Enclosing Behavior. Robert B. Bechtel. Stroudsburg, Pa.: Dowden, Hutchinson & Ross, Inc., 1977.

A readable book explaining the application of social theory and research methods to architecture; particular emphasis on behavior setting survey methodology.

Energy Audits, supplement of the *AIA Energy Notebook*. Washington, D.C.: The American Institute of Architects, 1979.

Energy Conservation Through Building Design. Donald Watson, ed. New York: Architectural Record Books, 1979.

Energy Conservation in Buildings: Techniques for Economical Design. C.W. Griffin. Washington, D.C.: Construction Specifications Institute, 1974.

Energy Estimate Analysis. CRS Energy Task Force. Houston, Texas: Caudill Rowlett Scott, 1978.

Energy Planning for Buildings. Michael Sizemore et al. Washington, D.C.: The American Institute of Architects, 1979.

Environmental Design Evaluation. Arnold Friedman, Craig Zimring and Ervin Zube. New York: Plenum Press, 1978.

A collection of case studies and research papers emphasizing the importance of a systematic method of appraisal in design.

Environmental Design Perspectives. Wolfgang F.E. Preiser and J. Thomas Regan, eds. Blacksburg, Va.: College of Architecture, VPI&SU, 1972.

Collection of papers surveying the educational, professional and research thrusts in man-environment system development. Includes articles dealing with some programming aspects, such as computer use and space planning.

Environmental Design Research Association (EDRA) Conference Reports:

EDRA 1—*Proceedings of the 1st Annual Environmental Design Research Association Conference*. Henry Sanoff and Sidney Cohn, eds. Stroudsburg, Pa.: Dowden, Hutchinson & Ross, Inc., 1970.

EDRA 2—*Proceedings of the 2nd Annual Environmental Design Research Association Conference, October 1970, Pittsburgh, Pennsylvania*. John Archea and Charles Eastman eds. Stroudsburg, Pa.: Dowden, Hutchinson & Ross, Inc., 1970.

EDRA 3—*Proceedings of the EDRA3/ AR8 Conference, University of California at Los Angeles, January 1972*, Vols. 1&2. William J. Mitchell, ed. Los Angeles: University of California, 1972.

EDRA 4—*Environmental Design Research*, Vols. 1 & 2. Wolfgang F.E. Preiser, ed. Stroudsburg, Pa.: Dowden, Hutchinson & Ross, Inc., 1973.

EDRA 5—*Man-Environment Interactions: Evaluations and Applications*, Vols. 1, 2 & 3. Daniel H. Carson, ed. Stroudsburg, Pa.: Dowden, Hutchinson & Ross, Inc. 1974.

EDRA 6—*Responding to Social Change*. Basil Honikman, ed. Stroudsburg, Pa.: Dowden, Hutchinson & Ross, Inc., 1975.

EDRA 7— *The Behavioral Basis of Design*, Vols. 1&2. Peter Suedfeld and James A. Russell, eds. Stroudsburg, Pa.: Dowden, Hutchinson & Ross, Inc., 1976.

EDRA 8—*Priorities for Environmental Design Research*, Vols. 1&2. Sue Weideman, James R. Anderson and Roger L. Brauer, eds. Washington, D.C.: EDRA, Inc., 1977.

EDRA 9—*New Directions in Environmental Design Research*. Walter E. Rogers and William H. Ittelson, eds. Washington, D.C.: EDRA, Inc., 1978.

EDRA 10—*Environmental Design: Research, Theory and Application*. Andrew Seidel and Scott Danford, eds. Washington, D.C.: EDRA, Inc., 1979.

Yearly collection of research papers representing the state-of-the-art in the rapidly developing interdisciplinary field of environmental design research. Conference reports are divided by seminar topic, and generally include social trends research techniques, user-needs studies, computer-aided approaches to design, and various other methods of viewing the environment from the social science perspective.

Environmental Interaction: Psychological Approaches to Our Physical Environment. David Canter, ed. New York: International Universities Press, 1976.

Environmental Knowing. Gary T. Moore and Reginald G. Golledge, eds. Stroudsburg, Pa.: Dowden, Hutchinson & Ross, Inc., 1976.

Collection of research papers concerning human cognitive mapping tendencies as measured across cultures and age groups. Includes a section on methodologies for measuring these tendencies.

Facility Programming. Wolfgang F.E. Preiser, ed. Stroudsburg, Pa.: Dowden, Hutchinson & Ross, Inc., 1978.

For detailed annotation see Exhibit 1-2.

Factor Analysis of Data Matrices. P. Horst. New York: Holt, Rinehart & Winston, 1965.

Graphic Problem Solving for Architects and Builders. Paul Laseau. Boston: Cahners Publishing Company, 1975.

Emphasizes use of thinking drawings as a way of facilitating the transformation of design requirements into design drawings. Heavily illustrated with example diagrams.

Handbook of Research Design and Social Measurement. D. Miller. New York: David McKay, 1970.

Handbook of Social Psychology, Vol. 2. G. Lindsey and E. Aronson, eds. Reading, Mass.: Addison-Wesley Publishing Co., 1968.

Hospital Planning Handbook. Rex Whitaker Allen and Ilona von Karolyi. New York: John Wiley & Sons, 1976.

Addressed to hospital planners or architects doing hospital design work. Examination of existing facilities, projected changes in hospital trends, and relation of both to design possibilities is the general thrust of the book.

Human Aspects of Urban Form: Towards a Man-Environment Approach to Urban Form and Design. Amos Rapoport. New York: Pergamon, 1977.

A study of human needs and characteristics, both physical and psychological, with respect to the urban environment.

Human Behavior and Environment, Vol. 1. Irwin Altman and Joachim F. Wohlwill, eds. New York: Plenum Press, 1976.

A collection of position papers by various authors, concerning human behavior and relationship with the environment, built and natural. First of a proposed series, this book deals with human perception and use of land and space for recreational as well as vocational purposes.

Information Methods for Design and Construction. John Paterson. New York: John Wiley & Sons, 1977.

Discussion of the process of architectural data collection and flow in the predesign to postconstruction phases. Focus of data applicable to programming ranges from client/user needs to construction specifications.

Interviewing in Social Research. H. Hyman. Chicago: University of Chicago Press, 1954.

Introduction to Architectural Programming. Edward T. White III. Tucson, Ariz.: Architectural Media, 1972.

For detailed annotation see Exhibit 1-2.

An Introduction to Environmental Psychology. William H. Ittelson, Harold M. Proshansky, Leanne G. Rivlin, Gary H. Winkle. New York: Holt, Rinehart and Winston, Inc., 1974.

Environmental psychology is an interdisciplinary study of the effects of architecture on human behavior and attitudes.

Introduction to Statistical Analysis (2nd ed.) Wilfred J. Dixon and Frank J. Massey Jr. New York: McGraw-Hill Book Co., 1957.

Life Cycle Cost Analysis: A Guide for Architects. Washington, D.C.: The American Institute of Architects, 1977.

Life Cycle Cost Analysis 2: Using It in Practice. David S. Haviland. Washington, D.C.: The American Institute of Architects, 1978.

The Measurement of Meaning. Charles E. Osgood, George J. Suci and Percy H. Tannenbaum. Champaign, Ill.: University of Illinois Press, 1957.

The standard reference to the application of the "semantic differential" technique in research on the measurement of meaning. Includes various applications of the concept and technique.

Methodology of Social Impact Assess-

ment. Kurt Finsterbusch and C.P. Wolf, eds. Stroudsburg, Pa.: Dowden, Hutchinson & Ross, Inc., 1977.

A partial inventory of methodologies, with specific reference to architecture.

Methods of Architectural Programming. Henry Sanoff. Stroudsburg, Pa.: Dowden, Hutchinson & Ross, Inc., 1977.

For detailed annotation see Exhibit 1-2.

Multidimensional Scaling and Related Techniques in Marketing Analysis. Paul E. Green and Frank I. Carmone. Boston: Allyn and Bacon, Inc., 1970.

Detailed explanation of computer-based techniques, developed in the behavioral and life sciences, for measuring market trends and public preferences. Techniques are applicable to human-needs/preferences aspects of facility programming.

NCARB Architectural Registration Handbook. Washington, D.C.: National Council of Architectural Registration Boards and New York: Architectural Record Books, updated annually.

Guidebook for architecture professional exam candidates. A section, usually comprising one-fourth of the handbook, is devoted to programming.

Neighborhood Space: User Needs and Design Responsibility. Randolph T. Hester Jr. Stroudsburg, Pa.: Dowden, Hutchinson & Ross, Inc., 1975.

A primer to introduce the student designer to neighborhood space, user needs and design responsibility.

Nonparametric Statistics. J. Hajek. San Francisco: Holden-Day Inc., 1969.

Nonparametric Statistics for the Behavioral Sciences. S. Siegel. New York:

McGraw-Hill Book Co., 1956.

Notes on the Synthesis of Form. Christopher Alexander. Cambridge, Mass.: Harvard University Press, 1967.

History and description of methods for representing, analyzing and solving design problems. An appendixed example is included.

Open Office Planning: A Handbook for Interior Designers and Architects. John Pile. New York: Whitney Library of Design, 1978.

Technical source book on office layout, providing guidelines for space-allocating matrices and diagrams, proximity analyses, multifloor arrangements and client participation. Illustrations and examples are given.

Optimization Techniques with FORTRAN. J.L. Kuester and J.H. Mize. New York: McGraw-Hill, 1973.

The Oregon Experiment. Christopher Alexander. New York: Oxford University Press, 1975.

A master plan proposal for the University of Oregon. Part three of a three-part series, this is an example of a community plan using the designing and building methods described in *A Pattern Language.*

The Participant Observer. G. Jacobs, ed. New York: George Braziller Inc., 1970.

A Pattern Language: Towns, Buildings, Construction. Christopher Alexander, et al. New York: Oxford University Press, 1977.

Provides a language for use with the process described in *The Timeless Way of Building.* In *A Pattern Language* the planned environment is described as a cohesive whole derived from interrelated parts. The "pattern language" is an ordered division which explains town planning and building design and construction in terms of 253 separate but interreled problems. The problems, and suggested solutions, vary in scope from those dealing with regional characteristics to those dealing with specific building features and building materials. Together, *The Timeless Way of Building* and *A Pattern Language* constitute a generalized programming process.

People and Buildings. Robert Gutman, ed. New York: Basic Books, 1972.

A collection of articles covering a wide variety of sociological aspects of the environment. The last of five sections is concerned with "The Application of Behavioral Science to Design."

People in Places. Jay Farbstein and Min Kantrowitz. Englewood Cliffs, N.J.: Prentice-Hall, 1978.

Clearly written, comprehensive description of the factors necessary in correctly fitting design to specific user needs. Forty-two subtopics illustrate six topics describing the built environment: experiencing places; using places; how places work; politics of places; changing places.

Performance Specification of Computer-aided Environmental Design (two volumes). Kaiman Lee. Boston: Environmental Design and Research Center, 1975.

Discusses the development of a package of computer programs to aid the design process. Focus is on 13 design considerations: feasibility study, architectural programming, relational planning, site planning, two-dimensional graphics, three-dimensional graphics, cost/quality control, environmental control, circulation analysis, text manipulation, project control, office management, and evaluation.

Personal Space: The Behavioral Basis of Design. Robert Sommer. Englewood Cliffs, N.J.: Prentice-Hall, 1969.

Discusses the human considerations involved in designing individual work and living areas.

The Place of Architecture in Sociology. Robert Gutman. Princeton, N.J.: Princeton University, 1975.

Treatise on the interdisciplinary relationship between architecture and sociology.

Planning and Producing Slide Programs, Publication S-30. Rochester, NY: Eastman Kodak Co., 1975.

Planning Flexible Learning Places. Stanton Leggett, C. William Brubaker, Aaron Cohodes, Arthur S. Shapiro. New York: McGraw-Hill, 1977.

Relates school operational needs to design of new educational facilities and remodeling of existing facilities. Emphasis is on adaptability to progress and subsequent change in utility as changes in need occur.

Planning the New Office. Michael Saphier. New York: McGraw-Hill, 1978.

Describes a process of determining need for renovation or relocation, planning for that need, and applying and developing the plan. User participation in the planning phase is emphasized. Chapter notes suggest the range of consultants who may provide specialized advice.

Planning the Office Landscape. Alvin E. Palmer and M. Susan Lewis. New York: McGraw-Hill, 1977.

Method for detecting and solving organizational problems. Topics include communication, paper flow, work groups and equipment. Concepts are illustrated with case studies.

Planning the Research Interview. J.C.

Scott and Eliska Chanlette. Chapel Hill, N.C.: Laboratories for Population Statistics, University of North Carolina, 1973.

Practical Charting Techniques. Mary Eleanor Spear. New York: McGraw-Hill Book Co., 1969.

Problem Seeking: An Architectural Programming Primer. William Peña, with William Caudill and John Focke. Boston: Cahners Books, 1977.

For detailed annotation see Exhibit 1-2.

Project Management with CPM and PERT. Joseph J. Moder and Cecil R. Phillips. New York: Reinhold Book Corp., 1970.

Psychology for Architects. David V. Canter. New York: John Wiley & Sons, 1974.

Discusses the psychological impact on humans of the built environment. Describes some research techniques for measuring this impact.

Publication Design. Allen Hurlburt. New York: Van Nostrand Press, 1976.

A guide to page layout, typography, format and style.

Questionnaire Design and Attitude Measurement. A.N. Oppenheim. New York: Basic Books, 1966.

Recording and Analyzing Child Behavior. Herbert Wright. New York: Harper & Row, 1967.

Reflections on Computer Aids to Design and Architecture. Nicholas Negroponte, ed. New York: Petrocelli/Charter, 1975.

Research Methods in the Behavioral Sciences. Leon Festinger and Daniel Katz, eds. New York: Dryden Press, 1953.

Research Methods in Social Relations. Claire Selitz et al. New York: Holt Reinhart & Winston, 1959.

Royal Institute of British Architects Handbook of Architectural Practice and Management. London: RIBA Publications, 1973.

Scheduling Handbook. James J. O'Brien. New York: McGraw-Hill Book Co., 1969.

Serious Games. C.C. Abt. New York: Viking Press, 1970.

Social Science Frontiers, Vol. 6, Sociology and Architectural Design. John Zeisel. New York: Russell Sage Foundation, 1975.

A theoretical explanation of programming in both the predesign and postconstruction stages. Main objective is to "help bridge the gap between the architect and his or her user client." The solution: social science research techniques.

Space Planning: Designing the Office Environment. Lila Shoshkes. New York: Architectural Record Books, 1976.

Applies the aesthetic, functional and psychological aspects of space planning to how people work within the limits of changing office technologies. Includes consideration of lighting, acoustics and power outlet access.

Spaces for People: Human Factors in Design. Corwin Bennett. Englewood Cliffs, N.J.: Prentice-Hall, 1977.

An aid to the interior space designer in providing the ergonomic (human factor) data necessary to satisfy human user needs. Concentration is on aspects of health and safety, performance, comfort and aesthetic pleasantness.

Spatial Synthesis in Computer-aided Building Design. Charles M. Eastman, ed. New York: John Wiley & Sons, 1975.

A collection of papers directed at the use of computers specifically for design formulation. Emphasis is on space allocation and organization.

Statistics for Psychology. William Mendenhall and Madelaine Ramey. North Scituate, Mass.: Duxbury Press, 1973.

Statistics Made Simple. H.T. Hayslett, Jr. Garden City, N.Y.: Doubleday & Co., Inc., 1968.

Survey Sampling. L. Kish. New York: John Wiley & Sons, 1965.

Synectics: The Development of Creative Capacity. William J.J. Gordon. New York: Collier Books, 1961.

Taking Part: A Workshop Approach to Collective Creativity. Lawrence Halprin and James Burns. Cambridge, Mass.: MIT Press, 1974.

A methodological approach to group workshop decision making.

Time Budgets of Human Behavior. Pitirim Sorokin and Clarence Berger. Cambridge, Mass.: Harvard University Press, 1939.

The Timeless Way of Building. Christopher Alexander et al. New York: Oxford University Press, 1974.

First of three-part series (Part II: *A Pattern Language*; Part III: *The Oregon Experiment*) describing Alexander's concept of designing a "whole" environment—one satisfying all cultural and physical requirements of the user.

Understanding Media. Marshall McLuhan. New York: McGraw-Hill, Inc., 1964.

Introductory communications media textbook.

Urban Environments and Human Behavior: An Annotated Bibliography. Gwen Bell, Edwina Randall and Judith E.R. Roeder. Stroudsburg, Pa.: Dowden, Hutchinson & Ross, Inc., 1973.

Of interest to designers in need of background sources for studying human activity with respect to urban space. Bibliographic entries are classified as dealing with either design approaches to the urban environment, social science approaches to the urban environment, or the framework of the urban environment.

Value Engineering in the Construction Industry (2nd ed.) Alphonse J. Dell'Isola. New York: Construction Publishing Co., 1974.

Visual Anthropology: Photography as a Research Tool. John Collier Jr. New York: Holt, Rinehart & Winston, 1967.

With Man in Mind: An Interdisciplinary Prospectus for Environmental Design. Constance Perin. Cambridge, Mass.: MIT Press, 1970.

A treatise on closing the gap Perin sees between actual human factors and the conceptions of those factors held by architects.

Index

Ackoff, Russell L., 156
Activity analysis, 95
Activity mapping. See Observation techniques, behavior mapping
Activity site model, 97
Activity system, 98, 100
Activity time chart, 118
Adams, Graham, 234
Adjacency matrix, 123
Adjective checklists, 84
Affinity matrix, 123
Agostini, Edward J.
    programming defined by, 4
Ambulatory Care and Research Facility, Laboratory Prototype, National Institutes of Health, Bethesda, Maryland, 247-255
    program, 254-255
    programming process, 248-254
"A" Mountain Neighborhood Center, Tucson, Arizona, 171-175
    program, 174
    programming process, 173-174
Analysis. See Data analysis; Morphological analysis; Program elements, analysis of
Architects Collaborative, The (TAC), 165
Architectural Record, 12
Architecture One, 171, 173
    program for a neighborhood center, 171-175
        program, 174
        program implementation, 174-175
        programming process, 171, 173-174
    programming model, 40-41
Arithmetic mean, 90-91
Arts center, 198-208
Arundel Center at Broad Creek, Anne Arundel County, Maryland, 241-246
    program, 245-246
    programming process, 243-245
        data analysis and organization, 244-245
        data collection, 244
        site analysis, 245
Ascertainments. See Program, conclusions
Attitude measurement, 79-87
    purpose of, 79-80
    tests for
        adjective checklists, 84
        attribute discrimination scale, 84
        ranking chart, 84-86
        semantic differential, 80-84
    see also Data collection
Attribute discrimination scale, 84
Audio-visual aids, 144, 146
    see also Observation techniques, instru-

mented; Presentations

Bailey, Robert L., 117
Bar chart, 117
Barker, Roger, 97
Bazjanac, Vladimir, 158
Beard, David, R., 241
Bechtel, Robert B., 97
Behavior mapping, 73-75
    see also Observation techniques
Behavior patterns. See Tracking
Behavior setting, 97
Behavior specimen record, 75-76
Behavioral Research Methods in Environmental Design, 98
BEPS, 110-112
Bergen County Cultural Arts Center, Bergen County, New Jersey, 198-208
    feasibility program, 202-206
    programming process, 199-202
        site analysis, 202
        user data analysis, 201-202
        user data collection, 201
Berger, Clarence, 99
Bergfeld, C. Daniel, 198
Bipolar scale, 81
Black Like Me, 72
Block diagram, 130
Boerger, John, 209
Booz, Allen and Hamilton, 27, 35
Box matrix, 85, 122
Brainstorming, 136-137
Bridge, 139
Brill, Michael
    programming defined by, 4
Broadbent, Geoffrey, 89
Brown sheets, 135
Bubble diagram, 128-129
Building Energy Performance Standards (BEPS), 110-112
Building Optimization Program (BOP), 163-165
Buzz/rap sessions, 137

Caudill Rowlett Scott (CRS), 12, 129, 134, 139, 166, 179
    program for a middle school, 176-183
        program, 180-183
        program implementation, 180
        programming process, 179-180
    programming model, 39
Caudill, William, 12, 131
Central tendency measures, 90

Charette books. See Presentation, workbooks
Charettes, 139-140
Charts, project scheduling, 117-120
    activity time, 118
    bar, 117
    milestone, 117-118
    network, 118-120
    see also Evaluation techniques
Cherry, Edith A., 191
Clayton, Pamela, 247
Client, 10, 36, 42
    contracts with, 267-278
    see also Programming case studies
Client/designer interests, 17
Cluster
    analysis, 165
    sampling, 59
CLUSTR, 159
Collection of data. See Data collection
Color study, 256-261
Coming of Age in Samoa, 72
Commodore Sloat Elementary School, San Francisco, California, 216-222
    program, 221-22
    programming process, 217-221
        feasibility study, 221
        project preparation, 218
        workshops, 218-221
Communication
    importance of, 135
    techniques, 136-149
        brainstorming, 136-137
        buzz/rap sessions, 137
        gaming, 138-139
        group planning, 139-140
        role playing 137-138
        synectics, 137
        workshops, 139, 219
    see also Presentations
Compensation, 267, 271
Computer-aided Architectural Design, 159
Computer Applications in Architecture, 158
Computer Programs in Environmental Design, 165
Computers in Architectural Practice, 157
Computers, use of for programming, 159-167
    analysis techniques with, 159-165
        problem structuring, 159-162
        feasibility analysis, 162-163
        space needs, 163-164
    applications, 160, 165
    capabilities, 158-159
    programs, 165-166
Conclusions. See Program, conclusions

Contracts
   forms of agreement, 267-270
   liability, 275
   scope of services, 270-271
Correlation diagrams, 123-130
Cost analysis, 112-115
   cost/benefit analysis, 115
   life cycle, 114-115
   value analysis, 115
Cost, Planning & Management International
      (CPMI), 128, 166, 184-185
   program for a research facility, 184-190
      program, 190
      program implementation, 190
      programming process, 186-190
Costs, unit, 113-114
Critical Path Method (CPM), 118-120
Current Techniques in Architectural Practice,
   14

Data analysis, 29-31, 42, 88-120
   participant interaction techniques, 136-140
   statistical, 88-94
      descriptive, 89-92
      functions of, 88
      inferential, 92-94
   see also Computers, Evaluation techniques;
      Program elements, analysis of
Data collection, 29, 42, 53-87
   background information, 53-55
      obtaining, 54-55
      resources, 55
      sources, 55-57
      types of, 53-54
   value of, 87
   see also Attitude measurement; Communi-
      cation, techniques; Forms, standard-
      ized; Interviews; Observation tech-
      niques; Presentations; Questionnaires;
      Surveys
Data forms. See Forms, standardized
Data logs, 65-66
Data management, 158
Data manipulation, 158
Data organization
   analysis cards, 130-133, 147
   correlation diagrams, 123-130
      block diagrams, 130
      bubble diagrams, 128-129
      interaction nets, 129-130, 132
      link-node diagrams, 129
      procedures, 125-126
      resources, 127

      social mapping, 127
      sociograms, 127-128
      relationship matrices, 121-123
      worksheets, 132, 134-135
Davis, C.F., 162
Davis, Gerald, 26, 63
   programming defined by, 4-5
   programming model, 29-32
Davis, Howard
   programming defined by, 5
Denardo, E.V., 164
Design
   factors, categories of, 18-20
   relation to programming, 6, 16-17, 25-27
Design and Planning Assistance Center
      (DPAC), 191
   program for a health clinic, 191-197
      program, 196
      program implementation, 196-197
      programming process, 191-196
Design in Architecture, 89
Design Methods: Seeds of Human Futures, 55,
   123, 156
Design of Social Research, The, 156
Designer, 11, 36, 42
Diagrams. See Data organization, correlation
   diagrams
Disciplined Creativity for Engineers, 117-118
Documentation, 140-144
   graphics, 142-144
   narrative, 141-142
   see also Presentations
Dynamic programming, 164

*Ecological Psychology Concepts and Methods
   for Studying the Environment of Human
   Behavior,* 97
Ecology mapping. See Observation tech-
   niques, behavior mapping
Educational facilities
   elementary school, 216-222
   middle school, 176-183
Eggers Group P.C., The, 199
   program for an arts center, 199-208
      program, 202-206
      program implementation, 206-208
      programming process, 199-202
*Emerging Methods in Environmental Design and
   Planning,* 159-162
Emerging Techniques of Architectural Practice,
   12
*Emerging Techniques 2: Architectural Program-
   ming,* 13

Enclosing Behavior, 97
Energy use analysis, 20, 104-112
   BEPS, 110-112
   budgeting, 109-112
   conservation, 108
   considerations in programming, 108
Engineering Organization, 163
Engineering Research Building, Research Triangle Institute, Research Triangle Park,
   North Carolina, 234-240
   program, 239
   programming process, 235-239
Environmental Analysis Group, The (TEAG), 26
   programming model, 29-32
Environmental Research Group, The, 97
   programming model, 37-38
Enzmann, Herbert K., 184
Evaluation techniques
   rating scales, 149, 151-154
      charts, 152-154
      ladder scale, 152
      procedures, 151-152
   weighting, 155-156
   see also Data analysis; Matrices

Facility Programming, 12, 14
Factor analysis, 88,93-94
Farbstein, Jay
   programming model, 33-34
Feasibility analysis. See Computers, analysis
   techniques
Feasibility studies/programs
   cultural arts center, 198-208
   elementary school, 216-221
   health clinic, 191-197
   hospital facilities, 209-215
Focke, John W., 12, 131
Forms, standardized, 66-70
   lighting survey, 68
   procedures, 69-70
   room requirements, 67, 69
Forums, 147
Frequency distribution, 89-90
Function analysis, 94-95

Gaming, 138-139
Gans, Herbert, 72
Gero, John S., 158, 163-165
Gould, Bryant P., 198
Government office building, 241-246
*Graphic Problem Solving for Architects and
   Builders,* 127

Grossmont Hospital Additions, Mental Health and Physical Rehabilitation Centers, La Mesa, California, 209-215
feasibility study and program, 211-215
programming process, 209-211
Guttridge, Bryan, 157

Half matrix, 86, 123
Hospital Planning Information Systems (HPIS), 163, 166
Human factors, 9, 19-20

Incompatibility matrix, 162
Information processing
functions of, 10
index to techniques, 50-52
levels related to design decisions, 24-25
see also Communication; Data analysis; Data collection; Data organization; Evaluation; Observation
Interaction network, 129-130, 132
Interval scale, 151-152
Interviews, 60-63
procedures, 60-61
resources, 63
structured, 62-63
unstructured, 61-62
Introduction to Architectural Programming, 13-14, 18
Introduction to Statistical Analysis, 88-89
Iterative process, 24, 27

Jones, J. Christopher, 55, 123, 156

Kaplan/McLaughlin, 209
program for a hospital, 209-215
program, 211-214
program implementation, 214
programming process, 209-211
Kaplan/McLaughlin/Diaz, 25, 139
Kline, Lawrence S., 191
Kuester, J.L., 163
Kurtz, John M., 27
programming model, 35-36

Ladder scale, 152
Laseau, Paul, 127
Lee, Kaiman, 165-167
Levy, Alan, 228

Lewis, M. Susan, 118
Liability, 275
Life cycle cost analysis, 114-115
Lighting study, 256-261
Lighting survey form, 68
Lindquist Center for Measurement, College of Education, University of Iowa, Iowa City, Iowa, 184-190
program, 190
programming process, 186-190
Link-node diagram, 129

Macklin, Liz, 247
Marathons, 139
Marquis Associates, 216-217
program for a school redesign, 216-222
program, 221-222
program implementation, 222
programming process, 217-221
Marquis, Robert, 216
Matrices
evaluation, 145-155
incompatibility, 162
preference, 86
relationship, 121-123
adjacency, 123
affinity, 123
box, 85, 122
half, 86, 123
McLaughlin, Herbert, 25, 209
programming defined by, 6
Mead, Margaret, 72
Mean. See Arithmetic mean
Meaning, measurement of, 81
Measurement of Meaning, The, 81
Median, 90-91
Medical facilities
health clinic, 191-197
hospital, 209-215
research laboratory, 247-255
Methods of Architectural Programming, 13-14, 127, 156
Michelson, William, 98
Middle school, Texas, 176-183
program, 180-183
programming process, 179-180
Milne, Murray, 159
Mitchell, William J., 159
Mize, J.H., 163
MLTW/Turnbull, Associates, 223
program for a residence, 223-227
program, 224-225
program implementation, 225-227

programming process, 223-224
Mode, 90
Models
programming, 27-37
sociophysical analysis, 97-99
see also Programming case studies
Moleski, Walter, 97-98
programming defined by, 6
programming model, 37-38
Morphological analysis, 162
Motion pictures, 77-78
Multidimensional scaling, 88, 94, 165
Multidisciplinary teams. See Programming, practice
Murphy Levy Wurman, 228-229
plan for riverfront development, 228-233
program, 232-233
program implementation, 233
programming process, 229-232

National Institute of Mental Health, Nursing Units of the Clinical Center, Bethesda, Maryland, 256-261
light and color study conclusions, 259-261
programming process, 257-260
data analysis, 259
data collection, 258-259
design and documentation, 260
National Institutes of Health. See Ambulatory Care and Research Facility
Negroponte, Nicholas, 158
Neighborhood services center, 171-175
Nominal scale, 151
Nonprobability samples, 59
North Carolina State University School of Design, Raleigh, North Carolina, 234-235
program for a research facility, 234-240
program implementation, 239-240
programming process, 235-239

Observation techniques, 70-79
behavior mapping, 73-75
behavior specimen record, 75-76
direct, 70-72
instrumented, 76-79
participatory, 72-73
see also Data collection
Optimization, 162-163
Optimization Techniques with FORTRAN, 163
Ordinal scale, 151-152
Organization of data. See Data organization
Owner, 42-43

Pacheco and Graham Architects, 191
Palmer, Alvin E., 118
Panel discussions, 147-148
Participants, 10-11, 36-43
 see also Programming, practice
Pattern language, 99
Peña, William M., 12, 14, 16, 18, 26, 131-132, 134
 programming defined by, 6-7
 programming model, 39
Penn's Landing Riverfront Development, Philadelphia, Pennsylvania, 228-233
 program, 232-233
 programming process, 229-232
Performance Specification of Computer-aided Environmental Design, 165
Perry Dean & Stewart, 166
Petronis, John P., 191
Photography, 76-78
 annotated, 76-77
 time-lapse, 77
Planning the Office Landscape, 118
Population, 92
Practice. See Programming, practice
Predictions. See Programming, conclusions
Preiser, Wolfgang F.E., 12-14, 191
 programming defined by, 8
Preliminary Office Building Design (PROB), 165
Presentations, 144-150
 audio-visual aids, 144, 146
 forums, 147
 oral, 146-147
 panel discussions, 147-148
 workbooks, 148-150
 see also Communication, techniques; Documentation
Problem Seeking: An Architectural Programming Primer, 12, 14, 16, 131, 134
Proceedings of the First Annual Environmental Design Research Association Conference, 98
Program, 6
 audience, 8-9
 comprehensiveness, 11, 22-23
 conclusions, 21-22, 23
 contents, 21
 development, 29-32, 43-44
 organization, 45-46
 reports, 44-45
 types of, 46
  component, 23
  facility, 23
  master, 23
Program elements, analysis of, 94-120

cost, 112-115
 construction estimate, 113-114, 116
 evaluation estimate, 114-115
 project estimate, 112-113
 resources, 115
energy use, 104-112
 budgeting, 109-112
 conservation, 108
 considerations in programming, 108
function and activity analysis, 94-97
scheduling, 115-120
 charts, 117-120
 procedure, 117
space needs, 99-104
 procedure, 100
 space unit standards, 103-104
Program Evaluation and Review Technique (PERT), 118-120
Programmer, 9, 11, 33-36, 42
Programming, 7
 architect's role in, 14-15
 as communication, 8-9, 44
 changes in, 267
 definitions of, 4-9
 evolution of, 11-14
 general concepts, 1
 goals, 33-34
 importance of, 3-4
 models, 29-39
  see also Programming case studies
 objectives, 4
 opportunities in, 275
 practice, 271-275
  client/programming team, 274-275
  multidisciplinary teams, 271-274
 preparation for, 33-35
 process, 10, 16-46
  participants, 10-11, 36
  procedural model, 31-32
  techniques, 11
  see also Data analysis; Data collection; Data organization; Program elements, analysis of; Programming case studies
 purpose, 7-8
 resources, 14
 scope of, 9-10, 17-21
 techniques related to information-processing functions, 50-52
 trends, 276-278
Programming case studies, 169-266
 cultural arts center, 198-208
 government office building, 241-246
 health clinic, 191-197
 hospital, 209-215

neighborhood services center, 171-175
 psychiatric residence units, 256-261
 research facilities
  educational, 184-190
  engineering, 234-240
  medical, 247-255
 residence, 223-227
 riverfront development, 228-233
 schools, 176-183, 216-222
 zoo, 262-266
Programming/designing interface, 16-17, 25-28, 277
 integrated approach, 25
 interactive approach, 26-27
 segregated approach, 26
Psychiatric residence units, 256-261

Questionnaires, 63-65
 procedure, 64-65
 resources, 65
Queuing models, 163

Raeke, Carolyn, 247
Ranking charts, 84-86
Ratio scale, 152
Recommendations. See Program, conclusions
Redevelopment project, 228-233
Reed, Paul, 98
Reflections on Computer Aids to Design and Architecture, 158
Relational planning programs, 166
Relationship matrices, 121-123
Research. See Data collection
Research facilities
 educational, 184-190
 engineering, 234-240
 medical, 247-255
Residence, Fairfax County, Virginia, 223-227
 program, 224-225
 programming process, 223-224
RIBA Handbook of Architectural Practice and Management, 5
Role playing, 137-138
RTKL Associates, 241, 243
 program for government offices, 241-246
 program, 245-246
 program implementation, 246
 programming process, 243-245

Samples, 93
Sampling, 59-60

Sanoff, Henry, 13-14, 55, 60, 127, 156, 234
    programming defined by, 8-9
Scales. See Attitude measurement, tests for;
        Evaluation techniques, rating scales
Scheduling, programming and project, 115-120
Semantic differential, 80-84
Services, scope of. See Contracts
Simon, Cathy, 216
Simplexes, 161
Site Feasibility Study Model (SFSM), 165
Site planning programs, 166
Skidmore, Owings & Merrill, 163, 166, 184
Smith, Ann, 234
Social mapping, 127
Sociogram, 127-128
Sorokin, Pitirim, 99
South Broadway Clinic, Albuquerque, New
        Mexico, 191-197
    program, 196
    programming process, 191-196
Space allocation programs, 166
Space analysis, 99-104
    see also, Computers, analysis techniques
        with
Space for Social Systems (SPACE 4), 247-248
    program for research facilities, 247-253
        program, 254
        program implementation, 255
        programming process, 248-254
Space normalization, 164
Space program, 45, 103-104
Spivack Associates, 257
    study for psychiatric units, 256-261
        program, 261
        program implementation, 261
        programming process, 257-260
Spivack, Mayer, 256
Squatters, 140
Statistics
    multivariate, 93-94
    nonparametric, 93
    see also Data analysis, statistical
Stratified sampling, 59
Sullivan Farbstein Associates
    programming model, 33-34
Surveys, 55-60
    behavior setting, 97
    lighting survey form, 68
    procedure, 56-58
    resources, 59-60
    sampling, 59
    types of, 58-59
Swenson, Alfred P., 165
Synectics, 137

Systematic sampling, 59
Szigeti, Francoise, 4-5

Tamer, Joanna
Team organization, 34, 36
    see also Programming, practice
Time budget analysis, 98
Time-Budgets of Human Behavior, 99
Timetable, 163
Topeka Zoological Park, Discovering Apes
        Complex, Topeka, Kansas, 262-266
    program, 266
    programming process, 264-266
Tracking, 71-73
Turnbull, William, Jr., 223

Unit cost standard, 113-114
Urban Villager, The, 72
User, 42
    needs, 18
    subjectivity of data, 60-61

Value analysis, 115
Variance, 88, 91-92
Videotape, 77-78

Wainwright, Jonathan R., 157
Watson, Donald, 98
Weighting, 155-156
White, Edward T., III, 13-14, 18, 171
    programming defined by, 9
    programming model, 40-41
Wilterding, Mark A., 184
Workbooks, 148-150, 220
Workshops, 139, 219
    see also Communication, techniques

Zoo exhibit complex, 262-266
Zooplan Associates, 262, 264
    program for a zoo complex, 262-266
        program, 266
        program implementation, 266
        programming process, 264-266